Islam, Muslims, and COVID-19

Muslim Minorities

VOLUME 42

The titles published in this series are listed at *brill.com/mumi*

Islam, Muslims, and COVID-19

The Intersection of Ethics, Health and Social Life in the Diaspora

Edited by

Aminah Al-Deen
Aasim I. Padela

BRILL

LEIDEN | BOSTON

The Library of Congress Cataloging-in-Publication Data is available online at https://catalog.loc.gov

Names: Al-Deen, Aminah, editor. | Padela, Aasim I., editor.
Title: Islam, Muslims, and COVID-19 : the intersection of ethics, health and social life in the diaspora / edited by Aminah Al-Deen, Aasim I. Padela.
Description: Boston : Brill, 2023. | Series: Muslim minorities, 1570-7571 ; 42 | Includes bibliographical references and index.
Identifiers: LCCN 2023031788 (print) | LCCN 2023031789 (ebook) | ISBN 9789004679764 (hardback) | ISBN 9789004679771 (ebook)
Subjects: LCSH: COVID-19 (Disease)–Religious aspects–Islam. | COVID-19 Pandemic, 2020—Religious aspects–Islam. | COVID-19 (Disease)–Social aspects. | COVID-19 Pandemic, 2020–Social aspects. | Islamic ethics–21st century.
Classification: LCC RA644.C67 I75 2023 (print) | LCC RA644.C67 (ebook) | DDC 362.1962/4144–dc23/eng/20230817
LC record available at https://lccn.loc.gov/2023031788
LC ebook record available at https://lccn.loc.gov/2023031789

Typeface for the Latin, Greek, and Cyrillic scripts: "Brill". See and download: brill.com/brill-typeface.

ISSN 1570-7571
ISBN 978-90-04-67976-4 (hardback)
ISBN 978-90-04-67977-1 (e-book)

Contents

Acknowledgments

This volume was seeded at a conference I hosted at the University of Chicago in October 2019 under the auspices of the Initiative on Islam and Medicine. That conference, *Advancing Muslim American Health Priorities: Exploring the Religious Dimensions of Mental, Reproductive and Sexual Health* [A-MAP], was sponsored, in part, by a grant from the Patient-Centered Outcomes Research Institute, and brought together Muslim religious leaders, clinicians, researchers, and advocates to discuss health and healthcare disparities among Muslim Americans. Prof. Al-Deen found the conversations illuminating and novel, and hence engaged me in conversation about how we may capture the rich discussions and research findings in print form. Fast forwarding a few months later, the COVID-19 pandemic took hold and we witnessed how marginalized and minoritized populations were bearing the brunt of the pandemic's social, economic, and health burdens. Simultaneously, ethical questions about religious life in the face of social restrictions were being raised in Muslim circles. We also witnessed many Muslim organizations rally to fill in healthcare and educational gaps. This history-in-action reshaped our thoughts, and we quickly pivoted to centering these experiences within the proposed edited volume. To our knowledge, this is the only volume of its kind, and we hope it provides the foundation for improving the plight of the marginalized in our society and addressing the religious, social, and ethical dimensions of health and healthcare.

As this book comes to light, I would like to thank all those who supported the 2019 conference that sparked this project, including the sponsors, presenters, and staff. I am truly indebted to Prof. Al-Deen for her confidence in our partnership and persistence in seeing this volume through and to our colleagues at Brill, especially Nienke Brienen-Moolenaar, who facilitated the review process and supported us throughout the publication process. An enormous note of appreciation is due to Dr. Lauren Nickel, Youa Xiong, and Thérèse Wassily Saba, who performed painstaking formatting and editing of the chapters and bibliography. As with any of my academic projects, I am grateful to my wife, Maryam, and our children, Aaleeyah, Maaria, Ahmed Fateh, and Faathima, who sacrifice on a daily basis to allow me to spend time on these efforts. And last but not least, all praise and gratitude are due to Allah for making all of this possible. I pray that He makes this work one of benefit to its readers.

Aasim I. Padela MD MSc

All of the above charts our journey with this collection. Additionally, I am indebted to all of the contributors and to my husband, Frederick, who just smiles at my projects and makes sure the coffee pot is on. Working again with Dr. Padela, a taskmaster in his own right, has been wonderful.

Aminah McCloud Al-Deen PhD

Figures and Tables

Figures

Tables

Abbreviations

ACA	Affordable Care Act
AMHP	American Muslim Health Professionals
AMJA	Assembly of Muslim Jurists of America
AMSA	American Medical Student Association
AMWA	American Medical Women's Association
APHA	American Public Health Association
APTC	Advanced Premium Tax Credit
BBSI	The British Board of Scholars and Imams
BIMA	British Islamic Medical Association
CAIR	Muslim Wellness Foundation Council on American-Islamic Relations
CAP	Center for American Progress
CBO	community-based organizations
CDC	Centers for Disease Control and Prevention
CISNA	Council of Islamic Schools in North America
CMP	Center for Muslim Philanthropy
DFA	Doctors for America
DPA	Defense Production Act
EANS	Emergency Assistance to Non-Public Schools
EUA	emergency use authorization
FCNA	*Fiqh* Council of North America
FRAC	Food Research & Action Center
FPL	federal poverty level
HHS	Health and Human Services
ICNA	Islamic Circle of North America
ICUS	intensive care units
IECN	Islamic Educators' Communication Network
II&M	The Initiative on Islam and Medicine
IMAN	Inner-City Muslim Action Network
IMANA	Islamic Medical Association of North America
IRB	Institutional Review Board
IRUSA	Islamic Relief USA
ISLA	Islamic Schools League of America
ISNA	Islamic Society of North America
MAS	Muslim American Society
MCB	Muslim Council of Britain
MHC	Muslim Health Consortium
MPAC	Muslim Public Affairs Council

MPI	Muslim Philanthropy Initiative
NAIF	North American Imams Federation
NBMCC	National Black Muslim COVID Coalition
NHS	National Health Service
NIH	National Institute of Health
NMA	National Medical Association
NMTF	National Muslim Task Force on COVID-19
PPP	Paycheck Protection Program
SEEMA	Support Embrace Empower Mental Health Advocacy
SEL	social emotional learning
SHOP	Small Business Health Options Program
SNAP	Supplemental Nutrition Assistance Program
WFC	Worry Free Community
WHO	World Health Organization

Notes on Contributors

Ummesalmah Abdulbaseer
is a fourth-year medical student at the University of Illinois at Chicago College of Medicine (UICOM). She is passionate about mentorship, medical education, and exploring the intersection of Islam and healthcare. She has had the opportunity to volunteer with many nonprofit organizations and serve the Chicago Muslim community. Currently, she is working on projects to explore healthcare gaps faced by Muslim patients and on how to promote religiously informed care.

Shafiq W. Ahmed
has over ten years' experience supporting healthcare data analytics, infectious disease epidemiology, and managing large-scale health research projects. He is a Senior Management Analyst supporting Health and Human Services and government entities including the Defense Health Agency and Navy Medicine in quantitative and qualitative health research. Additionally, Shafiq volunteers on the National Muslim Task Force on COVID-19, leading the healthcare professionals committee that has provided public health guidance and strategy for the Muslim community. He also volunteers as a guest lecturer on global infectious disease epidemiology at McDaniel College, Budapest. Shafiq holds a MS in Public Health focusing on Microbiology and Emerging Infectious Diseases.

Aminah Beverly (McCloud) Al-Deen
is professor emerita of Islamic Studies in the Department of Religious Studies at DePaul University, Chicago. In 2006, she founded the United States' first undergraduate baccalaureate program in Islamic World Studies. She is the former Editor in Chief of the *Journal of Islamic Law & Culture*. Her book publications include: *African American Islam*, *Questions of Faith*, *Transnational Muslims in America*, *Introduction to Islam in the 21st Century*, *Global Muslims in the 21st Century*, *History of Arab Americans: Exploring Diverse Roots*, and *Muslim Ethics in the 21st Century*.

Dr. Al-Deen is a Senior Fulbright Scholar, host of Critical Talk a Muslim Network TV production, board member of the Inner City Muslim Action Network, Soundvision, Muslim Mental Health, Muslim Arc, Greenwood Policy Institute and the American editor for the Muslim Minorities Series for Brill Publishers.

Miqdad Asaria
MD, is an Associate Professor at the Department of Health Policy at the London School of Economics and Political Science. He has extensive experience in both academic and policy-making settings. His research interests focus on the economics of health inequalities and health financing. His policy experience draws on his time working for the Ministry of Health and Family Welfare in India, the Department of Health and Social Care in the UK, and the World Health Organization.

Rania Awaad
MD, is a Clinical Associate Professor of Psychiatry at the Stanford University School of Medicine, where she is the Director of the Stanford Muslim Mental Health & Islamic Psychology Lab, Associate Chief of the Division of Public Mental Health and Population Sciences, and Co-Chief of the Diversity and Cultural Mental Health Section. On a community level, she is the Executive Director of the holistic mental health nonprofit Maristan.org. She serves as the Director of The Rahmah Foundation, a nonprofit organization dedicated to educating Muslim women and girls, and as a Senior Fellow at Yaqeen Institute and ISPU. Prior to studying medicine, she pursued traditional Islamic studies in Damascus, Syria.

Nazim Ghouri
MD, graduated from Edinburgh University and completed his specialist training in Diabetes, Endocrinology, and General Medicine. He completed his research doctorate thesis, titled "The Cardiometabolic Phenotype of UK South Asian Men," at the University of Glasgow. He was appointed as a consultant in 2015 at the Queen Elizabeth University Hospital, Glasgow and an Honorary Clinical Senior Lecturer at the University of Glasgow.

He is the joint senior editor of the British Islamic Medical Association Ramadan compendium—comprehensive informative guidance on the management of patients during Ramadan for HCPs covering a range of specialties.

Marium Husain
is a hematology/oncology fellow at the Ohio State University James Comprehensive Cancer Center. She graduated from the Ohio State University College of Medicine and completed a residency in Internal Medicine. As the Vice-President of the Islamic Medical Association of North America, she has been working on public health education and creating domestic campaigns for food insecurity, reproductive health, mental health, and climate change. She

is a member of the Policy Committee for the National Muslim Task Force on COVID-19.

Moina Hussain
is one of the four co-founders and a board member of Worry Free Community where she helped set up the Worry Free Health (WFH) program that now supports over 5,000 families with healthcare coverage options. She specializes in low-income dual eligible elderly immigrant folks ensuring low-cost medication coverage and least deductibles. Along with Affordable Care Act coverage, she helps people with Medicare and disability issues, while assessing their overall physical and mental well-being.

Shaza Khan
is the executive director of the Islamic Schools League of America, a non-profit that supports Islamic schools in by providing professional development, networking, resources, and critical research on Islamic education. Dr. Khan received her PhD in Teaching, Curriculum and Change from the Warner School of Education and Human Development at the University of Rochester. She has co-authored several peer-reviewed journal articles and book chapters which communicate the values and needs of full-time Islamic schools to the broader public.

Aafreen Mahmood
MD MPH, is a fourth-year medical student at UC Davis School of Medicine. Her research interests lie in exploring the mental health needs of immigrant and refugee populations resettling in the USA, as well as Muslim diaspora. Prior to entering the medical field, Aafreen worked in the public health sector to improve access to medical and psychiatric care among underserved patient populations in the San Francisco Bay Area and Baltimore, Maryland. She holds a Master's degree in Public Health from Johns Hopkins University, and intends to combine public health approaches to her clinical practice as a primary care physician.

Fatema Mirza
is also one of the four co-founders and executive director of Worry Free Community (WFC) that strives for health equity among immigrant communities. She has a long-standing background in healthcare IT and administration, which she channeled to develop community health infrastructure that allows WFC to establish programs catering to the three aspects of healthcare: cost, quality, and access. Additionally, she ensured WFC's participation in Patient-Centered Outcomes Research (PCORI) projects focusing on mosque-communities.

Maham Mirza
is a first-year college student, certified in Affordable Care Act enrollment and has been providing health coverage education to needy families for over four years. As a high school student, Maham volunteered at Worry Free Community since its inception by providing outreach in mosque-communities to support the new immigrant health education needs. Maham has a keen insight into community health data and loves to analyze the data gathered from the outreach activities.

Diane Ameena Mitchell
has degrees from Duquesne University, Pennsylvania State University, and Purdue University. She has worked as an English and Speech Communication teacher and as a guidance counselor in private and public school settings. Presently, Ms. Mitchell is a doctoral candidate in Education at the University of Illinois at Chicago. Her dissertation focuses on the relations between students' reported beliefs and desires about careers and the connection of those beliefs and desires with their school performance.

Karim Mitha
is a Public Health Registrar within the National Health Service in England. He has experience in both academic and public health settings: as an instructor in Public Health at the Usher Institute, University of Edinburgh and previously at De Montfort University; and at the local and national government levels, in the Department of Health and for public health teams in London boroughs. He works with the Health Protection team in London, providing public health guidance in infectious disease and supports the London-wide COVID-19 response. He is completing a PhD in Sociology at the University of Glasgow, exploring the inequalities experienced by ethnic minorities and migrants.

Aasim I. Padela
is an internationally recognized scholar in the fields of Muslim community health research and Islamic bioethics. He holds an MD from Weill Cornell Medical College, a MSc in Healthcare Research from the University of Michigan, a BS in Biomedical Engineering and a BA in Classical Arabic from the University of Rochester, and has studied Islamic theology and law in seminary and academic settings. He has authored over 140 peer-reviewed journal articles and book chapters, as well as three books, and has been featured in major news outlets including the *New York Times, USA Today*, the *Chicago Tribune, Washington Post*, National Public Radio, BBC, and CNN.

Rafaqat Rashid

MD, is a traditional Shariʿa scholar, general medical practitioner, and an educator. He is the co-founder of al-Balagh Academy and Director its medical *fiqh* programs and associated *takhassus* courses for *ʿulamāʾ*. He is an active researcher in the field of Islamic bioethics and medical law having obtained his Masters from the University of Manchester and contributing to many peer-reviewed chapters and journal articles on Islamic bioethics and Islamic medical jurisprudence.

Leena Raza

is a fourth-year medical student at Oakland University William Beaumont. Her research interests include healthcare disparities and healthcare delivery models in underserved communities. During her collegiate and medical school career, she worked on helping build a novel community mental health center in Chicago and worked with the Michigan Department of Health and Human Services as a fellow on COVID-19 testing strategy. She completed her undergraduate education at Harvard University. She hopes her clinical experiences as a primary care physician influence her future clinical research questions and life-long patient advocacy.

Urooj Rehman

is one of the four co-founders and a board member of Worry Free Community, supporting people with setting up their medical homes, and finding innovative solutions to support the access to care needs of multigenerational families, where every person may fall into a different bucket of health coverage options. She is now providing healthcare coverage consulting across the United States with licenses in all fifty states.

Constance D. Shabazz

MD, received her medical degree from Southern IL School of Medicine. She holds a Master of Business Administration and Master of Public Health from St. Xavier University in Chicago. Dr. Shabazz was a Public Service Fellow at the John F. Kennedy School of Government at Harvard University, where she received a Master of Public Administration. She is the CEO and founder of Salaam Community Wellness Center in Chicago. Dr. Shabazz was awarded the inaugural Distinguished Alumni Service Award from Southern Illinois University School of Medicine.

Mehrunisha Suleiman

is Director of Medical Ethics and Law Education at the University of Oxford and is responsible for leading and delivering a range of teaching activities for undergraduate and graduate students. She is a medically trained bioethicist and public health researcher, whose research experience spans healthcare systems analysis to empirical ethics evaluation.

Sana Syed
MD, is a neurologist working as a Senior Medical Director, Clinical Lead at Sanofi US. She graduated from King Edward Medical College and has a Masters in Public Health from Harvard School of Public Health. She completed her neurology training in Boston, including sub-specialty training in Demyelinating Disorders and Cognitive Neurology from Beth Israel Deaconess Medical Center, HMS. Dr. Syed is also involved in multiple public health and professional organizations including as the Health Policy and Advocacy Director for American Muslim Health Professionals and is currently also a Chair on the Policy Committee for the National Muslim Task Force on COVID-19.

Anam Tariq
MD, is a board-certified nephrologist and internist and epidemiologist. She is a Clinical Assistant Professor of Medicine at the George Washington University School of Medicine. As a clinical-researcher and educator, her focus is on nutrition, metabolomics, and cardio-metabolic disease in the kidney-diseased populations. Dr. Tariq is also involved in multiple public health and professional organizations, including as a Board Member of the Islamic Medical Association of North America. She is also a member of the Policy Committee for the National Muslim Task Force on COVID-19.

Osman Umarji
PhD MA, holds a Bachelor of Science in Electrical Engineering and a Master's and PhD in Educational Psychology from UC Irvine. He has studied Islam at al-Azhar University in Cairo, Egypt. His research interests include the development of human motivation, religious socialization, spirituality, and Islamic legal theory. Dr. Umarji is also an Adjunct Professor in the School of Education at UC Irvine. He has previously taught child development, adolescent development, and statistics. His expertise in both psychological and Islamic sciences allows him to conduct empirical research on contemporary issues facing Muslims.

Salman Waqar
MD, is an academic general practitioner at the University of Oxford, an Associate Medical Director at East Berkshire Primary Care, and the Clinical Lead for Cancer Inequalities at the Thames Valley Cancer Alliance. He has published

on the management of Ramadan and various long-term conditions and has an interest in the role of faith organizations in healthcare. He is also the Vice-President of the British Islamic Medical Association (BIMA) and was one of the founding executive members. He sits on several boards of national organizations in the National Health Service, addressing workforce and population inequalities.

Aisha Zafar
has been a certified healthcare counselor at Worry Free Community since 2016 and plays a vital role as an Affordable Care Act (ACA) enrollment expert by providing daily enrollments all around the Chicagoland area, educating immigrant families about essential health benefits, and filling in necessary gaps with respect to health equity, while ensuring all of the healthcare needs are met for each of the individuals in the families she serves. She is looking forward to celebrating the ten-year anniversary of ACA marketplace enrollments in the fall 2022.

Introduction

Aasim I. Padela and Aminah Al-Deen

1 Aims of the Volume

This collection describes how Muslim communities in several minority contexts responded to, and experienced, the early phases of the COVID-19 pandemic. In particular, the volume details several key challenges they faced and how they traversed them, with a specific focus on the interplay between religious values, public health mandates, social structures, and communal life. The diverse disciplinary perspectives offered by the authors on Muslim engagement with the pandemic was purposively encouraged, for we, as editors, sought to provide a multidisciplinary and multidimensional account of Muslim ethics operating in the COVID-19 era, one where scriptural values, lived experiences, societal structures, and cultural contexts combine together in fresh and diverse ways. Indeed, all too often, Islamic ethical evaluation ignores contributions from the social sciences, and contextual factors are not fully addressed in Islamic edicts.[1] And descriptions of Muslim life often overlook the significant interplay between religious beliefs, values, identity and behaviors. This volume thus aims at a more connected and a fuller account of how religious concerns generated challenges and how Muslims lived out their religious values during the pandemic. The chapters (as will be detailed shortly) cover multiple issues faced by Muslim diasporic communities, utilize different disciplinary approaches to describe and analyze these topics, and offer varied critiques of the global response to the ongoing pandemic.

It is important to underscore that this volume largely gathers accounts from the first year of the pandemic which was marred by significant uncertainties and novel stresses to social life. Critically, Ramadan, the Muslim month of fasting, coincided with the second month of the pandemic, April 2020, bringing concerns over how to accomplish religious rituals in the pandemic era to the forefront of Muslim minds. Indeed several chapters recount the significance of Ramadan to Muslim life which we, as editors, let stand at the risk of perceived overlap in order to underscore its prominence to Muslims. The immediate interaction between religious and social life in confronting the pandemic,

1 Aasim I. Padela, "Islamic Bioethics: Between Sacred Law, Lived Experiences, and State Authority," *Theoretical Medicine and Bioethics* 34, no. 2 (2013): 65–80. https://doi.org/10.1007/s11017-013-9249-1.

 | DOI:10.1163/9789004679771_002

and between biomedical and political concerns and theological ones, provided the impetus for this volume and makes this work unique and novel.

2 The Muslim Community Context

Several chapters describe how Muslims living in the United States and the United Kingdom coped with, strategized against, and otherwise experienced the COVID-19 pandemic, revealing a great deal about their place as minority communities living in the diaspora. Overall, there are approximately 2.7 million Muslims in England and Wales, representing about 4 percent out of a total population of 67.22 million before the pandemic. Immigrants of South Asian background comprise the dominant racial/ethnic group there.[2] Within the United States, accurate statistics regarding the Muslim population are harder to obtain because the census does not collect religious affiliation data. Estimates by community organizations, polling agencies, and research institutes vary widely, with some putting the population at around 2.5 million and others at 8 million. A modest estimate of 5 million[3] would put the group comprising about 1.5 percent of the approximately 330 million persons in the United States.[4] However, within the United States, the Muslim community is very diverse, with African Americans, South Asians, and Arabs being the largest groups, and nearly two-thirds of the community being migrants.[5] Beyond these differences, socio-economic indicators suggest that the American-Muslim community may have better economic indices relative to the community in the UK.

Although one may argue the populations and their social contexts are different enough to preclude comparisons, there are some remarkable unifying features that allow for aggregating their experiences together in this volume. First, religious identity is a unifying feature that informs their beliefs, behaviors, and

2 Office for National Statistics, "Research Report on Population Estimates by Ethnic Group and Religion," United Kingdom Government, December 4, 2019, https://www.ons.gov.uk/peoplepopulationandcommunity/populationandmigration/populationestimates/articles/researchreportonpopulationestimatesbyethnicgroupandreligion/2019-12-04#population-estimates-by-religion.

3 Tom W. Smith, "The Muslim Population of the United States: The Methodology of Estimates," *The Public Opinion Quarterly* 66, no. 3 (2002): 404–417. https://doi.org/10.1086/341669.

4 United States Census Bureau, "U.S. and World Population Clock," https://www.census.gov/popclock/.

5 Pew Research Center, "Demographic Portrait of Muslim Americans," July 26, 2017. https://www.pewresearch.org/religion/2017/07/26/demographic-portrait-of-muslim-americans/#muslims-in-the-us.

experiences. Religiosity is high in both communities and, in turn, religious values, beliefs, and identity impact health outcomes.[6] Relatedly, the set-up of community organizations and spokespersons is also similar. In the UK, the Muslim Council of Britain (MCB), a national umbrella body of over 500 mosques and educational and charitable associations, coordinated messaging and convened resources to help Muslims on the ground attend to pandemic-related issues.[7] Notably, the British Board of Scholars and Imams (BBSI),[8] a national network of dozens of Islamic scholars, researchers, and activists, served as a religious consultation body, often working with the MCB but sometimes on its own, to issue bioethical guidance to Muslim communities during the pandemic. In the United States, the MCB's role is carried out by several national organizations, including the Islamic Society of North America (ISNA), the Islamic Circle of North America (ICNA), the Muslim American Society (MAS), and parallel to the BBSI are religious councils such as the *Fiqh* Council of North America (FCNA) and the American Muslim Jurists Assembly (AMJA).[9] The USA's larger and more diverse community results in a much more diffuse set of communication and consultation lines. Indeed, this siloed and fractured nature motivated the creation of the National Muslim Task Force on COVID-19, which would

6 David Voss and Steve Bruce, "Religion: Identity, Behaviour and Belief Over Two Decades," in *British Social Attitudes: The 36th Report*, ed. J. Curtice, E. Clery, J. Perry, M. Phillips, and N. Rahim (London: The National Centre for Social Research, 2019), https://bsa.natcen.ac.uk/media/39293/1_bsa36_religion.pdf; Abulaziz Aflakseir, "Religiosity, Personal Meaning, and Psychological Well-Being: A Study Among Muslim Students in England," *Pakistan Journal of Social and Clinical Psychology* 10, no. 1 (2021): 27–31; Laird, Lance D., Mona M. Amer, Elizabeth D. Barnett, and Linda L. Barnes. "Muslim Patients and Health Disparities in the UK and the US," *Archives of Disease in Childhood* 92, no. 10 (2007): 922–926, https://doi.org/10.1136/adc.2006.104364; Aasim I. Padela and Farr A. Curlin, "Religion and Disparities: Considering the Influences of Islam on the Health of American Muslims," *Journal of Religion and Health* 52, no. 4 (2013): 1333–1345, https://doi.org/10.1007/s10943-012-9620-y; Skaiste Liepyte and Kareena McAloney-Kocaman, "Discrimination and Religiosity Among Muslim Women in the UK before and After the Charlie Hebdo Attacks," *Mental Health, Religion & Culture* 18, no. 9 (2015): 789–794, https://doi.org/10.1080/13674676.2015.1107890; Mohammed Fahim Uddin, Amanda Williams, and Katharine Alcock, "Visibility as Muslim, Perceived Discrimination and Psychological Distress Among Muslim Students in the UK," *Journal of Muslim Mental Health* 16, no. 1 (2022), https://doi.org/10.3998/jmmh.135; and Aziz Sheikh and Abdul Rashid Gatrad, eds., *Caring for Muslim Patients*, 2nd ed. (London: CRC Press, 2008).

7 Muslim Council of Britain, "Who We Are," https://mcb.org.uk/about/.

8 The British Board of Scholars and Imams, https://www.bbsi.org.uk/.

9 Islamic Society of North America (ISNA), https://isna.net/; Islamic Circle of North America (ICNA), https://icnany.org/; Muslim American Society (MAS), https://www.muslimamericansociety.org/; Fiqh Council of North America (FCNA), https://fiqhcouncil.org/; and Assembly of Muslim Jurists of America (AMJA), https://www.amjaonline.org/.

serve as a unified communication platform for Muslims (more details about this group are presented in subsequent chapters). In some ways, these communication channels mirror the larger societal health communication channels. In the UK, a more streamlined channel of health and health policy communication through the National Health Service and the Office of the Prime Minister was utilized for communicating COVID-19-related messages. Yet, in the United States, a diverse array of governmental organizations at the national, state, and local levels shared different messages throughout the pandemic. However, in both contexts, Muslim communities desired religious channels to filter and translate public health guidance.

Second, both communities live within highly advanced, biomedically driven societies that are global economic and political powers. Hence, the health infrastructure in these countries, particularly concerning healthcare services and health policy, are similar enough that Muslim experiences tell similar stories of engagement and challenge. Moreover, societal problems such as violence are often biomedicalized in both nations. This cultural dynamic was borne out in the responses to the pandemic, both positively and negatively. Again, the cultural context similarity allows for bringing together Muslim experiences from the USA and the UK in this volume.

Third, both nations have suffered terrorism-related tragedies and sociopolitical upheavals that have contributed to Muslim identity and Islam being highly scrutinized. In the United States, there was 9/11, and in the UK, 7/7, both instances of senseless loss of life which spurred negative reactions to Muslims living within these societies. Hate crimes increased, the social discourse was more cutting, and anti-Muslim sentiment climbed. Advancing forward in time from those events, both countries have seen a more recent rise in anti-immigrant sentiment with Trumpism in the United States and Brexit in the UK. Again, the similar social dynamic in these countries allows for aggregating the Muslim experiences together. Indeed, even in medical journals, Muslims are negatively portrayed, generally inferring that they should leave religious tradition and join the modern world.[10] And the caricature of Muslims as terrorists is pervasive despite the fact that few Muslims in either country were/are involved in any nefarious activity, and Muslims in both countries hold prominent governmental and legislative offices.[11] Moreover, Muslim immigrant communities

10 Lance D. Laird, Justine de Marrais, and Linda L. Barnes, "Portraying Islam and Muslims in MEDLINE: A Content Analysis," *Social Science & Medicine* 65, no. 12 (2007): 2425–2439, https://doi.org/10.1016/j.socscimed.2007.07.029.

11 For example, in the United Kingdom, prominent Muslims include Sadiq Khan who has been serving as Mayor of London since 2016, and was a member of parliament from 2005

are on at least their second generation of children born in the West in both countries, while African-American Muslim communities are in their fifth generation. The Muslim presence in American and British society is not new, yet the discourse around these groups has become charged, and it has impacted them in various ways during the pandemic.

Social scientists see the marginalization and demonization of Muslims as an extension of colonial efforts to stigmatize Muslims. This discourse inadvertently spills over to healthcare and contributes to healthcare disparities as care providers stereotype and discriminate against Muslim religious identity.[12] Indeed scores of studies point to this phenomenon of lesser quality care. In addition, prominent bioethicists consider religion, particularly Islam, as an inappropriate source of bioethical guidance, hence, it is understandable why Muslims and Islam are marginalized in healthcare and bioethical discourses. As noted, religious studies scholar and Islamic ethicist Abdulaziz Sachedina, states:

> My major concern with bioethics in the Muslim world today is that it has severed its partnership with faith communities in providing solutions to the moral problems that have arisen in clinical situations as well as public health around the world.[13]

When Professor Sachedina wrote this, he also noted an absence of knowledge on the part of clinicians about the local cultures and contexts which inform bioethical deliberation. He also noted that: "Translation or grafting of

to 2016. Similarly, Sajid Javid has been the Secretary of State for Health and Social Care since June 2021 and a Member of Parliament since 2010. In the United States, Ilhan Omar and Rashida Tlaib are prominent Muslims been serving in the House of Representatives since 2019.

12 Mary Brigid Martin, "Perceived Discrimination of Muslims in Health Care," *Journal of Muslim Mental Health* 9, no. 2 (2015), https://doi.org/10.3998/jmmh.10381607.0009.203; Goleen Samari, Héctor E. Alcalá, and Mienah Zulfacar Sharif, "Islamophobia, Health, and Public Health: A Systematic Literature Review," *American Journal of Public Health* 108, no. 6 (2018): e1-e9, https://doi.org/10.2105/AJPH.2018.304402; Marcia C. Inhorn, and Gamal I. Serour, "Islam, Medicine, and Arab-Muslim Refugee Health in America After 9/11," *The Lancet* 378, No. 9794 (2011): 935–943, https://doi.org/10.1016/s0140-6736(11)61041-6; and Aasim I. Padela and Michele Heisler, "The Association of Perceived Abuse and Discrimination after September 11, 2001, with Psychological Distress, Level of Happiness, and Health Status Among Arab Americans," *American Journal of Public Health* 100, no. 2 (2010): 284–291, https://doi.org/10.2105/AJPH.2009.164954.

13 Abdulaziz Sachedina, *Islamic Biomedical Ethics: Principles and Applications* (New York: Oxford University Press, 2009), 10.

the secular Western bioethics to the Muslim medical and healthcare institutions is unproductive without first investigating native epistemic and cultural resources ....”[14] Certainly a lack of religiously informed ethics prevents society from addressing the moral issues of medicine and a lack of knowledge coupled with a lack of appropriate communication channels obstructs Muslim communities from successfully navigating health concerns and bioethical quandaries.

Indeed, healthcare disparities and bioethics are related, and nowhere was this more apparent than during the pandemic. The allocation of life-saving ventilators was a bioethical issue, and just allocation policies can only be developed with cognizance of the structural inequities that contribute to disease burdens among specific minority populations.[15] In the United States, refugees are housed in poorer neighborhoods or in cities where there are no people of color to ally themselves with, thus contributing to less access to quality healthcare and poorer social capital to demand equitable treatment. And redlining, a discriminatory practice where financial and other services are withheld from potential customers classified as hazardous due to residing in specific neighborhoods, occurs in both countries. These two practices alone constrain incomes for many minorities, including Muslims, and induce healthcare disparities. If we ignored the fact that certain populations were succumbing to more severe disease because of structural inequities in healthcare access and education, to socio-economic policies that kept certain communities marginalized, we risked perpetuating inequities in ventilator allocation algorithms that tackle COVID-19 related health issues.

As faith communities with a religious system that incorporates health, legal, and moral standards as one, scholars and researchers remind us of the connections between Muslim healthcare disparities and Islamic bioethics. At least some of the observed healthcare disparities experienced by Muslims are on account of their commitment to faith values, more problematically they are rooted in inadequate accommodation of their religious needs and values on the part of the healthcare system.[16] These connections deserve greater explo-

14 Sachedina, *Islamic Biomedical Ethics*, 11.

15 Harald Schmidt, Dorothy E. Roberts, and Nwamaka D. Eneanya, “Rationing, Racism and Justice: Advancing the Debate Around ‘Colourblind’ COVID-19 Ventilator Allocation,” *Journal of Medical Ethics* 48, no. 2 (2022): 126–130, https://doi.org/10.1136/medethics-2020-106856; Douglas B. White and Bernard Lo, “A Framework for Rationing Ventilators and Critical Care Beds During the COVID-19 Pandemic,” *Jama* 323, no. 18 (2020): 1773–1774, https://doi.org/10.1001/jama.2020.5046; and Matthew J. Brown et al., “Allocating Medical Resources in the Time of Covid-19,” *New England Journal of Medicine 382*, no. 22 (2020): e79, https://doi.org/10.1056/NEJMc2009666.

16 Aasim I. Padela and Danish Zaidi, “The Islamic Tradition and Health Inequities: A Prelim-

ration. While this volume does not take on this topic directly, it does describe connections between Islam and Muslim health attitudes and experiences that may provide foundations for such dedicated study.

3 The COVID-19 Context

Much ink has been spilled describing the origin of the global pandemic and the varied local and international responses. Recounting this history in full seems unnecessary; for that, the reader is directed elsewhere.[17] For posterity, the noteworthy relevant milestones are that the virus, SARS-COV-2, popularly known as COVID-19, spread quietly and lethally worldwide in late 2019, as global travel enabled rapid dispersal across countries and continents. The origin was/is traced to live animal markets in Wuhan, China, in December 2019, and the WHO declared a global pandemic in March 2020. The first confirmed case in the United States was on January 19, 2020,[18] while in the United Kingdom, it was on January 29, 2020. Societal lockdowns, stay-at-home orders, and social distancing mandates were the mainstay of initial control measures until a rapid pharmaceutical race to find effective vaccines yielded success. For example, in the USA, in April 2020, ABC News reported that 46 states had closed what were deemed nonessential businesses such as restaurants, beauty/barber shops, and bookstores, and the number of cars and foot traffic in cities was drastically low.[19] The US Department of Education "ordered or recommended school building closures for the rest of the academic year, affecting at least 50.8 million public school students."[20] Initially, schools were temporarily closed,

---

inary Conceptual Model Based on a Systematic Literature Review of Muslim Health-Care Disparities," *Avicenna Journal of Medicine* 8, no. 1 (2018): 1–13, https://doi.org/10.4103/ajm.AJM_134_17.

17 "Covid-19: The Story of a Pandemic," *New Scientist*, March 10, 2021, https://www.newscientist.com/article/2270361-covid-19-the-story-of-a-pandemic/; David J. Sencer, "CDC Museum COVID-19 Timeline," CDC Museum, Atlanta, GA, https://www.cdc.gov/museum/timeline/covid19.html; Lawrence Wright, *The Plague Year: America in the Time of Covid* (London: Allen Lane, 2021); and Rachel Clarke, *Breathtaking: The UK's Human Story of Covid* (London: Little, Brown, 2021).

18 Michelle L. Holshue, et al., "First Case of 2019 Novel Coronavirus in the United States," *New England Journal of Medicine* 382, no. 10 (2020): 929–936, https://doi.org/10.1056/NEJMoa2001191.

19 Will Linendoll and Erin Schumaker, "Here are the States That Have Shut Down Nonessential Businesses," *ABC News*, April 3, 2020, https://abcnews.go.com/Health/states-shut-essential-businesses-map/story?id=69770806.

20 "The Coronavirus Spring: The Historic Closing of U.S. Schools (A Timeline)," *Education*

but eventually distance learning became the mainstay of education in 2021. This was no easy task as some students and teachers in rural and semi-rural areas had no internet access to carry out online learning; many public-school teachers and university professors were unfamiliar with, and thus ineffective at, online learning; and parents had to try to perform work duties from home while also tutoring their children learning online. Significant loss of employment occurred, further stressing families and putting daily life at risk. With multiple vaccines coming to market in late 2020, vaccination campaigns have been the cornerstone of public health measures to address the virus. Yet, disproportionate access and uptake have been the rule. Minority communities and socio-economically depressed ones have less access and greater vaccine hesitancy and rejection than their counterparts.[21] Mis- and disinformation have plagued the public health response to the pandemic. Nefarious bioweapon origin stories remain circulating; unproven cures and preventative measures continue to be advertised on social media and by prominent leaders and celebrities; and active protests against lockdowns and vaccines routinely occur.

Again, this volume takes up this aforementioned early phase of the pandemic right up to when vaccines became available to the general public. The chapters speak to how religious communities handled the multifaceted crisis brought by COVID-19 and offer stories about how religious life adapted to these societal dynamics.

We know that Muslims, as minority populations, found their communities to experience high mortality rates and troublesome mental health issues. Many Muslims thought the pandemic would be over relatively soon. As Ramadan approached (April–May 2020), they anticipated the restraints imposed during the month of fasting, the nightly feasts, and the nightly congregational prayers. Yet, as mosques closed, panic began. Fortunately, many larger mosques began online counseling services and prayer circles. Yet, smaller and less-resourced places of worship had less to offer. Islamic organizations began to mobilize and play triage to address the community's social, religious, physical, and mental needs. Overall, Muslims felt a conflict between religious obligations and public policy. Religious and scholarly leadership scoured traditional sources

Week, July 1, 2020, www.edweek.org/leadership/the-coronavirus-spring-the-historic-closing-of-u-s-schools-a-timeline/2020/07.

21 Jagdish Khubchandani et al., "COVID-19 Vaccination Hesitancy in the United States: A Rapid National Assessment," *Journal of Community Health* 46 (2021): 270–277, https://doi.org/10.1007/s10900-020-00958-x; and Elaine Robertson et al., "Predictors of COVID-19 Vaccine Hesitancy in the UK Household Longitudinal Study," *Brain, Behavior, and Immunity* 94 (May 2021): 41–50, https://doi.org/10.1016/j.bbi.2021.03.008.

for guidance so that they could provide some leadership. Muslim physicians and religious scholars thus played outsized roles, but their service also came with costs: some lost their lives due to being on the frontlines, and others suffered from exhaustion and burnout—the chapters in this volume dive into these responses and these struggles. Within the scholarly literature on COVID-19, Muslims are once again at the margins. This volume thus provides a timely and much-needed account that uplifts voices from within the community and highlights the connections between ethics, health, and social life in the Muslim diaspora as it faced the pandemic.

4 The Content of the Chapters

The chapters in this volume proceed in the following way. In Chapter 1, "Aligning Public Health Mandates with Religious Goals: Developing Islamic Bioethical Guidance During the COVID-19 Pandemic," Aasim I. Padela, a physician bioethicist, and Shafiq W. Ahmed, a research analyst, explore bridges between public health ethics and the Islamic moral tradition. Certainly, governments are tasked with containing morbidity and mortality from pandemics, and they have used every public health tool in their armamentarium to confront the COVID-19 pandemic. Under-investigated is what these policies and mandates mean for religious communities and how they match up with religious bioethical frameworks. Successful policies rely on motivating behavior change and social adherence to said policies. This chapter thus reports on how public health and religion-related values intersected in the Islamic bioethical guidance offered by the US-based National Muslim Task Force on COVID-19. This task force's Fiqh/Bioethics committee was charged with crafting guidance that took both public health mandates and religious practices into account. As such, this chapter provides critical insights into multidisciplinary Islamic bioethical deliberation.

In Chapter 2, "Islam, Muslims, and COVID-19: Examining the Intersection of Healthcare Advocacy, Religion, and Community During a Global Pandemic," Anam Tariq, Marium Hussain, and Sana Syed, a team of physicians, discuss the formation and work of the Taskforce's policy committee and the main issues they addressed. In particular, the chapter focuses its attention on the framework of cooperation among organizations and the scriptural statements that motivate collective action. They detail the Taskforce and Committee's stances on policy issues and how they jointly engaged over topics such as food insecurity and health education. This chapter speaks to how religious values were lived out through the Taskforce's work.

At the local level, many Muslim community-based organizations (CBO) answered the call to meet the social, healthcare, civic, and other needs of both Muslims and non-Muslims. Indeed, the turmoil and chaos created in all households by fears of contracting the deadly disease was exacerbated by concerns about being able to survive as a family, put food on the table, and have a roof over one's head, when people lost jobs as businesses closed and often with health insurance coverage tied to employment. Worry Free Community, a CBO located in a suburb of Chicago, Illinois, rose to the challenge of helping all comers navigate the maze of various social and health programs they could seek assistance through. They adapted to the pandemic by launching telephonic resources and hosting webinars and chats. They also collected data critical in identifying local needs during the pandemic so that government organizations, community-based entities, and other institutes could address the needs of those most vulnerable to the pandemic. Chapter 3, "Effects of COVID-19 on the Healthcare Coverages of Immigrant Populations", written by the team of Ummesalmah Abdulbaseer, Maham Mirza, Moina Hussain, Aisha Zafar, Urooj Rehman, and Fatema Mirza, draws upon Worry Free Community data to describe how COVID-19 impacted the health coverage of its clientele.

While the focus of Muslim communities and leaders was on serving others, the toll that this took is understudied. Chapter 4, "Muslim Healthcare Workers in the Time of COVID-19," co-authored by Aminah Al-Deen and Constance Shabazz, adds to that gap in the literature. Prof. Al-Deen (co-editor of this volume) and an emeritus professor of Islamic studies, and Dr. Shabaaz, a clinician, use a hybrid method of primary interviews and secondary literature analysis to dive into the experiences of Muslim healthcare workers. Taking an oath to save lives is different from taking that oath to the extreme during a pandemic where a hospital is full of crises. Some clinicians were exhausted and wondering if they had made mistakes, costing rather than saving lives. Others were overwhelmed by having to decide to terminate life support without family consultations. All were overburdened without spiritual guidance. The counseling of Muslims facing death and the performance of rituals preceding and at death are the traditional remit of hospital-based Muslim chaplains and local Imams. Muslim healthcare workers often had to answer the call during the pandemic because hospitals did not allow visitors and were understaffed. All too often, Muslim healthcare workers were not emotionally and educationally prepared for this role, and too many lamented over their incapacities afterward. This chapter offers insight into the inner life of Muslim healthcare workers as they confronted the pandemic.

Chapter 5, "Religiosity, Coping and Mental Health: An Empirical Analysis of Muslims Across the COVID-19 Pandemic," dives deeper to analyze mental health responses during the pandemic. Osman Umarji, Aafreen A. Mahmood, Leana Raza, and Rania Awaad, a group of Muslim community health researchers and educators, used international surveys and focused interviews to investigate relationships between mental health, religiosity, theological beliefs, and COVID-19 attitudes, which Muslims held during the early phases of the pandemic. The chapter not only reports on the diverse theological opinions that Muslims have about COVID-19, their concerns about social distancing, and attitudes toward closing mosques during the pandemic, it also investigates how psychological characteristics and religiosity associate with mental health, as well as how demographic, psychological, and religious factors influenced philanthropic attitudes and behaviors during the pandemic. The chapter, thus, focuses on core psychological and religious processes that permeated through the lives of Muslims to influence the way COVID-19 has been lived and experienced.

African-American Muslims are often neglected in extensive studies about Muslim-American health experiences and social attitudes. Chapter 6, authored by Diane Ameena Mitchell, a doctoral candidate in Education at the University of Illinois at Chicago, offers a narrative account of the shared experiences of seven African-American Muslims navigating issues of technology, food, housing, religious practice, and healthcare during the pandemic. Indeed, there are many academic reflections on the first year of the pandemic, but this small ethnographic look provides something more personal and understandable. It weaves interview content together with larger societal contexts that contributed to the situations the interviewees found themselves in and, as such, adds much-needed lived experiences to the volume.

Another gap in the literature is how Muslim schools responded to the pandemic. As noted above, public health concerns led to a near-total closure of public and private schools, Islamic schools being no exception. Shaza Khan, executive director of the Islamic Schools League of America, fills in the literature gap in Chapter 7, "COVID-19 and US Islamic Schools: Responsive, Resourceful, and Resilient." Using survey data and personal experiences as head of a social network of Islamic school leaders, she describes how Islamic school leaders responded to the COVID-19 pandemic and its impact on the instructional methods, enrollment, and finances of full-time Islamic schools. The author argues that the cumulative insights and data illustrate that school leaders demonstrated grit and resolve to address the ever-changing pandemic environment while delivering quality education to learners. Islamic schools are an essential American Muslim institution that deserve dedicated support and research.

The penultimate chapter in this volume, Chapter 8, takes the reader to the UK. In "An Examination of Ramadan Fasting and COVID-19 Outcomes in the

UK," Karim Mitha, Salman Waqar, Miqdad Asaria, Mehrunisha Suleiman, and Nazim Ghouri, a group of medical researchers in the UK, examine the contextual factors leading to health disparities among Muslims in the UK and how they played out during the COVID-19 pandemic. They specifically consider whether ritual fasting during Ramadan contributed to inequalities and discuss how structural factors largely explain the disproportionate impacts on Muslims observed in the early stages of the pandemic. This analysis lays bare the connections between health and healthcare inequities and social conditions.

The final chapter in the volume, Chapter 9, returns to the domain of normative ethics. Rafāqat Rashid, a physician and Islamic scholar, proposes "An Islamic Ethico-Legal Framework for Pandemics: The Case for COVID-19." Like Chapter 1, authored by Padela and Ahmed, this chapter addresses the interface between the Islamic ethico-legal tradition, medical science, and public health policy. The chapter examines scriptural sources and legal precedents to provide direction and guidance when there is a conflict between public health interventions and Islamic legal imperatives during pandemics like COVID-19. While Padela and Ahmed's chapter looked backward at how public health and religious goals were aligned, this chapter projects into the future to consider about how dialogue and deliberation should proceed. In this way, Chapters 1 and 9 offer comparable bookends to a volume dedicated to the intersection of Islamic ethics, health, and Muslim life.

Bibliography

Aflakseir, Abulaziz. "Religiosity, Personal Meaning, and Psychological Well-Being: A Study Among Muslim Students in England." *Pakistan Journal of Social and Clinical Psychology* 10, no. 1 (2021): 27–31.

British Board of Scholars and Imams. https://www.bbsi.org.uk/.

Brown, Matthew J., Justin Goodwin, Kathleen Liddell, Stevie Martin, Stephanie Palmer, Paul Firth, Nir Eyal, Adnan A. Hyder, Govind Persad, James Phillips, and Ezekiel J. Emanuel. "Allocating Medical Resources in the Time of Covid-19." *New England Journal of Medicine 382*, no. 22 (2020): e79. https://doi.org/10.1056/NEJMc2009666.

Clarke, Rachel. *Breathtaking: The UK's Human Story of Covid.* London: Little, Brown, 2021.

"The Coronavirus Spring: The Historic Closing of U.S. Schools (A Timeline)." *Education Week*, July 1, 2020. www.edweek.org/leadership/the-coronavirus-spring-the-historic-closing-of-u-s-schools-a-timeline/2020/07.

"Covid-19: The Story of a Pandemic." *New Scientist*, March 10, 2021, https://www.newscientist.com/article/2270361-covid-19-the-story-of-a-pandemic/.

Holshue, Michelle L., Chas DeBolt, Scott Lindquist, Kathy H. Lofy, John Wiesman, Hollianne Bruce, Christopher Spitters, Keith Ericson, Sara Wilkerson, Ahmet Tural, George Diaz, Amanda Cohn, LeAnne Fox, Anita Patel, Susan I. Gerber, Lindsay Kim, Suxiang Tong, Xiaoyan Lu, Steve Lindstrom, Mark A. Pallansch, William C. Weldon, Holly M. Biggs, Timothy M. Uyeki, and Satish K. Pillai, the Washington State 2019-nCoV Case Investigation Team. "First Case of 2019 Novel Coronavirus in the United States." *New England Journal of Medicine* 382, no. 10 (2020): 929–936. https://doi.org/10.1056/NEJMoa2001191.

Inhorn, Marcia C., and Gamal I. Serour. "Islam, Medicine, and Arab-Muslim Refugee' Health in America After 9/11." *The Lancet* 378, No. 9794 (2011): 935–943. https://doi.org/10.1016/s0140-6736(11)61041-6.

Khubchandani, Jagdish, Sushil Sharma, James H. Price, Michael J. Wiblishauser, Manoj Sharma, and Fern J. Webb. "COVID-19 Vaccination Hesitancy in the United States: A Rapid National Assessment." *Journal of Community Health* 46 (2021): 270–277. https://doi.org/10.1007/s10900-020-00958-x.

Laird, Lance D., Mona M. Amer, Elizabeth D. Barnett, and Linda L. Barnes. "Muslim Patients and Health Disparities in the UK and the US." *Archives of Disease in Childhood* 92, no. 10 (2007): 922–926. https://doi.org/10.1136/adc.2006.104364.

Laird, Lance D., Justine de Marrais, and Linda L. Barnes. "Portraying Islam and Muslims in MEDLINE: A Content Analysis." *Social Science & Medicine* 65, no. 12 (2007): 2425–2439. https://doi.org/10.1016/j.socscimed.2007.07.029.

Liepyte, Skaiste, and Kareena McAloney-Kocaman. "Discrimination and Religiosity Among Muslim Women in the UK before and After the Charlie Hebdo Attacks." *Mental Health, Religion & Culture* 18, no. 9 (2015): 789–794. https://doi.org/10.1080/13674676.2015.1107890.

Linendoll, Will, and Erin Schumaker. "Here are the States That Have Shut Down Nonessential Businesses." *ABC News*, April 3, 2020. https://abcnews.go.com/Health/states-shut-essential-businesses-map/story?id=69770806.

Martin, Mary Brigid. "Perceived Discrimination of Muslims in Health Care." *Journal of Muslim Mental Health* 9, no. 2 (2015). https://doi.org/10.3998/jmmh.10381607.0009.203.

Muslim Council of Britain, "Who We Are." https://mcb.org.uk/about/.

Office for National Statistics. "Research Report on Population Estimates by Ethnic Group and Religion." United Kingdom Government, December 4, 2019, https://www.ons.gov.uk/peoplepopulationandcommunity/populationandmigration/populationestimates/articles/researchreportonpopulationestimatesbyethnicgroupandreligion/2019-12-04#population-estimates-by-religion.

Padela, Aasim I. "Islamic Bioethics: Between Sacred Law, Lived Experiences, and State Authority." *Theoretical Medicine and Bioethics* 34, no. 2 (2013): 65–80. https://doi.org/10.1007/s11017-013-9249-1.

Padela, Aasim I., and Farr A. Curlin, "Religion and Disparities: Considering the Influences of Islam on the Health of American Muslims." *Journal of Religion and Health* 52, no. 4 (2013): 1333–1345. https://doi.org/10.1007/s10943-012-9620-y.

Padela, Aasim I., and Michele Heisler, "The Association of Perceived Abuse and Discrimination after September 11, 2001, with Psychological Distress, Level of Happiness, and Health Status Among Arab Americans." *American Journal of Public Health* 100, no. 2 (2010): 284–291. https://doi.org/10.2105/AJPH.2009.164954.

Padela, Aasim I., and D. Zaidi. "The Islamic Tradition and Health Inequities: A Preliminary Conceptual Model Based on a Systematic Literature Review of Muslim Health-Care Disparities." *Avicenna Journal of Medicine* 8, no. 1 (2018): 1–13.

Pew Research Center. "Demographic Portrait of Muslim Americans." July 26, 2017. https://www.pewresearch.org/religion/2017/07/26/demographic-portrait-of-muslim-americans/#muslims-in-the-us.

Robertson, Elaine, Kelly S. Reeve, Claire L. Niedzwiedz, Jamie Moore, Margaret Blake, Michael Green, Srinivasa Vittal Katikireddi, and Michaela J. Benzeval. "Predictors of COVID-19 Vaccine Hesitancy in the UK Household Longitudinal Study." *Brain, Behavior, and Immunity* 94 (May 2021): 41–50. https://doi.org/10.1016/j.bbi.2021.03.008.

Sachedina, Abdulaziz. *Islamic Biomedical Ethics: Principles and Applications*. New York: Oxford University Press, 2009.

Samari, Goleen. Héctor E. Alcalá, and Mienah Zulfacar Sharif. "Islamophobia, Health, and Public Health: A Systematic Literature Review." *American Journal of Public Health* 108, no. 6 (2018): e1–e9. https://doi.org/10.2105/AJPH.2018.304402.

Schmidt, Harald, Dorothy E. Roberts, and Nwamaka D. Eneanya. "Rationing, Racism and Justice: Advancing the Debate Around 'Colourblind' COVID-19 Ventilator Allocation." *Journal of Medical Ethics* 48, no. 2 (2022): 126–130. https://doi.org/10.1136/medethics-2020-106856.

Sencer, David J. "CDC Museum COVID-19 Timeline." CDC Museum, Atlanta, GA. https://www.cdc.gov/museum/timeline/covid19.html.

Sheikh, A. and Gatrad, A.R. eds., 2008. *Caring for Muslim Patients*. Radcliffe Publishing

Smith, Tom W. "The Muslim Population of the United States: The Methodology of Estimates." *The Public Opinion Quarterly* 66, no. 3 (2002): 404–417. https://doi.org/10.1086/341669.

Uddin, Mohammed Fahim, Amanda Williams, and Katharine Alcock. "Visibility as Muslim, Perceived Discrimination and Psychological Distress Among Muslim Students in the UK." *Journal of Muslim Mental Health* 16, no. 1 (2022). https://doi.org/10.3998/jmmh.135.

United States Census Bureau. "U.S. and World Population Clock." https://www.census.gov/popclock/.

Voss, David, and Steve Bruce, "Religion: Identity, Behaviour and Belief Over Two Decades." In *British Social Attitudes: The 36th Report*, edited by J. Curtice, E. Clery,

J. Perry, M. Phillips, and N. Rahim. London: The National Centre for Social Research, 2019. https://bsa.natcen.ac.uk/media/39293/1_bsa36_religion.pdf.

White, Douglas B., and Bernard Lo. "A Framework for Rationing Ventilators and Critical Care Beds During the COVID-19 Pandemic." *Jama* 323, no. 18 (2020): 1773–1774. https://doi.org/10.1001/jama.2020.5046.

Wright, Lawrence. *The Plague Year: America in the Time of Covid*. London: Allen Lane, 20

CHAPTER 1

Aligning Public Health Mandates with Religious Goals: Developing Islamic Bioethical Guidance during the COVID-19 Pandemic

Aasim I. Padela and Shafiq W. Ahmed

1 Introduction

Little did we know it at the time, but December 2019 marked a seismic shift in global society: a novel coronavirus outbreak first reported in Wuhan, China would lead to an international pandemic that continues to this day. Governments and health agencies hurried to craft social policies to stem contagion and deaths; biomedical researchers, epidemiologists, and pharmaceutical companies speedily sought to understand how the disease was spreading and evading the immune system, so as to mitigate these effects and develop countermeasures; and the public rushed to various media channels and local leaders seeking accurate guidance on how to protect themselves and their loved ones. While many different, and variably successful, social policies have been enacted at various points in the pandemic, and our understanding of the virus and how to prevent and treat it has grown significantly in these past two years, there remains much to learn and disaster continues to the loom large. While new variants with different infectivity profiles continue to appear on the global stage, there continues to be wide disparities within and across societies in the uptake of vaccines and masking, and ever-present campaigns of mis- and disinformation target at-risk communities and social circles.

This state of affairs, according to some scholars, reflects the confluence of a biomedical reality, a pandemic, with a social reality, an infodemic. According to the World Health Organization (WHO), a pandemic is an epidemic of disease that crosses international boundaries and affects a large number of people.[1] COVID-19 met the threshold and was declared a pandemic by WHO on March 11, 2020. This biomedical reality was/is marked by a new disease with posited significant morbidity, mortality, and infectivity risk. Certainly, the novel nature of

1 "World Health Organization (WHO) Pandemic Definition," Public Health Nigeria, April 19, 2021, https://www.publichealth.com.ng/world-health-organization-who-pandemic-definition/.

 | DOI:10.1163/9789004679771_003

the disease, by definition, was/is coupled with many uncertainties that need to be filled in through social, epidemiological, and biomedical research. As studies are undertaken and experience grows, our state of knowledge rapidly changes. These oft-changing understandings contribute to an infodemic. First coined by journalist and political scientist David Rothkopf, an infodemic represents a social circumstance where "a few facts, mixed with fear, speculation and rumor, [are] amplified and relayed swiftly worldwide by modern information technologies." In turn adverse impacts upon "national and international economies, politics and even security [occurs] in ways that are utterly disproportionate with the root realities,"[2] and effective public health responses are hampered by confusion and distrust. One need only look to any local news channel to observe that we are in the midst of an infodemic.

Against this backdrop of known knowns, for example, COVID-19 is a public health threat, and known unknowns, for example, what measures are most efficacious in controlling COVID-19 disease, state and public health authorities have been compelled to act. Societies are composed of conglomerations of individuals, and COVID-19 represented an existential threat at both the individual level and societal level. Individuals succumbing to the disease could be rendered disabled and/or dead leaving families torn apart, households without wage earners, and communities impoverished. At the same time, if too many essential workers fell ill or worse, basic functions within society would come to a halt leading to a vicious cycle of downstream impacts upon families and individuals who might be "saved" from the biological harms of COVID-19 but nonetheless were/are afflicted by the societal disruptions impacting their livelihoods. More significantly perhaps were/are concerns about the healthcare system. Widespread COVID-19 infectivity can effectively incapacitate healthcare systems such that not only are there not enough facilities and healthcare workers to attend to patients stricken by COVID-19, but also too many patients with COVID-19 may "clog" up the system by diverting resources away from other routine, urgent, and emergent healthcare needs. This crisis is exemplified by the "flatten" or "bend the curve" messaging that exhorts individuals to take preventive measures to stem disease spread by curtailing social activities.[3]

2 David J. Rothkopf, "When the Buzz Bites Back," *Washington Post*, May 11, 2003, https://www.washingtonpost.com/archive/opinions/2003/05/11/when-the-buzz-bites-back/bc8cd84f-cab6-4648-bf58-0277261af6cd/. [Accessed July 30th 2023]

3 "Interim Pre-Pandemic Planning Guidance: Community Strategy for Pandemic Influenza Mitigation in the United States: Early, Targeted, Layered Use of Nonpharmaceutical Interventions," Centers for Disease Control and Prevention, February 2007, https://stacks.cdc.gov/view/cdc/11425; and Joost Santos, "Reflections on the Impact of 'Flatten the Curve' on Inter-

In order to convey the gravity of the situation, some statistics bear mention. Since the WHO declared a global pandemic in March 2020, there have been over 434.1 million cases and 5.9 million deaths worldwide.[4] Within the United States, the first cases were identified in January 2020 and, as of February 2022, over 78.7 million individuals have suffered from the disease and over 945,000 died. A remarkable breakthrough occurred approximately nine months into the pandemic when novel mRNA-based technology led to the development of COVID-19 vaccines.[5] These preventive therapeutics were quickly brought to the public after several clinical trials showed efficacy in preventing mortality,[6] and rapid emergency authorizations led to the roll-out to essential workers at first and then to the wider public. By January 2022, over 9 billion doses of the vaccine had been administered worldwide. In the United States, 64.9 percent of the population had been fully vaccinated.[7] While vaccines and therapeutics have had successes in curbing cases and community spread, COVID-19 variants—changes caused by genetic mutations in the original strain—impact vaccine efficacy and challenge national and global mitigation strategies.

In the initial stages, and still to this day, policymakers around the globe designed social policies and legal mandates to mitigate disease spread and impact. From restrictions on public gatherings and travel to masking regulations and the closure of businesses, multiple different strategies are employed to limit COVID-19-related morbidity and mortality and preserve civil society. Religious practices and institutions have also been under scrutiny and constraint, insofar as they contribute to social life and inform COVID-19-related behaviors. Indeed, the pandemic has spurred Islamic jurists and medical experts, individually or as part of juridical councils, to consider religious practices in light of posited public health risks. Muslim stakeholders, that is, patients, clinicians, and community and mosque leaders, have looked to these scholars

dependent Workforce Sectors," *Environment Systems and Decisions* 40, no. 2 (June 2020): 185–188, https://doi.org/10.1007/s10669-020-09774-z.

4 "WHO Coronavirus (COVID-19) Dashboard," World Health Organization, accessed March 10, 2022, https://covid19.who.int; and "COVID Data Tracker," Centers for Disease Control and Prevention, accessed March 10, 2022, https://covid.cdc.gov/covid-data-tracker.

5 Azizul Haque and Anudeep B. Pant, "Efforts at COVID-19 Vaccine Development: Challenges and Successes," *Vaccines* 8, no. 4 (December 6, 2020): 739, https://doi.org/10.3390/vaccines8040739.

6 Lindsey R. Baden et al., "Efficacy and Safety of the MRNA-1273 SARS-CoV-2 Vaccine," *New England Journal of Medicine* 384, no. 5 (February 4, 2021): 403–416, https://doi.org/10.1056/NEJMoa2035389.

7 Defined as receiving two doses of the Moderna or Pfizer vaccines; "U.S. COVID-19 Vaccine Tracker: See Your State's Progress," Mayo Clinic, accessed March 10, 2022, https://www.mayoclinic.org/coronavirus-covid-19/vaccine-tracker.

and councils for guidance about how to structure their religious lives during the pandemic. Accordingly, this chapter delves into these needs through the lens of the *Fiqh* (Islamic Bioethics) Committee of the National Muslim Task Force on COVID-19 in the United States.[8]

Specifically, we begin by describing the context, personnel, and procedures by which the *Fiqh* Committee of the National Muslim Task Force on COVID-19 came to be and deliberated. Thereafter, we recount the ways in which biomedical data, state authority mandates, and Islamic ethico-legal imperatives were aligned to furnish Islamic bioethical guidance to mosques, community organizations, and other stakeholders. Specifically, we describe contentions regarding the applicability of the Islamic ethico-legal constructs of *maṣlaḥa* (public interest), *ḍarūra* (dire necessity), and ethico-legal objectives of *ḥifẓ al-nafs* (preservation of life), and *ḥifẓ al-dīn* (preservation of religion) as related to two issues at the interface of the biomedicine and the religion: (i) establishing congregational prayers; and (ii) vaccine uptake. To close the chapter, we comment on how the pandemic underscored discursive gaps between policymakers, religious scholars, and public health professionals, and how these gaps must be remedied in order to furnish Islamic bioethical guidance to its many consumers.

2 The National Muslim Task Force on COVID-19

The rapid spread and severity of COVID-19 illness created many challenges for the health and safety of communities. While US governmental agencies such as Health and Human Services (HHS), the National Institute of Health (NIH), and

8 Formally, this committee was designated the *Fiqh* Committee and its charge was to analyze pandemic-related issues through the lens of Islamic law and draft guidance for Muslim stakeholders. Yet, the remit of the committee was not to issue Islamic rulings. First, some members on the committee had no formal Islamic legal training, and none considered themselves qualified to issue independent legal rulings. Indeed, we collectively decided that we would rely on the moral status determinations of classical jurists and contemporary juridical bodies rather than conduct our own "new/fresh" *ijtihād* (ethico-legal normative analysis). Second, the focus of the committee was less on individual actions as is common to *fiqh* determination, and more on regulating communal life. This more expanded focus meant that the committee functioned to mediate between scriptural evidence, public health directives, and Muslim communal life. Said another way, the committee sought to align biomedical and religious imperatives by drawing upon evidence from both sources of knowledge, and as such was focused on matters of Islamic bioethics, not simply *fiqh*. As such, in this chapter, although we will use the formal title, *Fiqh* Committee, we want the reader to recognize that the committee operated on a different register.

the Centers for Disease Control and Prevention (CDC) provided updated information about COVID-19 risks and countermeasures, such information was often confusing and, at times, out of date and out of reach. Local community members thus sought advice from their leaders and developed grassroots-based communication channels, for example, social media and email listservs, to vet and disseminate COVID-19 information.

For the Muslim community, which is diverse and spread across the United States, one of the challenges was communicating critical information about the pandemic to ensure the health and safety of worshipers through community and religious leaders. Undertaking these challenges required a multidisciplinary and multisectoral approach to communicating information and addressing pressing questions at the ground level. Recognizing this urgent need, the Islamic Medical Association of North America (IMANA), American Muslim Health Professionals (AMHP), and Islamic Society of North America (ISNA) collaborated to create a nation-wide task force to provide leadership and a communication channel by which Muslim community needs would be served. In early 2020, the National Muslim Task Force on COVID-19 (NMTF)[9] was formed and brought together over thirty national Muslim organizations that specialized in healthcare/medicine, legal/policy, education, and relief.[10] The NMTF was organized though a steering committee that oversaw the activities of the NMTF along with five subcommittees:

1. Policy
2. Healthcare Professionals
3. Social Services
4. Mental Health
5. *Fiqh*/Bioethics

The Policy Committee oversaw advocacy efforts to ensure that resources, legal, and health policy efforts were addressed through contacting policymakers and

9 See National Muslim Task Force on COVID-19 statements at Islamic Medical Association of North America, https://imana.org/covid-19/national-muslim-taskforce-statements/.

10 The organizations included: Islamic Society of North America (ISNA), Islamic Relief, Islamic Medical Association of North America (IMANA), American Muslim Health Professionals (AMHP), Muslim Public Affairs Council (MPAC), Celebrate Mercy, Penny Appeal USA, American Muslim Community Foundation, Institute for Muslim Mental Health, Support Embrace Empower Mental Health Advocacy (SEEMA), American Muslim Bar Association, Muslim Health Consortium (MHC), Muslim Wellness Foundation Council on American-Islamic Relations (CAIR), *Fiqh* Council of North America (FCNA), The Initiative on Islam and Medicine (II&M), Muslim American Society (MAS), Islamic Schools League of America (ISLA), Poligon Education Fund, North American Imams Federation (NAIF), and Assembly of Muslim Jurists of America (AMJA).

translating newly issued policies into impacts to the Muslim community. The Healthcare Professional Committee supporting the detailing of statements to address the pandemic, strategies to prevent spread of the virus, as well as sharing pertinent information about the novel virus. The Social Services Committee oversaw efforts and needs of vulnerable and underserved communities. The Mental Health Committee supported programs to identify mental health needs among frontline workers, healthcare professionals, and community members (depression, domestic abuse, etc.). The *Fiqh*/Bioethics Committee oversaw issues pertaining to whether policies, vaccine development, and any changes that may affect worshipers. These groups together identified where the greatest needs were and prioritized them to address as quickly as the pandemic was evolving.

Each of the committee leads shared and briefed the steering committee of new concerns and emphasized how to address the needs. An example was that of the rapid development of the COVID-19 vaccine using mRNA technology. While the Healthcare Committee stayed abreast of the development of the vaccine and discussed how it could be distributed in the Muslim community, the *Fiqh* Committee identified where potential concerns would be regarding the ingredients of the vaccine and whether it would be considered *ḥalāl* (permissible) for Muslims to use. These were discussed with the steering committee to present what issues would be concerning the Muslim community. Another example was the social distancing and the implementation of preventing indoor and outdoor gatherings. The Policy and Healthcare Committee discussed the importance of preventing the spread of the COVID-19 virus, the *Fiqh* Committee drew up rationale and justification for keeping houses of worship closed during this period. Once this was discussed with the NMTF, a joint statement was written and published to the Muslim Community for religious leaders and worshipers to understand and adhere to.

The NMTF's *Fiqh* Committee grew out of a conversation between the newly installed president of the American Muslim Health Professionals (AMHP), Dr. Hasan Shanawani,[11] and myself (AIP)[12] from the Initiative on Islam and Medicine. Dr. Shanawani and I were on collegial terms having previously collab-

11 Dr. Hasan Shanawani was the president of AMHP (a voluntary position). He works at Blue Cross Blue Shield of Michigan as their Medical Director for Clinical Performance Improvement. He is board certified in internal medicine, pulmonary and critical care, and clinical informatics.

12 Dr. Aasim I. Padela is Chairperson and Director of the Initiative on Islam and Medicine (a voluntary position). He is also Professor with Tenure of Emergency Medicine, Bioethics and the Medical Humanities at the Medical College of Wisconsin. He is an internationally renowned clinician-researcher with scholarly foci at the intersections of healthcare,

orated on Muslim health disparities research projects and co-convened an Islamic bioethics conference at the University of Michigan in 2011.[13] We also were part of an ad hoc working group of clinicians and Islamic scholars critically examining Muslim discourses around brain death in partnership with Darul Qasim Islamic Institute in 2009–2010.

The first guidance statement on COVID-19 issued jointly by AMHP, IMANA, the Islamic Society of North America (ISNA), and endorsed by the *Fiqh* Council of North America (FNCA) in February 2020 (a precursor to the Task Force statements) was motivated by the incredible speed at which COVID had taken hold in the United States. With rising infections and alarming death rates in China and Italy, a global lockdown strategy was being invoked in many policy circles. Medical professionals from IMANA and AMHP conveyed an urgent need to restrict mosque activities in light of the exponentially rising disease incidence and sought out religious scholars to endorse this action. As such, this first communication was primarily authored by healthcare professionals, and various scriptural texts and religious concepts buttressed a strong recommendation to totally shutter mosques. The statement explicitly noted that "the preservation of human life and human rights" held sway over "the continuity of … essential practices of devotion."[14] That guidance was not well received by several prominent Islamic jurists as it privileged physical health over spiritual health and seemed to discount divergences of opinion regarding the public health risks of mosque-based prayer. The conversation between Dr. Shanawani and myself (AIP) focused on these concerns, and the necessity of aligning religious and biomedical imperatives by bringing a wide coalition of Islamic jurists to the dialogue table. A more nuanced approach to the statements would, in my view, allow for better uptake and behavioral change at the local level. At the conclusion of that meeting, Dr. Shanawani agreed to advocate for a *Fiqh* Com-

---

bioethics, and religion, and has formal training in Islamic theology and law, clinical medical ethics, and emergency medicine.

13 Titled "Where Religion, Bioethics and Policy Meet: An Interdisciplinary Conference on Islamic Bioethics and End of Life Care," this landmark two-day conference was jointly sponsored by The University of Michigan Medical School, Darul Qasim Islamic Institute, and the Institute for Social Policy and Understanding. It brought together Islamic scholars and religious leaders, social scientists, health professionals, and other stakeholders to discuss Islamic law, bioethics, medicine, and health policy in the American context. Videos from the conference are available at https://www.youtube.com/playlist?list=PLKPFd4mBCvIgDyDXmlqrqo_hwYERcYpWh.

14 "Joint Statement Regarding the Global Coronavirus Pandemic (Also Known as SARS-CoV-2 or COVID-19)," Islamic Medical Association of North America, accessed March 10, 2022, https://www.imana.org/wp-content/uploads/2023/06/National-Muslim-Task-Force-Statement-on-COVID-19_03-18-2020.pdf.

mittee that would participate in the drafting of Task Force statements, and I (AIP) agreed to bring jurists into dialogue.

As the NMTF came into being,[15] a multidisciplinary *Fiqh* Committee comprising organizational representatives was also established. No specific inclusion criteria was set for members, rather individuals were self-selected for volunteer service. Additionally, the *Fiqh* Committee was given the vague mandate of ensuring any statement issued by the Task Force was "Islamically appropriate." Members of the committee included individuals with biomedical and religious training, Dr. Hatem El Haj from the American Muslim Jurists Assembly (AMJA), Dr. Rania Awaad from Stanford Muslim Mental Health Lab, and myself (AIP); Imams Abdulhakim Mohamed from the North American Imams Federation and Suhaib Webb from the Suhaib Webb Institute of Sacred Sciences; a healthcare chaplain Khurram Ahmed from the Association of Muslim Chaplains; and physicians Drs. Hasan Shanawani and Afroz Hafeez from the American Muslim Health Professionals (AMHP). We convened in mid-March 2020 to set out our operational structure. Overall, committee members felt they lacked the intellectual and time resources needed to function as an independent juridical council and carry out ethico-legal deliberation. In addition, various juridical bodies already existed that had the trust of local mosque communities. Instead, the group agreed to reference the writings of existing juridical councils and scholarly bodies as grounds for Task Force guidance. Furthermore, our ethos was to be ecumenical; we decided to search for common ground among the various religious edicts and highlight plurality so that the NMTF's statements provided stakeholders with the flexibility needed to contextualize religious rulings.

Given that Dr. Hatem El Haj was/is part of the AMJA's fatwa body and I (AIP) was/am a consultant to the *Fiqh* Council of North America, the British Board of Scholars and Imams, and prominent Chicagoland religious scholars, the group decided to feature decrees from these councils in NMTF statements. Additionally, these connections allowed us to prod juridical bodies to deliberate over issues that the broader Muslim community was confronting. Furthermore, our links to these councils allowed us to maintain an informal channel of communication between religious scholars, health policy stakeholders, and clinicians as the Muslim community confronted the pandemic. The committee also tabbed myself (AIP) as Chair given my expertise in aligning religious and biomedical ethical imperatives.[16]

15 Importantly the Task Force was only open to organizations with a national footprint and each organization put forward one or more representatives on the Task Force.

16 I (AIP) nominated Dr. Hatem El Haj for leadership given that he is qualified to issue reli-

The process by which the Task Force developed their statements was generally as follows. Member organizations would present the need for guidance about a certain matter on a closed WhatsApp group and/or at monthly meetings of the Task Force. One or more of the various committees of the Task Force would be charged with drafting an appropriate statement to address these ground-level concerns. When the issue involved religious activities such as worship services, religious holidays, or other observances the *Fiqh* Committee was charged with drafting the communiqué. Members of the committee would collate any available juridical body statements relevant to the matter and share them with each other on their private communication channels. On the basis of the statements, the committee chair was charged with drafting an initial statement for review by the committee. Given the urgency involved with the communications, a short time period was given for open comment and revision of the statement. Often times silence by committee members was assumed to reflect that they had no concerns. Importantly, there was an open letter communication between the religious scholars on the committee as well as prominent jurists and juridical councils around the country to 'vet' the views the *Fiqh* Committee would promulgate. Once the *Fiqh* Committee Chair signed off on the statement, the larger Task Force would be invited to endorse the statement by affixing their organizational logo.

3 The Task Force's Statements and Islamic Bioethics

The Task Force continues to publish statements to guide Muslim communities throughout the United States. As the situation on the ground changes, Task Force members convene on social media, organize webinars, draft infographics, and craft position statements in order to respond to queries from mosque and community leaders. Illustratively, when stay-at-home orders and shutdown orders were being promulgated across various locales in the USA, the Task Force considered how to manage mosque activities; when the season of Ramadan and the holiday of Eid approached, the Task Force issued guidelines for the safe practice of these religious observances; and when COVID-19 vaccines were developed and rolled out among essential workers and then to the broader public, the Task Force advised Muslims to take vaccines, while recognizing the many unknowns associated with them.[17] The early stages of the pan-

gious verdicts, is a practicing pediatrician, and is on AMJA's fatwa committee. In lieu of accepting committee leadership, he convinced the group that I should be the Chair.

17 "Joint Statement from the National Muslim Task Force on COVID-19 (NMTF) and the

demic saw more frequent communiqués as public health authority guidance was rapidly changing alongside steep rises in cases in the country. Accordingly, mosque activities and religious observances were actively being scrutinized by governmental authorities as they sought to contain COVID-19. In the second year of the pandemic, Task Force statements became less frequent because the government shifted its focus from containment to mitigation strategies. The advent of COVID-19 vaccines provided a measure of protection to individuals and hence the urgency of the pandemic somewhat receded from individuals' minds. The increased experience of healthcare workers in treating COVID-19 patients led to better outcomes, and a relative leveling off of case incidence rates throughout the nation allowed for social life to return. Contributing to this reduced frequency of communiqués was/is that local juridical councils, for example, the Islamic *Shura* Council of Southern California, have somewhat supplanted the role played by the NMTF by providing targeted guidance to mosques and community organizations in their locales. A more significant contributor may be a general sense of fatigue that has pervaded Task Force members and organizations. Many organizations within the Task Force have served on the frontlines of the pandemic addressing the social and human needs of their communities leaving them with little bandwidth to participate in Task Force activities. Similarly, prominent members of the *Fiqh* Committee leadership have had to juggle professional responsibilities as frontline workers with service roles of giving lectures and providing consultation to policymakers. Adding to the exhaustion is no small measure of apathy across various sectors in American society, and segments within the Muslim-American community advance conspiracy theories and misrepresent epidemiological data which lessen the motive force Task Force statements contain. Indeed, the infodemic and pandemic intersects within Muslim-American communities as well.

That said, in this section, we use Task Force statements as source material for Islamic bioethics research. As I (AIP) have detailed elsewhere,[18] Islamic bioethics is a discourse that uses the Islamic tradition to address moral questions and ethical issues arising out of the biomedical sciences and allied health practice. Commonly, this discourse entails the bringing together of two bodies of knowledge: knowledge of Islamic theology, law, and ethics; and knowledge

National Black Muslim COVID Coalition (NBMCC) on Ramadan 2021 and COVID-19 Vaccines," Islamic Medical Association of North America, April 6, 2021, https://www.imana.org/wp-content/uploads/2020/02/NMTFC_NBMCC-and-COVID-vaccines.pdf.

18 Aasim I. Padela, "An Introduction to Islamic Bioethics: Its Producers and Consumers," in *Medicine & Shariah: A Dialogue in Islamic Bioethics*, ed. Aasim I. Padela (Notre Dame, IN: University of Notre Dame Press, 2021), 1–37.

of biomedicine. The former is typically represented by Islamic jurists, imams, or Islamic studies experts, and the latter by clinicians, allied health professionals, or health policy experts. Among the many producers of Islamic bioethics literature are Muslim health professional organizations that convene scholars to deliberate about questions of bioethical import, and among the many consumers are local religious leaders who seek to assure the guidance they provide community members is theologically sound.[19] Under this definition and framework, the Task Force statements qualify as Islamic bioethics literature. First, the pandemic certainly posed moral quandaries for Muslim community leaders, clinicians, and the laity as they sought to uphold religious life in the face of mounting public health risks. Hence, the questions were squarely Islamic bioethics-related ones. Second, the *Fiqh* Committee of the Task Force, and accordingly the Task Force statements, aligned biomedical and religious imperatives by engaging with data and ethical arguments coming from each domain of knowledge. As such, they reflect a discourse between the Islamic and the biomedical.

In analyzing the statements, our goal is to describe the strategy taken by the *Fiqh* Committee to align biomedical and religious evidences concerning congregational prayer and COVID-19 vaccines. We also highlight how the Islamic constructs of *maṣlaḥa* (public interest), *ḍarūra* (dire necessity), *ḥifẓ al-nafs* (preservation of life), and *ḥifẓ al-dīn* (preservation of religion) played into the ethical deliberations.

3.1 *Establishing Congregational Prayer*

3.1.1 Religious Dimensions

The Qur'an calls on believers not only to pray but also to *establish* prayer within their homes and communities (see Q.2:43, 2:110, 7:170, 9:11, among others). Beyond the communal duty to establish prayer, praying in congregation is meritorious. Various statements from the Prophet Muhammad relay that congregational prayer is rewarded over twenty times more than individual prayer.[20] Moreover, according to some jurists, congregational prayer is a communal obligation and when an able-bodied, adult, competent Muslim male hears the call to prayer from a mosque, it becomes obligatory for him to join in that congregational service, unless he has a valid excuse.[21] Beyond the daily ritual prayers,

19 Padela, "An Introduction to Islamic Bioethics: Its Producers and Consumers."

20 *Sunan al-Nasa'i*, no. 839; and *Ṣaḥīḥ al-Bukhārī*, no. 645.

21 "Ruling on Prayer in Congregation for Men," Islam Question & Answer, November 18, 2008, https://islamqa.info/en/answers/40113/ruling-on-prayer-in-congregation-for-men; and "Is

mosques host congregational Friday worship services (*Jumuʿa*), which are also a communal obligation to establish. This service is especially significant in that it is a hallmark of the religion. For example, the Prophet Muhammad is reported to have said:

> We [Muslims] are the last [to come] but [will be] the foremost on the Day of Resurrection though the former nations were given the Holy Scriptures before us … Allah gave us the guidance for [Friday] … the Jews' [holy day is] tomorrow [i.e., Saturday] and the Christians' [is] the day after tomorrow [i.e., Sunday].[22]

Relatedly, the Qurʾan exhorts "when the call to prayer is made on Friday, then proceed [diligently] to the remembrance of Allah and leave off [your] business (Q.62:9)." Consequently, it is considered sinful for able-bodied, adult, competent Muslim men to miss these congregational prayers without a legally valid excuse. Obviously, this obligation implicates the work life of Muslims living in diasporic countries where Friday is not a holiday. Hence, various Muslim communities have established Friday services at their places of work including hospitals, universities, and storefronts. As the place from which the call to prayer rings out five times a day and where Muslims gather to worship, mosques provide an avenue for fulfilling both individual and communal religious duties and are an integral part of Muslim life.

Beyond worship, mosques are also a sanctuary and emblem of the faith. Illustratively, a statement attributed to the Prophet Muhammad notes that a town in which the call to prayer is audible is saved from God's punishment, and other statements indicate that the call to prayer differentiates between a Muslim and non-Muslim locality.[23] In addition, mosques serve other vital functions in the American context: they are often venues for education and vocational training, places where food pantries and meal services are provided, sites for health education and free clinics, and settings for social clubs, particularly for the elderly. It is this fuller conceptualization of the mosque, as a place where multiple determinants of health beyond the spiritual are attended to, that the *Fiqh* Committee had to account for when evaluating the public health risks mosque activities posed.

Congregational Prayer Obligatory?" *IslamQA*, August 31, 2012, https://islamqa.org/shafii/shafiifiqh/30069/is-congregational-prayer-obligatory/.

22 *Ṣaḥīḥ al-Bukhārī*, no. 876.

23 Jon MC, "Church Bells and the Muslims Adhan," *faithfreedom.org*, June 27, 2018, accessed March 10, 2022, https://www.faithfreedom.org/church-bells-and-the-muslims-adhan/.

3.1.2 Public Health Risks and Policy Guidance Offered by Health and State Authorities

The COVID-19 virus is transmitted from person to person by means of respiratory droplets. A person can transmit the virus through exhaling while breathing and speaking, as well as by coughing and sneezing. Hence, exposure to the virus primarily occurs by: (1) inhalation of fine respiratory droplets; (2) respiratory droplets that come into contact with exposed mucous membranes in the eyes, nose, and mouth; and (3) coming into contact with mucous membranes that have been infected with the virus directly or indirectly through touching infected surfaces. Studies have shown that transmission of COVID-19 has been primarily through exposure to respiratory droplets spread from person to person.[24] While it is true that a person can get infected by touching an infected surface, this is considered a low-risk mode because the virus cannot survive long on a dry surface.[25] Once a person has become infected with the virus, symptoms can appear between 2–14 days after an exposure. Individuals that are infected present with a variety of symptoms including: fever, chills, cough, shortness of breath or difficulty breathing, fatigue, muscle or body aches, headache, loss of taste and/or smell, sore throat, nasal congestion, nausea or vomiting, and diarrhea. While some of these symptoms are common to other infections, the loss of smell or taste is almost pathognomonic. The severity of the disease is also dependent on whether an individual has co-morbidities. These co-morbidities include high blood pressure, diabetes, obesity, and lung disease each of which can contribute to increased severity of disease and prolonged hospitalizations and deaths.

For symptomatic individuals, public health practices such as quarantining for a recommended period of time, wearing a mask, and getting virtual care from a provider will help to limit the spread to other people.[26] The public

24 "Transmission," Centers for Disease Control and Prevention, July 12, 2021, https://www.cdc.gov/coronavirus/2019-ncov/transmission/index.html; and Anshika Sharma, Isra Ahmad Farouk, and Sunil Kumar Lal, "COVID-19: A Review on the Novel Coronavirus Disease Evolution, Transmission, Detection, Control and Prevention," *Viruses* 13, no. 2 (January 29, 2021): 202, https://doi.org/10.3390/v13020202.

25 "Science Brief: SARS-CoV-2 and Surface (Fomite) Transmission for Indoor Community Environments," Centers for Disease Control and Prevention, April 5, 2021, https://www.cdc.gov/coronavirus/2019-ncov/more/science-and-research/surface-transmission.html; and Eric A. Meyerowitz et al., "Transmission of SARS-CoV-2: A Review of Viral, Host, and Environmental Factors," *Annals of Internal Medicine* 174, no. 1 (January 2021): 69–79, https://doi.org/10.7326/M20-5008.

26 "What to Do If You Are Sick," Centers for Disease Control and Prevention, February 7, 2022, https://www.cdc.gov/coronavirus/2019-ncov/if-you-are-sick/steps-when-sick.html.

health challenge was/is that asymptomatic, infected individuals are able to spread the virus. Hence, population-based strategies are/were necessary to mitigate the spread of disease because policies cannot only focus on symptomatic individuals or those who tested positive because of the lag time between infection and symptoms or test positivity. Containing the spread of the virus has proven to be difficult and taxing for public health leaders and legislative authorities. For symptomatic individuals, testing and medical care provide insights into COVID-19 hotspots and contact tracing and quarantine health to limit the spread of infection. Yet, the asymptomatic could also be vectors of disease spread. As a result, many governments, including the United States, implemented policies such as social distancing, closing business, schools, and houses of worship, prohibiting large gatherings, wearing masks outdoors and indoors, and mandating vaccinations preserve preparations as they became available. However, these policies are not uniformly applied nor applicable; state legislators governed stay-at-home and lockdown policies, some locales made policies optional while others made them mandatory, and a significant proportion of individuals simply ignored public health guidance. Moreover, with respect to religious organizations, some states carved out exemptions to limits on public gatherings, while others did not. Throughout the pandemic, there has been significant variance by locale and, as such, a very ineffective containment of disease spread within the USA. Furthermore, with each wave of infection that increased national cases and deaths, different methods have been reenacted, again introducing variance and demonstrating poor coordination by local, state, and national authorities.

3.1.3 Islamic Bioethics Deliberation and Recommendations

At the outset of the pandemic, there was vigorous debate in juridical circles outside of the committee over a proposed total closure of mosques. On one hand, particularly in the first few months of the pandemic, there was scant data related to how much Muslim prayer services elevate the risk of infectivity from COVID-19. There were reports from South Korea and India where religious services became super-spreader events,[27] and preliminary studies suggested that

27 Youjin Shin, Bonnie Berkowitz, and Min Joo Kim, "How a South Korean Church Helped Fuel the Spread of the Coronavirus," *Washington Post*, March 25, 2020, https://www.washingtonpost.com/graphics/2020/world/coronavirus-south-korea-church/; and Sanghamitra, "The Tablighi Jamat has Become the Coronavirus Super-Spreader in Asia, Read How," *OpIndia*, March 31, 2020, https://www.opindia.com/2020/03/tablighi-jamat-india-nizamuddin-iztema-lahore-malaysia-tamil-nadu-coronavirus-positive-cases/.

church choirs elevated the risk of contagion.[28] Additionally, the effectiveness of broad shutdown policies reducing disease transmission was based on experiences in China and Taiwan where social norms are quite different than in the USA. When combined, these data indicated that mosque activities *probably* elevated the risk of disease spreading among the community.

These biomedical evidences suggested that mosque activities should be curtailed, if not totally suspended, to save individual lives and societal resources. Indeed, the mantra of 'flattening the curve' was invoked in social and public media channels, noting that the high transmissibility of the disease was exacerbating the lack of resources healthcare systems had to address both COVID-19 and non-COVID-19-related health issues. In many religious circles, these healthcare system resources were deemed a public good (*maṣlaḥa ʿāmm*) that Muslims were ethically required to protect. Accordingly, based on this biomedical evidence, several religious arguments for temporary closure of mosques were admissible. For example, an overarching Islamic legal maxim states that the "repelling of harms takes precedence over the procuring of benefits" (*darʾ al-mafāsid awlā min jalb al-maṣāliḥ*),[29] hence the posited harm to individuals and broader society from disease transmission through mosque activities required redress. Indeed, this maxim is based on a Prophetic statement that reads "There is no harm or harming in Islam."[30] Furthermore, according to the higher objectives-based legal theories of Islamic law, one of the cardinal and essential objectives of the law is to preserve human life (*ḥifẓ al-nafs*).[31] Carrying on worship services within mosques conveyed a potential threat to human life, and according to this framework, demanded that the religious law remove this threat by recourse to exemptions or allowances (*rukhaṣ*). Additionally, there was historical precedent for suspending mosque-based prayer at times of contagion.[32]

---

28 Nur Hayati et al., "COVID-19 Cluster Investigation After Choir Recording at Church X Bantul Regency in 2021," *BKM Public Health and Community Medicine* 37, no. 11 Suppl. (2021), https://doi.org/10.22146/bkm.v0i0.3154; and Nathalie Charlotte, "High Rate of SARS-CoV-2 Transmission Due to Choir Practice in France at the Beginning of the COVID-19 Pandemic," *Journal of Voice*, December 2020, https://doi.org/10.1016/j.jvoice.2020.11.029.

29 Zayn al-Dīn Ibn Nujaym, in *Al-Ashbāh wa-l-Naẓāʾir*, ed. Zakariyyā ʿUmayrāt (Beirut: Dār al-Kutub al-ʿIlmiyya, 1999).

30 *Sunan Ibn Mājah*, no. 2340.

31 Aḥmad Raysūnī and International Institute of Islamic Thought, *Imam Al-Shatibi's Theory of the Higher Objectives and Intents of Islamic Law* (London: International Institute of Islamic Thought, 2005).

32 Russell Hopley, "CONTAGION IN ISLAMIC LANDS: Responses from Medieval Andalusia and North Africa," *Journal for Early Modern Cultural Studies* 10, no. 2 (2010): 45–64; and Ayman Shabana, "From the Plague to the Coronavirus: Islamic Ethics and Responses to

On the other hand, according to some views, overturning a religious obligation requires certain, and not probable, evidence. Some viewed the biomedical evidence as not meeting this standard, and hence the community may sin should all mosque-based worship activities be suspended. Additionally, there was an argument to be made that according to the higher objectives-based legal theories of Islamic law, the preservation of life was subordinate to the preservation of religion (*ḥifẓ al-dīn*).[33] As such, individual and communal obligations to establish prayer could not be suspended. Furthermore, there was an undercurrent of societal critique about what constitutes essential services that influenced views on whether mosques should be closed. Some scholars felt that religious services were as important, if not more important, than educational and business activities. Hence, the closure of mosques should be considered only when a total shutdown or stay-at-home order was levied by the government. Otherwise, Muslims would be undermining the importance of religion at a time of calamity.

As noted above, the *Fiqh* Committee sought to base the Task Force's statements on the common grounds found within extant juridical views. Given the insights Drs. Haj and Padela had into the aforementioned debates and their connections to leading juridical bodies, both worked to set the stage for a nuanced and balanced approach to the issue. First, most jurists agreed that mosques activities were subject to state and public health authority rulings. If a public health authority aligned with the state judged mosque activities to convey public health risks and enacted restrictions, then Muslims would be ethically obligated to follow the guidance. Otherwise, Muslims would contribute to morally objectionable public disorder. Hence, Task Force statements came to foreground the necessity of following local public health and state authority rulings. For example, the Task Force's statement in March 2020 stated that "mosques and community centers should follow guidance from the US Centers for Disease Control and Prevention (CDC) in accordance with local and national public health authorities,"[34] and in July 2020 that they should "con-

the COVID-19 Pandemic," *Journal of Islamic Ethics*, April 13, 2021, 1–37, https://doi.org/10.1163/24685542-12340060.

33 Raysūnī and International Institute of Islamic Thought, *Imam Al-Shatibi's Theory of the Higher Objectives and Intents of Islamic Law*; Ibrāhīm ibn Mūsá Shāṭibī, Imran Ahsan Khan Nyazee, Raji M. Rammuny, and Centre for Muslim Contribution to Civilization, *The Reconciliation of the Fundamentals of Islamic Law* (Reading: Garnet, 2011); and Aasim I. Padela, "The Essential Dimensions of Health According to the Maqasid Al-Shari'ah Frameworks of Abu Ishaq al-Shatibi and Jamal-al-Din-'Atiyah," *IIUM Medical Journal Malaysia* 17, no. 1 (July 18, 2018), https://doi.org/10.31436/imjm.v17i1.1035.

34 "Joint Statement From the National Muslim Task Force on COVID-19 Regarding the Glob-

tinue to follow public health guidelines to prevent the spread of COVID-19 by practicing social distancing, wearing masks and staying at home, when possible."[35]

A second area of consensus was that social and educational mosque activities could be suspended in light of the probable risks of disease transmission. From a religious law perspective, the principal purpose of mosques is to establish prayer; these other functions are ancillary—despite being important. Similarly, counseling and other activities, which could be provided via online and telephonic methods, were to be switched to those channels. Accordingly, the March 2020 statement explicitly called for the suspension of all non-essential gatherings including social and educational events and the implementation of online and telephonic platforms, arguing that it accorded with the maxim "avoiding harm takes precedence over acquiring benefit."[36]

Finally, with respect to establishing prayer services in the mosque, the committee took the approach of drilling down into the communally obligatory aspects of prayer and allowing them to proceed in minimal fashion where local leaders judged it was safe to do so. This involved the following recommendations: (i) suspending mosque-based prayer services for those worship activities that were not a communal obligation to establish, for example, night vigil prayers (*tarāwīḥ*) in Ramadan; (ii) advising individuals on whom there is no obligation to attend congregational services to forgo attendance, obligating those who are sick to take the exemption and not attend services so as to also protect others, and reiterating that individuals who have risk factors that would make COVID-19 a credible life threat to have a justified exemption from establishing prayer in the mosque; and (iii) constraining the performance of congregational prayer to the minimum required for validity, for example, shortening the Friday sermon and completing recommended and supererogatory prayer circuits at home. Moreover, the Task Force reiterated the adoption of mitiga-

al Coronavirus Pandemic (Also Known as SARS-CoV-2 or COVID-19)," Islamic Medical Association of North America, March 18, 2020, https://www.imana.org/wp-content/uploads/2023/06/National-Muslim-Task-Force-Statement-on-COVID-19_03-18-2020.pdf; and "Toolkit for Community and Faith-Based Organizations," Centers for Disease Control and Prevention, January 14, 2021, https://www.cdc.gov/coronavirus/2019-ncov/communication/toolkits/community-faith-based.html.

35 "Joint Statement From the National Muslim Task Force and the National Black Muslim COVID Coalition on COVID-19 Regarding Eid ul-Adha," Islamic Medical Association of North America, July 27, 2020, https://www.imana.org/wp-content/uploads/2020/07/National-Muslim-Task-Force-Joint-Statement-for-Eid-ul-Adha_.pdf.

36 "Joint Statement From the National Muslim Task Force on COVID-19 Regarding the Global Coronavirus Pandemic (Also Known as SARS-CoV-2 or COVID-19)," March 18, 2020.

tion strategies by enforcing social distancing and masking, and room capacity limits. Indeed, the Task Force opted to prioritize safety by explicitly noting that mosque elders would be within their religious rights to suspend prayer services should they not be able to carry them out safely. Nearly every statement underscored this fact and when a phased reopening of society was implemented, the Policy Committee of the Task Force developed safe reopening checklists so that mosque elders could judge their readiness for re-establishing prayer services and other activities.[37] Finally, it is worth mentioning that every statement frames adherence to the proposed guidelines as part of living out a religious life, and when there were religious obligations that were suspended, these communiqués noted that there were alternative religious obligations that were maintained. For example, the suspension of congregating for Friday services was reframed as the continuing obligation to perform midday prayers.

Illustrating the first tactic of suspending prayer services that are not community obligations, the March 2020 statement declared:

> the 5 daily prayers are individual obligations. Although performing these prayers in congregation within mosques is highly recommended, when establishing prayer within mosques poses undue hardship or harm to oneself or others, performing prayer individually fulfills our religious obligation. Thus, in light of potential health risks to congregants … the Task Force urges mosques to suspend public congregational prayers.[38]

Similarly, the April 2020 guidance recommended that mosque leaders to not "establish communal night vigils (*taraweeh/qiyam ul-layl*). Rather these Ramadan-related prayers can be performed by families and individuals in their own residences." The second tactic was adopted in these same communiqués. The March 2020 statement called out that Friday prayers are "not obligatory in specific instances—such as for the sick—and there is significant Islamic legal precedent for exemption," and that if congregational prayer "poses undue hardship or harm to oneself or others, performing prayer individually fulfills our religious obligation," subtly hinting at the permissibility of taking exemptions

37 "Joint Statement From the National Muslim Task Force on COVID-19 Regarding a Phased Reopening of Mosques Across United States," Islamic Medical Association of North America, May 18, 2020, https://www.imana.org/wp-content/uploads/2023/07/Joint-Statement-on-Phased-Reopening-of-Mosques_05182020.pdf.

38 "Joint Statement From the National Muslim Task Force on COVID-19 Regarding the Global Coronavirus Pandemic (Also Known as SARS-CoV-2 or COVID-19)," March 18, 2020.

and allowances.[39] The April 2021 tip-sheet was more explicit noting that individuals over the age of 65, and those with co-morbidities such as high blood pressure, heart disease lung disease, and other such ailments should consider staying home.[40] Lastly, the third strategy was also explicit in the March 2020 statement where it was strongly recommended that the Friday prayer be "fulfilled by minimal gatherings (the weightier Hanafi view notes 3 individuals represent a quorum) and with minimal sermonizing (*hamd, salawat, tilawat,* and *dua*)."[41]

This nuanced approach was adopted throughout the pandemic and applied to the daily congregational prayers, Friday services, the night vigil prayers of Ramadan, as well as Eid prayers. Since daily congregational prayers are not generally obligated by Islamic law, the night vigil prayers are recommended but non-obligatory, and Eid prayers are considered nonobligatory most jurists, Friday services remain the essential worship activity that has required consistent address throughout pandemic. The initial curtailment voiced in March 2020 was gradually lifted as the case rates fell, for example, the May 2020 statement noted that "some mosques may reopen for communal services (e.g., Friday Jummah prayers) where allowed by law and through careful implementation of safe practices."[42] By October 2020, the Task Force recognize that society was opening up and advised that "mosques and Islamic centers … adhere to local regulations about public gatherings (and daily congregational) prayers can be performed safely in the [mosques] if guidelines are followed."[43] In this second year of the pandemic, nearly all mosques in the United States opened up for Friday and congregational prayers given that vaccines provided an additional layer of protection, and state and public health authorities no longer advocated for limited capacity within business and social establishments. While one may argue, given where we are at the time of this writing (January 2022) with

39 "Joint Statement from the National Muslim Task Force on COVID-19 (NMTF) and the National Black Muslim COVID Coalition (NBMCC) on Ramadan 2021 and COVID-19 Vaccines," April 6, 2021.

40 "Joint Statement from the National Muslim Task Force on COVID-19 (NMTF) and the National Black Muslim COVID Coalition (NBMCC) on Ramadan 2021 and COVID-19 Vaccines," April 6, 2021.

41 "Joint Statement From the National Muslim Task Force on COVID-19 Regarding the Global Coronavirus Pandemic (Also Known as SARS-CoV-2 or COVID-19)," March 18, 2020.

42 "Joint Statement from the National Muslim Task Force on COVID-19 Regarding a Phased Reopening of Mosques across United States," May 18, 2020.

43 "Joint Statement from the National Muslim Task Force on Covid-19 and the National Black Muslim Covid Coalition on the COVID-19 Surge," American Muslim Health Professionals, October 29, 2020, https://amhp.us/wp-content/uploads/2020/11/National-Muslim-Task-Force-Joint-Statement-for-COVID-19-Surge.pdf.

the Omicron-based widespread disease transmission and concurrent limited healthcare capacity, religious arguments for constraints on mosque activities may be actionable. Yet, without the state and public health authority cover, jurists, juridical bodies, and mosque leaders appear ill-motivated to restrict prayer in mosques.

3.2 *Taking COVID-19 Vaccines*

With the ever-increasing health, economic, and social toll the COVID-19 pandemic was having, biomedical scientists both within the academy and the pharmaceutical industry heavily invested in trying to develop vaccines that could mitigate disease morbidity and infectivity. Companies around the globe from Russia to the USA took part in the clinical research to develop and test various vaccine formulations. In late 2020, the food and drug administration granted emergency use authorization (EUA) to two vaccines—one developed by Pfizer/BioNTech and the other by Moderna—each of which are based on novel mRNA technology that targets immune response against the COVID-19 spike protein. Several weeks later, in early 2021, a third vaccine developed by Johnson & Johnson using more traditional methods of an adenovirus vector that also develops an immune response against the spike protein, was granted an EUA. The EUAs were based on internal pharmaceutical company data demonstrating effectiveness against disease morbidity and transmission, as well as early clinical trial data that demonstrated the same.[44] In the early stages, given limited supply and the need for ongoing clinical trials, the EUA authorized public health agencies to proceed with a limited deployment of the vaccines to essential workers and individuals at high risk of morbidity and mortality from COVID-19 disease. As supply and data streams were bolstered, a broader public vaccination strategy has been deployed over the past year, and various vaccine mandates have been used to motivate vaccination. As of Febru-

44 "Clinical Trial Data | Moderna COVID-19 Vaccine (EUA)," Modernatx, accessed March 10, 2022, https://www.modernatx.com/covid19vaccine-eua/providers/clinical-trial-data; "Pfizer and BioNTech Initiate Rolling Submission for Emergency Use Authorization of Their COVID-19 Vaccine in Children 6 Months Through 4 Years of Age Following Request From U.S. FDA | Pfizer," Pfizer, February 1, 2022, https://www.pfizer.com/news/press-release/press-release-detail/pfizer-and-biontech-initiate-rolling-submission-emergency; Sara Y. Tartof et al., "Effectiveness of MRNA BNT162b2 COVID-19 Vaccine up to 6 Months in a Large Integrated Health System in the USA: A Retrospective Cohort Study," *The Lancet* 398, no. 10309 (October 2021): 1407–1416, https://doi.org/10.1016/S0140-6736(21)02183-8; and Minal K. Patel et al., "Evaluation of Post-Introduction COVID-19 Vaccine Effectiveness: Summary of Interim Guidance of the World Health Organization," *Vaccine* 39, no. 30 (July 2021): 4013–4024, https://doi.org/10.1016/j.vaccine.2021.05.099.

ary 2022, 76.3 percent of the American population has received one dose of a vaccine with 64.9 percent being fully vaccinated.[45]

Certainly COVID-19 vaccine manufacture and deployment has been subject to intense public and professional scrutiny. There are various issues and narratives surrounding the vaccines that make its uptake a controversial matter, from concerns about the motivations of pharmaceutical and state actors in authorizing vaccination, to concerns about the limited oversight and speed with which the vaccines were developed, to controversies over the procedures and ingredients used to manufacture vaccines.[46] Any discussion of vaccine uptake must acknowledge the politicized narratives and the legitimate concerns various corners of society have about the vaccines. However, it is beyond the capacity and scope of this chapter to fully weigh in on how these issues and narratives impact Muslim behaviors. With respect to capacity, there is no population representative data regarding Muslim-American COVID-19 vaccination rates. Indeed, national healthcare and administrative databases, as well as national surveys, overlook religious affiliation thereby precluding disparities research based on religious identity. Additionally, local Muslim institutions lack the infrastructure to conduct prospective research on vaccine uptake within their own communities. Indeed, all Muslim-American healthcare disparities research suffers from this lack of attention and capacity.[47] With respect to scope, our focus is on the religious dimensions of this health behavior for the *Fiqh* Committee sought to address the religion-related bioethical concerns Muslims had with the vaccines. In that vein, there were two main issues to resolve. First, what is the moral status of taking a vaccine? And second are the ingredients in the vaccines judged to be religiously permissible to consume or partake of?

According to the classical Sunni schools of law, taking medicine is a permissible or recommended but non-obligatory. Said another way, an individual is not judged to be sinning should they decide not to take a certain therapeutic. This analysis is based on the fact that medicine is probabilistic, and treatments are not certain to relieve or cure illness; Qur'anic verses as well as Prophetic

45 Mayo Clinic, "U.S. COVID-19 Vaccine Tracker."

46 Josh Michaud and Jennifer Kates, "Distributing a COVID-19 Vaccine Across the U.S.—A Look at Key Issues," KFF, October 20, 2020, https://www.kff.org/report-section/distributing-a-covid-19-vaccine-across-the-u-s-a-look-at-key-issues-issue-brief/.

47 Aasim I. Padela and Afrah Raza, "American Muslim Health Disparities: The State of the Medline Literature," *Journal of Health Disparities Research and Practice* 8, no. 1 (2015): 1–9; and Amal Killawi et al., "Using CBPR for Health Research in American Muslim Mosque Communities," *Progress in Community Health Partnerships: Research, Education, and Action* 9, no. 1 (2015): 65–74, https://doi.org/10.1353/cpr.2015.0007.

reports unequivocally note that God has full dominion over disease, illness, healing, and cure.[48] Classical Islamic jurists have reconciled these notions by determining that the moral status of healthcare seeking is permissible save for exceptional circumstances. Those exceptions could elevate the action to be obligated when a proposed treatment is assuredly lifesaving.[49] A more contemporary juridical council involving scholars from across the various schools of law ruled that partaking of medicine can be obligatory if not doing so leads to disability and or conveys credible health risks to others.[50] Within Muslim scholarly and public circles, the contention over COVID-19 vaccines related to the evaluation of whether the vaccine is assuredly lifesaving, and whether not taking the vaccine would credibly harm others.

Some early clinical research data did suggest that the vaccines prevented mortality from COVID-19 within the study population. However, these study protocols were tightly controlled and the study samples did not fully represent American population. The weight of the evidence, both in the early stages of the pandemic and now with the Delta and Omicron variants, suggests a reduction in morbidity as well as mortality from vaccination, but not that it fully prevents death from the disease.[51] Similarly, research data suggests that disease transmission is greatly reduced by vaccination, that is, vaccinated individuals have lower shedding of the virus. Yet, individuals who have the disease and are vaccinated can still transmit the disease through droplets and respiration.[52] Consequently, the extant biomedical data does not bear out the fact that vaccination is assuredly lifesaving nor that not taking the vaccine would credibly

48 Omar Qureshi and Aasim I. Padela, "When Must a Patient Seek Healthcare? Bringing the Perspectives of Islamic Jurists and Clinicians into Dialogue," *Zygon®* 51, no. 3 (September 2016): 592–625, https://doi.org/10.1111/zygo.12273.

49 Qureshi and Padela, "When Must a Patient Seek Healthcare?"

50 Mohammed Ali Al-Bar and Hassan Chamsi-Pasha, *Contemporary Bioethics: Islamic Perspective* (Cham: Springer International Publishing, 2015); and Mohammed Ali Albar, "Seeking Remedy, Abstaining From Therapy and Resuscitation: An Islamic Perspective," *Saudi Journal of Kidney Diseases and Transplantation* 18, no. 4 (2007): 629–637, https://www.sjkdt.org/text.asp?2007/18/4/629/36527.

51 Ronen Arbel et al., "BNT162b2 Vaccine Booster and Mortality Due to Covid-19," *New England Journal of Medicine* 385, no. 26 (December 23, 2021): 2413–2420, https://doi.org/10.1056/NEJMoa2115624; and Amelia G. Johnson, "COVID-19 Incidence and Death Rates Among Unvaccinated and Fully Vaccinated Adults With and Without Booster Doses During Periods of Delta and Omicron Variant Emergence—25 U.S. Jurisdictions, April 4–December 25, 2021," *MMWR: Morbidity and Mortality Weekly Report* 71 (2022), https://doi.org/10.15585/mmwr.mm7104e2.

52 Michael A. Johansson et al., "SARS-CoV-2 Transmission From People Without COVID-19 Symptoms," *JAMA Network Open* 4, no. 1 (January 7, 2021): e2035057, https://doi.org/10.1001/jamanetworkopen.2020.35057.

harm others. Hence, the *Fiqh* Committee, and the juridical councils that committee members are affiliated with, did not consider it a moral obligation for Muslims to take the vaccine. Furthermore, there are contentions around every piece of evidence that supports public vaccination efficacy, some of which are legitimate and others baseless. This reality on the ground figured into the messaging the Task Force would take toward vaccination. A 'strong' statement of promotion could be seen as an overreach into co-option of religious lexicon for biomedical ends. Hence, the Task Force communiqués in April and August 2021 strongly recommended vaccination.[53]

A more pressing concern for the *Fiqh* Committee was to address issues related to juridically impure substances being part of, or utilized in manufacturing, the vaccines. It is well known that many vaccines utilize porcine gelatin as a stabilizer. Porcine products are particularly controversial for Muslims as pork is considered to be an impure substance, one that should not be used for human purposes.[54] Thankfully, none of the vaccines contained porcine gelatin and it was important for the Task Force to relay this message lest individual Muslims reject the vaccine perceiving it to be containing porcine products. Illustratively, the April 2021 statement noted that none of the three vaccines contained pork products and were *ḥalāl* (permissible to use).[55] Yet, there are concerns about the Johnson & Johnson vaccine having been manufactured using cell lines from aborted fetal stem cells. Certain Christian voices had raised alarms at this relationship between aborted tissue and the vaccine, and some Islamic jurists followed suit. For example, a prominent fatwa committee associated with Darul Qasim Institute in Chicago advised Muslims to stay away from the Johnson & Johnson vaccine because of its alleged association with a fetal cell line.[56] The religious concern was not so much the abortion that led to a fetal cell line, rather than the fetal cell lines contain a measure of inviolabil-

53 "Joint Statement from the National Muslim Task Force on COVID-19 (NMTF) and the National Black Muslim COVID Coalition (NBMCC) on Ramadan 2021 and COVID-19 Vaccines," April 6, 2021; and "Keeping Students Safe: Joint Statement on School Re-Openings and COVID Vaccines," *ISLA*, accessed March 10, 2022, https://theisla.org/keeping-students-safe/.

54 "The Ruling on Getting the COVID-19 (Coronavirus) Vaccine," Assembly of Muslim Jurists of America, December 13, 2020, https://www.amjaonline.org/fatwa/en/87763/the-ruling-on-getting-the-covid-19-coronavirus-vaccine.

55 "Joint Statement from the National Muslim Task Force on COVID-19 (NMTF) and the National Black Muslim COVID Coalition (NBMCC) on Ramadan 2021 and COVID-19 Vaccines," April 6, 2021.

56 Amin Kholwadia and Hisham Dawood, "Fatwā On COVID Vaccines" (Glendale Heights, IL: Darul Qasim, April 21, 2021), https://darulqasim.org/wp-content/uploads/2021/04/DI00489-Fatwa-COVID-Vaccine.pdf.

ity and sanctity and should not be used to manufacture medicaments. On the other hand, the Assembly of Muslim Jurists of America, and the British Board of Scholars and Imams did not find this argument to preclude taking the vaccine, and held the relationship to abortion to be so distant from the contemporary cell line that it did not figure into their moral evaluation.[57] Given the principle of Islamic law that juridical disagreement over a matter suggests that there is no singular determinative religious view, the *Fiqh* Committee and Task Force advanced that all three vaccines were considered religiously permissible and advised consultation with a medical professional about which one was right for the individual.

In their deliberations, *Fiqh* Committee members did consider that taking the vaccine could be backed as an action that aligned with the higher objective of *ḥifẓ al-nafs* (the preservation of life) and grounded in the construct of securing a *maṣlaḥa* (public interest) in stemming disease spread. It also considered that for certain individuals with the appropriate risk profile taking the vaccine could be viewed as a dire necessity (*ḍarūra*) because of the high risk they have for death should they contract COVID-19. However, given that the remit of the committee was not to issue their own verdict and that the statements were directed more at communities and not individuals, the committee did not include these arguments within the statements.

4 Discursive Gaps: The Task Force, Muslim Needs, and Islamic Bioethics

The National Muslim Task Force on COVID-19 was quickly stood up by enterprising leaders of AMHP, IMANA, and ISNA as they recognized the urgent need for a platform through which Muslim organizations could communicate and provide collective counsel and support to Muslim communities across the nation. They also recognized the need to draw attention to Muslim concerns on a national stage. Indeed, the very first statement released by the Task Force exclaimed that it is

> a time for unity across all boundaries ... (and) numerous entities including religious, civic, community, medical, and public health organizations

57 British Board of Scholars & Imams, "Top Ten Questions Imams & Scholars Get Asked About Vaccines," December 24, 2020, http://www.bbsi.org.uk/wp-content/uploads/2020/12/BBSI-Vaccines-2020-1.pdf.

> have come together to serve the educational, social, spiritual, and physical well-being of American Muslims and our society at large.[58]

This bold vision and broad mission has been powerfully channeled into community service; the Task Force has been an undeniable force of good in this time of trial coordinating numerous educational webinars, fundraising events, food banks, vaccination campaigns, and the like. Yet, as we move into this third year of the pandemic, collective exhaustion has taken root as many pandemic-related challenges remain to be tackled. In this closing section, we would like to point out several discursive gaps that constrain the reach and effectiveness of the Task Force. Attending to these gaps at the outset of such initiatives, or presently with respect to the Task Force, could bolster their impact.

The first gap draws attention to the disconnect between Muslim stakeholders and health policymakers. At its inception, and at various junctures during its operation, there has been confusion over the Task Force's primary audience. Certainly, Task Force members saw themselves as organizational representatives who were brought together to address the needs of Muslim Americans, however, it has remained ambiguous as to whether the Task Force should focus on *speaking to* Muslims, or alternatively *speaking about* Muslim needs to external policymakers. While the Task Force statements indicate that the Task Force saw its primary audience as the Muslim community for the statements seek to motivate Muslim behaviors, the choice of this primary audience, however, was made by default. Addressing Muslim-American needs through policy action requires communication channels that Task Force members did/do not possess. For example, outside of AMHP's connection to the Center for Faith-Based and Neighborhood Partnerships at the Health and Human Services Administration, and the White House's Office of Community and Faith-Based Partnerships, there is no direct link or history of collaboration between Task Force organizations and health policymakers at the state and/or national level. Relatedly, Task Force organizations had little experience with, or capacity for, creating data streams about Muslim community needs that could support policy action even if communication channels were established. As an example, although there are large Muslim mosque communities in California, Texas, and Illinois, Muslim voices were largely left out of policy conversations regarding exemptions for religious congregations from capacity limits on public gatherings. Similarly, while there has been a significant policy focus on getting

58 "Joint Statement From the National Muslim Task Force on COVID-19 Regarding the Global Coronavirus Pandemic (Also Known as SARS-CoV-2 or COVID-19)," American Muslim Health Professionals, accessed March 10, 2022, https://amhp.us/covid19-statement/.

vaccines and tailored educational material to communities disproportionately stricken by COVID-19 morbidity and mortality, as well as plagued by vaccine hesitancy, there is no data stream evidencing such among the Muslim community nationally. Muslim organizations that are part of the NMTF have little capacity to generate such data streams, which could draw the attention of policymakers. This issue is further compounded by the fact that healthcare disparities in the United States based on long-established policy regulations are primarily measured along racial/ethnic lines and religious affiliation is not a measured variable, as such data on the Muslim community because of its racial/ethnic diversity and its aggregation based on religious identity is out of reach. While the Task Force's primary goal was to address Muslim community needs during the pandemic, addressing these needs requires communication with health policymakers outside of Muslim communities. The disconnect between health policymakers and Muslim organizations hamstrings addressing these needs. Moreover, the ethical analyses undertaken through an Islamic lens, as is the case in the Task Force statements, are relevant beyond Muslim circles for they speak to issues of global ethics and equity. This relevance is obscured due to the aforementioned discursive gaps. For example, issues that Muslims may have about porcine or fetal stem cell-related ingredients in vaccines are shared by other religious communities and, insofar as they are not addressed, inequities in vaccine uptake may arise. Similarly, arguments against closing mosques which address the spiritual and religious determinants of health while social clubs remain open should be heard by policymakers for they speak to larger issues about privileging some aspects of health, and some societal activities, over others.[59] Establishing better connectivity between policymakers and Muslim stakeholders would go a long way in attending to the "educational, social, spiritual, and physical well-being of American Muslims and our society at large."[60]

The second disconnect relates to that between biomedical and religious expertise. As illustrated above, pandemic-related concerns—regarding religious activities such as prayer and health decisions such as taking COVID-19 vaccines—have both religious and biomedical dimensions. Addressing these

59 Aasim I. Padela, "Commentary: Religious Communities are Critical in the Fight Against COVID-19," *Chicago Tribune*, April 17, 2020, https://www.chicagotribune.com/opinion/commentary/ct-opinion-coronavirus-public-health-faith-leaders-padela-20200417-3dv5x6ex6nc6hlslceygp2llpe-story.html.

60 American Muslim Health Professionals, "Joint Statement From the National Muslim Task Force on COVID-19 Regarding the Global Coronavirus Pandemic (Also Known as SARS-CoV-2 or COVID-19)."

concerns, consequently, requires bridging biomedical and religious data and aligning the ethical imperatives of each domain of knowledge. The founding organizations of the NMTF, AMHP, and IMANA primarily comprised clinicians and allied healthcare providers. The leaders of these organizations are drawn from the membership and thus their expertise generally resides in the biomedical domain. Neither organization has a standing *fiqh* or bioethics committees where religious, ethical, and legal experts would be brought in for consultation. Absent religious law expertise within its fold, neither organization routinely engages with Islamic jurists and juridical bodies to address the religious determinants of health behaviors or the religious implications of health policies.[61] A similar critique could be leveled at American juridical councils such as the *Fiqh* Council of North America and the Assembly of Muslim Jurists of America (AMJA) in that they rarely collaborate with Muslim health professional organizations to address issues of bioethics and/or health policy.[62] Thus, healthcare professional organizations and religious councils operate in relative silos, not benefiting from each other's expertise and hamstring efforts at generating holistic solutions to the ethical challenges that they confront. These gaps lead to inaccurate conceptualizations of the problem space, partial answers, and disordered and confusing Islamic bioethics discourse. While it is laudable that the Task Force was able to fill in this discursive gap through the *Fiqh* Committee, it remains to be seen whether this sort of dialogue will outlast the Task Force. In our view, institutional commitments by AMHP and IMANA through structures such as bioethics committees are required to sustain channels of communication, and commitments by juridical bodies to seek out biomedical experts at these or other organizations when deliberating over bioethical issues is required to align religious and the biomedical imperatives. Islamic bioethics deliberation requires multi-sectoral and multidisciplinary engagement.

This pandemic has tried and tested many communities, nations, as well as the global community. The COVID-19 global pandemic put stress on collected resources and frontline workers who have worked to contain, treat, and care for those who were infected and suffered the severe consequences of the disease. For the Muslim community, the challenges were/are in being able to balance the needs and practices of faith, while adhering to public health rules

61 While individual members of these organizations may contain such research and theological expertise, the organizations themselves, arguably, do not see their missions as encompassing such work.

62 Dr. Hatem El Haj serves on AMJA's fatwa committee and as such biomedical expertise is present on the Council. The statement reflects that AMJA does not routinely collaborate with healthcare and clinician organizations.

and mandates. These challenges were also spurned by misinformation that was spread widely through various social media that required Muslim scholars, policy experts, and health and medical leaders to come together through the NMTF to promote the accurate information and share knowledge on how to practice their faith safely. While the NMTF was able to respond to needs, there were limitations due to the lack of research and available data on the Muslim community during the pandemic. There were numerous studies by the Kaiser Family Foundation and others that did not include findings on Muslims regarding the sentiment of pandemic, vaccine uptake, concerns, and other metrics that could help local and national leaders to address these concerns and challenges in order to limit the transmission of the COVID-19 pandemic.[63] Going forward, it will be critical to collect data on Muslim community needs and sentiment, and to forge connections between religious, biomedical, and policy experts.

Bibliography

Albar, Mohammed Ali. “Seeking Remedy, Abstaining from Therapy and Resuscitation: An Islamic Perspective.” *Saudi Journal of Kidney Diseases and Transplantation* 18, no. 4 (2007): 629–637. https://www.sjkdt.org/text.asp?2007/18/4/629/36527.

Al-Bar, Mohammed Ali, and Hassan Chamsi-Pasha. *Contemporary Bioethics: Islamic Perspective*. Cham: Springer International Publishing, 2015.

American Muslim Health Professionals. “Joint Statement from the National Muslim Task Force on COVID-19 and the National Black Muslim Covid Coalition on the COVID-19 Surge.” October 29, 2020. https://amhp.us/wp-content/uploads/2020/11/National-Muslim-Task-Force-Joint-Statement-for-COVID-19-Surge.pdf.

American Muslim Health Professionals. “Joint Statement From the National Muslim Task Force on COVID-19 Regarding the Global Coronavirus Pandemic (Also Known as SARS-CoV-2 or COVID-19).” Accessed March 10, 2022. https://amhp.us/covid19-statement/.

63 “KFF COVID-19 Vaccine Monitor Dashboard,” KFF, March 1, 2022, https://www.kff.org/coronavirus-covid-19/dashboard/kff-covid-19-vaccine-monitor-dashboard/; Annie Kibongani Volet et al., “Vaccine Hesitancy Among Religious Groups: Reasons Underlying This Phenomenon and Communication Strategies to Rebuild Trust,” *Frontiers in Public Health* 10 (February 7, 2022): 824560, https://doi.org/10.3389/fpubh.2022.824560; and “Religious Identities and the Race Against the Virus: Successes and Opportunities for Engaging Faith Communities on COVID-19 Vaccination,” PRRI, July 28, 2021, https://www.prri.org/research/religious-vaccines-covid-vaccination/.

Arbel, Ronen, Ariel Hammerman, Ruslan Sergienko, Michael Friger, Alon Peretz, Doron Netzer, and Shlomit Yaron. "BNT162b2 Vaccine Booster and Mortality Due to Covid-19." *New England Journal of Medicine* 385, no. 26 (December 23, 2021): 2413–2420. https://doi.org/10.1056/NEJMoa2115624.

Assembly of Muslim Jurists of America. "The Ruling on Getting the COVID-19 (Coronavirus) Vaccine." December 13, 2020. https://www.amjaonline.org/fatwa/en/87763/the-ruling-on-getting-the-covid-19-coronavirus-vaccine.

Baden, Lindsey R., Hana M. El Sahly, Brandon Essink, Karen Kotloff, Sharon Frey, Rick Novak, David Diemert, et al. "Efficacy and Safety of the MRNA-1273 SARS-CoV-2 Vaccine." *New England Journal of Medicine* 384, no. 5 (February 4, 2021): 403–416. https://doi.org/10.1056/NEJMoa2035389.

British Board of Scholars & Imams. "Top Ten Questions Imams & Scholars Get Asked About Vaccines." December 24, 2020. http://www.bbsi.org.uk/wp-content/uploads/2020/12/BBSI-Vaccines-2020-1.pdf.

Centers for Disease Control and Prevention. "COVID Data Tracker." Accessed March 10, 2022. https://covid.cdc.gov/covid-data-tracker.

Centers for Disease Control and Prevention. "Interim Pre-Pandemic Planning Guidance: Community Strategy for Pandemic Influenza Mitigation in the United States: Early, Targeted, Layered Use of Nonpharmaceutical Interventions." February 2007. https://stacks.cdc.gov/view/cdc/11425.

Centers for Disease Control and Prevention. "Science Brief: SARS-CoV-2 and Surface (Fomite) Transmission for Indoor Community Environments." April 5, 2021. https://www.cdc.gov/coronavirus/2019-ncov/more/science-and-research/surface-transmis sion.html.

Centers for Disease Control and Prevention. "Toolkit for Community and Faith-Based Organizations." January 14, 2021. https://www.cdc.gov/coronavirus/2019-ncov/com munication/toolkits/community-faith-based.html.

Centers for Disease Control and Prevention. "Transmission." July 12, 2021. https://www .cdc.gov/coronavirus/2019-ncov/transmission/index.html.

Centers for Disease Control and Prevention. "What to Do If You Are Sick." February 7, 2022. https://www.cdc.gov/coronavirus/2019-ncov/if-you-are-sick/steps-when -sick.html.

Charlotte, Nathalie. "High Rate of SARS-CoV-2 Transmission Due to Choir Practice in France at the Beginning of the COVID-19 Pandemic." *Journal of Voice*, December 2020. https://doi.org/10.1016/j.jvoice.2020.11.029.

Haque, Azizul, and Anudeep B. Pant. "Efforts at COVID-19 Vaccine Development: Challenges and Successes." *Vaccines* 8, no. 4 (December 6, 2020): 739. https://doi.org/10 .3390/vaccines8040739.

Hayati, Nur, Fitriana Puspitarani, Andri Setyo Dwi Nugroho, and Citra Indriani. "COVID-19 Cluster Investigation After Choir Recording at Church X Bantul Regency in 2021."

BKM *Public Health and Community Medicine* 37, no. 11 Suppl. (2021). https://doi.org/10.22146/bkm.v0i0.3154.

Hopley, Russell. "CONTAGION IN ISLAMIC LANDS: Responses from Medieval Andalusia and North Africa." *Journal for Early Modern Cultural Studies* 10, no. 2 (2010): 45–64.

Ibn Nujaym, Zayn al-Dīn. In *Al-Ashbāh wa-l-Naẓāʾir*, edited by Zakariyyā ʿUmayrāt. Beirut: Dār al-Kutub al-ʿIlmiyya, 1999.

ISLA. "Keeping Students Safe: Joint Statement on School Re-Openings and COVID Vaccines." Accessed March 10, 2022. https://theisla.org/keeping-students-safe/.

Islam Question & Answer. "Ruling on Prayer in Congregation for Men." November 18, 2008. https://islamqa.info/en/answers/40113/ruling-on-prayer-in-congregation-for-men.

Islamic Medical Association of North America. "Joint Statement from the National Muslim Task Force on COVID-19 (NMTF) and the National Black Muslim COVID Coalition (NBMCC) on Ramadan 2021 and COVID-19 Vaccines." April 6, 2021. https://www.imana.org/wp-content/uploads/2020/02/NMTFC_NBMCC-and-COVID-vaccines.pdf.

Islamic Medical Association of North America. "Joint Statement From the National Muslim Task Force on COVID-19 Regarding the Global Coronavirus Pandemic (Also Known as SARS-CoV-2 or COVID-19)." March 18, 2020. https://www.imana.org/wp-content/uploads/2023/06/National-Muslim-Task-Force-Statement-on-COVID-19_03-18-2020.pdf.

Islamic Medical Association of North America. "Joint Statement From the National Muslim Task Force on COVID-19 Regarding a Phased Reopening of Mosques Across United States." May 18, 2020. https://www.imana.org/wp-content/uploads/2023/07/Joint-Statement-on-Phased-Reopening-of-Mosques_05182020.pdf.

Islamic Medical Association of North America. "Joint Statement From the National Muslim Task Force and the National Black Muslim COVID Coalition on COVID-19 Regarding Eid ul-Adha." July 27, 2020. https://www.imana.org/wp-content/uploads/2020/07/National-Muslim-Task-Force-Joint-Statement-for-Eid-ul-Adha_.pdf.

Islamic Medical Association of North America. "Joint Statement Regarding the Global Coronavirus Pandemic (Also Known as SARS-CoV-2 or COVID-19)." Accessed March 10, 2022. hhttps://www.imana.org/wp-content/uploads/2023/06/National-Muslim-Task-Force-Statement-on-COVID-19_03-18-2020.pdf.

IslamQA. "Is Congregational Prayer Obligatory?" August 31, 2012. https://islamqa.org/shafii/shafiifiqh/30069/is-congregational-prayer-obligatory/.

Johansson, Michael A., Talia M. Quandelacy, Sarah Kada, Pragati Venkata Prasad, Molly Steele, John T. Brooks, Rachel B. Slayton, Matthew Biggerstaff, and Jay C. Butler. "SARS-CoV-2 Transmission From People Without COVID-19 Symptoms." *JAMA Network Open* 4, no. 1 (January 7, 2021): e2035057. https://doi.org/10.1001/jamanetworkopen.2020.35057.

Johnson, Amelia G. "COVID-19 Incidence and Death Rates Among Unvaccinated and Fully Vaccinated Adults With and Without Booster Doses During Periods of Delta and Omicron Variant Emergence—25 U.S. Jurisdictions, April 4–December 25, 2021." *MMWR: Morbidity and Mortality Weekly Report* 71 (2022). https://doi.org/10.15585/mmwr.mm7104e2.

Jon MC. "Church Bells and the Muslims Adhan." *faithfreedom.org*, June 27, 2018. Accessed March 10, 2022. https://www.faithfreedom.org/church-bells-and-the-muslims-adhan/.

KFF. "KFF COVID-19 Vaccine Monitor Dashboard." March 1, 2022. https://www.kff.org/coronavirus-covid-19/dashboard/kff-covid-19-vaccine-monitor-dashboard/.

Kholwadia, Amin, and Hisham Dawood. "Fatwā On COVID Vaccines." Glendale Heights, IL: Darul Qasim, April 21, 2021. https://darulqasim.org/wp-content/uploads/2021/04/DI00489-Fatwa-COVID-Vaccine.pdf.

Kibongani Volet, Annie, Cristina Scavone, Daniel Catalán-Matamoros, and Annalisa Capuano. "Vaccine Hesitancy Among Religious Groups: Reasons Underlying This Phenomenon and Communication Strategies to Rebuild Trust." *Frontiers in Public Health* 10 (February 7, 2022): 824560. https://doi.org/10.3389/fpubh.2022.824560.

Killawi, Amal, Michele Heisler, Hamada Hamid, and Aasim I. Padela. "Using CBPR for Health Research in American Muslim Mosque Communities." *Progress in Community Health Partnerships: Research, Education, and Action* 9, no. 1 (2015): 65–74. https://doi.org/10.1353/cpr.2015.0007.

Mayo Clinic. "U.S. COVID-19 Vaccine Tracker: See Your State's Progress." Accessed March 10, 2022. https://www.mayoclinic.org/coronavirus-covid-19/vaccine-tracker.

Meyerowitz, Eric A., Aaron Richterman, Rajesh T. Gandhi, and Paul E. Sax. "Transmission of SARS-CoV-2: A Review of Viral, Host, and Environmental Factors." *Annals of Internal Medicine* 174, no. 1 (January 2021): 69–79. https://doi.org/10.7326/M20-5008.

Michaud, Josh, and Jennifer Kates. "Distributing a COVID-19 Vaccine Across the U.S.—A Look at Key Issues." KFF, October 20, 2020. https://www.kff.org/report-section/distributing-a-covid-19-vaccine-across-the-u-s-a-look-at-key-issues-issue-brief/.

Moderna. "Clinical Trial Data | Moderna COVID-19 Vaccine (EUA)." Accessed March 10, 2022. https://www.modernatx.com/covid19vaccine-eua/providers/clinical-trial-data.

Padela, Aasim I. "An Introduction to Islamic Bioethics: Its Producers and Consumers." In *Medicine & Shariah: A Dialogue in Islamic Bioethics*, edited by Aasim I. Padela, 1–37. Notre Dame, IN: University of Notre Dame Press, 2021.

Padela, Aasim I. "Commentary: Religious Communities are Critical in the Fight Against COVID-19." *Chicago Tribune*, April 17, 2020. https://www.chicagotribune.com/opinion/commentary/ct-opinion-coronavirus-public-health-faith-leaders-padela-20200417-3dv5x6ex6nc6hlslceygp2llpe-story.html.

Padela, Aasim I. "The Essential Dimensions of Health According to the Maqasid Al-

Shari'ah Frameworks of Abu Ishaq al-Shatibi and Jamal-al-Din-'Atiyah." *IIUM Medical Journal Malaysia* 17, no. 1 (July 18, 2018). https://doi.org/10.31436/imjm.v17i1.1035.

Padela, Aasim I., and Afrah Raza. "American Muslim Health Disparities: The State of the Medline Literature." *Journal of Health Disparities Research and Practice* 8, no. 1 (2015): 1–9.

Patel, Minal K., Isabel Bergeri, Joseph S. Bresee, Benjamin J. Cowling, Natasha S. Crowcroft, Kamal Fahmy, Siddhivinayak Hirve, et al. "Evaluation of Post-Introduction COVID-19 Vaccine Effectiveness: Summary of Interim Guidance of the World Health Organization." *Vaccine* 39, no. 30 (July 2021): 4013–4024. https://doi.org/10.1016/j.vaccine.2021.05.099.

Pfizer. "Pfizer and BioNTech Initiate Rolling Submission for Emergency Use Authorization of Their COVID-19 Vaccine in Children 6 Months Through 4 Years of Age Following Request From U.S. FDA | Pfizer." February 1, 2022. https://www.pfizer.com/news/press-release/press-release-detail/pfizer-and-biontech-initiate-rolling-submission-emergency.

PRRI. "Religious Identities and the Race Against the Virus: Successes and Opportunities for Engaging Faith Communities on COVID-19 Vaccination." July 28, 2021. https://www.prri.org/research/religious-vaccines-covid-vaccination/.

Public Health Nigeria. "World Health Organization (WHO) Pandemic Definition." April 19, 2021. https://www.publichealth.com.ng/world-health-organization-who-pandemic-definition/.

Qureshi, Omar, and Aasim I. Padela. "When Must a Patient Seek Healthcare? Bringing the Perspectives of Islamic Jurists and Clinicians into Dialogue." *Zygon®* 51, no. 3 (September 2016): 592–625. https://doi.org/10.1111/zygo.12273.

Raysūnī, Aḥmad, and International Institute of Islamic Thought. *Imam Al-Shatibi's Theory of the Higher Objectives and Intents of Islamic Law*. London: International Institute of Islamic Thought, 2005.

Rothkopf, David J. "When the Buzz Bites Back." *Washington Post*, May 11, 2003. https://www.washingtonpost.com/archive/opinions/2003/05/11/when-the-buzz-bites-back/bc8cd84f-cab6-4648-bf58-0277261af6cd/.

Sanghamitra. "The Tablighi Jamat has Become the Coronavirus Super-Spreader in Asia, Read How." *OpIndia*, March 31, 2020. https://www.opindia.com/2020/03/tablighi-jamat-india-nizamuddin-iztema-lahore-malaysia-tamil-nadu-coronavirus-positive-cases/.

Santos, Joost. "Reflections on the Impact of 'Flatten the Curve' on Interdependent Workforce Sectors." *Environment Systems and Decisions* 40, no. 2 (June 2020): 185–188. https://doi.org/10.1007/s10669-020-09774-z.

Shabana, Ayman. "From the Plague to the Coronavirus: Islamic Ethics and Responses to the COVID-19 Pandemic." *Journal of Islamic Ethics* (April 13, 2021): 1–37. https://doi.org/10.1163/24685542-12340060.

Sharma, Anshika, Isra Ahmad Farouk, and Sunil Kumar Lal. "COVID-19: A Review on the Novel Coronavirus Disease Evolution, Transmission, Detection, Control and Prevention." *Viruses* 13, no. 2 (January 29, 2021): 202. https://doi.org/10.3390/v13020202.

Shāṭibī, Ibrāhīm ibn Mūsá, Imran Ahsan Khan Nyazee, Raji M. Rammuny, and Centre for Muslim Contribution to Civilization. *The Reconciliation of the Fundamentals of Islamic Law*. Reading: Garnet, 2011.

Shin, Youjin, Bonnie Berkowitz, and Min Joo Kim. "How a South Korean Church Helped Fuel the Spread of the Coronavirus." *Washington Post*, March 25, 2020. https://www.washingtonpost.com/graphics/2020/world/coronavirus-south-korea-church/.

Tartof, Sara Y., Jeff M. Slezak, Heidi Fischer, Vennis Hong, Bradley K. Ackerson, Omesh N. Ranasinghe, Timothy B. Frankland, et al. "Effectiveness of MRNA BNT162b2 COVID-19 Vaccine up to 6 Months in a Large Integrated Health System in the USA: A Retrospective Cohort Study." *The Lancet* 398, no. 10309 (October 2021): 1407–1416. https://doi.org/10.1016/S0140-6736(21)02183-8.

"Where Religion, Bioethics and Policy Meet: An Interdisciplinary Conference on Islamic Bioethics and End of Life Care." Conference at University of Michigan Medical School, April 2011. www.youtube.com/playlist?list=PLKPFd4mBCvIgDyDXmlqrqo_hwYERcYpWh.

World Health Organization. "WHO Coronavirus (COVID-19) Dashboard." Accessed March 10, 2022. https://covid19.who.int.

CHAPTER 2

Examining the Intersection of Healthcare Advocacy, Religion, and Community During a Global Pandemic

Anam Tariq, Marium Husain and Sana Syed

1 Introduction

A public health crisis as extensive as COVID-19 goes beyond normative standards of typical community healthcare. According to the Johns Hopkins COVID-19 tracker, over 5 million people have been infected by COVID-19 and nearly 164,000 people have died from the disease in the United States alone as of early August 2020.[1] The United States remains the epicenter of the pandemic as over 75 percent of the number of cases and deaths from the disease occur within its borders and cases continue to increase daily. The race to engineer a vaccine is ongoing but, to date, there is no vaccine to prevent transmission of, and mortality from, the disease, and there is no known early and effective treatment. This pandemic cries for the need of a multidisciplinary approach to a multisystem problem and prompts communities to organize themselves and rise to the occasion. For this reason, the pandemic brought the Muslim community together to collaborate around topics of public health, religious needs, public policy, and education leading with a coalition of over forty organizations under the umbrella of a National Muslim Task Force on COVID-19 in the United States. Muslims may be a minority in the United States, however, many Muslims are frontline health workers, essential workers, lawyers, public health officials, and teachers. Therefore, the Task Force was able to benefit from the diversity of expertise offered by our community. The Task Force dictated overall strategy by performing a needs assessment and then creating subcommittees to address social, healthcare, and policy needs. To that end, recognizing the intersection of religion, social justice, law, public health, and healthcare led to the creation of a policy framework, the "Policy Committee of the National Muslim Task Force on COVID-19." The Policy Committee provided an advocacy platform that stream-

1 "Coronavirus Resource Center," Johns Hopkins University & Medicine, n.d., https://coronavirus.jhu.edu/.

 | DOI:10.1163/9789004679771_004

lined efforts in promoting policies related to public health, healthcare, family and social welfare, and financial equity from the outset of the crisis. This discussion will particularly highlight the work of the Policy Committee in order to emphasize the importance of civic engagement and healthcare legislation as a humanitarian need, while at the same time presenting a unique endeavor from the perspective of overall healthcare advocacy.

This Task Force created scientific and Islamic guidelines in addition to recommendations to help Muslims safely live, work, and worship in this time of unprecedented suffering and isolation. As Muslims, we believe in the sanctity of human life and this is in reference to *Surah Al-Māʾidah* in the Qur'an, where it is eloquently stated: "Whoever saves one—it is as if he had saved mankind entirely." The sanctity of life is at the very core of our Islamic belief system and advocating for life-saving measures is well stated in this Qurʾanic verse.

2 Creation of the National Muslim Task Force on COVID-19

The Task Force has over forty organizations, bringing together public health and medical professionals, civic and faith leaders, social justice, and policy experts to provide a comprehensive response to the needs of all American Muslims and Americans in general during the COVID-19 crisis. The American Muslim Health Professionals (AMHP) and the Islamic Medical Association of North America (IMANA) were two of the key healthcare and public health organizations involved in the creation of this overall Task Force.

The initial objective of the Task Force was to create guidelines for religious practice, especially congregational prayers during the lockdown and, subsequently, in light of the public health policies of social distancing and masking after weeks of "stay-at-home" and "shelter-in-place" orders in March and April 2020. It was recognized that Islamic centers, Islamic schools, and mosques play many important roles in religious and communal life of Muslim Americans and are a critical part of their cultural identity. These institutions are vital not only for worship and education, but also for social services, a sense of community and many other duties (e.g., prayer, marriage, counseling, burial rights, '*aqeeqahs*' [joyous sacrifice of an animal on the occasion of childbirth] for newborns). For the Task Force, it was essential to carefully consider the important functions that these structures play and to implement practical measures that minimize harm, while allowing community members to fulfill communal obligations, *fardh kifaya* (moral religious duties), where moral duties thrust on every member of the community can be satisfied by the practice of a few members of the community in the mosque. In developing these guidelines, the

Task Force used updates from the Centers for Disease Control and Prevention (CDC) and World Health Organization (WHO) to ensure compliance with the most current safety protocols, therefore, striking a balance between religious requirements and public health necessity.

3 The Task Force's Response to COVID-19 Crisis in Spring 2020

To further expand on the activities of the Task Force, other notable Islamic societies (i.e., the Islamic Society of North America, the *Fiqh* Council of North America, Assembly of Muslim Jurists of America, Chicagoland Ulema, and the Initiative on Islam and Medicine) worked in close consultation with AMHP and IMANA to develop provisional guidelines related to Friday (*Jumuʿa*) prayers, which are both an individual and communal responsibility. *Jumuʿa* prayers can attract anywhere from a handful of people to hundreds of worshipers. In March 2020, under the guidance of the Task Force, the special obligation of Friday prayers was suspended and replaced by the routine obligation of midday prayers (*dhuhr*) for most of the Muslim-American community. Moreover, Muslims were advised to limit the number of people gathering to ten people, as per recommendations of local state authorities. Based on the legal precedent of choosing lots (*qurra*), mosque administrations were advised to implement a lottery system with advanced sign-up by which community members are assigned and notified about the specific *Jumuʿa* service they can attend (either which week and/or which time slot). Most importantly, individuals upon whom *Jumuʿa* prayer is not obligatory (e.g., children, disabled, sick, elderly) were instructed to stay at home; this guideline was also for individuals at high risk of death should they get infected with COVID-19. It is important to acknowledge that this recommendation came at a crossroads for many; there were some disagreements between various parties about the permissibility of suspending *Jumuʿa* when there was NOT a state prohibition on holding them. While some leaders felt it was appropriate to do so given the intention to save lives, others felt it was not permissible given it was a *fard* (religious obligation or duty). Regardless, there was a consensus achieved that allowed leaders to open or close depending on their local situation. In addition, mosque leadership and staff were strongly educated to implement screening for sick individuals at the entrances of mosques and during Friday prayer sign-up, provide facial masks to individuals who do not have them, have plentiful hand sanitizing stations, and encourage *wudu* (ablution) to be performed prior to coming to the mosque. The Task Force also advised those centers that remained open to perform *Jumuʿa* prayer outside on the grounds of the mosque or in parking lot spaces, with six feet of separation, where practical and possible. Other minor guidelines were related to signage and hygiene. Educational checklists and information of these guidelines were dispersed via email listservs, letters, institutional signage, Zoom meetings, telehealth, and community officials via each Task Force members' network, reaching Islamic communities nationwide.

A piece from the Task Force statement in May 2020, written in English:

> Public ablution, Wudu, areas were advised to be kept closed as respiratory droplets can propagate in these areas, and individual restrooms can be kept open for dire needs and once used must be thoroughly cleaned … Islamic centers and mosques should create a dedicated cleaning and disinfection team that uses EPA-approved disinfectants to clean doors, doorknobs, tables, chairs, restrooms on a routine schedule. Prayer rugs and carpets should be cleaned with a disinfectant after each prayer service.[2]

Second, the Task Force was instrumental in identifying Muslim leaders to close all mosques and areas of gatherings during important Muslim practices, Friday congregational prayers, daily five prayers, Ramadan (April–May 2020), Muslim holidays (Eid al-Fitr on May 23, 2020, and Eid al-Adha on July 31, 2020), and at children's schools. In consultation with public health and religious experts, the Task Force implemented crucial statements that set out the principles and practices by which Islamic centers and mosques could implement both closings and reopening of their services for routine prayers and subsequently for religious holidays. Here is an excerpt from the May 12, 2020 statement:

> With respect to principles, our statement recognizes (i) God sends down both disease and cure and that we must believe in His Divine Wisdom and pray for Divine deliverance from this trial; (ii) that the shutting of Islamic centers and mosques has and continues to greatly impact the religious and social lives of the Muslim American community as well as its overall well-being; (iii) that the health risks posed by COVID-19 remain credible to both individuals and communities and will likely continue for months; (iv) that every mosque community is unique with respect to the surrounding public health context, state authority guidance, and capabil-

2 "Joint Statement From the National Muslim Task Force on COVID-19 Regarding a Phased Reopening of Mosques Across United States," Islamic Medical Association of North America, May 12, 2020, https://imana.org/imana-backup/wp-content/uploads/2020/05/Joint-Statement-on-Phased-Reopening-of-Mosques_05182020.pdf.

ities to safely implement reopening; and (v) that mitigating health risks while reopening aspects of mosque-based communal religious life will require significant changes in rituals and social practices for the foreseeable future.[3]

4 Evolution of the Task Force to Activities in Summer–Fall 2020

After mobilizing large organizations to come together on the Task Force (mentioned at the beginning of this chapter), to generate unified religious guidance across the United States, the next step for this Task Force was to address the overall daily needs of the communities. In accordance with preserving the sanctity of life, the Task Force was striving to follow in the footsteps of our beloved Prophet Muhammad (Peace Be Upon Him), as he instructed that "every one of you is a shepherd and will be asked about [how well you took care of] those in your flock."[4] A needs assessment revealed many additional areas of deficits for this Task Force to focus further efforts on. This led to the creation of further committees within the Task Force to streamline next steps. These needs were informed by review of research and statistics on the impact of the pandemic on the American people at large. The Pew Research Center reported that over 15 million were unemployed in May 2020,[5] substantially greater than the increase due to the Great Recession during 2007–2010 where approximately 8 million were unemployed. As per the United States Bureau of Labor Statistics, the total unemployment rate was 10.2 percent by July 2020.[6] Unfortunately, the exact number of unemployed Americans may actually have been higher since the entire population was likely not captured during measurements and surveys. In regards to unemployment, food insecurity hit several communities throughout the country. In 2020, approximately 38.3 million Americans lived in food-insecure households in the United States,

3 "Joint Statement From the National Muslim Task Force on COVID-19 Regarding a Phased Reopening of Mosques Across United States," May 12, 2020.

4 *Ṣaḥīḥ al-Bukhārī*, no. 6719; and *Ṣaḥīḥ Muslim*, no. 1829.

5 Rakesh Kochhar, "Unemployment Rose Higher in Three Months of COVID-19 Than It Did in Two Years of the Great Recession," Pew Research Center, June 11, 2020, https://www.pewresearch.org/fact-tank/2020/06/11/unemployment-rose-higher-in-three-months-of-covid-19-than-it-did-in-two-years-of-the-great-recession/.

6 "The Employment Situation—July 2020," Bureau of Labor Statistics, August 7, 2020, https://www.bls.gov/news.release/archives/empsit_08072020.pdf.

including more than 6.1 million children.[7] Additionally, 5.2 million seniors, or 7.1 percent of the senior population, were food insecure in 2019.[8] As of an April 2020 U.S. Bureau of Labor Statistics report, the unemployment rate shot up from 4.4 percent to 14.7 percent in one month.[9] Americans were, therefore, applying for unemployment and food assistance benefits in record numbers. Emergency food assistance measures were not able to address the immediate needs of this crisis, creating difficult situations for food pantries to meet supply with the increased demand. Many small business owners (i.e., barbers, hair salons, restaurants, gyms, etc.) were hit the hardest due to the mandated government shutdowns. The unemployment rate peaked the highest at 12 percent for those with education at a high school level or below.[10] The National Muslim Task Force on COVID-19 factored in this data by creating dedicated committees including Healthcare Professionals and Social Services Committees. These groups quickly addressed a variety of issues by promoting local community leaders, mosques, and organizations to raise funds for providing groceries and/or prepared meals to those most deserving (i.e., unemployed, frontline workers, homeless) during the months of April, May, and June. These activities went above and beyond traditional humanitarian efforts, as the cross-functional nature of the Task Force allowed the organizations to recognize the need for specific medical supplies as well. Therefore, Muslim relief organizations also procured and delivered medical-grade N95/KN95 masks to the hardest hit communities, domestically (e.g., New York City, Chicago) and even internationally (Pakistan June 2020 and Beirut in August 2020). Logistically, lifesaving 50,000 N95/KN95 masks that aligned with CDC specifications and standards were procured and distributed to hospitals in need throughout the country, through the collaboration between IMANA, Islamic Relief, Penny Appeal, and Dar El Salam. Another example of a similar effort domestically involved AMHP's initiative of the National Mask Making Campaign which was also started with support from the Task Force and had been instrumental in organizing coordinated efforts by American Muslims across the country to sew and distribute masks to their local communities with a framework provided by AMHP. This

7 "Food Security in the U.S.," U.S. Department of Agriculture Economic Research Service, January 19, 2022, https://www.ers.usda.gov/topics/food-nutrition-assistance/food-security-in-the-u-s/.

8 "Facts about Senior Hunger in America," Feeding America, n.d., https://www.feedingamerica.org/hunger-in-america/senior-hunger-facts.

9 "The Employment Situation—April 2020," Bureau of Labor Statistics, May 8, 2020, https://www.bls.gov/news.release/archives/empsit_05082020.pdf.

10 Kochhar, "Unemployment Rose Higher in Three Months of COVID-19 Than It Did in Two Years of the Great Recession."

effort was publicized and supported by the overall Task Force therefore leading to a greater impact and with successful distribution of thousands of much needed masks nationally.

During this crisis, raising money and procuring supplies was intuitive for the Muslim community, especially because Ramadan occurred during the height of the COVID-19 pandemic, which reminded us of our obligations to help our communities and to put the needs of others before our own. The Prophet Muhammad (Peace Be Upon Him) urged charity in Ramadan and has mentioned its ample reward and its virtue of importance: "He who breaks the fast (provides *ifṭār*) of another fasting person shall earn a reward equivalent to the fasting person without detracting from the reward of the latter." The Companions said: "O Messenger of Allah! Some of us do not have enough to break the fast (*ifṭār*) of another." Thereupon, our Prophet (Peace Be Upon Him) said: "Allah Gives this reward even to those who give a sip of milk (for *ifṭār*) to a fasting man."[11]

Fundraising was not the only step the Task Force coordinated; additional work was also done to address the mental health needs of the community. This in particular was critical due to ingrained prejudices against mental health concerns in our religious communities, despite the extraordinary emotional stress the pandemic created for society at large. There remains deep cultural stigma against seeking professional, medical counseling and therapy and the emphasis remains on being grateful and relying on faith to improve the mental state even though depression, anxiety, and other psychiatric illnesses have a biological basis. Again, a collaborative effort with mental health experts, religious leaders, and policy experts allowed our organizations to put together meaningful programming by the Khalil Center, Family Youth Institute, Support Embrace Empower Mental Health Advocacy (SEEMA), among others. This served to highlight the mental health needs and also provided an infrastructure to support the Muslim community during this stressful period.

It is important to note that during this time of crisis, Muslim organizations were able to coalesce their expertise and unique perspectives to create a coalition that worked toward a common goal of humanitarian beneficence. It is also worth noting that as a result of this coalition of cross-functional experts, the philanthropic endgame was achieved by innovative means and one of those innovations was the Policy Committee of the National Muslim Task Force on COVID-19.

---

11 *Ṣaḥīḥ al-Bukhārī*, no. 6719.

5 The Branching of the Task Force and Formation of a Policy Committee

As the pandemic surged on, a number of issues surfaced over the course of time including the fact that physicians, healthcare providers, essential workers who were on the front lines, and health systems faced severe shortages of PPE associated with the status of COVID-19 in the state, especially at the outset of the pandemic.[12] Personal protective equipment, commonly referred to as "PPE," is equipment worn to minimize exposure to hazards that cause serious workplace injuries and illnesses. For a hospital in the time of COVID-19, PPE included gowns, N95 masks, eyewear, and gloves needed to maintain COVID-19 precautions. When COVID-19 cases increased, the PPE shortage worsened, and when cases were stable the need still persisted, and appropriate PPE added to the stability. Appropriate supplies for hospitals and nursing homes, who were at the forefront of this pandemic, were critical to ending this crisis. An account sent in by one of AMHP's featured frontline healthcare workers, Dr. Rowza Rumma, a General Surgery resident at Brigham and Women's Hospital, Harvard Medical School clearly captured the direness of the circumstances in the hospitals:

> I served as the senior surgical resident in the emergency room caring for trauma and emergent surgical patients who ranged from screening negative for COVID-19 symptoms to having tested positive for COVID-19. It was a challenge to say the least, running traumas in the ED with little notice ahead of their arrival and with patients who arrived with GCS8 (coma scale—meaning non-responsive patient) or less, unable to screen for COVID-19. Additionally, while we were experiencing an extreme shortage of N95s, we were seeing patients with a surgical mask, since examining patients at bedside were not considered aerosol-generating procedures.[13]

Tedros Adhanom Ghebreyesus, director-general of WHO, said at a news conference at the organization's Geneva headquarters, "Supplies are rapidly depleting. WHO estimates that, each month, 89 million medical masks will be required for the COVID-19 response, 76 million examination gloves and 1.6 million

12 Benjamin Siegel and Josh Margolin, "Doctors, Nurses Warn of Another Protective Gear Shortage as Coronavirus Surges," ABC News, July 15, 2020, https://abcnews.go.com/Health/doctors-nurses-warn-protective-gear-shortage-coronavirus-surges/story?id=71778380.

13 Featured Frontline Worker—Stories from the Frontline American Muslim Health Professionals Newsletter (April 2020).

goggles." He added that manufacturers were needed to increase personal protective gear supplies by 40 percent.[14] The path to a resolution for the pandemic was not restricted to the wearing of masks for healthcare providers and others, but also in the appropriate use of measures such as increased testing and contact tracing that contributed to preventing the spread of COVID-19. Resolving this pandemic was not only essential for the health and well-being of all, but also had an impact on the economy. Goldman Sachs stated that if the pandemic is brought under control, it will increase GDP by 5 percent.[15]

Furthermore, as the pandemic evolved, sobering statistics emerged from across the country showing that COVID-19 was disproportionately impacting minority groups with African Americans accounting for one-third of virus cases nationwide, despite making up just 13 percent of the population. In at least ten states, Asian Americans had a case fatality rate that was disproportionately higher as well. Approximately 20 percent African Americans and approximately 10 percent Asian Americans, identified as Muslims. Black and brown communities had been hit particularly hard by the virus due to underlying disparities like higher rates of chronic illness, lack of healthcare, and lower household incomes that have made them more susceptible to illness and poor outcomes. People of color comprised the majority of service workers, and without the option of staying home, they continued performing the essential jobs that provided the rest of us with what we needed (e.g., groceries, trash pick-up, cleaning services, ancillary healthcare services) further exposing them to the virus. Another stark factor that contributed to these disparate numbers was that African Americans also made up more than half the prison population in Michigan, Illinois, Louisiana, and Maryland—all states reported higher rates of infection and in African Americans testing positive for COVID-19. By June 6, 2020, the COVID-19 case rate for prisoners was 5.5 times higher than the US population case rate and the death rate in the prison population was 3.0 times higher than would be expected if the age and sex distributions of the United States and prison populations were equal.[16] Prisons were not tracking or disclosing race data related to COVID-19-associated deaths, however, from some data that has been made available, there was a racial disparity in diagnosed

14 Berkeley Lovelace Jr., "HHS Clarifies US has About 1% of Face Masks Needed for 'Full-Blown' Coronavirus Pandemic," CNBC, March 4, 2020, https://www.cnbc.com/2020/03/04/hhs-clarifies-us-has-about-1percent-of-face-masks-needed-for-full-blown-pandemic.html.

15 "Face Masks and GDP," Goldman Sachs, July 1, 2020, https://www.goldmansachs.com/insights/pages/the-link-between-face-masks-and-gdp.html.

16 Brendan Saloner et al., "COVID-19 Cases and Deaths in Federal and State Prisons," *JAMA* 324, no. 6 (August 11, 2020): 602, https://doi.org/10.1001/jama.2020.12528.

cases of COVID-19. According to the Marshall Project data from Vermont, by May 20, black prisoners accounted for 18 percent of positive tests, even though they only made up 9 percent of the prison population (and just 1 percent of the state's population was black).[17] These were all factors contributing to the grim reality that the black population is facing in the midst of a pandemic.

The Policy Committee of the National Muslim Task Force on COVID-19 was created given the gravity of the situation and the need for a stronger response from state and federal administration. AMHP has been a key organization in the Policy Committee along with IMANA, Muslim Public Affairs Council, Islamic Relief USA (IRUSA) and Emgage. This newly formed Policy Committee focused on advocacy/civic engagement for legislation that supported our communities during the pandemic.

6 Framework for the Policy Committee of the National Muslim Task Force on COVID-19

Our strategy centered on incorporating civic engagement in our advocacy efforts to mobilize our communities to engage in changing the landscape of health policy for the betterment of the health of all Americans. This resonates well with our religious obligations to inspire others to acts of righteousness which, in this case, encompasses legislation that could impact people's healthcare and therefore their lives. As guided in *Surah Al-ʿAsr*,

> Indeed mankind is in loss, except those who believe and do good, righteous deeds, and exhort one another to truth, and exhort one another to steadfast patience (in the face of misfortunes, and suffering in God's way, and in doing good deeds, and not committing sins) (Q.103:3).

In order to address the pressing issues outlined above, the Policy Committee prioritized PPE/testing, frontline worker protections and food insecurity through advocacy and civic engagement.

17 Maurice Chammah and Tom Meagher, "Is COVID-19 Falling Harder on Black Prisoners? Officials Won't Tell Us.," The Marshall Project, May 28, 2020, https://www.themarshallproject.org/2020/05/28/is-covid-19-falling-harder-on-black-prisoners-officials-won-t-tell-us.

7 PPE/Testing

The Policy Committee began advocating to invoke the Defense Production Act (DPA) for increasing PPE and testing, the testing provision of HEROES Act, and the TRACE Act; these all represent the array of legislation that incorporated funding for steps to achieve a public health solution for thepandemic and for the prevention of a potential second wave. The testing provision of the HEROES Act allocated increased funding for COVID-19 testing overall but the TRACE Act (House Resolution 6666) went further, not only supporting funding for increased testing but also making provisions for additional measures required in the crisis, including mobile health units for coronavirus testing especially in underserved areas, supporting quarantine and contact tracing efforts along with other measures. Senator King (I-ME) introduced the TRACE Act (S. 4315). The bill would have established a $100 billion grant program run by the Centers for Disease Control and Prevention (CDC) to award grants to eligible entities to conduct diagnostic testing for COVID-19, to trace and monitor the contacts of infected individuals, and to support the quarantine and isolation of such contacts. Funding could be used to support programs that develop mobile health units, test individuals, and for programs that provide individuals who are quarantining or in isolation with services related to testing at their residences. Special preference would be given to grantees operating in hot spots and medically underserved communities. A grant recipient may use the grant funds: (1) to hire, train, compensate, and pay expenses of individuals; and (2) to purchase personal protective equipment ("PPE") in support of such contact tracing and other activity. Priority is given to applicants proposing to: (1) conduct activities in "hot spots and medically underserved communities"; and (2) hiring residents of the area or community where the activities will occur. The harsh reality about the disparities in the impact of and response to COVID-19 prompted the Policy Committee to advocate for not only an overall increase in testing but also to support legislation that included proposals for an equitable response to the pandemic, especially as relates to COVID-19 testing and the ancillary measures as outlined in the TRACE Act. The emphasis that the Policy Committee has placed on testing for the virus is in recognition of the global response to COVID-19. Testing has emerged as an extremely effective measure in containing the virus and, even though testing is available in most places in the United States, some communities are suffering, underscoring the need for a community-based approach.

8 Frontline Worker Protections

Another important issue that has surfaced during the pandemic concerns the safety of healthcare workers as it relates to their exposure to the virus. The most immediate measure to ameliorate this safety concern was to increase funding for proper equipment and appropriate workplace standards. To that end, as mentioned earlier, the Policy Committee worked on advocating for increased PPE from the outset of this crisis and also reached out to the CDC to update occupational safety standards for healthcare workers at risk of exposure to COVID-19 to align with international WHO standards. In Congress, they were(in winter 2021) discussing health worker protections in the new COVID-19 relief package, while we have seen some momentum in individual states, with Virginia implementing emergency temporary standards. The increased political attention that protection standards were receiving, at both the federal and state levels, was a step in the right direction that this committee has been advocating for since the beginning of the pandemic. However, with the evolution of the situation across the country, there was a rise in intimidation and retaliation against healthcare workers who spoke up about dire work conditions. For example, we were seeing physicians, nurse practitioners, and nurses being threatened with job termination if they revealed the lack of PPE in their hospital on social media or to local media outlets. To that end, AMHP, as representative of the Policy Committee joined a coalition led by Physicians for Human Rights and AMHP in collaboration with eleven leading healthcare organizations—American Public Health Association (APHA), Doctors for America (DFA), American Medical Women's Association (AMWA), American Medical Student Association (AMSA), National Medical Association (NMA) and others—drafted a letter to the National Governors Association calling for better protections for workers in healthcare settings, exemplifying the ability of this Policy Committee to engage broadly in order to achieve the shared goal of making a difference in the overall community.

> Unto every one of you have we appointed a [different] law and way of life. And if Allah had willed it, He would surely have made you all one single community: but [He willed it otherwise] in order to test you by means of what He has vouch safed unto you. Vie, then, with one another in doing good works! Unto Allah you all must return; and then He will make you truly understand all that on which you were wont to differ. (Q.5:48)

This quote signifies that people of different opinions or cultural ways can form a coalition in situations of natural disasters or emergency for the greater good of humanity.

9 Food Insecurity

Furthermore, as a crucial aspect of public health includes nutrition, one of the key advocacy areas identified by the Policy Committee was food insecurity. This aspect of the advocacy work was also supported by the Food Research & Action Center (FRAC), Feeding America, Center for American Progress (CAP), Muslim Humanitarian Working Group on Domestic Needs, and other national, state, and community-based organizations across the country. These organizations signed onto a letter urging Congress and the White House to immediately boost Supplemental Nutrition Assistance Program (SNAP) benefits during the crisis and make investments in other critical nutrition programs with proven health and economic impacts.

10 Methodology

In order to achieve these time-sensitive goals, the Policy Committee conducted an advocacy campaign by writing letters directly to the responsible officials which included, as mentioned, Vice-President Pence (2017–2021) (as head of the White House COVID-19 Task Force), Health and Human Services (HHS) Secretary Azar (2018–2021), CDC, and House and Senate members. These letters were supported by a number of organizations who participated in the overall National Muslim Task Force on COVID-19 and additionally by other partner public health and healthcare organizations including: American Public Health Association (APHA), Doctors for America (DFA), Community Catalyst, American Medical Women's Association (AMWA), American Medical Student Association (AMSA), and National Medical Association (NMA). Another element of our advocacy strategy involved civic engagement by using action alerts to engage our members on these issues and by which they are able to directly send letters on these same concerns, as constituents to their representatives. The third pillar of our advocacy strategy has included virtual meetings with legislative aides at the US Senate Offices for several states (Maryland, Pennsylvania, Arizona, and Ohio completed so far) to discuss public health concerns delineated in our advocacy letters related to COVID-19 in a bipartisan manner. These meetings were conducted through an alliance between AMHP, IMANA, and IRUSA and we ensured that there were constituents from that state who had a healthcare or public health background present at all of these meetings. These constituents were an integral part of the conversation and in all of the meetings thus far, physicians from the state have participated; this added legitimacy to our policy asks. This strategy allowed us to relay the facts from the front lines and from the experts who are dealing with the disease in different capacities in the respective states making for a very constructive conversation. The Policy Committee discussion during these meetings were related to the legislations described earlier and more specifically on the TRACE Act and Supplemental Nutrition Assistance Program (SNAP) expansion. In addition, advocacy letters related to SNAP expansion were also reviewed with correspondents at the Senators' offices. The work on the SNAP program was seen as a priority during this pandemic, since the program had a twofold objective by alleviating food insecurity, that is, improving public health and stimulating the economy. The SNAP program allows low-income households to buy food at grocery stores and not just rely on emergency service programs like food banks, improving their nutritional intake. By promoting these food purchases, this allows these low-income households to engage in the economy. A public health crisis cannot be contained without equity in our management by providing the basic needs of the most vulnerable.

Understanding and advocating for the needs of the community is extremely important, however, it is also essential to educate the community on these civic obligations. For that reason, AMHP with Poligon and Emgage, as part of the Policy Committee, organized and conducted congressional training to review Congressional Outreach basics. More focused trainings were also organized as a collaboration between IRUSA and AMHP with community members who had volunteered for the Senate meetings mentioned earlier. These trainings were an ongoing effort and encompassed various aspects of advocacy including the importance of coalitions, Op-Ed writing, and all the activities described above as well. This work follows our overarching theme to engage with our community and beyond to urge others to be part of a movement to advance the health and well-being of all by harnessing the legislative process.

Narrated ʿAbdullah bin Masʿūd (may Allah be pleased with him):

> The Prophet (Peace Be Upon Him) said, "Do not wish to be like anyone except in two cases. (The first is) A person, whom Allah has given wealth and he spends it righteously; (the second is) the one whom Allah has given wisdom (the Holy Qur'an) and he acts according to it and teaches it to others."[18]

Advocacy is a long-term endeavor without an immediate outcome measure, therefore, there is no means to assess the success of our efforts; although one

18 Fath-al-Bari, Vol. 1, 177; *Ṣaḥīḥ al-Bukhārī*, 73.

improvement that occurred overall was the increase in PPE. Other elements will be followed and reviewed over time, however, the fact that the various Muslim organizations and community members came together and recognized the importance of bettering society is a favorable measure in itself.

11 Conclusion

The Policy Committee and overall Task Force work has been extremely timely, not only due to the initial need for a cohesive response within the Muslim community and the continued need secondary to the resurgence in cases across a number of states, but also due to the obligation on all Muslims to enact change in the face of adversity.

On the authority of Abu Saʿīd al-Khudrī (may Allah be pleased with him) who said:

> I heard the Prophet (Peace Be Upon Him) say, "Whosoever of you sees an evil, let him change it with his hand; and if he is not able to do so, then [let him change it] with his tongue; and if he is not able to do so, then with his heart—and that is the weakest of faith." (Al-Nawai, Hadith 34)

Our work highlights the importance of advocacy as an essential tool to make a difference especially when utilized for healthcare issues. Since healthcare can influence an individual's right to life, therefore policies that improve healthcare access and delivery are a means to save lives. In Muslim communities, the mainstay of good deeds and charitable works tend to be focused on monetary contributions and material donations. Even though these aspects are a critical element of societal obligations, advocacy to inform policies that can have a lasting impact on communities is a responsibility with potentially less tangible immediate results, but definitely long-term impact in reforming our communities for the better in the long run. We are constantly reminded of raising our voice and taking action (i.e., civic engagement) as a core requirement of our teachings. Living the faith is *ibada*, service to God through service to humankind.

12 Summary

The National Muslim Task Force on COVID-19 framework was based on protecting the sanctity of life, a core value of our Islamic belief system that is mentioned in *Surah Al-M ā'idah*. The Task Force urged individuals, households, community organizations, and mosques to adhere to public health and state authority guidance, and CDC guidelines. The COVID-19 pandemic led to a public health crisis and economic downturn, prompting the Task Force to immediately activate a cohesive humanitarian effort to provide a comprehensive response to the spiritual, economic, and public health needs of Americans. Throughout this tumultuous period, the Task Force continued to communicate about the rapidly evolving situation and provide the Muslim communities with innovative solutions. The Task Force's strength was its cross functional approach: from raising money for PPE to providing healthcare guidance to mosques to advocating for life-saving health policy at federal and state levels.

The Policy Committee of the National Muslim Task Force on COVID-19 advocated for COVID-19-related regional and national policy issues, particularly PPE production/access, testing/contact tracing, food insecurity, and health education. The work of the Policy Committee during this pandemic highlighted that public health advocacy and civic engagement are crucial elements of Islamic foundational principles. The Task Force showcases the power of unity in the Muslim community and how it can lead to a transformative ability to be more influential within our communities and beyond.

Bibliography

Bureau of Labor Statistics. "The Employment Situation—April 2020." May 8, 2020. https://www.bls.gov/news.release/archives/empsit_05082020.pdf.

Bureau of Labor Statistics. "The Employment Situation—July 2020." August 7, 2020. https://www.bls.gov/news.release/archives/empsit_08072020.pdf.

Chammah, Maurice, and Tom Meagher. "Is COVID-19 Falling Harder on Black Prisoners? Officials Won't Tell Us." The Marshall Project, May 28, 2020. https://www.themarshallproject.org/2020/05/28/is-covid-19-falling-harder-on-black-prisoners-officials-won-t-tell-us.

Feeding America. "Facts about Senior Hunger in America." n.d. https://www.feedingamerica.org/hunger-in-america/senior-hunger-facts.

Goldman Sachs. "Face Masks and GDP." July 1, 2020. https://www.goldmansachs.com/insights/pages/the-link-between-face-masks-and-gdp.html.

Islamic Medical Association of North America. "Joint Statement From the National Muslim Task Force on COVID-19 Regarding a Phased Reopening of Mosques Across United States." May 18, 2020. https://imana.org/imana-backup/wp-content/uploads/2020/05/Joint-Statement-on-Phased-Reopening-of-Mosques_05182020.pdf.

Johns Hopkins University & Medicine. "Coronavirus Resource Center." n.d. https://coronavirus.jhu.edu/.

Kochhar, Rakesh. "Unemployment Rose Higher in Three Months of COVID-19 Than It Did in Two Years of the Great Recession." Pew Research Center, June 11, 2020. https://www.pewresearch.org/fact-tank/2020/06/11/unemployment-rose-higher-in-three-months-of-covid-19-than-it-did-in-two-years-of-the-great-recession/.

Lovelace Jr., Berkeley. "HHS Clarifies US Has About 1% of Face Masks Needed for 'Full-Blown' Coronavirus Pandemic." CNBC, March 4, 2020. https://www.cnbc.com/2020/03/04/hhs-clarifies-us-has-about-1percent-of-face-masks-needed-for-full-blown-pandemic.html.

Saloner, Brendan, Kalind Parish, Julie A. Ward, Grace DiLaura, and Sharon Dolovich. "COVID-19 Cases and Deaths in Federal and State Prisons." *JAMA* 324, no. 6 (August 11, 2020): 602. https://doi.org/10.1001/jama.2020.12528.

Siegel, Benjamin, and Josh Margolin. "Doctors, Nurses Warn of Another Protective Gear Shortage as Coronavirus Surges." *ABC News*, July 15, 2020. https://abcnews.go.com/Health/doctors-nurses-warn-protective-gear-shortage-coronavirus-surges/story?id=71778380.

U.S. Department of Agriculture Economic Research Service. "Food Security in the U.S." January 19, 2022. https://www.ers.usda.gov/topics/food-nutrition-assistance/food-security-in-the-u-s/.

CHAPTER 3

Effects of COVID-19 on the Healthcare Coverage of Immigrant Populations

Ummesalmah Abdulbaseer, Maham Mirza, Moina Hussain, Aisha Zafar, Urooj Rehman and Fatema Mirza

1 Background

The effects of COVID-19 not only created turmoil and disrupted all economies of mass scale—industry, employment including healthcare insurances and education—its depth of penetration even challenged major relief packages floated nationally to help the underserved. The most deleterious effect was on access to healthcare where minor gaps between poverty levels became matters of life and death. In the United States, with one of the most advanced healthcare systems in place, with built-in laws for emergency access further augmented by equitable access implemented under the Affordable Care Act (ACA), it was deemed useless as people responded in many different ways to the pandemic stimulus packages. Despite being one of the highly developed and outcomes-based medically responsive systems, pockets of disparities prevail throughout the US healthcare landscape as flags of a class system and differences in acculturation prevail.[1] Likewise, for the immigrant population, income and residency in relationship to both type and quality of healthcare are also inversely related. This fragmentation based on income and residency status, required meticulous planning for the rolling out of the equity compliance relief packages for which the administration of that time lacked capacity. Stimulus packages which were designed to assist families who lost employment and/or had lost healthcare coverage often created reverse effects on the most deserving communities and defeated the purposes for which they were created. This paper seeks to highlight the healthcare coverage disparities faced by immigrant Muslim communities created by the pandemic and the negative impact it had on health insurance and healthcare access.

1 "The State of Health for Blacks in Chicago: 2021 Data Brief," Chicago Department of Public Health (CDPH), https://www.chicago.gov/content/dam/city/depts/cdph/CDPH/HealthyChicago/CDPH_BlackHealth7c_DIGITAL.pdf.

 | DOI:10.1163/9789004679771_005

1.1 *Health Coverage Under Affordable Care Act*

The ACA tackled the uninsured and underinsured disparities in several different ways, including the establishment of Marketplace exchange, expansion of existing Medicaid programs, tax subsidies from government to people within lower tax brackets, and the introduction of the Small Business Health Options Program (SHOP) for small businesses.[2] It became the main source of health coverage for those who were/are unable to get private or employer-based insurance. Uninsured people qualified for ACA marketplace exchange coverage if they fall within certain tax brackets as measured by Federal Poverty Levels (FPL).[3]

FPL is a measure of the income that individuals make in relation to the predetermined poverty level set by the government. It does not vary based on state of residence but varies depending on the number of people in a household. An individual making $12,760 in 2020 is said to be at a 100 percent FPL, whereas an individual making $17,609 annually is at 138 percent of the FPL. Individuals making 138–400 percent FPL are eligible to be enrolled in the health insurance plans offered on marketplace exchange. If an individual makes less than 100 percent of FPL, they will qualify for health coverage, food stamps, and, in some cases, cash assistance. However, they must either be citizens or eligible for citizenship. Eligible citizens who are over 100 percent of the FPL but fall at or below 138 percent of the FPL will receive only health coverage benefits from the state. In most states, the health coverage offered by the state government is Medicaid.

Citizens and immigrants with incomes over 138 percent but below 250 percent of the FPL receive government subsidies in the form of Advanced Premium Tax Credit (APTC) to make the ACA monthly health insurance premiums affordable to the beneficiaries. The lower the FPL, the higher the tax subsidy. However, these subsidies stop at around 250 percent FPL and there is no tax credit available to pay for the health insurance of those over 250 percent FPL. Therefore, many folks who earn close to 250 percent FPL or higher find ACA health coverage very expensive due to no tax credits.

The ACA does have certain rules that determine how well it works for certain communities. People with salaries over 400 percent FPL do not qualify for it and have to find other modes of insurance. Thus, it becomes clear that FPL's plays a critical role in determining health insurance eligibility. In addition to

2 "Small Business Health Options Program (SHOP)," Centers for Medicare & Medicaid Services, https://www.cms.gov/CCIIO/Programs-and-Initiatives/Health-Insurance-Marketplaces/SHOP.

3 http://www.healthreformbeyondthebasics.org/wp-content/uploads/2019/10/REFERENCE-GUIDE Yearly-Guideline-and-Thresholds CoverageYear2020.pdf.

TABLE 3.1 HHS Poverty guidelines for 48 contiguous states for the year 2020

Household/ family size	100% FPL	138% FPL	150% FPL	200% FPL	250% FPL	300% FPL	400% FPL
1	$12,760	$17,609	$19,140	$25,520	$31,900	$38,280	$51,040
2	$17,240	$23,791	$25,860	$34,480	$43,100	$51,720	$68,960
3	$21,720	$29,974	$32,580	$43,440	$54,300	$65,160	$86,880
4	$26,200	$36,156	$39,300	$52,400	$65,500	$78,600	$104,800
5	$30,680	$42,338	$46,020	$61,360	$76,700	$92,040	$122,720
6	$35,160	$48,521	$52,740	$70,320	$87,900	$99,480	$140,640
7	$39,640	$54,703	$59,460	$79,280	$99,100	$118,920	$158,560
8*	$44,120	$60,886	$66,180	$88,240	$110,300	$132,360	$176,480

* For households with more than 8, add $4,480 for each additional person

SOURCE: "POVERTY GUIDELINES" FROM THE OFFICE OF THE ASSISTANT SECRETARY FOR PLANNING AND EVALUATION, 2020, HTTPS://ASPE.HHS.GOV/TOPICS/POVERTY-ECONOMIC-MOBILITY/POVERTY-GUIDELINES

the FPL requirements, ACA does require a valid immigration or residency status such as a Visa or Green Card. Thus, those who are undocumented or are in the process of obtaining a status are unable to use this federal program or take part in the lower deductibles and premiums, which can be too high for them to afford.

1.2 *Affordable Care Act Under Trump Administration*

During the recent Trump administration, tax credits were also becoming a large topic of discussion as he spoke of repealing the ACA. Instead of tax credits, he implemented tax deductions, which saved less money for families, who on average had to now increase spending by $3,500 a year.[4] This change had brought significant financial losses to especially those in the lower- and moderate-income group, which often included new immigrants who were now having to pay out more or choose to forego insurance altogether.[5]

4 Evan Saltzman and Christine Eibner, "Donald Trump's Health Care Reform Proposals: Anticipated Effects on Insurance Coverage, Out-of-Pocket Costs, and the Federal Deficit," The Commonwealth Fund, September 23, 2016, https://doi.org/10.26099/94f4-8d17.

5 Aviva Aron-Dine and Tara Straw, "House Tax Credits Would Make Health Insurance Far Less Affordable in High-Cost States," Center on Budget and Policy Priorities, March 16, 2017, https://www.cbpp.org/research/health/house-tax-credits-would-make-health-insurance-far-less-affordable-in-high-cost.

As a result of this and other policy changes that increased premiums or removed individual mandate penalties,[6] the number of uninsured individuals during his presidency grew by over 2.3 million, even before the pandemic.[7]

Another new policy mandated immigrants to find insurance to pay for potential healthcare within thirty days of arrival—which also proved to be difficult given most insurances will not consider them for long-term plans until they are here and situated.[8]

The ACA had filled in a gap of care that unfortunately was recreated as a result of such policy changes. Individuals who could not afford private/employer insurance, but still made enough to not qualify for Medicaid were able to take advantage of its services. As a result, 7.8 million were able to gain some coverage and uninsured rates for US immigrants were greatly reduced.[9]

1.3 *Effect of COVID-19 on Low-Income and Immigrant Communities*

The pandemic created significant economic pressures for vulnerable and low-income populations across the USA, which in turn exacerbated existing health coverage gaps that minority communities face. Unprecedented rises in unemployment claims came about as many companies furloughed employees to reduce costs.[10] Loss of jobs also resulted in a loss of healthcare coverage, as a large portion of healthcare coverage in the United States is tied to their employment.

Some of those who lost jobs received unemployment benefits that were higher than their previous salaries. Their efforts to obtain healthcare through the ACA were challenging as now they were in a different income bracket. This was compounded by the fact that the government sent two stimulus checks

6 Emily Gee, "Less Coverage and Higher Costs: The Trump's Administration's Health Care Legacy," Center for American Progress, September 25, 2020, https://www.americanprogress.org/article/less-coverage-higher-costs-trumps-administrations-health-care-legacy/.

7 Adam Gaffney, David Himmelstein, and Steffie Woolhandler, "How Much has the Number of Uninsured Risen Since 2016—And at What Cost to Health and Life?" *Health Affairs*, October 29, 2020, https://www.healthaffairs.org/do/10.1377/forefront.20201027.770793/full/.

8 Kristina Cooke and Mica Rosenberg, "Trump Rule on Health Insurance Leaves Immigrants, Companies Scrambling for Answers," *Reuters*, October 31, 2019, https://www.reuters.com/article/us-usa-immigration-insurance-idUSKBN1XA1G6.

9 Arturo Vargas Bustamante et al., "Health Care Access and Utilization Among U.S. Immigrants Before and After the Affordable Care Act," *Journal of Immigrant and Minority Health* 21, no. 2 (April 1, 2019): 211–218, https://doi.org/10.1007/s10903-018-0741-6.

10 Maria Nicola et al., "The Socio-Economic Implications of the Coronavirus Pandemic (COVID-19): A Review," *International Journal of Surgery* 78 (June 1, 2020): 185–193, https://doi.org/10.1016/j.ijsu.2020.04.018.

which temporarily also increased their annual income and thus threw them into a higher income bracket for applying for healthcare. A disaster.

During this time, the needs of low-waged essential workers grew greatly. However, given their lower salaries, they were often uninsured and unable to pay for testing or treatment. Being on the front line, these workers, many of whom already have chronic diseases, were at an increased risk of getting sick. Unfortunately, staying home was not an option because they needed their jobs as a source of livelihood and, if they got sick, they not only lacked insurance but also paid sick leave.

The outbreak in the USA has disproportionately affected urban and suburban areas, which includes multiple racial minorities.[11] In Illinois, the Department of Public Health (IDPH) implemented complete isolation measures when the COVID-19 transmission rates reached 95 cases per 100,000 people.[12] As the country went into isolation, these measures widened the gap for access to care, as some health practitioners were now only providing telehealth services. Individuals without previous primary care connections or lack of proper internet services often had no choice but to go to the emergency departments for any issues, only to find emergency rooms filled beyond capacity.

Specifically in Chicago, before the pandemic, varying economic conditions and lack of access to care are reasons why there is a thirty-year difference in life expectancy among the sickest and wealthiest zip codes in Chicago.[13] The difference stems from inequalities that have been exacerbated by food insecurity, poverty, and higher rates of incarceration especially among Black and Brown citizens.[14] COVID-19 has infected African-American and Latino communities at

11 Leo Lopez III, Louis H. Hart, and Mitchell H. Katz, "Racial and Ethnic Health Disparities Related to COVID-19," *JAMA* 325, no. 8 (2021): 719–720, https://doi.org/10.1001/jama.2020.26443. For maps and tables of the disproportion affects throughout the USA, see Chicago Department of Public Health (CDPH), "The State of Health for Blacks in Chicago: 2021 Data Brief."

12 "Suburban Cook County Among 30 Illinois Counties at COVID-19 Warning Level: IDPH," *WTTW News*, August 29, 2020, https://news.wttw.com/2020/08/29/suburban-cook-county-among-30-illinois-counties-covid-19-warning-level-idph.

13 Kelly Gooch, "Health Disparities among Chicago Hospitals' Most Pressing Public Health Concerns," *Becker's Hospital Review*, March 12, 2020, https://www.beckershospitalreview.com/care-coordination/health-disparities-among-chicago-hospitals-most-pressing-public-health-concerns.html.

14 Stephen Nkansah-Amankra, Samuel Kwami Agbanu, and Reuben Jonathan Miller, "Disparities in Health, Poverty, Incarceration, and Social Justice among Racial Groups in the United States: A Critical Review of Evidence of Close Links with Neoliberalism," *International Journal of Health Services* 43, no. 2 (April 2013): 217–240, https://doi.org/10.2190/HS.43.2.c.

higher rates, with many citing that chronic medical conditions, lack of proper healthcare access, and working low-wage essential jobs all play a role in their situation.[15] Additionally, since the beginning of the pandemic, more individuals have been trying to find ways to reduce personal or household expenditures, to adjust to their current income status, and increase methods for saving money for essentials and potential medical emergencies.[16] For many, the pandemic changed their conceptions of economic class and mobility.

A significant number of immigrants joined those who had been disproportionately impacted as a result of the pandemic. With many of them in low-wage work because of visa status, immigrants struggled with out-of-pocket costs and navigating coverage. Due to the pandemic, immigrants and undocumented workers have also increasingly lost their jobs, further fueling severe financial insecurity.[17] Often, many immigrants and undocumented individuals waited until their sickness was life threatening to come see a doctor, as they lacked coverage and could not pay large sums for care.

One specific community in Chicago that has been greatly impacted is the immigrant Muslim population. According to the Pew Research Center, 58 percent of American-Muslim adults are immigrants.[18] American Muslims are often referred to as being a group that is racially, ethnically, and socio-economically diverse.[19] Those who were already in vulnerable situations were substantially affected, as it has been shown that lower-income populations have been the most financially impacted by COVID-19.

As Muslims, there were specific social impacts of COVID-19 to deal with, such as the closure of mosques, cancellation of large religious gatherings, Ramadan, and *Hajj* (the pilgrimage to Makkah).[20] These situations were experienced

15 Rachel Nania, "Blacks, Hispanics Hit Harder by the Coronavirus, Early U.S. Data Show," AARP, May 8, 2020, https://www.aarp.org/health/conditions-treatments/info-2020/minority-communities-covid-19.html.

16 Suborna Barua, "Understanding Coronanomics: The Economic Implications of the Coronavirus (COVID-19) Pandemic," April 1, 2020, http://dx.doi.org/10.2139/ssrn.3566477.

17 George Borjas and Hugh Cassidy, "The Adverse Effect of the COVID-19 Labor Market Shock on Immigrant Employment" (Cambridge, MA: National Bureau of Economic Research, May 2020), https://doi.org/10.3386/w27243.

18 "Muslim Americans: Immigrants and U.S. Born See Life Differently," Pew Research Center's Religion & Public Life Project, April 17, 2018, https://www.pewforum.org/essay/muslims-in-america-immigrants-and-those-born-in-u-s-see-life-differently-in-many-ways/.

19 America Indivisible et al., "Muslim Civic Engagement Toolkit for Community Members," 2020, https://www.poligonnational.org/uploads/8/2/8/6/82865960/muslim_civic_engagement_toolkit_for_community_members.pdf.

20 Ziad A. Memish et al., "Pausing Superspreader Events for COVID-19 Mitigation: International Hajj Pilgrimage Cancellation," *Travel Medicine and Infectious Disease* 36 (July 2020): 101817, https://doi.org/10.1016/j.tmaid.2020.101817.

with the same impact among those with differing immigration and insurance status as those who were citizens. COVID-19 leveled harnessed access to religious observances. At least 33 percent of American-Muslim families live at or below the poverty line, making them the most disadvantaged faith group in America.[21] According to the National Black Muslim COVID Coalition, Chicago's Muslim population comprises more than 20–25 percent Black Muslims, who have been found to have higher rates of infection.[22] Also, according to the "Muslim Civic Engagement Toolkit for Community Members," because many African-American Muslims are on that lower end of income, they have been severely vulnerable to disparities in healthcare and economic changes brought on by this pandemic, as they struggle to find care they can afford.[23] Thus, it becomes clear that this community experienced health coverage gaps during this time.

For the immigrant Muslim community in Chicago to eliminate gaps in healthcare, many local organizations are taking time to promote the ACA coverage options. Organizations such as the Inner-City Muslim Action Network (IMAN) and Worry Free Community (WFC) have stepped up to provide services to those who need them most. These organizations are centered on improving access to care and, since the pandemic began, have continued to work to provide more access and support. WFC and its founders have been serving the Muslim community in Chicago within a forty-mile radius since 2013. They aim to improve access to healthcare for immigrants by enrolling them into ACA programs.

1.4 *Methods*

Worry Free Community has primarily focused their work on increasing coverage for the immigrant community, with 95 percent of them from a Muslim background. They screen community members with an assessment of needs and eligibility and then discuss health coverage enrollment into Medicaid, ACA, or a temporary program. Staff also provides coverage for care counseling, individually speaking with all clients regarding their status. Calls are also made regularly to those identified as un- or underinsured to explain criteria and eligibility to enroll in different programs. Since even before the pandemic,

21 Petra Alsoofy and Katherine Coplen, "Community in the Time of Corona: Documenting the American Muslim Response to the COVID-19 Crisis," *ISPU*, May 18, 2020, https://www.ispu.org/community-in-the-time-of-corona-documenting-the-american-muslim-response-to-the-covid19-crisis/.

22 National Black Muslim COVID Coalition, n.d., https://www.blackmuslimcoalition.com.

23 America Indivisible et al., "Muslim Civic Engagement Toolkit for Community Members."

they were able to look at how policy changes affected FPLs of the local immigrant community. They also were able to collect data on how the healthcare coverage rates changed through the pandemic, which they believe will bring great insight into understanding the sheer impact of the pandemic on such immigrant-based communities. With this and the acknowledgment that the Muslim immigrant community does rely on such programs for guidance, it becomes imperative to explore the degree of the impact they faced between the pre-COVID-19 and COVID-19 periods. This will then allow local healthcare organizations to see how certain groups in these communities have been more negatively impacted, enabling work to develop strategies and policies needed to help them overcome such challenges.

Healthcare coverage data was collected via the ACA and Medicaid enrollment programs and applications processed by Worry Free Community's staff from November 1, 2019 to July 31, 2020. Clients are enrolled on the government's US Centers for Medicare & Medicaid Services website's Marketplace via www.healthcare.gov and the State of Illinois's Application for Benefits Eligibility website, www.ABE.illinois.gov.

Data from the pre-COVID-19 period was collected from November 1–December 15 in 2019. This is when open enrollment for ACA is typically done and will be referred to as the Open Enrollment period. Data from the COVID-19 period was collected from February 1–July 31 in 2020. When staff provides insurance counseling for clients, they do ask about immigration status and religious preferences.

All of the program data was captured in a health coverage case management software. All data analysis, graphs, and enrollment comparisons were done through Microsoft Excel.

2 Results

All ACA enrollments mentioned here took place from November 1, 2019–July 31, 2020. There were 1,875 applications received during the COVID-19 period, from February 1, 2020 to July 31, 2020. Of these, 1,002 were processed for ACA, 536 were processed for Medicaid, 273 were processed for employer and private plans, and 76 were for clients that wanted to remain uninsured. Of their clients, 54 percent of clients are Green Card holders, 39 percent of clients are citizens or eligible to be citizens, 3 percent of clients have unknown status, 3 percent of clients have Mixed Residency (some family members have had Green Cards for less than five years and the other household members are citizens), and 1 percent of clients are on Employment Authorization.

TABLE 3.2 Enrollment application breakdown during the COVID-19 period, November 1–December 15, 2019

Location/type	ACA applications	Medicaid applications	Total applications
Suburban	841	360	1,201
Urban	161	164	325
Total	1,002	524	1,526*

* Pre- and during COVID-19

SOURCE: WORRY FREE COMMUNITY'S DATA COLLECTION OF ACA AND MEDICAID ENROLLMENT PROGRAMS AND APPLICATIONS

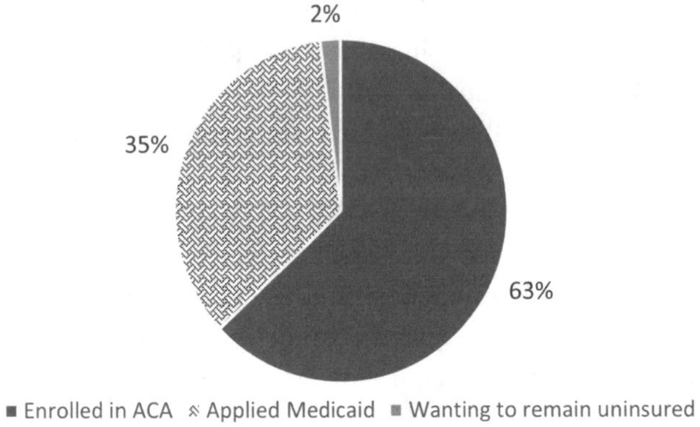

FIGURE 3.1 Application types during open enrollment/pre-COVID-19 period

SOURCE: WORRY FREE COMMUNITY'S DATA COLLECTION OF ACA AND MEDICAID ENROLLMENT PROGRAMS AND APPLICATIONS

The following are a series of tables and graphs that came from analyzing data of Muslims' insurance applications from a pre-COVID-19 to COVID-19 period. Applications can be representative of individuals or families.

Table 3.2 shows the breakdown of health coverage applications between urban (Chicago) and suburban areas. For technical purposes, any zip codes that were not part of the city of Chicago, as they did not have the Chicago zip codes pattern of a 606—were from neighboring suburbs and were referred to as suburban. Suburban clients filled out 1,201 enrollment applications to apply for a specific insurance type, with 70 percent or 84 being for ACA and 30 percent or 260 being for Medicaid. Urban clients filled out 325 enrollment applications, with nearly equal numbers of both applications, with 161 for ACA and 164 for Medicaid applications. Overall, the applications of both suburban and urban clients were 66 percent for ACA and 34 percent for Medicaid.

Figure 3.1 shows the percentage of enrollments processed during the Open Enrollment or pre-COVID-19 period. Of the applications, 63 percent were for

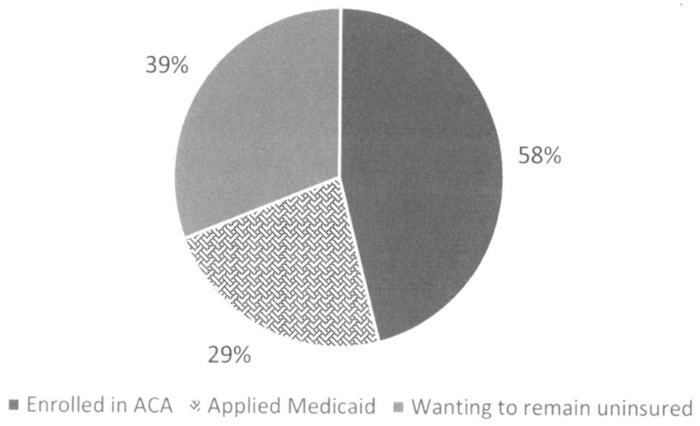

FIGURE 3.2 Application types during COVID-19
SOURCE: WORRY FREE COMMUNITY'S DATA COLLECTION OF ACA AND MEDICAID ENROLLMENT PROGRAMS AND APPLICATIONS

TABLE 3.3 Residency status and household poverty levels of clients based on applications during the COVID-19 period

Residency status/FPL	Below 100%	Below 138%	Below 150%	Below 200%	Below 250%	Below 300%	Below 400%	Above 400%	Unknown
Eligible citizens	58	40	38	116	67	52	45	42	0
Mixed Residency	10	6	5	6	4	4	2	0	0
Employment Authorization	3	0	0	2	0	0	0	0	1
F1 + F2	2	0	1	0	0	0	0	0	0
Green Card < 5 Years	267	141	44	95	20	22	17	5	20
Unknown	11	3	2	13	2	0	2	0	8

SOURCE: WORRY FREE COMMUNITY'S DATA COLLECTION OF ACA AND MEDICAID ENROLLMENT PROGRAMS AND APPLICATIONS

ACA, 35 percent were for Medicaid, and 2 percent were for individuals who wanted to remain uninsured.

Figure 3.2 shows the enrollments processed during the COVID-19 period. Of the applications, 58 percent were for ACA, 29 percent were for Medicaid, and 13 percent were for individuals who wanted to remain uninsured.

Table 3.3 classifies the residency status and the poverty level of the individuals who filled out applications during the COVID-19 period.

Eligible citizens are those who already have been awarded citizenship or who legally have been in the USA for more than five years. They make up the largest number of applications received for those in the below 200–400 percent

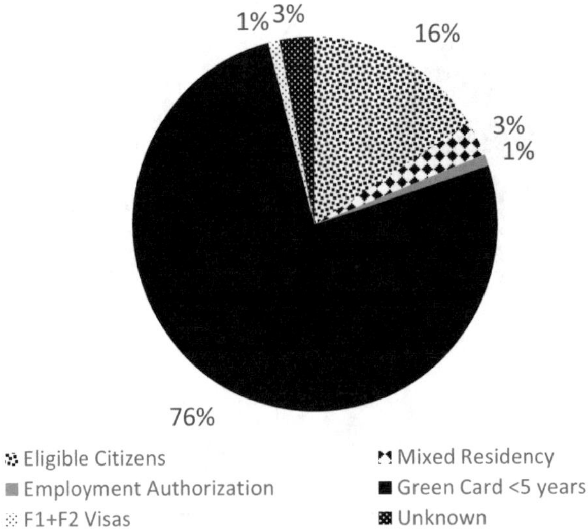

FIGURE 3.3 Residency status of clients based on applications below 100 percent FPL during the COVID-19 period
SOURCE: WORRY FREE COMMUNITY'S DATA COLLECTION OF ACA AND MEDICAID ENROLLMENT PROGRAMS AND APPLICATIONS

FPL range. Green Card holders who have been in the USA for less than five years make up the largest number of applications received for those in the below 100–150 percent FPL range. Green Cards gives permanent residency status to individuals from outside the USA to live and work there. It is filed differently depending on an immigrants' reason for residence, such as employment, family, asylum, etc. Unknown is for applications where clients did not specify their residency status. Mixed Residencies are households whose members have varying residency statuses, for example, the primary member can be a citizen while their spouse is a Green Card holder. F1 visas belong to students relocating to the USA for academic reasons, while F2 visas are for immediate family members of F1 visa holders.

Figure 3.3 further elaborates on information from Table 3.3. Focusing in on the lowest poverty level of below 100 percent FPL, this figure shows that of these individuals who applied in this poverty level range during the COVID-19 period, 76 percent are Green Card holders who have been in the USA for less than five years. Of the other groups, 16 percent are Eligible Citizens, 3 percent are Mixed Residency, 3 percent are Unknown, 1 percent are under Employment Authorization, and the remaining 1 percent are under F1+F2 visas.

Figure 3.4 highlights why ACA applications were terminated by clients during the COVID-19 period. Of the 213 ACA applications that WFC received during

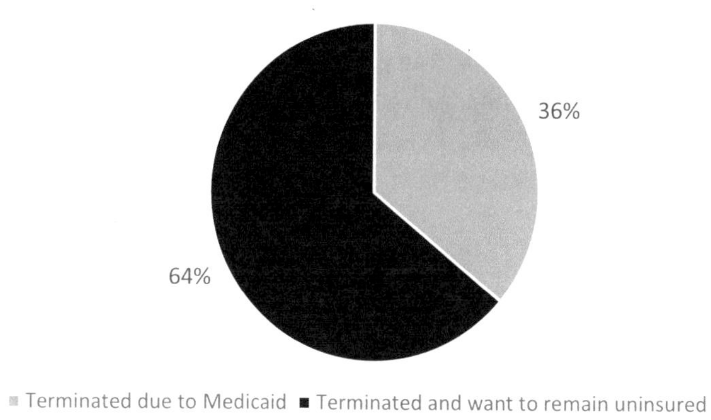

FIGURE 3.4 Terminated ACA plans during the COVID-19 period
SOURCE: WORRY FREE COMMUNITY'S DATA COLLECTION OF ACA AND MEDICAID ENROLLMENT PROGRAMS AND APPLICATIONS

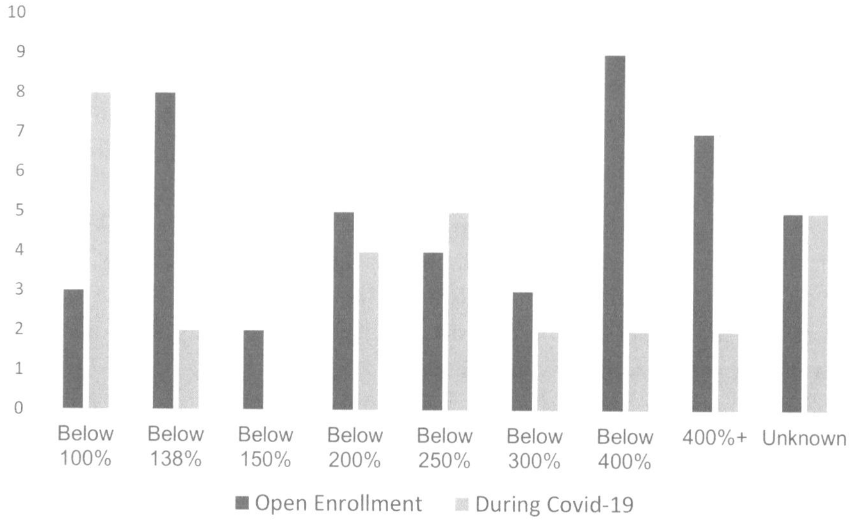

FIGURE 3.5 Comparison of terminated ACA plans between the open enrollment/pre-COVID-19 period, and the COVID-19 period
SOURCE: WORRY FREE COMMUNITY'S DATA COLLECTION OF ACA AND MEDICAID ENROLLMENT PROGRAMS AND APPLICATIONS

this time, 64 percent or 137 were terminated by clients because they were able to receive Medicaid due to changes in their income, while 36 percent or 76 were terminated because clients opted to become uninsured and forego insurance altogether.

Figure 3.5 highlights how ACA plans were terminated pre-COVID-19 versus during the COVID-19 period based on clients' household poverty level. Clients in the range from below 300–400+ percent and below 138–250 percent FPL had more terminations during the pre-COVID-19 period. Clients in the range below 100 percent FPL had more ACA terminations during the COVID-19 period.

3 Discussion

Through these data sets, there are several things to observe about the financial conditions of Muslim immigrants in Chicago in terms of their changed needs during COVID-19 and their response.

Table 3.2 shows the data for classifying enrollment applications for ACA and Medicaid by geography: in Chicago (urban) and outside of Chicago (suburban). Through these, it becomes clear that during the COVID-19 period, there were significantly more applications from suburban clients for both ACA and Medicaid compared to the applications from urban clients. For these suburban clients, ACA applications made up 70 percent of total enrollment applications and Medicaid applications made up 30 percent. Thus, for these clients it is clear that something was changing for them, whether it was income, job status, increased expenses, that was greatly affecting their ability to keep their current insurance and change it outside of the normal Open Enrollment period.

Both groups had significantly more ACA enrollment applications than for Medicaid. This could be because they were no longer covered under Medicaid due to stimulus checks and packages, causing them to surpass the financial limits set for Medicaid. For example, although the checks were one time only, by increasing household income, they decreased the accessibility of Medicaid for many poor and underinsured families.

Figure 3.1 demonstrates the types of enrollment applications received by clients during the Open Enrollment or pre-COVID-19 period. This is the general time for ACA applications to come in, which would explain why the majority of the total applications, at 63 percent, were for enrolling in ACA; 35 percent of applications were for Medicaid and 2 percent of applications were for clients who wanted to remain uninsured.

Figure 3.2 demonstrates the types of enrollment applications received by clients during the COVID-19 period. Similar to Figure 3.1, the majority of the applications received were for ACA at 58 percent, followed by Medicaid at 29 percent, and then for clients wanting to remain uninsured at 13 percent. From the pre-COVID-19 to COVID-19 period, there was an 11 percent increase in total clients wanting to remain uninsured. This increase in uninsured clientele can be attributed to the unemployment benefits that were provided to these households, rendering them ineligible for Medicaid or increased their monthly premiums, which resulted in the premiums perceived to be unaffordable. These caused clients to have to forego any type of insurance in an effort to save money, as what they were being offered now was too expensive for them to afford.

Table 3.3 classifies clients who have filled out applications during the COVID-19 period based on their residency status and household poverty level. It demonstrates two key findings. First, eligible citizens who applied were more likely to be in the upper portions of the poverty level, constituting the majority of applicants in the below 200–400+ percent FPL range. Second, Green Card holders who have legally been in the USA for less than five years constitute the majority of applicants in the below 100–150 percent FPL. Of the clients at WFC, eligible citizens are the group with the highest income brackets and least applications, suggesting they have more economic stability than other groups who are not citizens yet. This is most likely because of governmental mechanisms in place to financially help citizens, which are generally not extended to immigrants or residents who have been in the USA less than five years.

Thus, that would explain why Green Card holders who have not reached the five-year mark represent the residency status group with the lowest percentages of FPL and, thus, the lowest amount of economic and financial stability. This suggests that this group of Green Card holders are the most vulnerable populations among those of varying residency status in this group, considering how many live below 150–100 percent FPL. This makes it clear that the most vulnerable population for healthcare is the immigrant population that is under five years of permanent residency. To help pay for basic coverage, this group requires premium tax credits, and recent policy changes have been putting their coverage at risk.

Figure 3.3 highlights the residency status breakdown of the applicant group with the lowest percentage of the FPL, at less than 100 percent, which was also shown in Table 3.3. This group has the lowest FPL, suggesting that they are facing the highest level of economic burden and financial insecurity of any group; 76 percent of this group is represented by Green Card holders who have been in the USA less than five years. This further acknowledges that they are the most vulnerable group among the other residency status groups. The second largest group in this bracket is Eligible citizens with 13 percent in this below 100 percent FPL, which suggests that although they do get national assistance for being citizens or residing in the USA for over five years, they can still find themselves in lower poverty levels due to a variety of reasons.

Figure 3.4 shows the types of clients that wanted to terminate ACA coverage for their household. There were a total of 213 termination requests. Majority or 64 percent wanted to terminate ACA and enroll into Medicaid because of income changes brought about by COVID-19. The remaining 36 percent wanted to remain uninsured because of the monthly premium prices that were perceived to be unaffordable. As more terminations are happening, a lot of people in the lower-income brackets are moving into Medicaid. They do not have to pay anything, but those who got an increase with unemployment, did not want to pay higher insurance premiums. However, those who received stimulus packages, in the below the 100 percent FPL group, had higher premiums and were unable to qualify for Medicaid.

Figure 3.5 demonstrates how clients terminated ACA plans during the pre-COVID-19 times compared to COVID-19 times. From Figures 3.1 and 3.2, it is clear that the number of uninsured clients went up during the COVID-19 period by 10 percent. As mentioned, many opted to remain uninsured in this period because lost jobs and wages led to filing of unemployment. Many received unemployment benefits and stimulus packages that either made them ineligible for federal coverage or increased their premiums. This graph suggests how clients in the higher-income brackets were more likely to terminate ACA plans during the Open Enrollment or pre-COVID-19 period, most likely because they did not fall under certain economic parameters or were able to afford other insurances. Clients in the lowest-income bracket, below 100 percent FPL, were more likely to terminate ACA plans during the COVID-19 period, because of the aforementioned changes to ACA eligibility or premiums due to provisions from unemployment and stimulus packages.

4 Conclusion

Through this data, WFC is able to explore the economic impact that COVID-19 had on the Muslim immigrant community of Chicago. This data suggests that immigrants have been impacted considerably more than citizens, especially those who are Green Card holders and have been residents in the USA for less than five years. It is this group and others in the below 100 percent and 138 percent FPL that have been the most impacted.

Unfortunately for this group, their immigrant status of being a Green Card holder makes them ineligible for food stamps and they are not given other government benefits to help improve their financial status. Thus, at this level, having the premium tax credit from the government to pay for their health coverage is the only way they can be covered. If given more money through any means, via work or government checks, they become part of a higher-income bracket and will then need to pay a higher subsidy, which they often are unable to. However, once their unemployment benefits end and their stimulus runs out, they do return to the lower FPL percentage if another source of income is not found.

Among all of the groups of Muslims that WFC caters to, it is clear for the immigrants that there is a strong reliance on federal forms of insurance. Many are not able to afford private insurance or work in jobs that do not provide employer insurance. However, even with the threat of COVID-19 to health conditions, there was a substantial 10 percent increase in the number of those who chose to now become uninsured. Because of unemployment and/or additional sources of income from the government, they would have to begin paying more for insurance, and this expense was greater for these clients than the threat of COVID-19. Thus, they chose to forego healthcare insurance altogether.

With the ACA, individuals in these communities were receiving lower premiums. However, with the high rate of unemployment, they would often lose their jobs and suffer income changes. They would no longer be able to pay their existing premiums and would choose to forego insurance, as it seems unaffordable. Others would receive unemployment or stimulus checks, which would increase their income levels, causing their premiums to rise. The rise in premium is proportional to the increase in their current income, but because the amount is higher, many will see it now as unaffordable. The educational and financial literacy barriers experienced by immigrants also limits their ability to understand how to access more benefits and see that higher premiums are still affordable if they are making more money.[24] Here, the uninsured rate jumped from 3 percent to 13 percent, most likely due to perceptions of premiums being too high, even though they remained 8.5 percent of total income.

Unfortunately, given that immigrants are often the most vulnerable in their communities, policy changes often affect them greatly. Not all government policies that are implemented to ease burdens are equally beneficial to every segment of the population. Thus, it is imperative that policies that are implemented need to be equitably beneficial and not equally beneficial. Special attention must be paid in the next few years to how healthcare coverage policies will change, and how that will affect the economic burdens of all communities, especially those already impacted the most.

Moving forward, it would be worth taking this research further to see how more of the financial healthcare burdens immigrants in and outside of the

---

24 Silvia Helena Barcellos et al., *Barriers to Immigrant Use of Financial Services: The Role of Language Skills, U.S. Experience, and Return Migration Expectations* (Santa Monica, CA: RAND Corporation, 2012), https://doi.org/10.7249/WR923.

Muslim-American community. It would also be important to look at the financial and sociological impacts of opting to remain uninsured for all of these groups during the COVID-19 period. At WFC in this time, more clients chose to remain uninsured, more clients lost coverage under previous Medicaid, and more had to change around their plans to accommodate for other things happening in their lives. Although this problem is not unique to any particular group here, the complexities are well represented through analyzing the Muslim-American community in Chicago. Their diverse representation among residency/immigration status and household poverty levels (percentage FPL) was able to elucidate many things. Organizations, such as WFC, will have to continue working with Muslim immigrants, such as Green Card holders with less than a five-year residency, to help them obtain adequate coverage. It will be through these methods that they can ensure proper, equal access to care for all, regardless of lower-income status, employment changes, and lower financial literacy.

Acknowledgments

We would like to thank the entire Worry Free Community (WFC) team for giving back to the Muslim community in Chicago with their work in improving access to healthcare and insurance coverage.

Bibliography

Alsoofy, Petra, and Katherine Coplen. "Community in the Time of Corona: Documenting the American Muslim Response to the COVID-19 Crisis." ISPU, May 18, 2020. https://www.ispu.org/community-in-the-time-of-corona-documenting-the-americ an-muslim-response-to-the-covid19-crisis/.

America Indivisible, Emgage Action, MPower Change, Muslim Public Affairs Council, and Poligon Education Fund. "Muslim Civic Engagement Toolkit for Community Members." 2020. https://www.poligonnational.org/uploads/8/2/8/6/82865960/ muslim_civic_engagement_toolkit_for_community_members.pdf.

Aron-Dine, Aviva, and Tara Straw. "House Tax Credits Would Make Health Insurance Far Less Affordable in High-Cost States." Center on Budget and Policy Priorities, March 16, 2017. https://www.cbpp.org/research/health/house-tax-credits-would-ma ke-health-insurance-far-less-affordable-in-high-cost.

Barcellos, Silvia Helena, James P. Smith, Joanne K. Yoong, and Leandro Carvalho. "Barriers to Immigrant Use of Financial Services: The Role of Language Skills, U.S. Experience, and Return Migration Expectations." Santa Monica, CA: RAND Corporation, 2012. https://doi.org/10.7249/WR923.

Barua, Suborna. "Understanding Coronanomics: The Economic Implications of the Coronavirus (COVID-19) Pandemic." April 1, 2020. http://dx.doi.org/10.2139/ssrn.3566477.

Borjas, George, and Hugh Cassidy. "The Adverse Effect of the COVID-19 Labor Market Shock on Immigrant Employment." Cambridge, MA: National Bureau of Economic Research, May 2020. https://doi.org/10.3386/w27243.

Bustamante, Arturo Vargas, Jie Chen, Ryan M. McKenna, and Alexander N. Ortega. "Health Care Access and Utilization Among U.S. Immigrants Before and After the Affordable Care Act." *Journal of Immigrant and Minority Health* 21, no. 2 (April 1, 2019): 211–218. https://doi.org/10.1007/s10903-018-0741-6.

Centers for Medicare and Medicaid Services. "Small Business Health Options Program (SHOP)." https://www.cms.gov/CCIIO/Programs-and-Initiatives/Health-Insurance-Marketplaces/SHOP.

Chicago Department of Public Health (CDPH). "The State of Health for Blacks in Chicago: 2021 Data Brief." https://www.chicago.gov/content/dam/city/depts/cdph/CDPH/Healthy Chicago/CDPH_BlackHealth7c_DIGITAL.pdf.

Cooke, Kristina, and Mica Rosenberg. "Trump Rule on Health Insurance Leaves Immigrants, Companies Scrambling for Answers." *Reuters*, October 31, 2019. https://www.reuters.com/article/us-usa-immigration-insurance-idUSKBN1XA1G6.

Gaffney, Adam, David Himmelstein, and Steffie Woolhandler. "How Much has the Number of Uninsured Risen Since 2016—And at What Cost to Health and Life?" *Health Affairs*, October 29, 2020. https://www.healthaffairs.org/do/10.1377/forefront.20201027.770793/full/.

Gee, Emily. "Less Coverage and Higher Costs: The Trump's Administration's Health Care Legacy." Center for American Progress, September 25, 2020. https://www.americanprogress.org/article/less-coverage-higher-costs-trumps-administrations-health-care-legacy/.

Gooch, Kelly. "Health Disparities Among Chicago Hospitals' Most Pressing Public Health Concerns." *Becker's Hospital Review*, March 12, 2020. https://www.beckershospitalreview.com/care-coordination/health-disparities-among-chicago-hospitals-most-pressing-public-health-concerns.html.

Health Reform Beyond Basics. October 2019. http://www.healthreformbeyondthebasics.org/wp-content/uploads/2019/10/REFERENCE-GUIDE_Yearly-Guideline-and-Thresholds_CoverageYear2020.pdf.

Lopez III, Leo, Louis H. Hart, and Mitchell H. Katz. "Racial and Ethnic Health Disparities Related to COVID-19." *JAMA* 325, no. 8 (2021): 719–720. https://doi.org/10.1001/jama.2020.26443.

Memish, Ziad A., Yusuf Ahmed, Saleh A. Alqahtani, and Shahul H. Ebrahim. "Pausing Superspreader Events for COVID-19 Mitigation: International Hajj Pilgrimage Cancellation." *Travel Medicine and Infectious Disease* 36 (July 2020): 101817. https://doi.org/10.1016/j.tmaid.2020.101817.

Nania, Rachel. "Blacks, Hispanics Hit Harder by the Coronavirus, Early U.S. Data Show." AARP, May 8, 2020. https://www.aarp.org/health/conditions-treatments/info-2020/minority-communities-covid-19.html.

National Black Muslim COVID Coalition. n.d. https://www.blackmuslimcoalition.com.

Nicola, Maria, Zaid Alsafi, Catrin Sohrabi, Ahmed Kerwan, Ahmed Al-Jabir, Christos Iosifidis, Maliha Agha, and Riaz Agha. "The Socio-Economic Implications of the Coronavirus Pandemic (COVID-19): A Review." *International Journal of Surgery* 78 (June 1, 2020): 185–193. https://doi.org/10.1016/j.ijsu.2020.04.018.

Nkansah-Amankra, Stephen, Samuel Kwami Agbanu, and Reuben Jonathan Miller. "Disparities in Health, Poverty, Incarceration, and Social Justice among Racial Groups in the United States: A Critical Review of Evidence of Close Links with Neoliberalism." *International Journal of Health Services* 43, no. 2 (April 2013): 217–240. https://doi.org/10.2190/HS.43.2.c.

Office of the Assistant Secretary for Planning and Evaluation. "Poverty Guidelines", 2020. https://aspe.hhs.gov/topics/poverty-economic-mobility/poverty-guidelines.

Pew Research Center's Religion & Public Life Project. "Muslim Americans: Immigrants and U.S. Born See Life Differently." April 17, 2018. https://www.pewforum.org/essay/muslims-in-america-immigrants-and-those-born-in-u-s-see-life-differently-in-many-ways/.

Saltzman, Evan, and Christine Eibner. "Donald Trump's Health Care Reform Proposals: Anticipated Effects on Insurance Coverage, Out-of-Pocket Costs, and the Federal Deficit." The Commonwealth Fund, September 23, 2016. https://doi.org/10.26099/94f4-8d17.

WTTW News. "Suburban Cook County Among 30 Illinois Counties at COVID-19 Warning Level: IDPH." August 29, 2020. https://news.wttw.com/2020/08/29/suburban-cook-county-among-30-illinois-counties-covid-19-warning-level-idph.

CHAPTER 4

Muslim Healthcare Workers in the Time of COVID-19

Aminah Al-Deen and Constance Shabazz

1 Introduction

The first formal mention of the virus to the rank and file of our medical clinic comes in the weekly staff email, on January 24:

- This is a novel coronavirus with its epicenter in Wuhan, China, with a ~14-day incubation period and potential for person-to-person transmission (though limited)
- Thus far this virus appears to have a milder illness compared to MERS or SARS

  …
- There are currently 830 confirmed cases worldwide, 26 deaths, and 2 confirmed US cases.[1]

Nevertheless, following on the heels of SARS, H1N1, and MERS, the medical community at the beginning of 2020 found itself faced with a category 5 hurricane-equivalent pandemic named COVID-19, though they did not know it at the time. Even now, in 2021, the pandemic continues to instill fear even though vaccines are available with an almost equal amount of lack of information. Thus, this writing attempts to relate the state of healthcare at the beginning of the pandemic, and the thoughts and feelings of Muslim healthcare practitioners from initial awareness to action. We frame our inquiry around Muslim healthcare personnel who were actually working during the early months of the pandemic especially since Ramadan began during the second month. No one knew what to expect or the strains a pandemic would place on them. Disruption of normalcy was the norm; indeed many of our interviews had to be done in parts as hospital emergencies constantly interrupted.

1 Danielle Ofri, "A Bellevue Doctor's Pandemic Diary," *New Yorker Magazine*, October 1, 2020. https://www.newyorker.com/science/medical-dispatch/a-bellevue-doctors-coronavirus-pandemic-diary.

 | DOI:10.1163/9789004679771_006

How could we pose questions that let Muslim healthcare personnel express the anxiety that lack of clear communication caused them? We knew that a fixed set of interview questions or a closed-ended survey would not do justice to their experiences nor were they practical as all healthcare workers were overburdened and stressed. While the backdrop was healthcare worker anxiety and overwork, we imagined that there was something to Muslim experiences that deserved telling; that there would be unique perspectives that would arise. Hence we set out to speak (interview being too formal a notion) with Muslim healthcare workers across the country and listen to their stories. The largest challenge was to make those we spoke with comfortable enough to share. We initially posed the following guiding questions to Muslim physicians and medical staff and wove their responses along with information garnered from other articles into this chapter. Unless a conversationalist is specified, the narrators of accounts are the authors of this chapter, or a quote is from another source.

1. How did you feel when you first realized that COVID-19 was likely to spread in your area or after cases in your area had been reported?
2. What did the pandemic make you think regarding how it was going to affect you and your family/friends/neighbors?
3. What were your greatest concerns regarding your patients?
    a. Was I now sure about my diagnosis of symptoms? Is it COVID-19 or non-COVID-19?
4. How prepared was your health center to handle this pandemic?
5. How prepared were you (educationally, training-wise, and mentally) to handle this pandemic?
6. What has been the most challenging aspect for you as a healthcare provider or someone working with patients during this pandemic?
7. What role has your faith played in dealing with this pandemic?
8. How have you tended to your spiritual health?
    a. What changed or did not change in your practices?
    b. Did you expand your practices?
    c. How did your spiritual health affect your medical practice?

We found that these questions could not be asked in a series, as our conversationalists just wanted to talk more freely and we let them, taking note of special remarks, and using our guiding questions periodically but unsystematically.

Our informal conversations using the platform Zoom began in March 2020 and as of this writing, by January, 2021, we had spoken with physicians, physician assistants, nurse practitioners, administrative physicians, and receptionists. We chose to speak with different kinds of Muslim healthcare workers to indicate the scope of experiences of persons in conversation with us, not to establish statistical relevance. We were able to contact Muslim workers first in the Federally Qualified Health Centers because Dr. Shabazz was one of the auditors. Other workers were referred to us or were known to us through our personal circles. We had two focus groups, each with just a few participants. These groups were productive in that the depth of experiences was found to be common. We felt the intensity of workers' experiences as often our conversations were interrupted by emergencies. We did not record the conversations to comply with the wishes of the participants, but we used the conversations to highlight topics for inquiry. Our focus was on getting Muslim healthcare workers to share what was happening in their environments and what they thought about preparedness, how they were reacting and behaving spiritually in the pandemic. We used journal articles, newspaper reports, and other healthcare workers' reports of the status of environments and their personal feelings as complements to our conversations. We engaged these professionals in New York, Houston, Chicago, Los Angeles, San Francisco, and New Haven. Participants asked for anonymity for their names and the names of their clinics, whether freestanding or hospital-associated and for the hospitals where they were employed.

As a result of this lack of formality in our conversations, even though we had guiding questions, we did not obtain substantial data for quantitative analysis. We did not rely on any particular method but sought to provide a record of the impact of the pandemic on Muslim healthcare professionals from their point of view. Though the number of workers we were able to contact was small, we felt it important to have this kind of exploration of the pandemic.

2 Media Influences

Media first inundated US viewers with footage of overflowing patients being intubated in hospitals in Wuhan in the province of Hubei, China. Reports explained that a respiratory disease had infected many in the city and seemed to be spreading quickly. There was also a report of a physician who was sounding alarms and that he had been quieted.[2] He was exposed and died shortly

2 This physician was an ophthalmologist who was treating a case of conjunctivitis combined with an upper respiratory infection. His alert contained a warning to treat this eye inflammation at home, unless patient needed to come to an office or hospital because something unusual was present. In the United States, this differential diagnosis was translated to "wear shields to protect eyes."

after—apparently from this disease. This city was soon quarantined, and residents were not allowed out of their homes. At first, the origin was suspected to be from the raw foods in the marketplace. Since a significant amount of the food in the markets in this city was raw, it was suspected that it was the vector. The focus shifted to an armadillo-like animal called a pangolin, which is used in Chinese medicine as its scales are understood as therapeutic. That there was a pandemic was not in the news in December 2019 or in January 2020. There was little angst in the United States as China is thousands of miles away and media was not detailing any outbreaks in the United States. Although the World Health Organization (WHO) was first alerted of several cases of pneumonia on December 31, 2019, which rapidly increased to forty-four by January 3, no world alarm was sounded for COVID-19 in the United States. Physicians in the United States also experienced levels of heightened concern about the reports coming from WHO and other global health organizations but this was not initially communicated in the media. The first recorded case was diagnosed at Providence Regional Medical Center in Snohomish Country in Washington State on January 20, 2020. The patient had returned from Wuhan, China. The second case occurred in Chicago, Illinois on January 30, 2020, when a woman who had traveled to China returned home. She infected her husband. Although this was reported in the media, the alarm was sounded only for people who had recently traveled to China and their close contacts since their return. The government restricted travel to China but not Europe or between states within the USA. Even after the restrictions were in place, it was reported that an additional 40,000 people had entered into the USA from all over the world. It was then that both state and federal officials began the process of determining the appropriate responses. Some of the responses involved isolating patients in hospitals and nursing homes and requiring the use of personal protective equipment (PPE). Initial medical treatments were varied but the use of intubation became a primary response to respiratory failure along with isolation/quarantine of exposed contacts.

President Trump's White House had dissolved the White House's National Security Council Directorate for Global Health Security and Biodefense in 2018 to the shock and dismay of those who ran this office. Thus, there was "no organized, accountable leadership to prepare for and respond to pandemic threats."[3] With the dismantling of this office, the government could not mount a speedy and measured response.

---

3 Beth Cameron, "I Ran the White House Pandemic Office. Trump Closed It," *Washington Post*, March 13, 2020, https://www.washingtonpost.com/outlook/nsc-pandemic-office-trump-closed/2020/03/13/a70de09c-6491-11ea-acca-80c22bbee96f_story.html.

Initially physicians struggled to: (1) get personal protective equipment (PPE) for themselves and staff; and (2) read up on the latest information regarding protocols for COVID-19. They quickly realized that there was no standardized approach or system for care of patients, and that there were supply chain issues, which impacted the availability of and access to PPE.[4]

The Centers for Disease Control and Prevention (CDC) guidelines for every citizen were not only confusing but also impossible for some to follow and calls to physicians for clarity increased as the general public began to follow rules as they were presented. Both special reports on television from the government and authoritative reports from the CDC crowded television screens. Initially, family members who had to go outside the home were told to wear masks and gloves and distance themselves from others or avoid contact with potentially infected objects or surfaces. Upon returning home, healthcare workers were asked to bag their clothing, put them in the washing machine, and take a shower. Media emphasized the need to sanitize homes for everyone, preferably with Lysol spray ignoring the effect of the constant spraying of aerosols in closed spaces. Home isolation for those with mild–moderate COVID-19 was also idyllically described: isolate in a room; do not come into contact with others; use a separate bathroom and utensils. These guidelines were problematic for many people and especially low-income persons living in crowded spaces. Notably, as time progressed, these guidelines continued to change.

News media had become the "go to doctor" for many in the public to gauge what to do with their health. The government questioned the efficacy of the scientists at the CDC but found itself in continual reliance on them. Again, the media was over-reporting without details. Listeners are not apprised of the severity of the cases, recovery rates, incidents of recurrences, or re-hospitalizations unless they are sensational.[5]

4 Ian Munro, "State Performing Reviews of Essential Supply Lines," *Daily News-Record*, July 6, 2021, https://www.dnronline.com/dnronline/state-performing-reviews-of-essential-supply-lines/article_3ee5615b-96ad-5991-9d65-95089f61d3d1.html; Jordan Drupal, "Blog: The Health Care Supply Chain Before and in the Midst of COVID-19," *American Hospital Association News*, September 9, 2020, https://www.aha.org/news/blog/2020-09-09-blog-health-care-supply-chain-and-midst-covid-19; and Stephany Lapierre, "The PPE Supply Chain Problem and 5 Ways to Solve it," *Industry Today*, April 27, 2020, https://industrytoday.com/the-ppe-supply-chain-problem-and-5-ways-to-solve-it/.

5 Mary Beth Schweigert, "A Surgeon's Survival Story: Five Phone Calls, a Long Recovery, and Lessons Learned from COVID," *Penn Medicine*, June 23, 2020, https://www.pennmedicine.org/news/news-blog/2020/june/a-surgeons-survival-story; Madeline Heim, "'It's Just Going to Be like This Now': These Wisconsinites Survived Covid-19, but 'Recovery' Hasn't Meant a Return to Normal," *The Post-Crescent*, August 4, 2020, https://www.postcrescent.com/in-depth/news/2020/08/03/wisconsin-coronavirus-some-covid-19-recovery-stories-long-hauls/5522928002/.

Media had become a portal for raising fears and trepidation about travel as millions were determined to travel for various holidays. One recent report was on one man collapsing with COVID-19 on a flight and potentially infecting everyone on plane, resulting in them having to immediately go into isolation. This report, of course, made some cash in tickets while others decided to risk it. As numbers of reported cases declined, news reporters and physicians continued asking people to stay home and have small gatherings while reporting on lines of people waiting to travel. Confusion and more anxiety had not ceased in the latter months of 2020. The trend of media to raise panic also has not ceased in this continuing pandemic and the rise of vaccine availability. In 2021, misinformation, lack of accurate information on what vaccines do, how they were developed so quickly, how safe they are, and their availability—especially to low-income and uninsured people—created hesitancy in people signing up to receive them. Stories about sites running out of vaccines and costs added to this hesitancy.

3 Emergency Rooms and Clinics

The staggering number of issues that medical professionals have encountered and still have to encounter remains and is anxiety-producing even as the pandemic continues and has resurfaced in second and third waves. The total numbers of cases in the United States as of November 7, 2020, stood at 10,078,415 with 242,417 deaths and rising daily.[6] On March 15, 2021, the number of cases was 30,095,234, deaths thus far stood at 547,446 with fortunately 22,184,811 known cases of recovery.[7] In June 2021, though the number of deaths was declining and the number of persons vaccinated increasing, there was concern about another spike.[8] By the winter of 2021, scientists were learning more. The virulence of the virus increases in temperatures below 31 degrees Fahrenheit, so cases rose again. It was often unreported that deaths accounted for 2 percent of diagnosed cases while the number of patients who recovered is 98 percent. Recovery is now revealing a rising number of "long haulers."[9]

6 "United States Coronavirus," Worldometer, November 7, 2020, https://www.worldometers.info/coronavirus/country/us/.

7 "United States Coronavirus," Worldometer, November 7, 2020.

8 Jared Ortaliza et al., "Covid-19 Continues to be a Leading Cause of Death in the U.S. in June 2021," Peterson-KFF Health System Tracker, July 1, 2021, https://www.healthsystemtracker.org/brief/covid-19-continues-to-be-a-leading-cause-of-death-in-the-u-s-in-june-2021/.

9 Published studies (see Angelo Carfì et al., "Persistent Symptoms in Patients After Acute

In 2020, across the nation, hospital emergency rooms along with clinics were the first line of responders and physicians found themselves on the front lines. Meanwhile, hospital administrators scrambled to assess the efficiency of their structural designs (rooms and waiting areas) in the setting of an airborne pandemic, to enlarge intensive care units (ICUs), and cordon off ambulatory units. Administrators suspended elective surgeries while further expanding their infection control processes without closing down. Community clinics were faced with different challenges. The rapid reshuffling of personnel, sanitizing rooms, finding out how to access telehealth programs, and dampening down their own and their staff's panicked, exhausted physicians and medical staff.[10] To properly sanitize, many clinics had to shut down for a few days and some workers found themselves exposed and sick.[11] Receptionists had to reschedule regular patient visits and limit walk-in patients. Clinics attached to hospitals had to follow hospital protocols and some of them in many states were turned into triage centers for emergency rooms. One nurse expressed dismay when thinking about it,

> We did not have enough money in our small clinic to hire a cleaning company since all of the companies' rates went sky high, so we had to buy the chemicals and get the equipment and do it ourselves all the time worrying if we got it right.[12]

Emergency rooms and all clinics were given the protocol: "Remain vigilant at all points of entry … and screen every person for fever, cough, rash and travel history."[13] In some clinics, this became untenable as patients overcrowded

COVID-19," *JAMA* 324, no. 6 (2020): 603–605, https://doi.org/10.1001/jama.2020.12603; and Mark W. Tenforde et al., "Symptom Duration and Risk Factors for Delayed Return to Usual Health Among Outpatients with COVID-19 in a Multistate Health Care Systems Network—United States, March–June 2020," *MMWR: Morbidity and Mortality Weekly Report* 69, no. 30 (2020): 993–998, https://doi.org/10.15585/mmwr.mm6930e1) and surveys conducted by patient groups indicate that 50–80 percent of patients continue to have bothersome symptoms three months after the onset of COVID-19—even after tests no longer detect virus in their body; see Anthony L. Komaroff, "The Tragedy of the Long COVID," *Harvard Health*, March 1, 2021, https://www.health.harvard.edu/blog/the-tragedy-of-the-post-covid-long-haulers-2020101521173.

10 Instances of exhaustion were reported daily in news, journal op-eds, and in our interviews.

11 This information was gleaned from several interviews with clinic medical staff during May, 2020.

12 Anonymous nurse at clinic on west coast. Interview April 8, 2020.

13 Ibid.; and Ofri, "A Bellevue Doctor's Pandemic Diary."

waiting rooms. "It didn't feel right to ask patients, especially elderly folks to wait outside."[14]

Meanwhile as healthcare workers in hospitals and clinics quickly began to run out of PPE—situations became untenable. No one trusted usual sources of equipment as most of it was manufactured in China. American companies began to retool to fill the overwhelming need for ventilation equipment, masks, and gowns.[15] They were only able to produce these items in small quantities. This really demonstrated how the USA had outsourced the manufacture and production of critical healthcare resources putting its own population at risk. Counterfeit PPE began to appear in the market. Further inspection was instituted and, in some cases, equipment supplies were found to be defective. One Muslim organization, Zakat Foundation, found that it had received hundreds of masks destined for clinics and nursing homes that were counterfeit. They had to "just give them away to non-medical people in neighborhoods in suburban Chicago and people in surrounding states."[16]

Initially, the US government's response set the tone for the overall response to the pandemic. Cruise ships were marooned in offshore waters with passengers quarantined as some of them, along with staff, were infected or exposed.[17] There were not enough available testing kits and, when they were available, many of them were found to be defective or missing parts. As stockpiles of usable masks, gloves, and gowns dwindled, physicians were asked to reuse their PPE, which is contradictory to protection. One ophthalmologist reported, "I had staff take off white coats as they were potential carriers of the virus. At my office, we used surgical masks as the N95 masks did not fit."[18]

It is important to reassert that Muslim healthcare workers practice everywhere: in ethnic communities of Muslims, poor communities, in emergency rooms, and in hospitals. Muslim patients tend to feel more comfortable when the clinical staff is Muslim and initially patients were accompanied by family

---

14 Anonymous nurse practitioner on west coast. April, 2020.

15 It should be noted that when the exorbitant costs charged for ventilators was revealed in investigative journalism, this emergency was removed from the daily news broadcasts.

16 Interview with Donna Demir, RN at Zakat Foundation, April 16, 2020.

17 It was reported that:

> countries around the world are strengthening their border control measures in order to prevent the further spread of COVID-19 and port authorities continue to be in heightened state of alert in order to identify crew members or passengers displaying symptoms compatible with the disease.

"Coronavirus—Implications for Ships and Crew," *Gard*, March 24, 2020, https://www.gard.no/web/updates/content/29112071/coronavirus-implications-for-ships-and-crew.

18 Interview on March 2, 2021.

members and began coming to clinics in large numbers.[19] Fear and anxiety rose because of the spiritual implications along with the reality of COVID-19 and we found that we needed to discuss religious matters. For many Muslims, hearing on webinars and Zoom seminars, how to understand the pandemic from a spiritual point of view became critical.[20]

Religion is an overriding concern in healthcare issues. Knowledge of the physician and medical staff of Muslim ethical norms and decorum are extremely important, especially when there is the possibility of admission for hospital care. Our participants expressed that Muslim patients and healthcare workers find great comfort in expressions of a common religious belief or even when their religious belief is acknowledged like other religious community members. These concerns continue in 2021 as many clinics have returned to almost normal schedules while observing masking and distancing protocols.

As mentioned previously, there was much confusion caused by conflicting information from the government and CDC on the care or referral for further care of patients exhibiting symptoms. This made clinics' first responders wary. Shortness of breath, dry cough, listlessness, and absence of taste and smell were said to be symptoms of COVID-19 but these were also symptoms of cold and flu. Some clinics were overrun with families thinking they had the virus and some of them did indeed and had to be referred to emergency rooms or advised to isolate at home to the best of their ability. How to provide processes for quarantining at home became difficult. There were no manuals, no flyers in the face of the multiple kinds of family environment until early May 2020. Physicians and medical staff could not feel good ethically about sending patients home to crowded environments. Some families were inter-generational. Some lived in dwellings where the space to move around was limited.

The absence of access to emergency rooms (some were filled as patients lay in ambulances) provided physicians and patients with many anxious moments.[21] Anecdotal evidence of patients having heart attacks and or serious

19 One Muslim clinic in the southwest reported that the majority of its patient population was South Asian and they often stated that they felt more comfortable when their treatment was given by same ethnic physicians and medical staff.

20 Andrew Hanna, "What Islamists are Doing and Saying on Covid-19 Crisis," Wilson Center, May 14, 2020, https://www.wilsoncenter.org/article/what-islamists-are-doing-and-saying-covid-19-crisis; and Petra Alsoofy and Katherine Coplen, "Community in the Time of Corona: Documenting the American Muslim Response to the COVID-19 Crisis," Institute for Social Policy and Understanding, February 18, 2021, https://www.ispu.org/community-in-the-time-of-corona-documenting-the-american-muslim-response-to-the-covid19-crisis/.

21 Pauline W. Chen, "No Room at the Inn," *The New York Times*, March 12, 2020, https://www

situations like renal failure was daunting. The reality of not finding hospitals which could admit them because they were not only filled but what is more filled with COVID-19 patients, was and now is again startling.[22]

Entering into a world of increasingly necessary telehealth has been problematic. Many physicians and especially patients were skeptical. Some patients did not have access to computers. This was especially the case since schools were closed and young people were using them or other adults were working remotely or there was no computer or tablet or smartphone to ease the transition.[23] Telehealth served patients with minor illnesses, those who just needed to check-in, and those who wanted consolation. The visual phone consultation could not treat more serious issues nor really see what could be impending issues that perhaps could be detected with the touch or close visual examination.

Disputes between political and governmental authorities and the scientific communities led to confusion. At first, the USA's chief infectious disease expert, Dr. Fauci, was giving the nation information. Unfortunately, his information was not in line with the president's continual discounting of the spread of the pandemic. This caused even more confusion and led to a new team composed of Dr. Birx, who had been the AIDS coordinator for two past presidents, the Vice-President Mr. Pence (not a physician), and the president's son-in-law, Jared Kushner (also not a physician). Now the public saw incomplete graphs and heard language that better suited what the president wanted.

What was credible information? Healthcare providers passed on information given in alerts from the CDC guiding immediate care and follow up. There were now outside sources intervening in healthcare recommendations and patients began to use these mythical sources and question their physician's advice. Conspiracy theories, issues of personal freedom, fake medical advice

.nytimes.com/2020/03/12/well/live/coronavirus-emergency-rooms-hospital-crowding.html; and Simon Judkins, "Ed Overcrowding, Under-Resourcing 'Worst in 30 Years,'" *InSight+*, April 26, 2021, https://insightplus.mja.com.au/2021/14/ed-overcrowding-under-resourcing-worst-in-30-years/.

22 Nevada Governor's Office and Nevada Department of Health and Human Services, "Crisis Standards of Care—Coronavirus (COVID-19) in Nevada," Nevada Health Response, July 15, 2020, https://nvhealthresponse.nv.gov/wp-content/uploads/2020/07/NV_DHHS_DPBH_CSCRecommendations_COVID-19_071520_ADA.pdf; and Mark É. Czeisler et al., "Delay or Avoidance of Medical Care Because of COVID-19-Related Concerns—United States, June 2020," Centers for Disease Control and Prevention, September 11, 2020, https://www.cdc.gov/mmwr/volumes/69/wr/mm6936a4.htm.

23 The telehealth system itself was unreliable many times for medical staff. Patients experienced dropped calls and frustration with trying to reconnect and sometimes just gave up.

coming from the Office of the President caused a lot of trauma and anger among medical staff. By March 2020, when states began to shutter with at home orders, panic really began as the nation's issues with healthcare, food deserts, and inadequate housing were exposed. Minorities, who had always been underserved, found themselves even more marginalized.[24] Social distancing raised police suspicion to the point that thirty-five of forty arrests were Black. In Chicago, Blacks are 30 percent of the population but accounted for 60 percent of COVID-19 deaths. There were numerous stories about Black people being turned away from hospitals leading to increased concern over bias in treatment.[25]

Today, clinicians and technicians have more knowledge on how to treat patients with a wide variety of infections at various stages. They are adept with managing these infections, including COVID-19, along with providing continual care for other emergencies such as heart attacks, renal failure, aneurysms, and so on. What seems to be most problematic today, as mentioned in the section on media, is holiday celebrations in groups and the resultant surge in infections. This surge is being met at a time when healthcare workers' physical health is declining, as is their mental health.

Traveling nurses have been forced to stay in their home areas to treat surges. Seasoned physicians, nurses, and other healthcare workers have become teachers of recent graduates to expand the workforce. Some medical schools even graduated student months earlier than planned to address the need to have all hands onboard. The anxiety that this produces in the "just graduated" or "ready to graduate" groups is significant.[26] Physicians and nurses are also finding themselves switching specialties by demand or increased interest. As elective surgeries and procedures are put on hold, there is a critical need for ICU, respiratory, physical therapy, and occupational therapy specializations. The shift in specialties is most intriguing.[27] Specialties such as pulmonary care, emer-

---

24 Shanoor Seervai, "Why Are More Black Americans Dying of Covid-19?" Commonwealth Fund, June 26, 2020, https://www.commonwealthfund.org/publications/podcast/2020/jun/why-are-more-black-americans-dying-covid-19.

25 Bill Hutchinson, "Black Doctor Dies of COVID after Alleging Hospital Mistreatment: 'This Is How Black People Get Killed'," *ABC News*, December 24, 2020, https://abcnews.go.com/US/black-doctor-dies-covid-alleging-hospital-mistreatment-black/story?id=74878119.

26 Sandra Knispel, "Medical Students Graduate Early to Join Pandemic Fight," University of Rochester, April 9, 2020, https://www.rochester.edu/newscenter/medical-students-graduate-early-to-join-pandemic-fight-423812/; and Michail Papapanou et al., "Medical Education Challenges and Innovations During COVID-19 Pandemic," *Postgraduate Medical Journal* 98, no. 1159 (2021): 321–327, https://doi.org/10.1136/postgradmedj-2021-140032.

27 Brendan Murphy, "Covid-19 Capsizes the Physician Job Market: Trends You Should Know,"

gency medicine, critical care, and infectious diseases have become the premier needs. Ironically, just as healthcare workers began to strategize these specialties, states are opening up hospitals for elective surgeries in all areas. We have to wait and see what happens next regarding this quandary.[28]

In the advent of more telehealth, there is a shift in the regularity and intensity of chronic care. Patients who can, prefer this visit primarily because of its convenience. As a result, the "hands-on" approach becomes questionable. Many Muslim physicians still attempt to demand some person-to-person care but realize that the environment, especially in the current surge, is not conducive.

4 The Spiritual Quandary

In previous studies carried out by Nabil Khan (Harvard T.H. Chan School of Public Health) and Lance Laird (Boston University School of Medicine), there were about seventy Muslim-led free clinics across the United States.[29] These clinics served about 50,000 patients annually, the majority of whom were low income, uninsured or underinsured, Muslim and non-Muslim. "Several of the clinics began with the intention to address the unmet needs of local Muslim communities."[30] The need for continuing education conferences on Islamic biomedical issues is more apparent now. An Islamic perspective is needed as technologies expand without accompanying ethical concern. There is a pressing need for ethical thought as some technological advances push religious considerations of death and dying beyond their limits.

Muslim biomedical ethicists held, over at least the last two if not the last three decades, seminars and conferences to provide Muslim perspectives on issues in the field. Since most medical professionals have had all of their train-

---

American Medical Association, December 4, 2020, https://www.ama-assn.org/residents-students/transition-practice/covid-19-capsizes-physician-job-market-trends-you-should.

28 Association of American Medical College, "New AAMC Report Confirms Growing Physician Shortage," AAMC, June 26, 2020, https://www.aamc.org/news-insights/press-releases/new-aamc-report-confirms-growing-physician-shortage; and Darren Schulte, "Industry Voices—After COVID-19, There Will be a Tectonic Shift in How Medicine is Practiced," *Fierce Healthcare*, May 25, 2020, https://www.fiercehealthcare.com/practices/industry-voices-after-covid-19-coming-tectonic-shift-how-medicine-practiced.

29 Fran Quigley, "Muslim Health Care for All," *Foreign Policy*, June 27, 2019, https://foreignpolicy.com/2019/06/27/muslim-health-care-for-all/.

30 Ibid.

ing in Western schools where the emphasis is on the rights of the autonomous individual, it was deemed absolutely necessary to provide a religious point of view on subjects such as in-vitro fertilization, death and dying, and transplants. "Islamic discourse on concerns of a spiritually and morally autonomous individual incapable of attaining salvation outside of the nexus of community oriented Sharia, with its emphasis on the integrated system of law and morality," was a primary focus.[31] Muslim healthcare professionals worried about the extremes of care in attempts to override a perhaps impending death, the absence of the traditional rituals with guidance from spiritual leadership, and the absence of prayers at death and with family. COVID-19 caused concerns about the extremes of treatment and the lack of ethical concern about the use of some technologies and medicines as Muslim physicians walk a thin line in their thoughts about "doing all that can be done, and the rest is on Allah's timetable for that individual." Bio-medical ethicists are concerned and perhaps this pandemic has made those concerns more immediate. Since in most initial cases consultation with the patient was not possible, Muslim physicians worried about the patient's and their families' feelings about their spiritual states, whether the patient was Muslim or not.[32] The emphasis was primarily on saving a life.[33] Muslim healthcare professionals found themselves in consistent ethical quagmires, not because they did not want to save lives, but that they thought about not considering themselves the arbiters of life and death.

COVID-19 and now its variants have brought an especially difficult quandary to the Muslim healthcare community. Initially, many Muslims, along with the majority of society in the USA, thought that although people travel across the world hourly and it was a pandemic (across the world) that it would be over quickly so as not to inconvenience their daily lives.[34] Still in 2021, a year later, as hospitals continue to strain from patient loads, deaths mount, and vaccines are difficult to find or non-existent, millions of Americans refuse

31 Abdulaziz Abdulhussein Sachedina, *Islamic Biomedical Ethics: Principles and Application* (New York: Oxford University Press, 2009).

32 Keri Heath, "For Health-Care Workers, a Year of Adapt and Overcome," *The Daily News*, October 16, 2020, https://www.galvnews.com/news/specialreports/free/article_2d074c56-181e-5971-a81d-a6b69016f8c9.html.

33 Kenneth V. Iserson, "Principles of Biomedical Ethics," *Emergency Medicine Clinics of North America* 17, no. 2 (May 1999): 283–306, https://doi.org/10.1016/s0733-8627(05)70060-2.

34 Jan Cortes, "What COVID-19 Taught Us: All the Healthy Habits We Should Keep Even in a Post-Pandemic World," *International Business Times*, January 11, 2021, https://www.ibtimes.com/what-covid-19-taught-us-all-healthy-habits-we-should-keep-even-post-pandemic-world-3118898.

to believe there is a pandemic.[35] Nevertheless, when the pandemic and its attendant concerns became prominent, as mentioned previously, community webinars elicited and attempted to abate fears over death and dying, distancing from family members, and hypervigilance about touching others in family.[36]

According to the faith tradition of Islam, Allah is the determiner of both the moment of life and of death. Many Muslims believe that if it is your time to die, no medical intervention can stop this process. Others believe that one should avail themselves of medical care and Allah determines the outcome. Still others attempt to ward off the moment of death with blessings, prayers, talisman, holy water, and so on from those claiming a special relationship with God and thus, special powers to intervene in the crisis. These positions bring a host of questions to our conversations.

Medieval Islamic sources provide some foundational information on how epidemics and other plagues were encountered so that twenty-first-century believers can build strategies for spiritual care. In this pandemic, we are confronted with numerous situations. The sheer explosion of dead bodies caused concern about human dignity in death. Whether the cause of death was unavailability of healthcare in overworked hospitals creating the crisis of too many people to treat at one time, or actual death from too many modalities, or death due to fatalism on part of patient, the communal spiritual grief was and is great. We also know that issues of race, class, and religion demand our attention as we strategize. During the pandemic, there were ongoing Islamophobia incidents and fear of treatment in the hospital by potentially staff holding anti-Muslim biases.[37] These secular concerns have an important impact on treatments and survival or not.

While most Muslim healthcare professionals know that machines can mimic life and that with drugs and other modalities they can "start the heart" or "increase brain activity." Some physicians working in Intensive Care Units found themselves wondering about this quandary, since treating COVID-19

35 Christi A. Grimm, "Hospitals Reported That the COVID-19 Pandemic has Significantly Strained Health Care Delivery," U.S. Department of Health and Human Services Office of Inspector General, March 2021, https://oig.hhs.gov/oei/reports/OEI-09-21-00140.pdf.

36 Mehmet Ozalp, "How Coronavirus Challenges Muslims' Faith and Changes Their Lives," *The Conversation*, January 14, 2021, https://theconversation.com/how-coronavirus-challenges-muslims-faith-and-changes-their-lives-133925.

37 Mobashra Tazamal, "Islamophobia in 2020: Covid-19 and Conspiracy Theories," *Bridge Initiative*, December 22, 2022, https://bridge.georgetown.edu/research/islamophobia-in-2020-covid-19-and-conspiracy-theories/.

patients required this mimicry.[38] As previously stated, most in the medical community assumed that treatments would be intense but that patients would recover, and semblances of normalcy would return in a few months. The attack of COVID-19 on the brain, lungs, heart, pancreas, liver, and so on shredded ordinary protocols and the effects have destroyed understanding of normalcy for too many people and added to their hospital stays and therapies.

Many questions thus are raised—has the physician tried to interfere with God's decree? Is there a punishment for this? Is the physician acting contrary to the wishes of the patient who cannot respond and exists without family to make a determination? COVID-19 has caused extraordinary circumstances where family cannot visit, Muslim chaplains are not present, and the rapidity of the viral attack leaves no time for words of comfort from anyone.

Islamic faith imbues believers with the concept of death as a "transition to life after death," sometimes translating this understanding as "suffering in this world alleviates it in the next world." How can Muslims comprehend this in a pandemic? How much pain and discomfort should one endure or is the perception of another's pain a cause for more drugs? What does the intervention of powerful drugs for pain relief do to the need for spiritual awareness? Given this, how do we then view the disastrous results of COVID-19 treatments especially for those who believe that suffering sometimes perhaps at death is a part of living?

While in general healthcare providers want survival and healing, faith considerations must be taken into account somewhere in the discussion along with cultural deployments of those faith considerations.[39] In the West, again speaking generally, some lives are considered inherently more valuable, based on what that human contributes to society and race. In Islamic thought, human life is not inherently valuable but valuable because it is a "trust" from God.

Muslim healthcare providers find themselves rushing to save lives, while struggling with their spiritual position. Many expressed their confusion, anxi-

38 Emma Goldberg, "Life Lessons: What a Doctor Learned from Death and Dying in Covid Wards," *The Guardian*, July 22, 2021, https://www.theguardian.com/lifeandstyle/2021/jul/22/covid-doctor-confronts-death-dying.

39 Christine M. Lomiguen, Ivelys Rosete, and Justin Chin, "Providing Culturally Competent Care for Covid-19 Intensive Care Unit Delirium: A Case Report and Review," *Cureus* 12, no. 10 (October 9, 2020): e10867, https://doi.org/10.7759/cureus.10867; Meryl Bailey, "Culturally Competent Healthcare: Lessons from Covid-19," *HealthCity*, May 12, 2020, https://healthcity.bmc.org/population-health/culturally-competent-healthcare-lessons-covid-19; and Basem Attum et al., *Cultural Competence in the Care of Muslim Patients and Their Families* (Treasure Island, FL: StatPearls Publishing, 2018).

ety, frustration, and feelings of depression with how to think about this COVID-19 situation.[40] What has been shared at Friday prayers, done virtually to calm the community-at-large, does not get to these issues. It is the medical community which is making life and death decisions constantly and they need to share.[41] How do Muslims feel about themselves in the non-Muslim setting of the hospital, in an ICU, unclothed without spiritual guidance?

5 The Realities of Needed Care

The brutal face of the poverty, anxiety, and demands for care of patients left many in our conversations feeling inadequate regarding what their response could be.[42] One physician assistant said: "I began buying ten of everything I thought some of the patients might need when I could find it. Then everything shut down and I had no way to get it to them."[43] Almost all Muslim healthcare professionals in our conversations found themselves burning out and spiritually challenged, while feeling that there was more they could do. Many of them worked 12–14-hour days barely able to stand, taking over medical practices for colleagues who had fallen to COVID-19 and exhausting themselves while worrying about everyone else. Other colleagues' fears, anxieties, and exhaustion have caused a significant rise in sick leave, personal days, and vacation days unintentionally leaving significant burdens on those left behind to provide care. Patients have begun to experience shortages in staff as the burnouts and exposures are rising significantly. Nurses who flew across the country in some instances and retirees who came back to work in hot spots of the virus are finding the circumstances difficult as they leave their loved ones in places which are now experiencing surges in the virus.

---

40 Robin Zlotnick, "Doctor Tries to Explain What It's like Treating a Patient Who Doesn't Believe Covid-19 is Real," *Distractify*, May 27, 2020, https://www.distractify.com/p/doctor-patient-doesnt-believe-covid-real; and "Managing Mental Health during COVID-19," American Medical Association, March 29, 2021, https://www.ama-assn.org/delivering-care/public-health/managing-mental-health-during-covid-19.

41 Jason Phua et al., "Intensive Care Management of Coronavirus Disease 2019 (Covid-19): Challenges and Recommendations," *The Lancet* 8, no. 5 (May 2020): 506–517, https://doi.org/10.1016/s2213-2600(20)30161-2.

42 Heather A. Howard-Bobiwash, Jennie R. Joe, and Susan Lobo, "Concrete Lessons: Policies and Practices Affecting the Impact of COVID-19 for Urban Indigenous Communities in the United States and Canada," *Frontiers in Sociology* 6 (April 23, 2021), https://doi.org/10.3389/fsoc.2021.612029.

43 Anonymous Physician Assistant in Midwest, Interviewed April 26, 2020.

6 Muslim(-Owned or -Operated) Clinics

In 2010, the Islamic Medical Association of North America, reported,

> Muslim owned/operated clinics have been in existence for at least since the last decade of the 20th century in a variety of ways. They are pain centers dispensing narcotics, dental clinics, small healthcare offices who accept Medicare and Medicaid. A few accepted the uninsured with protracted (sliding scale for ability to pay).[44]

By 2018, the American Muslim Health Professionals group published a survey on muslim community-based health organizations.[45] This document thoroughly examined sixty-nine Muslim healthcare clinics. Most usefully, they defined a Muslim clinic:

> if its public presentation (online, in name, mission statement, media) included indications of being founded by, staff(ed) by, or inspired by Muslim individuals, Islam or a Muslim organization (e.g., mosque, Islamic Center, the Islamic Circle of North America, the Islamic Society of North America).[46]

According to this study, "the majority are small volunteer clinics open for a few hours on weekends." Despite what seems like small operations, these clinics served "from 50 to 10,080 patients per year." This bespeaks an incredible dedication to serving the uninsured, under-insured, low-income, and immigrant populations when and often where possible in American society. Almost all clinics provided "primary care, chronic disease management, preventive care and healthcare education." These services put these clinics at the center of pandemic care, of the diagnosis of COVID-19 and referrals to emergency rooms. It also put them at the center of primary mental and behavioral healthcare along with financial risks.[47] Primary care workers were inundated with patients

44 Shaukat Aziz Ashai, "Muslim Community Center Medical Clinic a Safety Net Clinic in Maryland," *Journal of the Islamic Medical Association of North America* 42, no. 3 (October 19, 2010): 117–123, https://doi.org/10.5915/42-3-5374.

45 Nabil Khan and Lance Laird, "Muslim Community Based Health Organizations in the United States," *American Muslim Health Professionals*, 2018, https://doi.org/10.1332/204080521X16573417795625

46 Survey Report p. 8.

47 Taylor Strickland, "MGMA Report Reveals Extent of COVID-19 Impacts to Financial Health of Physician and Hospital-Owned Medical Practices," *TMCnet*, July 28, 2021, https://www.tmcnet.com/usubmit/2021/07/28/9419158.htm.

seeking care for chronic conditions because these conditions were widely publicized as underlying conditions that would make them at higher risk of COVID-19 infection and death. Because of the higher number of patients who required evaluation for COVID-19, the quality of care for patients with chronic illnesses lapsed.

> Swollen joints, fevers, and abdominal pain have to be evaluated without a physical exam; some of my diabetic patients have started rationing their insulin; home-care arrangements for my elderly patients are splintering because necessary forms have gone missing.[48]

The plight of patients of all religious communities and, thus, their families has caused an exponential increase in the severity of some chronic conditions.[49] As healthcare practitioners, the ability to handle the sheer number of prescriptions to assist patients with three-month supplies of medicines dwindled. Patients and their doctors again panicked. Patients who got medicines through the US Postal Service noted that the mail slowed to a crawl or stopped abruptly in some neighborhoods. Postal workers became symptomatic and were sent home or to the hospital. There are even a few almost tragedies as patients self-rationed drugs for type 2 diabetes, and congestive heart failure.

Furthermore, media repeatedly asserted that the elderly were the most susceptible and needed close monitoring—though from afar. Many of the elderly in minority communities either lived with children, by themselves, or in nursing homes. For those living with children, the threat of contracting COVID-19 was perceived as high and indeed some cases of entire families with the virus emerged. Elderly living alone found themselves cut off from physical contact as homecare workers could not visit and family visits were discouraged. This was extremely harrowing for their mental and emotional well-being. The fairly recent increase in mobile units for treating patients confined to home care for a variety of reasons, ceased. Nursing homes and shelters around the country were in many cases toxic centers as medical staff had little PPE.[50]

---

48 Strickland, "MGMA Report Reveals Extent of COVID-19 Impacts to Financial Health of Physician and Hospital-Owned Medical Practices"; and Ofri, "A Bellevue Doctor's Pandemic Diary."

49 Susan Kansagra, Keith C. Ferdinand, and Jack Pitsor, "Chronic Disease Management During COVID-19," *National Conference of State Legislators*, October 7, 2020, https://www.ncsl.org/documents/health/Chronic-Disease-Management-During-COVID-19-webinar.pdf.

50 Madeline Holcombe, "Tip Leads Police to 17 Bodies at a New Jersey Nursing Home," *CNN: Cable News Network*, April 16, 2020, https://www.cnn.com/2020/04/16/us/bodies-found-new-jersey-nursing-home/index.html.

Clinics, irrespective of whether weekend, full-time or connected to hospitals, had to get PPE for staff, expand their sanitizing procedures, restructure their waiting rooms, and reduce scheduling and set-up for virtual visits. For some clinics, the hours were expanded and/or changed to accommodate the surge in patients. The stress, as mentioned previously, was daunting.

As the shelves in grocery stores and pharmacies emptied, many healthcare professionals found themselves overly anxious, as they had to care for nuclear and extended family members. Almost all of the physicians we spoke with experienced heightened anxiety around their own family members who expected that they direct their care. When family members lived overseas, anxiety increased exponentially. The simple act of getting information on the conditions of family members was and continues to be difficult. Some physicians lost a number of family members who were living together as was the tradition in large Muslim families overseas and also in the United States and Canada.

Moreover, healthcare workers had to apply extra personal methods to be sure not to carry any contaminants home. In most cities, the extended work hours and the shortages of intubation equipment and PPE, drove medical staff burn-out. In some cities, hospitals and workers even rented out rooms in hotels so they could be close to hospitals. This added anxiety and probably depression as they could not see loved ones and elderly family members except by video platforms such as FaceTime or Zoom. This fear was even evident for clinic workers. One nurse spoke of the fact that she had not seen her son or parents for months and had become "fidgety." The constant worry about the potential for family members to contract COVID-19 accelerated fears and sometimes led to depression.

Across the nation, people began to put up signs of all sorts letting medical staff know how much their efforts were appreciated and respected in these turbulent times. Nevertheless, the psychological weight of so many deaths, refrigerated trucks on sites, families in mourning over deaths they could not witness, the absence of funerals, and the fact that physicians and nurses were contracting COVID-19 was heavy. Healthcare workers quarantined themselves at home between shifts and thus, brought the anxiety and sometimes COVID-19 home. While we cannot measure all of the psychological toll, our interviews seemed to provide a cathartic space that was much needed.

Some emergency room physicians and other ICU medical staff found themselves in television news stories sharing their fears and anxieties with millions of strangers as they found themselves nearing breaking points and extremely vulnerable. Many immigrants and second-generation immigrants were too terrified of deportation to go to the hospital.[51] In a *New York Times* article, a Muslim woman found her care at an urgent care center troubling.[52]

Religion and its ministrations, usually sitting in the middle of life and death conversations, was given reports on some of the major broadcasting stations and by organizations such as the Gallup Poll.[53] Islam and its believers' responses to COVID-19 seemed to appear in articles about healthcare workers and Ramadan. Many articles focused on the challenges of other faiths in live-streaming services such as Easter for Christians and Passover for Jews.[54] Still other articles speculated as to whether or not the pandemic caused those who were not religious to turn to religion. Articles on Islam featured Pakistan and the other majority Muslim states.[55]

We thought about the fact the physicians, physician assistants, nurse practitioners, and nurses are caregivers who are "never supposed to get sick" or "never have mental health issues." The fact that they are groomed to be unassailable and not vulnerable made them reticent when it came to "opening up" about their own mental and physical health at any time because it would be seen is an expression of vulnerability (consider weakness of faith to avid redundancy). Here comes a pandemic and they knew more than the average person but the information to all was fractured, some untrue and other information was misleading. Medical journal articles were often unclear, sometimes foreboding, and other times just renditions of what was unknown mostly functioning without thoroughly reviewed research.

As the pandemic has continued, healthcare professionals have faced additional personal challenges. One group of physicians in Texas is asking for a Marshall Plan for physicians.[56] To remind readers, the Marshall Plan was an

51 "Fear Keeps Us Undocumented from Hospitals Despite Coronavirus," *The Straits Times*, May 7, 2020. https://www.straitstimes.com/world/united-states/fear-keeps-us-undocumented-from-hospitals-despite-coronavirus.

52 Roni Caryn Rabin, "Respecting Muslim Patients' Needs." *The New York Times*, November 1, 2010, https://www.nytimes.com/2010/11/01/health/01patients.html.

53 Frank Newport, "Religion and the COVID-19 Virus in the U.S," *Gallup*, April 6, 2020, https://news.gallup.com/opinion/polling-matters/307619/religion-covid-virus.aspx.

54 Jenesse Miller, "How Are Religious Groups Responding to the Coronavirus Pandemic?" *USC News*, April 9, 2020, https://news.usc.edu/168381/religious-groups-coronavirus-pandemic-religion-passover-easter/; and Jenesse Miller, "How are Religious Groups Responding to the Coronavirus Pandemic?" *USC Annenberg School for Communication and Journalism*, April 10, 2020, https://annenberg.usc.edu/news/research-and-impact/how-are-religious-groups-responding-coronavirus-pandemic.

55 Hanna, "What Islamists are Doing and Saying on Covid-19 Crisis."

56 Will Maddox, "The 'Marshall Plan' to Save Primary Care," D Magazine, April 28, 2020, https://www.dmagazine.com/healthcare-business/2020/04/the-marshall-plan-to-save-pr

American initiative present in 1948 for foreign aid to Western Europe. The United States transferred $12 billion in economic recovery after World War Two.[57] Physicians pointed out that telehealth visits did not generate enough revenue to cover operating expenses especially with a lower patient contact ratio. This resulted in a decrease in the paycheck of workers and for some put their own families in economic jeopardy. The media did not count clinics as small businesses, but clinics are small businesses, and many were and continue to be devastated by the pandemic. The traditional fee-for-service payment model "where physicians are paid based on the number of services provided, or the number of procedures ordered" is not functioning during this pandemic.[58] Some healthcare workers found themselves increasingly unable to provide for their families' heightened needs such as at home learning for children without childcare and the general standards of living had to be adjusted just like their patients.

As some clinics moved to telehealth, all sorts of issues arose as mentioned previously and some now unnecessary staff found themselves furloughed. Direct care professionals found themselves overwhelmed with calls which extended well into the night and over weekends. Many of these calls entailed longer contact as patients were charged to explain more about their condition in the absence of the face-to-face encounter and healthcare professionals inquired more. Physician angst was heightened by the need to maintain employment since student loans were not alleviated or delayed.

> I was scared beyond reason, but I have to work as I am the main support of my family, and my school loan payments are very large. I never thought I would be in this position. I definitely have PSTD. I was not sleeping and totally exhausted. Now I am just a barely functioning zombie.[59]

---

imary-care/; and Edgar Walters, "Texas Doctors are Losing Money During the Pandemic. They Want Lawmakers to Make Insurers Pay Up," *KERA News*, September 10, 2020, https://www.keranews.org/health-science-tech/2020-09-10/texas-physicians-are-losing-money-during-the-pandemic-they-want-lawmakers-to-make-health-insurers-pay-up.

57 Alexandra Hart and Shelly Brisbin, "Texas Physicians Say a 'Marshall Plan' is Needed to Protect Primary Care Practices," *Texas Standard*, September 14, 2020, https://www.texasstandard.org/stories/texas-physicians-say-a-marshall-plan-is-needed-to-protect-primary-care-practices/.

58 Jonathan Nelson, "The Primary Care Marshall Plan—TAFP," *TAFP: Texas Academy of Family Physicians*, September 16, 2020, https://tafp.org/Media/Default/Downloads/advocacy/primary_care_marshall_plan.pdf.

59 Interview with physician in free-standing clinic in May, 2020.

Clinics did get the stimulus financial relief and monies to get PPE and some other equipment plus monies to keep staff salaries. This was enormously helpful and did work to alleviate some of the stress, but the application process was daunting. Small weekend clinics, which relied on donations from religious communities, found themselves at the back of the line in that process and at banks. On the other hand, with reduced payments from insurance companies, many incomes suffered more than a 50 percent decrease and, thus, the call for a Marshall Plan.

7 Mental and Skill Preparedness

Some physicians we interviewed revealed that while in residency they had contracted H1N1 and MERS. Others had been on medical teams working with the spread of these viruses in the United States. The possibilities of pandemic were known but the specifics and actuality of a virus like COVID-19 were not. COVID-19 and its devastating effects on the entire body is novel. As mentioned previously, there was no central government coordination, and leadership from the CDC was hampered by the Office of the President. Healthcare workers found themselves engaged in marathon reading to keep up with the latest information. The differential diagnostics necessary in a pandemic called for heightened skill and attention to details of symptoms.

Muslims working in clinics attached to hospitals or emergency rooms were overwhelmed by the sheer numbers of patients and some felt that they were underprepared. "I was so tired I think I forgot the basics."[60] The shortcomings of modern medical education were and are on display as well as the efforts to quickly apply a fix. Specialty medical practice and the dreams of extremely high incomes or for female Muslim practitioners, the opportunity for work largely with women and children had steered many away from primary care, surgery, and the emergency room. The pandemic forced respiratory specialists, X-ray technicians, ICU, and other nurses along with hospital pharmacists into new roles and put their skills to the test. For some physicians who were commandeered from specialties like psychiatry to the emergency room, panic set in.

> We received an email that some of us were being shifted to the emergency room. I searched for my *Harrisons Principle of Medicine* and remembered that I had not even opened or dusted off this book in years. I was terri-

60 Pediatrician moved to ER in Detroit on moment's notice in an interview in April, 2020.

> fied, couldn't sleep, and prayed that Allah would have mercy on me and patients for any mistakes I made.[61]
>
> My mom had a catastrophic car accident at the beginning of the pandemic in South Korea. Here I am in the Midwest of the United States and because of the pandemic, she can't talk, and the physicians are all busy. I have to go to work double shifts because two members of my team have gone on mental health days. My oncology patients are high needs, and they think they are going to be disposed of in order to get their beds. I am exhausted and literally on-call 24-hours, seven days a week. My family has not seen me in several weeks. Just Zoom.[62]

Nurses proved to be the most resilient regarding stamina and keeping order. Most of them never lost their basic skills and older nurses proved to be a mercy to all teams. Older ICU nurses knew procedures by rote memory and adapted to the intensity of care with exhaustion but with competence. Despite this, many nurses oftentimes watched their skills not result in patient improvement and resolution.[63] Nurses traveled to volunteer help and many also volunteered for extra shifts. Holding the hands of patients dying by the dozens, watching them lying in hallways, listening to decisions on who would get extraordinary care and who would be just allowed to die was psychologically excruciating.

Nurses continue to speak out about their exhaustion and the attitudes of family.[64] Articles shock with information about patients in the hospital with COVID-19, protesting that they could not possibly have COVID-19.[65] They argue about their care up to the time of their intubation. Some citizens are not get-

61 Interview on April 25, 2020 with psychiatric fourth-year resident in Midwestern hospital.

62 Interview on April 28, 2020 with oncology physician in Midwestern hospital.

63 Lisette Hilton, "Critical Care Nurse Shows Unbreakable Commitment During Pandemic," *Nurse.com*, October 25, 2020, https://www.nurse.com/blog/2020/10/21/critical-care-nurse-shows-unbreakable-commitment-during-pandemic/.

64 Kim Chaudoin, "Pandemic Leads to Compassion Fatigue, Burnout for Health Care Workers," Lipscomb University, July 27, 2020, https://www.lipscomb.edu/news/pandemic-leads-compassion-fatigue-burnout-health-care-workers; and Brett Sholtis, "Facing Burnout, Worker Shortages, Nurses Say Covid-19 Shows Need for Staffing Ratios," *Transforming Health*, June 17, 2021, https://transforminghealth.org/2021/05/03/facing-burnout-worker-shortages-nurses-say-covid-19-shows-need-for-staffing-ratios/.

65 Esther Wang, "Patients are Denying the Existence of Covid-19 While Dying of Covid-19," *Jezebel*, November 16, 2020, https://jezebel.com/patients-are-denying-the-existence-of-covid-19-while-dy-1845690073; and Joel Shannon, "'It's Not Real': In South Dakota, Which Has Shunned Masks and Other Covid Rules, Some People Die in Denial, Nurse Says," *USA Today*, November 18, 2020, https://www.usatoday.com/story/news/health/2020/11/17/south-dakota-nurse-jodi-doering-covid-19-patients-denial/6330791002/.

ting tested and remain at home with COVID-19, infecting other family members until forced to go to the hospital where their encounter with intense treatment is guaranteed.

8 Where Are We Now?

Now, many people in the United States are removing their masks yet almost as many are keeping masks on. Vaccinations continue covering younger and younger children. The numbers of "long-haulers" continues to grow and mental health concerns are paramount. Hospital, pharmacy, and food deserts continue in poor neighborhoods across the country and the stimulus checks have been spent. The exorbitant costs of healthcare have rendered some citizens' indigent and homeless who were middle class prior to COVID-19. Global travel is picking up speed and those traveling to hot spots for the virus will certainly bring it back to some people. Medical personnel have tremendously increased their skill level and even if COVID-19 returns, or some variant of it, the sheer panic and chaos probably will not return as people have experienced getting outside again and likely will resist any quarantine. The fallout for a year plus under varying stages of quarantine has played havoc with the economy, people's livelihood, health, and mental health.

Bibliography

Alsoofy, Petra, and Katherine Coplen. "Community in the Time of Corona: Documenting the American Muslim Response to the COVID-19 Crisis." *Institute for Social Policy and Understanding*, February 18, 2021. https://www.ispu.org/community-in-the-time-of-corona-documenting-the-american-muslim-response-to-the-covid19-crisis/.

American Medical Association. "Managing Mental Health during COVID-19." March 29, 2021. https://www.ama-assn.org/delivering-care/public-health/managing-mental-health-during-covid-19.

Ashai, Shaukat Aziz. "Muslim Community Center Medical Clinic A Safety Net Clinic in Maryland." *Journal of the Islamic Medical Association of North America* 42, no. 3 (October 19, 2010): 117–123. https://doi.org/10.5915/42-3-5374.

Association of American Medical College. "New AAMC Report Confirms Growing Physician Shortage." *AAMC*, June 26, 2020. https://www.aamc.org/news-insights/press-releases/new-aamc-report-confirms-growing-physician-shortage.

Attum, Basem, Sumaiya Hafiz, Ahmad Malik, and Zafar Shamoon. *Cultural Competence in the Care of Muslim Patients and Their Families.* Treasure Island, FL: StatPearls Publishing, 2018.

Bailey, Meryl. "Culturally Competent Healthcare: Lessons from Covid-19." *HealthCity*, May 12, 2020. https://healthcity.bmc.org/population-health/culturally-competent-healthcare-lessons-covid-19.

Carfì, Angelo, Roberto Bernabei, Francesco Landi, and Gemelli Against COVID-19 Post-Acute Care Study Group. "Persistent Symptoms in Patients After Acute COVID-19." *JAMA* 324, no. 6 (2020): 603–605. https://doi.org/10.1001/jama.2020.12603.

Chaudoin, Kim. "Pandemic Leads to Compassion Fatigue, Burnout for Health Care Workers." *Lipscomb University*, July 27, 2020. https://www.lipscomb.edu/news/pandemic-leads-compassion-fatigue-burnout-health-care-workers.

Chen, Pauline W. "No Room at the Inn." *The New York Times*, March 12, 2020. https://www.nytimes.com/2020/03/12/well/live/coronavirus-emergency-rooms-hospital-crowding.html.

"Coronavirus—Implications for Ships and Crew." *Gard*, March 24, 2020. https://www.gard.no/web/updates/content/29112071/coronavirus-implications-for-ships-and-crew.

Cortes, Jan. "What COVID-19 Taught Us: All the Healthy Habits We Should Keep Even in a Post-Pandemic World." *International Business Times*, January 11, 2021. https://www.ibtimes.com/what-covid-19-taught-us-all-healthy-habits-we-should-keep-even-post-pandemic-world-3118898.

Czeisler, Mark É., Kristy Marynak, Kristie E.N. Clarke, Zainab Salah, Iju Shakya, JoAnn M. Thierry, Nida Ali, et al. "Delay or Avoidance of Medical Care Because of COVID-19-Related Concerns—United States, June 2020." Centers for Disease Control and Prevention, September 11, 2020. https://www.cdc.gov/mmwr/volumes/69/wr/mm6936a4.htm.

Drupal, Jordan. "Blog: The Health Care Supply Chain before and in the Midst of COVID-19." *American Hospital Association News*, September 9, 2020. https://www.aha.org/news/blog/2020-09-09-blog-health-care-supply-chain-and-midst-covid-19.

"Fear Keeps Us Undocumented from Hospitals despite Coronavirus." *The Straits Times*, May 7, 2020. https://www.straitstimes.com/world/united-states/fear-keeps-us-undocumented-from-hospitals-despite-coronavirus.

Goldberg, Emma. "Life Lessons: What a Doctor Learned from Death and Dying in Covid Wards." *The Guardian*, July 22, 2021. https://www.theguardian.com/lifeandstyle/2021/jul/22/covid-doctor-confronts-death-dying.

Grimm, Christi A. "Hospitals Reported That the COVID-19 Pandemic has Significantly Strained Health Care Delivery." U.S. Department of Health and Human Services Office of Inspector General, March 2021. https://oig.hhs.gov/oei/reports/OEI-09-21-00140.pdf.

Hanna, Andrew. "What Islamists Are Doing and Saying on Covid-19 Crisis." *Wilson Cen-*

ter, May 14, 2020. https://www.wilsoncenter.org/article/what-islamists-are-doing-and-saying-covid-19-crisis.

Hart, Alexandra, and Shelly Brisbin. "Texas Physicians Say a 'Marshall Plan' is Needed to Protect Primary Care Practices." *Texas Standard*, September 14, 2020. https://www.texasstandard.org/stories/texas-physicians-say-a-marshall-plan-is-needed-to-protect-primary-care-practices/.

Heath, Keri. "For Health-Care Workers, a Year of Adapt and Overcome." *The Daily News*, October 16, 2020. https://www.galvnews.com/news/specialreports/free/article_2d074c56-181e-5971-a81d-a6b69016f8c9.html.

Heim, Madeline. "'It's Just Going to Be like This Now': These Wisconsinites Survived Covid-19, but 'Recovery' Hasn't Meant a Return to Normal." *The Post-Crescent*, August 4, 2020. https://www.postcrescent.com/in-depth/news/2020/08/03/wisconsin-coronavirus-some-covid-19-recovery-stories-long-hauls/5522928002/.

Hilton, Lisette. "Critical Care Nurse Shows Unbreakable Commitment during Pandemic." *Nurse.com*, October 25, 2020. https://www.nurse.com/blog/2020/10/21/critical-care-nurse-shows-unbreakable-commitment-during-pandemic/.

Holcombe, Madeline. "Tip Leads Police to 17 Bodies at a New Jersey Nursing Home." *CNN: Cable News Network*, April 16, 2020. https://www.cnn.com/2020/04/16/us/bodies-found-new-jersey-nursing-home/index.html.

Howard-Bobiwash, Heather A., Jennie R. Joe, and Susan Lobo. "Concrete Lessons: Policies and Practices Affecting the Impact of COVID-19 for Urban Indigenous Communities in the United States and Canada." *Frontiers in Sociology* 6 (April 23, 2021). https://doi.org/10.3389/fsoc.2021.612029.

Hutchinson, Bill. "Black Doctor Dies of COVID after Alleging Hospital Mistreatment: 'This Is How Black People Get Killed'." *ABC News*, December 24, 2020. https://abcnews.go.com/US/black-doctor-dies-covid-alleging-hospital-mistreatment-black/story?id=74878119.

Iserson, Kenneth V. "Principles of Biomedical Ethics." *Emergency Medicine Clinics of North America* 17, no. 2 (May 1999): 283–306. https://doi.org/10.1016/s0733-8627(05)70060-2.

Judkins, Simon. "Ed Overcrowding, under-Resourcing 'Worst in 30 Years.'" *InSight+*, April 26, 2021. https://insightplus.mja.com.au/2021/14/ed-overcrowding-under-resourcing-worst-in-30-years/.

Kansagra, Susan, Keith C. Ferdinand, and Jack Pitsor. "Chronic Disease Management during COVID-19." *National Conference of State Legislators*, October 7, 2020. https://www.ncsl.org/documents/health/Chronic-Disease-Management-During-COVID-19-webinar.pdf.

Knispel, Sandra. "Medical Students Graduate Early to Join Pandemic Fight." *University of Rochester*, April 9, 2020. https://www.rochester.edu/newscenter/medical-students-graduate-early-to-join-pandemic-fight-423812/.

Komaroff, Anthony L. "The Tragedy of the Long COVID." *Harvard Health*, March 1, 2021. https://www.health.harvard.edu/blog/the-tragedy-of-the-post-covid-long-haulers-2020101521173.

Lapierre, Stephany. "The PPE Supply Chain Problem and 5 Ways to Solve It." *Industry Today*, April 27, 2020. https://industrytoday.com/the-ppe-supply-chain-problem-and-5-ways-to-solve-it/.

Lomiguen, Christine M, Ivelys Rosete, and Justin Chin. "Providing Culturally Competent Care for Covid-19 Intensive Care Unit Delirium: A Case Report and Review." *Cureus* 12, no. 10 (October 9, 2020): e10867. https://doi.org/10.7759/cureus.10867.

Maddox, Will. "The 'Marshall Plan' to Save Primary Care." *D Magazine*, April 28, 2020. https://www.dmagazine.com/healthcare-business/2020/04/the-marshall-plan-to-save-primary-care/.

Miller, Jenesse. "How Are Religious Groups Responding to the Coronavirus Pandemic?" *USC Annenberg School for Communication and Journalism*, April 10, 2020. https://annenberg.usc.edu/news/research-and-impact/how-are-religious-groups-responding-coronavirus-pandemic.

Miller, Jenesse. "How Are Religious Groups Responding to the Coronavirus Pandemic?" *USC News*, April 9, 2020. https://news.usc.edu/168381/religious-groups-coronavirus-pandemic-religion-passover-easter/.

Munro, Ian. "State Performing Reviews of Essential Supply Lines." *Daily News-Record*, July 6, 2021. https://www.dnronline.com/dnronline/state-performing-reviews-of-essential-supply-lines/article_3ee5615b-96ad-5991-9d65-95089f61d3d1.html.

Murphy, Brendan. "Covid-19 Capsizes the Physician Job Market: Trends You Should Know." *American Medical Association*, December 4, 2020. https://www.ama-assn.org/residents-students/transition-practice/covid-19-capsizes-physician-job-market-trends-you-should.

Nelson, Jonathan. "The Primary Care Marshall Plan—TAFP." *TAFP: Texas Academy of Family Physicians*, September 16, 2020. https://tafp.org/Media/Default/Downloads/advocacy/primary_care_marshall_plan.pdf.

Nevada Governor's Office and Nevada Department of Health and Human Services. "Crisis Standards of Care—Coronavirus (COVID-19) in Nevada." *Nevada Health Response*, July 15, 2020. https://nvhealthresponse.nv.gov/wp-content/uploads/2020/07/NV_DHHS_DPBH_CSCRecommendations_COVID-19_071520_ADA.pdf.

Newport, Frank. "Religion and the COVID-19 Virus in the U.S." *Gallup*, April 6, 2020. https://news.gallup.com/opinion/polling-matters/307619/religion-covid-virus.aspx.

Ofri, Danielle. "A Bellevue Doctor's Pandemic Diary." *The New Yorker*, October 1, 2020. https://www.newyorker.com/science/medical-dispatch/a-bellevue-doctors-coronavirus-pandemic-diary.

Ortaliza, Jared, Kendal Orgera, Cynthia Cox Twitter, and Krutika Amin. "Covid-19 Continues to Be a Leading Cause of Death in the U.S. in June 2021." *Peterson-KFF Health*

System Tracker, July 1, 2021. https://www.healthsystemtracker.org/brief/covid-19-continues-to-be-a-leading-cause-of-death-in-the-u-s-in-june-2021/.

Ozalp, Mehmet. "How Coronavirus Challenges Muslims' Faith and Changes Their Lives." *The Conversation*, January 14, 2021. https://theconversation.com/how-coronavirus-challenges-muslims-faith-and-changes-their-lives-133925.

Papapanou, Michail, Eleni Routsi, Konstantinos Tsamakis, Lampros Fotis, Georgios Marinos, Irene Lidoriki, Marianna Karamanou, et al. "Medical Education Challenges and Innovations during COVID-19 Pandemic." *Postgraduate Medical Journal* 98, no. 1159 (2021): 321–327. https://doi.org/10.1136/postgradmedj-2021-140032.

Phua, Jason, Li Weng, Lowell Ling, Moritoki Egi, Chae-Man Lim, Jigeeshu Vasishtha Divatia, Babu Raja Shrestha et al. "Intensive Care Management of Coronavirus Disease 2019 (Covid-19): Challenges and Recommendations." *The Lancet Respiratory Medicine* 8, no. 5 (May 2020): 506–517. https://doi.org/10.1016/s2213-2600(20)30161-2.

Quigley, Fran. "Muslim Health Care for All." *Foreign Policy*, June 27, 2019. https://foreignpolicy.com/2019/06/27/muslim-health-care-for-all/.

Rabin, Roni Caryn. "Respecting Muslim Patients' Needs." *The New York Times*, November 1, 2010. https://www.nytimes.com/2010/11/01/health/01patients.html.

Sachedina, Abdulaziz Abdulhussein. *Islamic Biomedical Ethics: Principles and Application*. New York: Oxford University Press, 2012.

Schulte, Darren. "Industry Voices—After COVID-19, There Will Be a Tectonic Shift in How Medicine is Practiced." *Fierce Healthcare*, May 25, 2020. https://www.fiercehealthcare.com/practices/industry-voices-after-covid-19-coming-tectonic-shift-how-medicine-practiced.

Schweigert, Mary Beth. "A Surgeon's Survival Story: Five Phone Calls, a Long Recovery, and Lessons Learned from COVID." *Penn Medicine*, June 23, 2020. https://www.pennmedicine.org/news/news-blog/2020/june/a-surgeons-survival-story.

Seervai, Shanoor. "Why Are More Black Americans Dying of Covid-19?" Commonwealth Fund, June 26, 2020. https://www.commonwealthfund.org/publications/podcast/2020/jun/why-are-more-black-americans-dying-covid-19.

Shannon, Joel. "'It's Not Real': In South Dakota, Which Has Shunned Masks and Other Covid Rules, Some People Die in Denial, Nurse Says." *USA Today*, November 18, 2020. https://www.usatoday.com/story/news/health/2020/11/17/south-dakota-nurse-jodi-doering-covid-19-patients-denial/6330791002/.

Sholtis, Brett. "Facing Burnout, Worker Shortages, Nurses Say Covid-19 Shows Need for Staffing Ratios." *Transforming Health*, June 17, 2021. https://transforminghealth.org/2021/05/03/facing-burnout-worker-shortages-nurses-say-covid-19-shows-need-for-staffing-ratios/.

Strickland, Taylor. "MGMA Report Reveals Extent of COVID-19 Impacts to Financial Health of Physician and Hospital-Owned Medical Practices." *TMCnet*, July 28, 2021. https://www.tmcnet.com/usubmit/2021/07/28/9419158.htm.

Tazamal, Mobashra. "Islamophobia in 2020: Covid-19 and Conspiracy Theories." *Bridge Initiative*, December 22, 2022. https://bridge.georgetown.edu/research/islamophobia-in-2020-covid-19-and-conspiracy-theories/.

Tenforde, Mark W., Sara S. Kim, Christopher J. Lindsell, Erica Billig Rose, Nathan I. Shapiro et al. "Symptom Duration and Risk Factors for Delayed Return to Usual Health Among Outpatients with COVID-19 in a Multistate Health Care Systems Network—United States, March–June 2020." *MMWR: Morbidity and Mortality Weekly Report* 69, no. 30 (2020): 993–998. https://doi.org/10.15585/mmwr.mm6930e1.

"United States Coronavirus." *Worldometer*, November 7, 2020. https://www.worldometers.info/coronavirus/country/us/.

Walters, Edgar. "Texas Doctors Are Losing Money during the Pandemic. They Want Lawmakers to Make Insurers Pay Up." *KERA News*, September 10, 2020. https://www.keranews.org/health-science-tech/2020-09-10/texas-physicians-are-losing-money-during-the-pandemic-they-want-lawmakers-to-make-health-insurers-pay-up.

Wang, Esther. "Patients are Denying the Existence of Covid-19 While Dying of Covid-19." *Jezebel*, November 16, 2020. https://jezebel.com/patients-are-denying-the-existence-of-covid-19-while-dy-1845690073.

Zlotnick, Robin. "Doctor Tries to Explain What It's Like Treating a Patient who Doesn't Believe Covid-19 is Real." *Distractify*, May 27, 2020. https://www.distractify.com/p/doctor-patient-doesnt-believe-covid-real.

CHAPTER 5

Religiosity, Coping, and Mental Health: An Empirical Analysis of Muslims Across the COVID-19 Pandemic

Osman Umarji, Aafreen A. Mahmood, Leena Raza and Rania Awaad

The COVID-19 global pandemic has significantly disrupted life, leading to elevated psychological distress in the general population.[1] During this period of uncertainty, many individuals turned to religion as a means of coping with pandemic-induced stressors.[2] Although participation in religious activities has been identified as a protective factor against poor mental health,[3] social distancing guidelines aimed at reducing the spread of COVID-19 have drastically changed how faith communities are able to perform religious rituals.[4] Therefore, understanding how religiosity, coping mechanisms, and mental health intersect during the COVID-19 pandemic is of particular interest.

The impact of COVID-19 for Muslim communities across the globe has been multifaceted. In adherence to public health guidelines, many mosques suspended daily congregational prayers, *Jumuʿa* (Friday) prayers, along with other services.[5] Communal *ifṭār*s (fast-breaking meals) and *tarāwīḥ* (night vigil)

1 Hannah Rettie and Jo Daniels, "Coping and Tolerance of Uncertainty: Predictors and Mediators of Mental Health during the COVID-19 Pandemic," *American Psychologist* 76, no. 3 (April 2021): 427–437, https://doi.org/10.1037/amp0000710.

2 Simon Dein et al., "COVID-19, Mental Health and Religion: An Agenda for Future Research," *Mental Health, Religion & Culture* 23, no. 1 (January 2, 2020): 1–9, https://doi.org/10.1080/13674676.2020.1768725; and Steven Pirutinsky, Aaron D. Cherniak, and David H. Rosmarin, "COVID-19, Mental Health, and Religious Coping Among American Orthodox Jews," *Journal of Religion and Health* 59, no. 5 (October 2020): 2288–2301, https://doi.org/10.1007/s10943-020-01070-z.

3 Linda M. Chatters et al., "Religious Participation and DSM-IV Disorders Among Older African Americans: Findings From the National Survey of American Life," *The American Journal of Geriatric Psychiatry* 16, no. 12 (December 2008): 957–965, https://doi.org/10.1097/JGP.0b013e3181898081; Hongtu Chen et al., "Religious Participation as a Predictor of Mental Health Status and Treatment Outcomes in Older Persons," *International Journal of Geriatric Psychiatry* 22, no. 2 (February 2007): 144–153, https://doi.org/10.1002/gps.1704.

4 Dein et al., "COVID-19, Mental Health and Religion"; and Sayed A. Quadri, "COVID-19 and Religious Congregations: Implications for Spread of Novel Pathogens," *International Journal of Infectious Diseases* 96 (July 2020): 219–221, https://doi.org/10.1016/j.ijid.2020.05.007.

5 Regarding the suspensions of mosque activities, both the *Fiqh* Council of North America and the Muslim Council of Britain made official announcements on March 16, 2020.

 | DOI:10.1163/9789004679771_007

prayers were also canceled during Ramadan. Furthermore, the Saudi government temporary suspended the ʿ*Umra* pilgrimage and dramatically scaled back *Hajj* pilgrimage attendance from 2.5 million to 1,000 attendees.[6] Within the Islamic tradition, numerous rituals are practiced communally, especially in the mosque, to foster a sense of unity, belonging, and collective responsibility within the community.[7] For diasporic Muslims, mosques play a crucial role in maintaining their affiliation with a religious community. Unlike mosques in Muslim-majority countries that are primarily for worship, mosques for diasporic Muslims serve broader purposes as community centers for legal and financial resources, education, professional networking, and social events.[8] Among American Muslims, a "built-in community," diversity, religious practice, and unity with community members were found to be essential to their identity and sense of belonging.[9] Mosques and congregational activities therefore play an instrumental role in cultivating this community for Muslims to enhance their spiritual and social engagement.

Furthermore, participating in mosque activities can be beneficial for Muslims' mental health and social functioning.[10] Mosque attendance has been

6 Shahul H. Ebrahim and Ziad A. Memish, "Saudi Arabia's Drastic Measures to Curb the COVID-19 Outbreak: Temporary Suspension of the Umrah Pilgrimage," *Journal of Travel Medicine* 27, no. 3 (May 18, 2020): taaa029, https://doi.org/10.1093/jtm/taaa029; and Ziad A. Memish et al., "Pausing Superspreader Events for COVID-19 Mitigation: International Hajj Pilgrimage Cancellation," *Travel Medicine and Infectious Disease* 36 (July 2020): 101817, https://doi.org/10.1016/j.tmaid.2020.101817.

7 Alean Al-Krenawi and John R. Graham, "Islamic Theology and Prayer: Relevance for Social Work Practice," *International Social Work* 43, no. 3 (July 2000): 289–304, https://doi.org/10.1177/002087280004300303.

8 Al-Krenawi and Graham, "Islamic Theology and Prayer: Relevance for Social Work Practice"; and Ann W. Nguyen et al., "Mosque-Based Emotional Support Among Young Muslim Americans," *Review of Religious Research* 55, no. 4 (December 2013): 535–555, https://doi.org/10.1007/s13644-013-0119-0.

9 Sherry C. Wang, Aysha H. Raja, and Sabreen Azhar, "'A Lot of Us Have a Very Difficult Time Reconciling What Being Muslim Is': A Phenomenological Study on the Meaning of Being Muslim American," *Cultural Diversity and Ethnic Minority Psychology* 26, no. 3 (July 2020): 338–346, https://doi.org/10.1037/cdp0000297.

10 Ahmed M. Abdel-Khalek et al., "The Relationship Between Religiosity and Anxiety: A Meta-Analysis," *Journal of Religion and Health* 58, no. 5 (October 2019): 1847–1856, https://doi.org/10.1007/s10943-019-00881-z; Nada Eltaiba and Maria Harries, "Reflections on Recovery in Mental Health: Perspectives From a Muslim Culture," *Social Work in Health Care* 54, no. 8 (September 14, 2015): 725–737, https://doi.org/10.1080/00981389.2015.1046574; and David R. Hodge, Tarek Zidan, and Altaf Husain, "Depression among Muslims in the United States: Examining the Role of Discrimination and Spirituality as Risk and Protective Factors: Table 1," *Social Work* 61, no. 1 (January 2016): 45–52, https://doi.org/10.1093/sw/swv055.

found to relate to greater levels of support given and received from community members,[11] and community support is considered a protective factor against distress during times of adversity.[12] Thus, in the COVID-19 era, the rapid suspension of group prayers and congregational activities may have significantly impacted Muslim well-being, for those who had hitherto found support and belonging through attending mosques and participating in communal religious activities. To address this void in communal activities, particularly during the month of Ramadan, many mosques and religious organizations transitioned to offering sermons, classes, and community support groups online during the pandemic, and little is known about the efficacy of such programming on faith and well-being.[13]

1 Mental Health and Coping Behaviors

The COVID-19 pandemic and its associated health, social, and economic stressors have had detrimental consequences to the general population's mental health and well-being. Adults in the USA reported higher symptoms of depression and anxiety disorders during April–June 2020 relative to the same period in 2019.[14] Various strategies to cope with psychological distress experienced during the pandemic among adult populations are documented in the literature. Negative coping strategies included substance use, denial, self-blame, behavioral disengagement, excessive eating, and news watching. Positive strategies included regular exercise, relaxation, seeking emotional and

11 Nguyen et al., "Mosque-Based Emotional Support Among Young Muslim Americans."

12 Harold G. Koenig, "Maintaining Health and Well-Being by Putting Faith into Action During the COVID-19 Pandemic," *Journal of Religion and Health* 59, no. 5 (October 2020): 2205–2214, https://doi.org/10.1007/s10943-020-01035-2.

13 Dein et al., "COVID-19, Mental Health and Religion"; Arwa Ibrahim, "Praying in Time of COVID-19: How World's Largest Mosques Adapted," *Al Jazeera*, April 6, 2020, https://www.aljazeera.com/news/2020/4/6/praying-in-time-of-covid-19-how-worlds-largest-mosques-adapted; and Nargis Rahman, "Mosques Go Virtual During a COVID-19 Ramadan," Michigan Radio, May 21, 2020, https://www.michiganradio.org/families-community/2020-05-21/mosques-go-virtual-during-a-covid-19-ramadan.

14 Mark É. Czeisler et al., "Mental Health, Substance Use, and Suicidal Ideation During the COVID-19 Pandemic—United States, June 24–30, 2020," *MMWR: Morbidity and Mortality Weekly Report* 69, no. 32 (August 14, 2020): 1049–1057, https://doi.org/10.15585/mmwr.mm6932a1; and Nirmita Panchal et al., "The Implication of COVID-19 for Mental Health and Substance Use," *KFF*, February 10, 2021, https://www.kff.org/coronavirus-covid-19/issue-brief/the-implications-of-covid-19-for-mental-health-and-substance-use/.

social support, humor, and positive reframing and acceptance.[15] Additionally, coping flexibility, which refers to a person's ability to use different coping strategies based on the situation, has been found to be adaptive, and therefore considering the number of coping behaviors used rather than the frequency of using them has been suggested.[16]

During such times of distress and adversity, religion can also serve as a coping mechanism for individuals to find a sense of meaning and purpose, personal control, intimacy with others, and spiritual or emotional comfort.[17] However, mental health outcomes are dependent on how individuals use religion to frame their adversities.[18] Positive religious coping encompasses reframing adversity as an opportunity to form a closer relationship with God, search for greater meaning, and spiritually connect with others.[19] Whereas negative reli-

---

15 Caroline Gurvich et al., "Coping Styles and Mental Health in Response to Societal Changes during the COVID-19 Pandemic," *International Journal of Social Psychiatry* 67, no. 5 (August 2021): 540–549, https://doi.org/10.1177/0020764020961790; Sujita Kumar Kar et al., "Coping with Mental Health Challenges During COVID-19," in *Coronavirus Disease 2019 (COVID-19)* (Singapore: Springer, 2020), 199–213; Kevin Stainback, Brittany N. Hearne, and Monica M. Trieu, "COVID-19 and the 24/7 News Cycle: Does COVID-19 News Exposure Affect Mental Health?" *Socius: Sociological Research for a Dynamic World* 6 (January 2020): 237802312096933, https://doi.org/10.1177/2378023120969339; and Emre Umucu and Beatrice Lee, "Examining the Impact of COVID-19 on Stress and Coping Strategies in Individuals with Disabilities and Chronic Conditions," *Rehabilitation Psychology* 65, no. 3 (August 2020): 193–198, https://doi.org/10.1037/rep0000328.

16 Taylor Heffer and Teena Willoughby, "A Count of Coping Strategies: A Longitudinal Study Investigating an Alternative Method to Understanding Coping and Adjustment," ed. Scott McDonald, *PLOS ONE* 12, no. 10 (October 5, 2017): e0186057, https://doi.org/10.1371/journal.pone.0186057.

17 Richard A. Jenkins and Kenneth I. Pargament, "Religion and Spirituality as Resources for Coping with Cancer," *Journal of Psychosocial Oncology* 13, no. 1–2 (August 15, 1995): 51–74, https://doi.org/10.1300/J077V13N01_04; Chaeyoon Lim and Robert D. Putnam, "Religion, Social Networks, and Life Satisfaction," *American Sociological Review* 75, no. 6 (December 2010): 914–933, https://doi.org/10.1177/0003122410386686; and Kenneth I. Pargament et al., "Patterns of Positive and Negative Religious Coping with Major Life Stressors," *Journal for the Scientific Study of Religion* 37, no. 4 (December 1998): 710, https://doi.org/10.2307/1388152.

18 Pirutinsky, Cherniak, and Rosmarin, "COVID-19, Mental Health, and Religious Coping Among American Orthodox Jews."

19 Hisham Abu Raiya and Kenneth I. Pargament, "Religiously Integrated Psychotherapy with Muslim Clients: From Research to Practice," *Professional Psychology: Research and Practice* 41, no. 2 (2010): 181–188, https://doi.org/10.1037/a0017988; and Justin Thomas and Mariapaola Barbato, "Positive Religious Coping and Mental Health Among Christians and Muslims in Response to the COVID-19 Pandemic," *Religions* 11, no. 10 (September 29, 2020): 498, https://doi.org/10.3390/rel11100498.

gious coping can involve feeling punished or abandoned by God, harboring anger toward a higher power, or foregoing personal accountability in an effort leave all matters up to God.[20]

Among diasporic Muslim populations, positive religious coping has a strong protective effect on mental health outcomes. Religiosity and maintaining a community religious affiliation has been associated with decreased odds of depression and anxiety, improved family functioning, and increased post-traumatic growth among American Muslims.[21]

However, knowledge gaps on religious coping and mental health in Muslim diasporas still remain. The few existing studies have found positive religious coping to be associated with better life satisfaction, but its relationship with symptoms of depression and anxiety remains unclear.[22] With regards to the pandemic, research on Muslims' religious coping and mental health is mainly limited to studies based in Muslim-majority countries. One study in particular found positive religious coping to be associated with lower rates of depression but not anxiety among Muslims in the United Arab Emirates.[23] Indefinite conclusions regarding religious coping and how it impacts mental health during stressful periods such as the COVID-19 pandemic underscore the complex relationship between religion and mental health.

20 Bryan Goodman, "Faith in a Time of Crisis," *American Psychological Association*, May 11, 2020, https://www.apa.org/topics/covid-19/faith-crisis; and Thomas and Barbato, "Positive Religious Coping and Mental Health Among Christians and Muslims in Response to the COVID-19 Pandemic."

21 Abdel-Khalek et al., "The Relationship Between Religiosity and Anxiety"; Hisham Abu-Raiya, Kenneth I. Pargament, and Annette Mahoney, "Examining Coping Methods with Stressful Interpersonal Events Experienced by Muslims Living in the United States Following the 9/11 Attacks," *Psychology of Religion and Spirituality* 3, no. 1 (2011): 1–14, https://doi.org/10.1037/a0020034; and Mona M. Amer and Joseph D. Hovey, "Socio-Demographic Differences in Acculturation and Mental Health for a Sample of 2nd Generation/Early Immigrant Arab Americans," *Journal of Immigrant and Minority Health* 9, no. 4 (August 7, 2007): 335–347, https://doi.org/10.1007/s10903-007-9045-y.

22 Abu-Raiya, Pargament, and Mahoney, "Examining Coping Methods with Stressful Interpersonal Events Experienced by Muslims Living in the United States Following the 9/11 Attacks"; and Zeenah Adam and Colleen Ward, "Stress, Religious Coping and Wellbeing in Acculturating Muslims," *Journal of Muslim Mental Health* 10, no. 2 (December 2016), https://doi.org/10.3998/jmmh.10381607.0010.201.

23 Thomas and Barbato, "Positive Religious Coping and Mental Health Among Christians and Muslims in Response to the COVID-19 Pandemic."

2 The Role of Theological Beliefs and Attitudes Toward Uncertainty

As the COVID-19 pandemic is a time of increased uncertainty, attitudes related to uncertainty can impact individuals' coping behaviors and overall mental health.[24] Islam provides substantial guidance on the nature of plagues and pandemics, which may be tests or punishments from Allah, and the uncertainty that they cause.[25] Theologically, certainty only lies with Allah and uncertainty should be expected, tolerated, and be a means for seeking support from Allah.[26] However, individuals who are intolerant of uncertainty may consider it unacceptable that a negative event may occur, however small the probability of its occurrence.[27] Uncertainty intolerance thus functions as a cognitive bias influencing how a person perceives, interprets, and responds to uncertain situations. Uncertainty intolerance has been associated with maladaptive coping and psychological distress prior to and during the pandemic.[28] Diasporic Muslims' attitudes toward uncertainty and how these attitudes inform coping and

24 Brooke M. Smith, Alexander J. Twohy, and Gregory S. Smith, "Psychological Inflexibility and Intolerance of Uncertainty Moderate the Relationship between Social Isolation and Mental Health Outcomes during COVID-19," *Journal of Contextual Behavioral Science* 18 (October 2020): 162–174, https://doi.org/10.1016/j.jcbs.2020.09.005.

25 Rania Awaad, Danah Elsayed, and Hosam Helal, "Holistic Healing: Islam's Legacy of Mental Health," Yaqeen Institute for Islamic Research, May 27, 2021, https://yaqeeninstitute.org/read/paper/holistic-healing-islams-legacy-of-mental-health; and Osman Umarji, Hassan Elwan, and Mustafa Umar, "A Punishment or a Mercy? What We Can Learn from COVID-19," Yaqeen Institute for Islamic Research, April 14, 2020, https://yaqeeninstitute.org/osman-umarji/a-punishment-or-a-mercy-what-we-can-learn-from-the-coronavirus/.

26 Osman Umarji and Hassan Elwan, "Embracing Uncertainty: How to Feel Emotionally Stable in a Pandemic," Yaqeen Institute for Islamic Research, March 30, 2020, https://yaqeeninstitute.org/read/paper/embracing-uncertainty-how-to-feel-emotionally-stable-in-a-pandemic.

27 K. Buhr and M.J. Dugas, "The Intolerance of Uncertainty Scale: Psychometric Properties of the English Version," *Behaviour Research and Therapy* 40, no. 8 (August 2002): 931–945, https://doi.org/10.1016/S0005-7967(01)00092-4.

28 Gaëtan Mertens et al., "Fear of the Coronavirus (COVID-19): Predictors in an Online Study Conducted in March 2020," *Journal of Anxiety Disorders* 74 (August 2020): 102258, https://doi.org/10.1016/j.janxdis.2020.102258; Rettie and Daniels, "Coping and Tolerance of Uncertainty"; Begum Satici et al., "Intolerance of Uncertainty and Mental Wellbeing: Serial Mediation by Rumination and Fear of COVID-19," *International Journal of Mental Health and Addiction*, May 15, 2020, https://doi.org/10.1007/s11469-020-00305-0; and Smith, Twohy, and Smith, "Psychological Inflexibility and Intolerance of Uncertainty Moderate the Relationship between Social Isolation and Mental Health Outcomes during COVID-19."

mental health have not been well studied. However, their attitudes are essential to understand in order to gain insight on how Muslims experienced the COVID-19 pandemic.

3 Socially Isolated Ramadan

The Ramadan experience during the COVID-19 pandemic was unique in modern Islamic history. Whereas it traditionally consists of group prayers, community *ifṭār* (fast-breaking meals), and increased social interactions centered around spiritual growth,[29] due to quarantine, Muslims worldwide could not partake in communal Ramadan activities. Though deprived of the communal experience, Muslims were encouraged to increase their prayer, reflection, and acts of service as is traditionally done during the holy month.[30] Ramadan in isolation was framed as an opportunity to perform these acts with utmost focus and sincerity, free from social expectations, and cultivate one's individual relationship with Allah.[31] In the spirit of Ramadan and in accordance with the Islamic responsibility to ensure the well-being of others, Muslims mobilized to feed those in need while also donating generously to charitable causes and pandemic relief efforts.[32] However, no published research has investigated how Muslims actually experienced Ramadan and the changes in behaviors due to the pandemic.

4 The Present Study

We have provided an overview of how the pandemic has presented challenges to Muslim communities and their mental health. However, empirical research about the beliefs and lived experiences of diasporic Muslim communities in coping with the COVID-19 pandemic is extremely limited. In the present study, through three large-scale surveys administered at different stages of the

29 Sana Loue, *Handbook of Religion and Spirituality in Social Work Practice and Research* (New York: Springer, 2017).

30 Umarji, Elwan, and Umar, "A Punishment or a Mercy?"

31 Koenig, "Maintaining Health and Well-Being by Putting Faith into Action During the COVID-19 Pandemic."

32 Al-Krenawi and Graham, "Islamic Theology and Prayer"; and Julie Zauzmer Weil, "Ramadan During Coronavirus: A Holiday like None before It," *Washington Post*, April 22, 2020, https://www.washingtonpost.com/religion/2020/04/22/washingtons-muslim-community-begins-ramadan-like-no-other/.

pandemic, we seek to address important knowledge gaps related to Muslims' beliefs and experiences during the pandemic. Specifically, this study investigates the mental health, religious beliefs and practices, and the Ramadan experience of Muslims in diasporic lands. In doing so, we hope to understand how core psychological and religious processes influenced the way that Muslims experienced the COVID-19 pandemic. We seek to answer the following research questions:

1. Stage 1 Questions (Initial Social Isolation)
   a. What theological beliefs did Muslims hold about COVID-19 and what were the correlates of these beliefs?
   b. What coping behaviors did Muslims engage in and what were the correlates of these coping behaviors?
   c. To what extent do various types of coping, religious practice (Qur'an reading and daily prayers), uncertainty tolerance, and frequency of news watching correlate with anxiety?
   d. What concerns did Muslims have and what were the correlates of these concerns?
2. Stage 2 Questions (Pre-Ramadan)
   a. How prevalent was depression and what were the correlates of depressive disorder? Specifically, how did various types of coping, religious practice (Qur'an reading and daily prayers), uncertainty intolerance, trait mindfulness, and self-esteem correlate with depression disorder?
   b. What coping behaviors did Muslims engage in and what were the correlates of these coping behaviors?
   c. What concerns did Muslims have and what were the correlates of these concerns?
   d. How did relationships with Allah change over the past month and what were the correlates of change?
   e. What were Muslims' attitudes about spending Ramadan in social isolation?
3. Stage 3 Questions (Post-Ramadan)
   a. How was well-being after Ramadan and how did it compare to well-being prior to Ramadan?
   b. Compared to last Ramadan, how did religious behaviors differ during Ramadan in social isolation?
   c. To what extent do religious practices (e.g., Qur'an reading, *Tarāwīḥ* enjoyment, donating money, and accessing mosque services online), self-regulation, and mindfulness predict Ramadan experiences during the pandemic?

For research question 1c, we hypothesize that anxiety will be positively correlated with negative coping behaviors, watching the news, uncertainty tolerance, and being female. General coping and religious behaviors are hypothesized to be negatively correlated with anxiety. For research question 2a, we hypothesize that the likelihood of depression will be positively related to negative coping and uncertainty intolerance, whereas we hypothesize it will be negatively related to general coping, religious behaviors, mindfulness, and self-esteem. For research question 3c, we hypothesize that all religious behaviors will be positively associated with positive Ramadan experiences.

5 Methods

5.1 *Participants*

The Yaqeen Institute for Islamic Research administered three large online surveys to Muslims all over the world during different stages of the COVID-19 pandemic. Requests to complete the surveys were shared online and on social media (e.g., YouTube, Facebook, WhatsApp), thus creating a convenience sample.[33] The data used in this study come from 4,271 Muslims. The majority of the sample is North American (72 percent), followed by European (24 percent), New Zealand/Australian (3 percent), and other lands of Muslim diaspora (1 percent). The sample in each of the three surveys was generally educated (holding a bachelor's degree on average). South Asians (~50 percent), Arabs (~18 percent), Whites (10 percent), and Blacks (8 percent) were the largest racial groups. Females comprised 73 percent of the sample. Table 5.1 summarizes the data used.

TABLE 5.1 Stages of the pandemic and participants per stage

Stage	Survey administered	Months into the pandemic	Sample size (*N*)
1. Initial Quarantine	March 17–24, 2020	0	1,163
2. Pre-Ramadan	April 15–26, 2020	1+	560
3. Post-Ramadan	May 24–June 1, 2020	2+	2,548

33 As convenience samples do not rely on random sampling of a population, it is important to note that our sample may not be representative of the larger population of Muslims in lands of diaspora.

5.2 *Measures*

Demographics. Participants were asked about their sex (male or female), age category (18–24, 25–34, 35–44, 45–54, 55+), and highest level of education completed (less than high school degree [1], high school graduate [2], some college [3], bachelor's degree [4], Master's degree [5], doctoral degree [PhD], or Professional degree [JD, MD]).

5.3 *Stage 1 Measures*

Anxiety. We constructed a three-item measure of anxiety similar to items on the Generalized Anxiety Disorder 7 (GAD-7), with each item on a scale of (1) Never to (5) Always. The three items were, "During the past few days, how often have you felt anxious?"; "During the past few days, how often have you felt nervous?"; and "During the past few days, how often have you felt calm?" (α=.86).[34]

COVID-19 theological beliefs. We created five items to understand Muslim beliefs about their theological beliefs related to COVID-19 on a scaled of (1) none at all to (5) a great deal. A question stem of "How much do you think the Coronavirus is …" preceded the four questions "A punishment from Allah," "A wake-up call from Allah," "A test from Allah," and "A sign of the end of times." A final question asked, "When the Coronavirus first spread in China, how much did you believe that it was a punishment from Allah for how they oppressed the Muslims?"

COVID-19 concerns. We created three items to understand COVID-19 health and societal concerns on a scale of (1) Not At All Concerned to (5) Extremely Concerned. Questions included "How concerned are you about getting the Coronavirus?"; "How concerned are you about beloved friends or family getting the Coronavirus?"; and "How concerned are you about the societal consequences of the Coronavirus?"

Change in relationship with Allah. One item asked, "How has your connection with Allah been over the past week?" from 1 (Much Worse) to 5 (Much Better).

Seeing blessings. A single item was created to measure the extent to which blessings had been observed due to COVID-19. On a scale of (1) None At All to (5) A Great Deal, respondents were asked, "How many blessings do you see from Allah in allowing the Coronavirus to spread?" This item was also asked in Stage 2.

Gratitude. A single item was created to measure trait gratitude. On a scale of (1) Never to (5) Very Often, respondents were asked, "How often do you count your blessings in life?"

---

34 We also conducted a confirmatory factor analysis of the items and found the items to load well onto a common factor. The standardized factor loadings were .88, .88, and .70.

Qur'an reading. A single item asked about Qur'an reading. On a scale of (1) Hardly Ever to (5) Daily, respondents were asked, "How often do you read the Qur'an?"

Prayer. A single item was created to measure frequency of prayer. On a scale of (1) Zero to (5) 5+sunnahs, respondents were asked, "How often do you pray daily (on average)?"

Coping behaviors. In order to measure coping behaviors, we asked, "Which of the following things have you done as a reaction to the Coronavirus? (check all that apply)". Options included reading Qur'an, listening to the Qur'an, making *duʿāʾ*, seeking forgiveness, praying regularly, listening to religious lectures related to the Coronavirus, deep breathing, exercise, walking outdoors, spending quality time with beloved family/friends, speaking on the phone with beloved family/friends, donating money, buying a lot of extra household supplies, watching a lot more entertainment, and emotional eating. We categorized these behaviors into three categories of religious coping, general coping, and negative coping.

Activities missed. One item asked, "Due to social isolation policies, what activities will you miss the most? (rank the top 3)". Options included: hanging out with friends, going out to places such as malls, movies, restaurants, coffee, etc.; not being able to attend Friday prayers; possible cancellation of Ramadan *tarāwīḥ* prayers and *ifṭār*s (dinners); school and educational activities; playing sports; and watching sports.

Masjid attitudes. Two items assessed attitudes toward the *masjid* offering in-person services. On a scale of (1) Extremely Unreasonable to (5) Extremely Reasonable, respondents were asked, "How reasonable do you think it is for the *masjid* to offer Friday prayers at the current time?" and "Do you think that *masjids* should completely close for the time being?"

Checking news. One item asked, "During the past few days, how often have you been checking social media or the news for Coronavirus info?" on a scale of (1) Never to (5) Always.

Uncertainty intolerance. Three items were taken from the intolerance of uncertainty scale.[35] On a scale of (1) Strongly Disagree to (5) Strongly Agree, respondents were asked to rate the following two statements, "Uncertainty makes life intolerance," "My mind can't be relaxed if I don't know what will happen tomorrow," and "Uncertainty makes me uneasy, anxious, or stressed." (α=.78).[36] The same questions were asked in Stage 3.

35 Buhr and Dugas, "The Intolerance of Uncertainty Scale."

36 We also conducted a confirmatory factor analysis of the items and found the items to load well onto a common factor. The standardized factor loadings were .60 .80, and .81.

5.4 *Stage 2 Measures*

General well-being. One item asked, "How well have you been doing over the past month?" The scale was from (1) Terrible to (5) Excellent. This item was also asked in Stage 3.

Anxiety. Three items from the General Anxiety Disorder-7 (GAD-7) were administered.[37] Respondents were asked how often they felt anxious, had trouble relaxing, and been unable to stop worrying (α=.75). Confirmatory factor analysis showed the items to load on a common factor, with standardized loadings of .84 (anxiety), .54 (worry), and .79 (relaxing).

Depression. Depressive symptoms were measured with two items from the Patient Health Questionnaire-2 (PHQ-2).[38] The question stem was "Over the past 2 weeks, how often have you been bothered by any of the following problems?" on a scale of (0) Not At All to (3) Nearly Every Day. The statements responded to were, "Little interest or pleasure in doing things" and "Feeling down, depressed, or hopeless" (α=.73). Based on the PHQ-2 guidelines, a cut score of three was used to classify a person as depressed.

Mindfulness. Two items from the Mindful Attention Awareness Scale (MAAS) were used to measure trait mindfulness.[39] On a scale of (1) Almost Never to (6) Almost Always, respondents were asked to endorse the following statements, "I find it difficult to stay focused on what's happening in the present" and "I find myself preoccupied with the future or the past" (α=.72).

Self-esteem. One item was taken from the Lifespan Self-Esteem Scale.[40] On a scale of (1) Really Sad to (5) Really Happy, respondents were asked, "When you think about yourself, how do you feel?"

Religious coping. One question asked, "Since the start of the pandemic, I find myself doing these behaviors: (check all that apply)" Behaviors included: seeking forgiveness and *duʿāʾ*; reading/listening to religious content related to

---

37 Robert L. Spitzer et al., "A Brief Measure for Assessing Generalized Anxiety Disorder: The GAD-7," *Archives of Internal Medicine* 166, no. 10 (May 22, 2006): 1092, https://doi.org/10.1001/archinte.166.10.1092.

38 Kurt Kroenke, Robert L. Spitzer, and Janet B.W. Williams, "The Patient Health Questionnaire-2: Validity of a Two-Item Depression Screener," *Medical Care* 41, no. 11 (November 2003): 1284–1292, https://doi.org/10.1097/01.MLR.0000093487.78664.3C.

39 Kirk Warren Brown and Richard M. Ryan, "The Benefits of Being Present: Mindfulness and Its Role in Psychological Well-Being," *Journal of Personality and Social Psychology* 84, no. 4 (2003): 822–848, https://doi.org/10.1037/0022-3514.84.4.822.

40 Michelle A. Harris, M. Brent Donnellan, and Kali H. Trzesniewski, "The Lifespan Self-Esteem Scale: Initial Validation of a New Measure of Global Self-Esteem," *Journal of Personality Assessment* 100, no. 1 (January 2, 2018): 84–95, https://doi.org/10.1080/00223891.2016.1278380.

the coronavirus; reading/listening to Qur'an; praying more; deep breathing; walking outdoors; artwork; watching more television; gaming more; snacking more; sleeping more; sleeping less; buying lots of extra household supplies (12); cleaning more, watching illicit material; smoking/drinking/drug use; being in conflict with family more; and withdrawing from responsibilities more. Again, we categorized these into religious, general, and negative coping. The coping behaviors in Stage 2 were more exhaustive than in Stage 1.

COVID-19 concerns. We created two items to understand COVID-19 health and finance concerns on a scale of (1) Not At All Concerned to (5) Extremely Concerned. Questions included "How concerned are you about getting the Coronavirus?" and "How worried are you about your financial situation or employment?"

5.5 *Stage 3 Measures*

Ramadan perceptions. Two questions investigated subjective perceptions of Ramadan during the pandemic. The first question asked, "How was your Ramadan this year?" on a scaled of (1) Not very good to (5) Amazing. The second question asked, "How was your Ramadan compared to last year?" on a scale of (1) Much Worse to (5) Much Better.

Qur'an reading. One question investigated Qur'an reading, asking, "How much Qur'an did you read this Ramadan compared to last year?" on a scale of (1) Much Less to (5) Much More.

Tarāwīḥ prayer. Four questions probed experiences and practices related to recommended prayers after *ifṭār*. The first item asked, "Did you pray *tarāwīḥ* at home this year?" (Yes or No). If yes, three follow-up questions were asked: "How much *tarāwīḥ* did you pray this Ramadan compared to last year?" on a scale of (1) Much Less to (5) Much More; "How much did you enjoy praying *tarāwīḥ* at home this year?" on a scale of (1) Not Too Enjoyable to (5) Absolutely Enjoyable; and "How was the spiritual experience of *tarāwīḥ* at home compared to *tarāwīḥ* in the *masjid*?" on a scale of (1) *Masjid* Far Better to (5) Home A Lot Better.

Masjid online access. One item assessed online *masjid* engagement. Respondents were asked, "How much content did you access from your local *masjid* this Ramadan?" on a scale of (1) None to (5) A Lot.

Exercise. One item asked, "How often did you exercise this Ramadan?" on a scale of (1) Not At All to (5) Daily.

Self-regulation. One item asked how true the following statement was of them. "I am able to resist temptations and stay focused on a task." The scale was from (1) Not At All True to Completely True.

Ramadan philanthropy. Four items investigated philanthropic behavior. One direct donation item asked, "How much money did you donate this Ramadan in total?" on a scale of (1) $0 to (8) $5000+. Three other items investigated donations to specific causes compared to last Ramadan on a scale of (1) A Lot Less to (5) A Lot More. "How much did you donate to the *masjid*/educational organizations/relief organizations this Ramadan compared to last year?"

Mindfulness. Three items from the Mindful Attention Awareness Scale were used to measure trait mindfulness. In addition to the two items from Stage 2, respondents were also asked to endorse how often, "I rush through activities without being really attentive to them." The alpha for the three-item scale was .85. Confirmatory factor analysis also showed the items loaded on a common factor with loadings of .68, .90, and .85.

5.6 *Analytic Approach*

We use regression techniques to answer all of our inferential questions. We use multiple linear regression to investigate the correlates of anxiety (RQ1c) and reporting a positive Ramadan experience (RQ3c). We use logistic regression to investigate the correlates of depression (RQ2a). We analyzed the patterns of missing data using t-tests and determined the missing data was not systematically biased (i.e., not missing not at random; MNAR). For example, survey fatigue was a common cause of non-completion, which did not differ based on demographics (p>.05). Therefore, listwise deletion was used for multivariate analyses with missing data, resulting in complete case analyses.

6 Results

6.1 *Stage 1: Initial Quarantine*

6.1.1 Theological Beliefs about COVID-19

Just as social distancing and isolation policies were being instituted by governments all over the world, we investigated Muslims' theological beliefs about the COVID-19 pandemic. See Figure 5.1 for a detailed breakdown of theological beliefs. The vast majority of Muslims believed COVID-19 was a great test (M=4.39)[41] and wake-up call from Allah (M=4.19). Ten percent believed COVID-19 was a great punishment, although the majority did not feel it was much of a punishment (M=2.52). Similarly, 13 percent believed it a great punishment

41 *M* refers to the mean value.

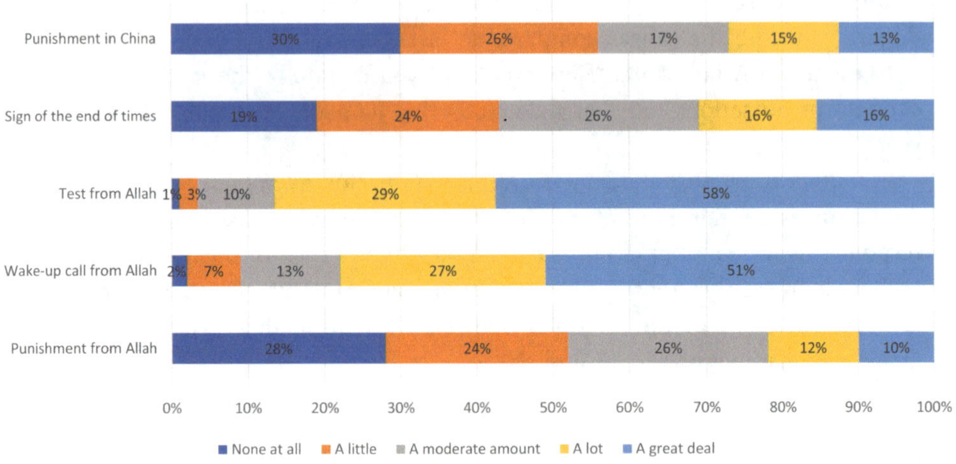

FIGURE 5.1 Theological beliefs about COVID-19

to China, as COVID-19 is thought to have originated in Wuhan, China. However, 56 percent felt it was either not a punishment at all or just a little bit of a punishment to China (M=2.54). Nearly one in three (32 percent) considered COVID-19 to be a sign of the end of times more than a moderate amount (M=2.85).

We then investigated the correlates of Muslims' theological beliefs. For example, believing COVID-19 was a punishment was negatively correlated with level of education (r=-.13), whereas it was positively correlated with reading the Qur'an frequently (r=.10), believing it was a wake-up call (r=.36), a test from Allah (r=.27), and believing it was a sign of the end of times (r=.42). Believing COVID-19 was a test from God was positively correlated with reading the Qur'an frequently (r=.14). These theological beliefs were not mutually exclusive. Therefore, we investigated beliefs about COVID-19 being a punishment and a test. Respondents who rated punishment or test beliefs as greater than a moderate amount were scored as being high in that belief. Twenty-two percent were high in believing COVID-19 was both a punishment and a test, 65 percent were high in test but not in punishment, and 13 percent were low in both. Believing that COVID-19 was both a substantial punishment and test was correlated with engaging in more religious coping (r=.10), whereas believing that COVID-19 was neither a substantial punishment or test was correlated with engaging in less religious coping (r=-.16). Lastly, we inquired about changes in people's relationship with Allah. Less than 1 percent said their relationship with Allah had gotten worse, 4 percent said it was about the same, 38 percent said it was somewhat better, and 35 percent said it was much better.

TABLE 5.2 Coping behaviors during stage 1

	Percentage
Religious coping	
Read Qur'an	44.09%
Listen Qur'an	38.36%
Seek Forgiveness	74.06%
Make *duʿāʾ*	86.90%
Listen to Lectures	52.83%
Donate	26.88%
General coping	
Deep Breathing	26.97%
Exercise	22.60%
Walking Outdoors	22.25%
See Family/Friends	54.37%
Call Family/Friends	53.00%
Negative coping	
Binge Watching	27.48%
Emotional Eating	19.69%
Panic Buying	31.76%

6.1.2 Coping Behaviors

Muslims reacted to Stage 1 of the pandemic and social isolation in a variety of ways. We asked respondents about their engagement in various types of religious, general, and negative coping behaviors. Religious coping included behaviors such as reading the Qur'an, listening to the Qur'an, making *duʿāʾ*, listening to religious lectures, seeking forgiveness, and giving charity. General coping included deep breathing, exercise, walking outdoors, spending time with family and friends, and speaking on the phone with family and friends. Negative coping included buying extra household supplies (i.e., panic buying), excessively consuming entertainment (i.e., binge watching), and emotional eating. See Table 5.2 for percentages of engaging in each coping behavior. Respondents were also asked about how often they checked social media or the news for COVID-19-related information. Negative coping was positively correlated with checking the news (r=.31) and anxiety (r=-.27). Religious coping was positively correlated with reading the Qur'an (r=.20), age (r=.14), and seeing

TABLE 5.3 Predictors of anxiety

	B	SE	*t*	*p*-value	*B*
Female	.19***	0.05	4.10	0.000	0.10
Age	-.06*	0.02	-2.92	0.004	-0.08
Education	.00	0.02	-0.07	0.942	0.00
Negative Coping	.12***	0.03	4.50	0.000	0.11
General Coping	.01	0.02	0.76	0.447	0.02
Prayer	-.07**	0.02	-3.17	0.002	-0.09
Qur'an Reading	.03	0.02	1.77	0.078	0.05
Uncertainty Intolerance	.42***	0.02	19.41	0.000	0.47
Checking the News	.14***	0.02	7.61	0.000	0.18
R^2	.40				

SE=standard error
B in the first column represent unstandardized values
B in the final column represent standardized values
* p<0.05, ** p<0.01, *** p<0.001

blessings (*r*=.27). General coping was correlated with being female (*r*=.11) and anxiety (*r*=.06).

6.1.3 Mental Health

Understanding anxiety during the pandemic was a central concern. The mean anxiety score was 2.13, which corresponded to sometimes feeling anxiety. Higher scores indicate experiencing anxiety more often. Of the sample reported, 11 percent experiencing anxiety either most of the time or always, and 48 percent reported experiencing it little to never. Anxiety was correlated with numerous psychological, religious, and demographic factors. Anxiety was positively correlated with uncertainty intolerance (*r*=.57): concerns of contracting COVID-19 (*r*=.37); concerns for beloved others contracting COVID-19 (*r*=.34); and concern for societal consequences of COVID-19 (*r*=.27). Anxiety was negatively correlated with seeing blessings during the pandemic (*r*=-.17), gratitude (*r*=-.13), age (*r*=-.15), praying five times a day (*r*=-.16), and reading the Qur'an (*r*=-.12). Women had significantly higher anxiety than men (*t*=-5.34, *p*<.001) during this time.

We investigated the correlate of anxiety further using linear regression (for details, see Table 5.4). Being female (*B*=.10, p<.001), engaging in negative coping behaviors (*B*=.11, p<.001), and uncertainty intolerance (*B*=.47, p<.001) were

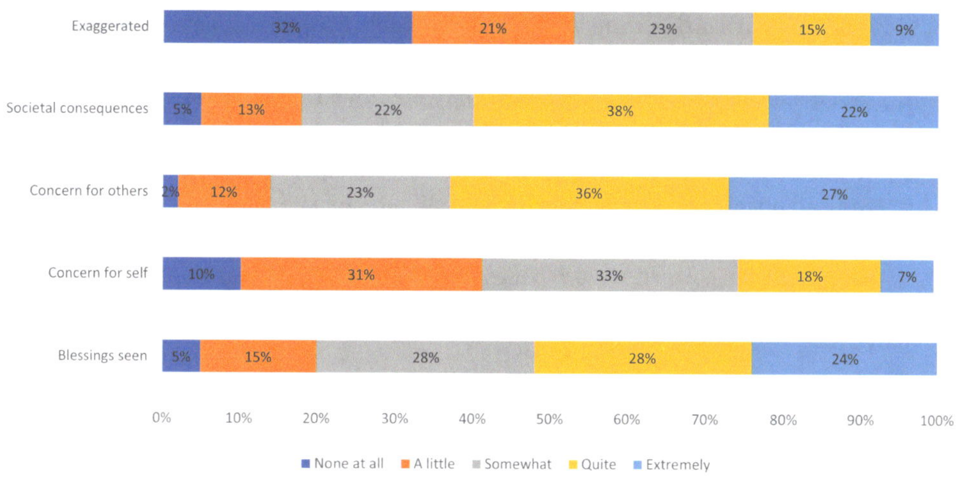

FIGURE 5.2 General perceptions of COVID-19 during stage 1

positively associated with anxiety. Age (*B*=-.08, p<.05) and daily prayer (*B*=-.09, p<.01) were negatively associated with anxiety. Education level, general coping behaviors, and Qur'an reading were not predictive of anxiety (p>.05).

6.1.4 General and Religious Concerns Toward COVID-19

We investigated both general and religious attitudes toward COVID-19 (for details, see Figure 5.2). Although there was some concern for contracting COVID-19 (*M*=2.80), people were substantially more concerned that close friends and family members may contract it (*M*=3.76). People were on average quite concerned about the societal consequences, and less than one in four (24 percent) felt the reaction to the pandemic was quite a bit or extremely exaggerated. Fifty-two percent of people reported seeing a lot or a great deal of blessings since COVID-19 spread (*M*=3.52). Seeing blessings during COVID-19 was positively correlated with gratitude (*r*=.19), age (.14), praying five times a day (*r*=.19), and reading Qur'an (*r*=.20). It was negatively correlated with being concerned with getting COVID-19 (*r*=-.11), concern for others (*r*=-.10), and concern for societal consequences (*r*=-.13).

People were asked to rank the activities they would miss the most due to social isolation policies. Choices included hanging out with friends, going out to malls, movies, restaurants, not being able to attend Friday prayers, possible closure of the masjid in Ramadan, school, playing sports, and watching sports. Not being able to attend Friday prayers (22 percent) and masjid closure in Ramadan (28 percent) were the activities most likely to be most missed. However, despite the concern for not being able to attend the masjid, the majority of people felt it was unreasonable for the masjid to offer Friday prayers (71 percent) during this time. Only 13 percent felt it was reasonable. Forty-nine percent felt the masjid should completely close for the time being, 21 percent said it should not close, and 30 percent were not sure. Being concerned about getting COVID-19 (r=.-08), being concerned for others getting COVID-19 (r=-.14), and being concerned about the societal consequences of COVID-19 (r=-.15) were all negatively correlated with believing the masjid should be open for Friday prayers. However, believing that the reaction to COVID-19 was exaggerated was positively correlated with believing the masjid should stay open for Friday prayers (r=.29).

7 Stage 2: Pre-Ramadan

7.1 *Mental Health and Depression*

We wanted to investigate anxiety and mental health in more depth during Stage 2, which occurred approximately one month into the pandemic. The mean anxiety score was 2.35, which corresponds to sometimes feeling anxiety. Nine percent of the sample reported feeling anxious either most of the time or always and 28 percent reported little to no anxiety. We also investigated depressive symptoms using the Patient Health Questionnaire-2 (PHQ-2). Twenty-four percent of the sample met the cutoff for major depressive disorder. We investigated the correlates of depression further using logistic regression. Uncertainty intolerance (OR[42]=1.60, p<.01) and negative coping (OR=1.69, p<.001) were associated with greater odds of reporting depression, whereas mindfulness (OR=.62, p=.001) and self-esteem (OR=.52, p<.001) were associated with decreased odds of reporting depression. Age, general coping, prayer, and frequency of reading the Qur'an did not correlate with depression (p>.05). A standard deviation increase in uncertainty tolerance increased the odds of depression by 60 percent. A standard deviation increase in mindfulness decreased the odds of depression by 38 percent. The full model explained 30 percent of the variance in depression. See Table 5.4 for the details of the logistic regression.

42 *OR* stands for odds ratio. Odds ratios express the likelihood, odds, or chance of being in one of two categories under different conditions. Odds ratios greater than 1 indicate increased odds, whereas odds ratios less than 1 indicate decreased odds of an outcome.

TABLE 5.4 Logistic regression predicting major depressive disorder

	OR	SE	*t*	*p*-value
Female	1.06	0.35	0.19	0.849
Age	0.99	0.15	-0.07	0.948
Education	0.86	0.11	-1.23	0.221
Negative Coping	1.69***	0.22	3.91	0.000
General Coping	0.86	0.11	-1.11	0.267
Prayer	1.10	0.22	0.47	0.637
Qur'an Reading	0.97	0.10	-0.27	0.784
UI	1.60**	0.27	2.79	0.005
Mindfulness	0.62**	0.09	-3.19	0.001
Self-Esteem	0.52***	0.08	-4.40	0.000
R^2	0.30			

OR=odds ratio
SE=standard error
* $p<0.05$, ** $p<0.01$, *** $p<0.001$

7.2 *Coping Behaviors*

Compared to Stage 1, we included a larger battery of religious, negative, and general coping behaviors. Religious coping included making *duʿāʾ*, reading or listening to the Qur'an, praying more, and reading or listening to religious content related to COVID-19. Negative coping included behaviors such as watching illicit material, smoking/drinking/drug use, being in conflict with family more, withdrawing from responsibilities more, sleeping more or less, and buying extra household supplies. General coping included walking outdoors, deep breathing, cleaning more, and engaging in artwork (for percentages of engagement in each type of behavior, see Table 5.5). Religious coping was frequently observed, as more than three in four (76 percent) made *duʿāʾ* and two in three people (66.03 percent) engaged with the Qur'an. The most common general coping behaviors were walking outdoors and cleaning more (33 percent). Negative coping was not reported as frequently. Only 1 percent reported using drugs or alcohol and 6 percent reported watching illicit material. Religious coping was negatively correlated with uncertainty intolerance (r=-.12) and positively correlated with seeing blessing (r=.21) and mindfulness (r=.10). Negative coping was positively correlated with anxiety (r=.29), uncertainty intolerance (r=.20), and financial concerns (r=.11). It was negatively correlated with reading the

TABLE 5.5 Coping behaviors in stage 2

	Percentage
Religious coping	
Duʿāʾ (Invoking God)	76.28%
Listen/Read Religious Content on COVID-19	55.98%
Listen/Read Qur'an	66.03%
Praying More	48.01%
General coping	
Deep Breathing	27.13%
Walking Outdoors	33.21%
Artwork	14.99%
Cleaning More	33.21%
Negative coping	
Sleeping More	37.76%
Sleeping Less	16.70%
Buying a Lot of supplies	11.01%
Watching Illicit Material	6.07%
Smoking/Alcohol/Drugs	1.14%
Family Conflict	11.57%
Withdrawing From Responsibilities	16.70%

Qur'an (r=-.22), age (r=-.19), seeing blessings (r=-.17), and mindfulness (r=-.31). Women were more likely to engage in general coping than men (r=.12).

7.3 *General and Religious Perceptions Toward COVID-19*

Nearly three of four people (73 percent) reported seeing a lot or a great deal of blessings (M=3.98), compared with 52 percent a month earlier (M=3.52). The mean difference was statistically significant (t=9.20, p<.001). Personal concerns for contracting COVID-19 were also significantly lower (M=2.51) than the previous month (t=5.38, p<.001). The median for personal financial concerns was to be a little worried, although 16 percent were quite or extremely concerned about finances. Concern for getting COVID-19 was positively correlated with financial concerns (r=.33), age (r=.19), education (r=.18), uncertainty intolerance (r=.21), and negatively correlated with mindfulness (r=.18). Financial concern was positively correlated with uncertainty intolerance (r=.17) and neg-

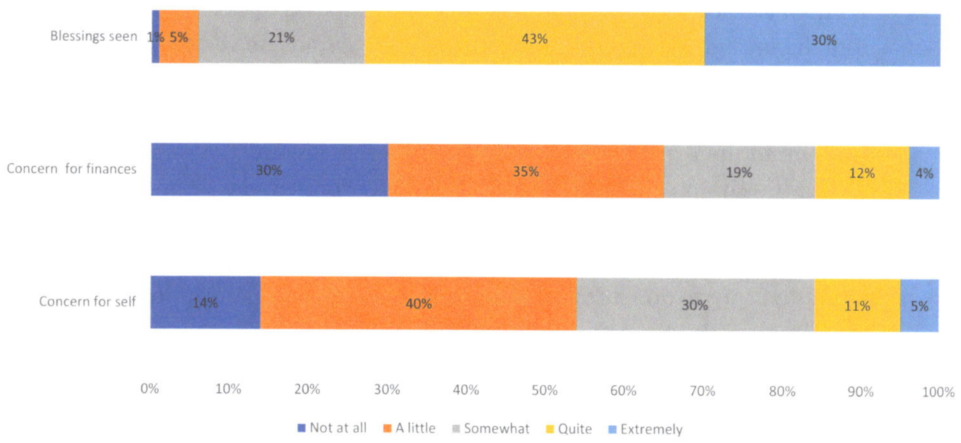

FIGURE 5.3 General perceptions about COVID-19 during stage 2

atively correlated with mindfulness (-.22). Seeing blessings had the opposite pattern, being negatively correlated with uncertainty intolerance (*r*=-.19) and positively correlated with mindfulness (*r*=.20), praying five times a day (*r*=.13), and reading Qur'an (.26). Gender was not correlated with these perceptions (for a detailed breakdown, see Figure 5.3).

We asked how people's relationship with Allah had changed over the past month: 2 percent responded that their relationship was "much worse"; 6 percent responded that it was "somewhat worse"; 22.5 percent responded that it was "about the same"; 44 percent responded it was "somewhat better"; and 25.5 percent responded that it was "much better." Overall, the mean was 3.8, ("somewhat better"). Change in one's relationship with Allah was positively correlated with religious coping (*r*=.45), seeing blessings (*r*=.26), concerns for contracting COVID-19 (*r* =.12), and mindfulness (*r*=.15). It was negatively correlated with negative coping (*r* =-.27) and uncertainty intolerance (*r* =-.12).

7.4 *Ramadan Anticipation and Intentions*

As Ramadan in 2020 was going to be spent in isolation at home, we asked respondents about their attitudes and intentions for the month of Ramadan. The majority of people anticipated Ramadan in social isolation being better. Of the respondents, 3.5 percent anticipated it being much worse, 20.5 percent somewhat worse, 14 percent about the same, 37 percent somewhat better, and 24.5 percent much better. Thus, approximately 24 percent felt Ramadan would be worse and 62 percent said it would be better. Consistent with these expectations of having a better Ramadan, 72 percent anticipated reading more Qur'an this Ramadan than the previous year. Less than 1 percent anticipated reading less than last year. To gauge potential concerns about spending Ramadan away from the masjid and community, we asked, "How much do you think you need a community to thrive in Ramadan?" Nine percent of people did not think they needed a community to thrive, whereas nearly 15 percent said they needed the community a great deal (*Mdn*=3, "a moderate amount"). Feeling that one needed the community to thrive was negatively correlated with anticipating a better Ramadan this year (r=-.27).

As Ramadan is the time of increased giving, we asked respondents about their intentions to donate to relief causes, educational organizations, and masjids. Although the average intention was to give the same as last year, approximately one in three intended to donate more this year. Intentions to donate to the three types of recipients (relief, education, masjid) were positively correlated with reading the Qur'an regularly (r=.16) and negatively correlated with uncertainty intolerance (r=-.13) and financial concerns (r=-.15). Age, gender, and education were not correlated with these intentions.

8 Stage 3—Post-Ramadan

Our focus in the post-Ramadan stage was to capture the Ramadan experience in social isolation, including well-being, religious worship, and philanthropy. To capture how people felt after Ramadan, we asked one item about global well-being. The mean well-being was 3.84 (between fair and good). Well-being after Ramadan was significantly higher than before Ramadan, where the mean was 3.56 (t=5.72, p<.001).

8.1 *Ramadan Experiences*

We asked about people's subjective perceptions of Ramadan this year. The median response was that Ramadan was "very good" (4) on a scale of (1) Not Very Good to (5) Amazing. Furthermore, 73 percent of people reported having a better Ramadan this year than last year, whereas 9 percent reported having a worse Ramadan than last year. Seventy-three percent reported reading more Qur'an than last year, whereas 14 percent reported reading less. Seventy-three percent of people reported praying *tarāwīḥ* at home this year. Of those that prayed *tarāwīḥ*, 52 percent prayed more *tarāwīḥ* this year compared to last year, whereas 18 percent prayed less than last year (for Qur'an, *tarāwīḥ*, and Ramadan comparisons from last year, see Figure 5.4).

We investigated the predictors of experiencing a good Ramadan in social isolation. Experiencing a good Ramadan was positively associated with accessing

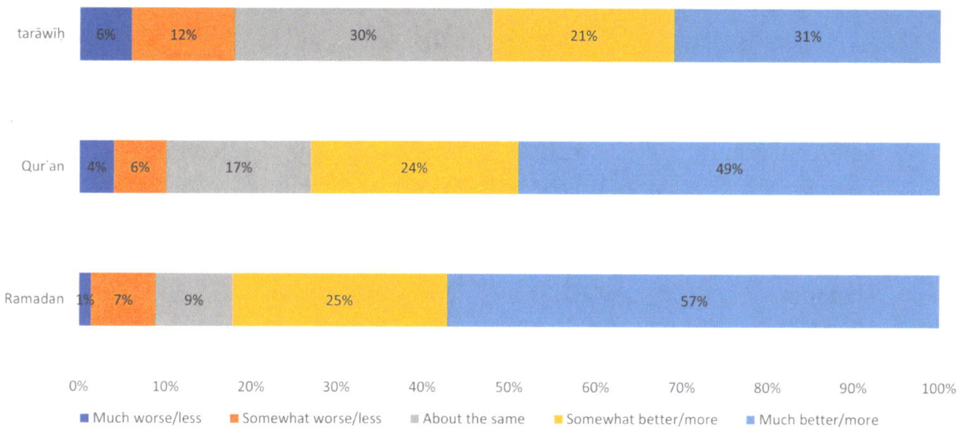

FIGURE 5.4 Ramadan perceptions in 2020 compared to 2019

masjid content online (B=.09), self-reported self-regulation (B=.11), exercising regularly (B=.06), reading more Qur'an than last year (B =.29), enjoying one's *tarāwīḥ* prayers (B=.33), giving charity (B=.06), and mindfulness (B =.12). Thus, a one standard deviation increase in enjoying *tarāwīḥ* prayers was associated with a one-third standard deviation increase in experiencing a good Ramadan. Age, gender, and education level were not associated with one's Ramadan experience. The model explained 33 percent of the variance in experiencing a good Ramadan (for detailed regression results, see Table 5.6).

9 Discussion

The present study drew from perspectives on Islam, religious coping, and mental health to understand the beliefs and experiences of Muslims during the COVID-19 pandemic. By utilizing three large samples of Muslims during different stages of the COVID-19 pandemic, we have contributed to the growing literature on the intersection of religion, coping with uncertainty, and mental health. Our discussion focuses on three themes informed by our results: (1) the relationship between theological beliefs, coping, and mental health; (2) religious thriving during Ramadan in social isolation; and (3) changes in religiosity.

9.1 *Theological Beliefs and Coping Behaviors*

The COVID-19 pandemic has been a time of incredible uncertainty regarding people's health, wealth, and future. Our findings highlight the diverse ways in which Muslims cope with uncertainty caused by the pandemic, as well as

TABLE 5.6 Predictors of Ramadan experience

	B	SE	*t*	*p*-value	*B*
Mosque Online Access	0.05***	0.01	4.30	0.000	0.09
Self-regulation	0.10***	0.02	4.94	0.000	0.11
Exercise	0.03**	0.01	2.76	0.006	0.06
Qur'an compare	0.25***	0.02	13.23	0.000	0.29
Tarāwīḥ enjoyment	0.30***	0.02	14.89	0.000	0.33
Donations	0.03*	0.01	2.25	0.024	0.06
Mindfulness	0.10***	0.02	5.16	0.000	0.12
Age	0.03	0.02	1.55	0.121	0.04
Female	0.07	0.05	1.50	0.133	0.03
Education	-0.02	0.02	-0.75	0.453	-0.02
R^2	0.33				

SE=standard error
B in the first column represent unstandardized values
B in the final column represent standardized values
$^{*}p<0.05$, $^{**}p<0.01$, $^{***}p<0.001$

their theological beliefs related to these coping behaviors. The high frequency of Muslim engagement in religious coping, including prayer, seeking forgiveness, and reading scripture, is in line with recent findings about religiosity during the pandemic across members of different faiths in ninety-five countries.[43]

What might explain the high rates of religious coping in Muslims? We believe that the holistic nature of the Islamic belief system is inherently conducive to religious coping. Mainstream Islamic theology rejects deism, and posits that Allah actively responds to his Servants. Therefore, Muslims are motivated to turn to Allah who is Omnipotent, Omnipresent, and always in control of all things that occur. As such, Muslims do not ascribe to the belief that God brought creation into existence and then allowed it to run its course without knowing or having control over what will happen. Furthermore, through structured daily and weekly practices, such as prayer, reading scripture, and

43 Jeanet Sinding Bentzen, "In Crisis, We Pray: Religiosity and the COVID-19 Pandemic," *Journal of Economic Behavior & Organization* 192 (December 2021): 541–583, https://doi.org/10.1016/j.jebo.2021.10.014.

gratitude, Islamic guidance addresses the physical, emotional, and spiritual well-being of both the individual and society.[44]

Islamic guidance extends beyond the legal guidelines of dress, diet, and business, and provides a theological worldview through which one sees, interprets, and responds to all events, expected or unexpected. Therefore, a religious worldview may prompt Muslims to turn to Islamically oriented coping mechanisms in lieu of professional help, social support, or general coping.[45] Our findings support this notion, as during the initial stages of the pandemic, Muslims were more likely to seek forgiveness and make *duʿāʾ* than to engage in any other coping mechanism, such as walking outside or sleeping more. Additionally, even one month into quarantine, religious coping was still the most frequently observed coping mechanism among our sample, as more than three in four Muslims (76 percent) made *duʿāʾ* and two in three (66 percent) recited the Qurʾan.

Religious coping is related to core theological beliefs about the pandemic. Specifically, beliefs about the nature of calamities frames how a person sees the pandemic and responds to it. Numerous Qurʾanic verses and hadith (Prophetic statements) address the nature of this life as a test and the possibility of worldly punishment for transgression and oppression. The Qurʾan states, "And We will surely test you with something of fear, hunger, a loss of wealth, lives, and fruits, but give good tidings to the patient (Q.2:155)." The Qurʾan further explains the purpose behind these events. "And We tested them with good [times] and bad that perhaps they would return [to God] (Q.7:168)." Punishments operate similarly to tests in Islam.[46] A religiously appropriate response to such events involves patience, repentance, and seeing blessings in the difficulty.

Plagues have received substantial attention in Islamic literature, and have historically been perceived as a punishment that can offer great rewards if one remains steadfast in faith.[47] The Qurʾan and hadith frame calamities as events intended to bring one closer to God. Therefore, it is not surprising that Muslims

44 C.A. Che Mohamad et al., "Muslims Responses to Pandemics: Lessons from the Best Generation," *IIUM Medical Journal Malaysia* 19, no. 2 (October 28, 2020), https://doi.org/10.31436/imjm.v19i2.1609.

45 Kate Miriam Loewenthal et al., "Faith Conquers All? Beliefs About the Role of Religious Factors in Coping with Depression Among Different Cultural-Religious Groups in the UK," *British Journal of Medical Psychology* 74, no. 3 (September 2001): 293–303, https://doi.org/10.1348/000711201160993.

46 Mira Bajirova, *The Divine Cure of Coronavirus and Widespread Diseases* (Singapore: PartridgeSingapore, 2020); and Umarji, Elwan, and Umar, "A Punishment or a Mercy?"

47 Awaad, Elsayed, and Helal, "Holistic Healing: Islam's Legacy of Mental Health"; and Bajirova, *The Divine Cure of Coronavirus and Widespread Diseases.*

would respond to the pandemic within a religious framework. Beliefs about the COVID-19 pandemic highlighted this connection: Believing that COVID-19 was both a substantial punishment and a test was correlated with engaging in more religious coping, whereas believing that COVID-19 was neither a substantial punishment nor a test was correlated with engaging in less religious coping. Interestingly, seeing blessings during COVID-19 was positively correlated with religious coping and praying five times a day and reading Qur'an. Religiosity thus shapes how a person perceives life events and, in this case, it allows a person to see blessings in times of difficulty and to respond in a religiously appropriate manner to a calamity.

9.2 *Mental Health*

Increased rates of anxiety and depression have been observed during the pandemic.[48] Pre-pandemic, per WHO, the proportion of depression in the global population is estimated to be around 4.4 percent, while females (5.1 percent) being more impacted than men (3.6 percent).[49] During the pandemic, a meta-analysis of fourteen studies including 44,531 people found the prevalence of depression in the general population to be 33.7 percent.[50] In our sample, 24 percent of Muslims met the cut-off for major depressive disorder a month into the pandemic.

Interestingly, after controlling for other factors, the religious behaviors of prayer and reading Qur'an were not associated with depression and showed mixed findings with anxiety, agreeing with previous research. For example, religious coping behaviors such as daily prayer was negatively correlated with anxiety but reading the Qur'an was not. Thus, despite Islam providing a holistic worldview of hardships and how to respond to them, there are other important psychospiritual factors related to mental health of which Muslims must be aware. Prayer and reading Qur'an alone do not capture the breadth of religious practices and beliefs likely related to mental health. Alternatively, it may be that religious behavior does not have a direct effect on mental health, but indirectly related to mental health through other psychological processes. For

48 Catherine K. Ettman et al., "Prevalence of Depression Symptoms in US Adults Before and During the COVID-19 Pandemic," *JAMA Network Open* 3, no. 9 (September 2, 2020): e2019686, https://doi.org/10.1001/jamanetworkopen.2020.19686.

49 World Health Organization, "Depression and Other Common Mental Disorders: Global Health Estimates" (Geneva: World Health Organization, 2017), WHO IRIS, https://apps.who.int/iris/handle/10665/254610.

50 Nader Salari et al., "Prevalence of Stress, Anxiety, Depression Among the General Population During the COVID-19 Pandemic: A Systematic Review and Meta-Analysis," *Globalization and Health* 16, no. 1 (December 2020): 57, https://doi.org/10.1186/s12992-020-00589-w.

example, we found that religious coping was positively associated with mindfulness, and that mindfulness was associated with lower rates of depression. Additionally, religious coping was correlated with seeing blessings during times of calamity, a trait also associated with overall well-being. Even during Stage 2, a stronger connection with Allah was correlated with seeing blessings and mindfulness and was negatively correlated with uncertainty intolerance. Furthermore, during Stage 3, well-being was higher after Ramadan than before it. Therefore, despite no clear conclusion regarding religious coping and its impact on depression and anxiety, our findings indicate a positive relationship between religious practice and coping on mental health.

This relationship between religious coping and mental health is especially amplified when comparing religious coping to other forms of coping. Negative coping was negatively correlated with mindfulness and general coping had no correlation with mindfulness. Furthermore, negative coping and general coping were both positively correlated with anxiety. Even after inclusion of numerous covariates in linear regression, engaging in negative coping behaviors was still correlated with higher anxiety.

Uncertainty intolerance was shown to be a cognitive bias with adverse effects. Despite a person's religiosity, a high degree of uncertainty intolerance increased the odds of suffering from major depressive disorder by 60 percent. Uncertainty intolerance was also correlated with less religious coping, more negative coping behaviors, and more financial worry. Thus, uncertainty intolerance was like a thorn in the side of the believer, affecting their life in multiple ways. Islam encourages believers to acknowledge that certainty only lies with God and to accept the unpredictable nature of life. However, uncertainty beliefs are related to many factors, including culture and upbringing, and uncertainty intolerance may therefore persist in religious people.[51] As uncertainty intolerance is associated with numerous negative outcomes, we believe future research on uncertainty tolerance and religiosity is essential to improving the lived experiences of Muslims in all facets of life, especially their mental health. Cognitive behavior therapy interventions targeting uncertainty intolerance have been successful in reducing worry and generalized anxiety disorder.[52] Similarly, mindfulness interventions may also reduce uncertainty intol-

---

51 Michael Minkov and Geert Hofstede, "A Replication of Hofstede's Uncertainty Avoidance Dimension Across Nationally Representative Samples From Europe," *International Journal of Cross Cultural Management* 14, no. 2 (August 2014): 161–171, https://doi.org/10.1177/1470595814521600.

52 J. Bomyea et al., "Intolerance of Uncertainty as a Mediator of Reductions in Worry in a Cognitive Behavioral Treatment Program for Generalized Anxiety Disorder," *Journal of Anxiety Disorders* 33 (June 2015): 90–94, https://doi.org/10.1016/j.janxdis.2015.05.004.

erance and health-related anxieties.[53] Therefore, we believe that both mechanisms are potential avenues for research on Muslim mental health.

9.3 *The COVID-19 Ramadan Experience*

The impact of COVID-19 upon the Ramadan experience was monumental. As a response to the pandemic, many nations restricted social gatherings, thus limiting the role that mosques could play in Ramadan. Especially in diaspora communities, mosques are a prominent part of a Muslim's social, spiritual, and cultural development, offering religious classes, financial resources, political knowledge workshops, and more.[54] This is in stark contrast to the role mosques play in Muslim-majority countries, where they are often just a place for prayer. In fact, the role of the mosque in the Muslim diaspora most closely mirrors the role of the church in the Black-American community.[55] As a result, one might predict that closed mosques would negatively impact the Ramadan experience.

Despite mosque closures, 73 percent of people reported having a better Ramadan this year than last year. Additionally, well-being after Ramadan was significantly higher than before Ramadan. It was also interesting to note that even communal prayers unique to Ramadan (*tarāwīḥ*) and typically prayed in the mosque were not only still heavily engaged in at home but were also on the rise: 73 percent of people reported praying *tarāwīḥ* at home this year. Of those that prayed *tarāwīḥ*, 52 percent prayed more *tarāwīḥ* this year compared to last year. It seems that social isolation had a more positive impact on religiosity than was predicted and that Muslims in our sample were able to maintain their connection to God from home. Yet, having some connection to the mosque was found to be beneficial, as experiencing a good Ramadan was positively associated with accessing masjid content online. Therefore, both worship in seclusion and worship with a virtual community were positively related to the Ramadan experience.

---

53 David Victorson et al., "Feasibility, Acceptability and Preliminary Psychological Benefits of Mindfulness Meditation Training in a Sample of Men Diagnosed with Prostate Cancer on Active Surveillance: Results from a Randomized Controlled Pilot Trial: Mindfulness and Active Surveillance," *Psycho-Oncology* 26, no. 8 (August 2017): 1155–1163, https://doi.org/10.1002/pon.4135.

54 Hope Collins, "The Mosque as a Political, Economic, and Social Institution 622–Present" (2011), Syracuse University Honors Program Capstone Projects (282), https://surface.syr.edu/honors_capstone/282/.

55 "A Religious Portrait of African-Americans," Pew Research Center, January 30, 2009, https://www.pewforum.org/2009/01/30/a-religious-portrait-of-african-americans/.

Religious practice was not the only predictor of a good Ramadan. It seems that non-religious coping mechanisms were also important in ensuring a positive Ramadan experience. For example, exercise was positively associated with a positive Ramadan experience, indicating that non-religious activities that encourage general well-being can also impact religious practice. This reinforces our previous findings on general coping also being helpful during the pandemic. Thus, general healthy life habits should be emphasized as part of optimizing spiritual experiences.

Ramadan itself had a positive impact on mental health. We found that well-being was significantly higher after Ramadan than before it. As rates of anxiety and depression increased during the pandemic, observing Ramadan after two months of quarantine was an uplifting experience. This finding corroborates existing research that religiosity and religious coping are protective factors against poor mental health. It also suggests that in addition to Ramadan improving one's spiritual growth, it can also improve mood and mental health.

9.4 *Changes in Religiosity*

One of the biggest takeaways from our study was the role of religiosity for Muslims during the pandemic. Whether it was during the initial stage of social isolation in March 2020 or a month later, the vast majority of Muslims reported an improved relationship with God. Although relationship with God is just one dimension of religiosity, it remains an important subjective measure of changes in religiosity due to the pandemic. Although levels of religiosity were found to increase in other populations, the Muslim religious renewal during the COVID-19 pandemic has been substantially more pronounced. In April 2020, 24 percent of Americans overall felt their faith had strengthened since the pandemic,[56] whereas 69.5 percent Muslims reported having an improved relationship with God. The Black Christian community, one of the most religious Christian communities in the United States, reported an increase in faith of 56 percent, which was still lower than the Muslim response. These findings highlight how the Muslim reaction to the pandemic was in accordance with what Islam advocates: returning to God in all situations.

56 Claire Gecewicz, "Few Americas Say Their House of Worship is Open, but a Quarter Say Their Faith Has Grown Amid Pandemic," Pew Research Center, April 30, 2020, https://www.pewresearch.org/fact-tank/2020/04/30/few-americans-say-their-house-of-worship-is-open-but-a-quarter-say-their-religious-faith-has-grown-amid-pandemic/.

10 Limitations and Conclusion

This study is one of the first studies focused on the diverse beliefs and practices of Muslims throughout different stages of the COVID-19 pandemic. In addition to the descriptive statistics presented, the multivariate analyses provide deeper insights into the relationship between religiosity, mental health, psychological mechanisms, and coping. However, there are a few limitations that must be considered when interpreting the results. As the study relied on cross-sectional correlational data, no strong causal inferences can be made. Second, our convenience samples may limit generalizability to all Muslims in diasporic lands, as the sample was overrepresented by woman and those higher in religious practice. Finally, due to the novel circumstances and sudden nature of the pandemic, our newly created measures did not go through rigorous testing and refinement in advance, possibly limiting their effectiveness in uncovering the complex relationships among constructs. We recommend that future research on mental health and coping, especially in Muslim samples, would greatly benefit by incorporating a larger array of religious beliefs and practices than frequency of reading scripture and prayer. Religious beliefs, practices, and coping behaviors have major implications for public health and need to be carefully considered when providing support to those in need, especially during times of uncertainty.

Bibliography

Abdel-Khalek, Ahmed M., Laura Nuño, Juana Gómez-Benito, and David Lester. "The Relationship Between Religiosity and Anxiety: A Meta-Analysis." *Journal of Religion and Health* 58, no. 5 (October 2019): 1847–1856. https://doi.org/10.1007/s10943-019-00881-z.

Abu Raiya, Hisham, and Kenneth I. Pargament. "Religiously Integrated Psychotherapy with Muslim Clients: From Research to Practice." *Professional Psychology: Research and Practice* 41, no. 2 (2010): 181–188. https://doi.org/10.1037/a0017988.

Abu-Raiya, Hisham, Kenneth I. Pargament, and Annette Mahoney. "Examining Coping Methods with Stressful Interpersonal Events Experienced by Muslims Living in the United States Following the 9/11 Attacks." *Psychology of Religion and Spirituality* 3, no. 1 (2011): 1–14. https://doi.org/10.1037/a0020034.

Adam, Zeenah, and Colleen Ward. "Stress, Religious Coping and Wellbeing in Acculturating Muslims." *Journal of Muslim Mental Health* 10, no. 2 (December 2016). https://doi.org/10.3998/jmmh.10381607.0010.201.

Al-Krenawi, Alean, and John R. Graham. "Islamic Theology and Prayer: Relevance for Social Work Practice." *International Social Work* 43, no. 3 (July 2000): 289–304. https://doi.org/10.1177/002087280004300303.

Amer, Mona M., and Joseph D. Hovey. "Socio-Demographic Differences in Acculturation and Mental Health for a Sample of 2nd Generation/Early Immigrant Arab Americans." *Journal of Immigrant and Minority Health* 9, no. 4 (August 7, 2007): 335–347. https://doi.org/10.1007/s10903-007-9045-y.

Awaad, Rania, Danah Elsayed, and Hosam Helal. "Holistic Healing: Islam's Legacy of Mental Health." Yaqeen Institute for Islamic Research, May 27, 2021. https://yaqeeninstitute.org/read/paper/holistic-healing-islams-legacy-of-mental-health.

Bajirova, Mira. *The Divine Cure of Coronavirus and Widespread Diseases*. Singapore: PartridgeSingapore, 2020.

Bentzen, Jeanet Sinding. "In Crisis, We Pray: Religiosity and the COVID-19 Pandemic." *Journal of Economic Behavior & Organization* 192 (December 2021): 541–583. https://doi.org/10.1016/j.jebo.2021.10.014.

Bomyea, J., H. Ramsawh, T.M. Ball, C.T. Taylor, M.P. Paulus, A.J. Lang, and M.B. Stein. "Intolerance of Uncertainty as a Mediator of Reductions in Worry in a Cognitive Behavioral Treatment Program for Generalized Anxiety Disorder." *Journal of Anxiety Disorders* 33 (June 2015): 90–94. https://doi.org/10.1016/j.janxdis.2015.05.004.

Brown, Kirk Warren, and Richard M. Ryan. "The Benefits of Being Present: Mindfulness and Its Role in Psychological Well-Being." *Journal of Personality and Social Psychology* 84, no. 4 (2003): 822–848. https://doi.org/10.1037/0022-3514.84.4.822.

Buhr, K., and M.J. Dugas. "The Intolerance of Uncertainty Scale: Psychometric Properties of the English Version." *Behaviour Research and Therapy* 40, no. 8 (August 2002): 931–945. https://doi.org/10.1016/S0005-7967(01)00092-4.

Chatters, Linda M., Kai McKeever Bullard, Robert Joseph Taylor, Amanda Toler Woodward, Harold W. Neighbors, and James S. Jackson. "Religious Participation and DSM-IV Disorders Among Older African Americans: Findings From the National Survey of American Life." *The American Journal of Geriatric Psychiatry* 16, no. 12 (December 2008): 957–965. https://doi.org/10.1097/JGP.0b013e3181898081.

Che Mohamad, C.A., M.A. Shahar, M.F. Md Tahir, and S.A.K. Syed Abd. Hamid. "Muslims Responses to Pandemics: Lessons from the Best Generation." *IIUM Medical Journal Malaysia* 19, no. 2 (October 28, 2020). https://doi.org/10.31436/imjm.v19i2.1609.

Chen, Hongtu, Karen Cheal, Elizabeth C. McDonel Herr, Cynthia Zubritsky, and Sue E. Levkoff. "Religious Participation as a Predictor of Mental Health Status and Treatment Outcomes in Older Persons." *International Journal of Geriatric Psychiatry* 22, no. 2 (February 2007): 144–153. https://doi.org/10.1002/gps.1704.

Collins, Hope. "The Mosque as a Political, Economic, and Social Institution 622–Present." 2011. Syracuse University Honors Program Capstone Projects (282). https://surface.syr.edu/honors_capstone/282/.

Czeisler, Mark É., Rashon I. Lane, Emiko Petrosky, Joshua F. Wiley, Aleta Christensen,

Rashid Njai, Matthew D. Weaver, et al. "Mental Health, Substance Use, and Suicidal Ideation During the COVID-19 Pandemic—United States, June 24–30, 2020." *MMWR: Morbidity and Mortality Weekly Report* 69, no. 32 (August 14, 2020): 1049–1057. https://doi.org/10.15585/mmwr.mm6932a1.

Dein, Simon, Kate Loewenthal, Christopher Alan Lewis, and Kenneth I. Pargament. "COVID-19, Mental Health and Religion: An Agenda for Future Research." *Mental Health, Religion & Culture* 23, no. 1 (January 2, 2020): 1–9. https://doi.org/10.1080/13674676.2020.1768725.

Ebrahim, Shahul H., and Ziad A. Memish. "Saudi Arabia's Drastic Measures to Curb the COVID-19 Outbreak: Temporary Suspension of the Umrah Pilgrimage." *Journal of Travel Medicine* 27, no. 3 (May 18, 2020): taaa029. https://doi.org/10.1093/jtm/taaa029.

Eltaiba, Nada, and Maria Harries. "Reflections on Recovery in Mental Health: Perspectives From a Muslim Culture." *Social Work in Health Care* 54, no. 8 (September 14, 2015): 725–737. https://doi.org/10.1080/00981389.2015.1046574.

Ettman, Catherine K., Salma M. Abdalla, Gregory H. Cohen, Laura Sampson, Patrick M. Vivier, and Sandro Galea. "Prevalence of Depression Symptoms in US Adults Before and During the COVID-19 Pandemic." *JAMA Network Open* 3, no. 9 (September 2, 2020): e2019686. https://doi.org/10.1001/jamanetworkopen.2020.19686.

Gecewicz, Claire. "Few Americas Say Their House of Worship is Open, but a Quarter Say Their Faith has Grown amid Pandemic." Pew Research Center, April 30, 2020. https://www.pewresearch.org/fact-tank/2020/04/30/few-americans-say-their-house-of-worship-is-open-but-a-quarter-say-their-religious-faith-has-grown-amid-pandemic/.

Goodman, Bryan. "Faith in a Time of Crisis." *American Psychological Association*, May 11, 2020. https://www.apa.org/topics/covid-19/faith-crisis.

Gurvich, Caroline, Natalie Thomas, Elizabeth H.X. Thomas, Abdul-Rahman Hudaib, Lomash Sood, Kali Fabiatos, Keith Sutton, et al. "Coping Styles and Mental Health in Response to Societal Changes During the COVID-19 Pandemic." *International Journal of Social Psychiatry* 67, no. 5 (August 2021): 540–549. https://doi.org/10.1177/0020764020961790.

Harris, Michelle A., M. Brent Donnellan, and Kali H. Trzesniewski. "The Lifespan Self-Esteem Scale: Initial Validation of a New Measure of Global Self-Esteem." *Journal of Personality Assessment* 100, no. 1 (January 2, 2018): 84–95. https://doi.org/10.1080/00223891.2016.1278380.

Heffer, Taylor, and Teena Willoughby. "A Count of Coping Strategies: A Longitudinal Study Investigating an Alternative Method to Understanding Coping and Adjustment." Edited by Scott McDonald. *PLOS ONE* 12, no. 10 (October 5, 2017): e0186057. https://doi.org/10.1371/journal.pone.0186057.

Hodge, David R., Tarek Zidan, and Altaf Husain. "Depression Among Muslims in the

United States: Examining the Role of Discrimination and Spirituality as Risk and Protective Factors: Table 1." *Social Work* 61, no. 1 (January 2016): 45–52. https://doi.org/10.1093/sw/swv055.

Ibrahim, Arwa. "Praying in Time of COVID-19: How World's Largest Mosques Adapted." *Al Jazeera*, April 6, 2020. https://www.aljazeera.com/news/2020/4/6/praying-in-time-of-covid-19-how-worlds-largest-mosques-adapted.

Jenkins, Richard A., and Kenneth I. Pargament. "Religion and Spirituality as Resources for Coping with Cancer." *Journal of Psychosocial Oncology* 13, no. 1–2 (August 15, 1995): 51–74. https://doi.org/10.1300/J077V13N01_04.

Kar, Sujita Kumar, S.M. Yasir Arafat, Russell Kabir, Pawan Sharma, and Shailendra K. Saxena. "Coping with Mental Health Challenges During COVID-19." In *Coronavirus Disease 2019 (COVID-19)*, 199–213. Singapore: Springer, 2020.

Koenig, Harold G. "Maintaining Health and Well-Being by Putting Faith into Action During the COVID-19 Pandemic." *Journal of Religion and Health* 59, no. 5 (October 2020): 2205–2214. https://doi.org/10.1007/s10943-020-01035-2.

Kroenke, Kurt, Robert L. Spitzer, and Janet B.W. Williams. "The Patient Health Questionnaire-2: Validity of a Two-Item Depression Screener." *Medical Care* 41, no. 11 (November 2003): 1284–1292. https://doi.org/10.1097/01.MLR.0000093487.78664.3C.

Lim, Chaeyoon, and Robert D. Putnam. "Religion, Social Networks, and Life Satisfaction." *American Sociological Review* 75, no. 6 (December 2010): 914–933. https://doi.org/10.1177/0003122410386686.

Loewenthal, Kate Miriam, Marco Cinnirella, Georgina Evdoka, and Paula Murphy. "Faith Conquers All? Beliefs about the Role of Religious Factors in Coping with Depression Among Different Cultural-Religious Groups in the UK." *British Journal of Medical Psychology* 74, no. 3 (September 2001): 293–303. https://doi.org/10.1348/000711201160993.

Loue, Sana. *Handbook of Religion and Spirituality in Social Work Practice and Research.* New York: Springer, 2017.

Memish, Ziad A., Yusuf Ahmed, Saleh A. Alqahtani, and Shahul H. Ebrahim. "Pausing Superspreader Events for COVID-19 Mitigation: International Hajj Pilgrimage Cancellation." *Travel Medicine and Infectious Disease* 36 (July 2020): 101817. https://doi.org/10.1016/j.tmaid.2020.101817.

Mertens, Gaëtan, Lotte Gerritsen, Stefanie Duijndam, Elske Salemink, and Iris M. Engelhard. "Fear of the Coronavirus (COVID-19): Predictors in an Online Study Conducted in March 2020." *Journal of Anxiety Disorders* 74 (August 2020): 102258. https://doi.org/10.1016/j.janxdis.2020.102258.

Minkov, Michael, and Geert Hofstede. "A Replication of Hofstede's Uncertainty Avoidance Dimension Across Nationally Representative Samples from Europe." *International Journal of Cross Cultural Management* 14, no. 2 (August 2014): 161–171. https://doi.org/10.1177/1470595814521600.

Nguyen, Ann W., Robert Joseph Taylor, Linda M. Chatters, Aaron Ahuvia, Elif Izberk-Bilgin, and Fiona Lee. "Mosque-Based Emotional Support Among Young Muslim Americans." *Review of Religious Research* 55, no. 4 (December 2013): 535–555. https://doi.org/10.1007/s13644-013-0119-0.

Panchal, Nirmita, Rabah Kamal, Cynthia Cox, and Rachel Garfield. "The Implication of COVID-19 for Mental Health and Substance Use." *KFF*, February 10, 2021. https://www.kff.org/coronavirus-covid-19/issue-brief/the-implications-of-covid-19-for-mental-health-and-substance-use/.

Pargament, Kenneth I., Bruce W. Smith, Harold G. Koenig, and Lisa Perez. "Patterns of Positive and Negative Religious Coping with Major Life Stressors." *Journal for the Scientific Study of Religion* 37, no. 4 (December 1998): 710. https://doi.org/10.2307/1388152.

Pew Research Center. "A Religious Portrait of African-Americans." January 30, 2009. https://www.pewforum.org/2009/01/30/a-religious-portrait-of-african-americans/.

Pirutinsky, Steven, Aaron D. Cherniak, and David H. Rosmarin. "COVID-19, Mental Health, and Religious Coping Among American Orthodox Jews." *Journal of Religion and Health* 59, no. 5 (October 2020): 2288–2301. https://doi.org/10.1007/s10943-020-01070-z.

Quadri, Sayed A. "COVID-19 and Religious Congregations: Implications for Spread of Novel Pathogens." *International Journal of Infectious Diseases* 96 (July 2020): 219–221. https://doi.org/10.1016/j.ijid.2020.05.007.

Rahman, Nargis. "Mosques Go Virtual During a COVID-19 Ramadan." Michigan Radio, May 21, 2020. https://www.michiganradio.org/families-community/2020-05-21/mosques-go-virtual-during-a-covid-19-ramadan.

Rettie, Hannah, and Jo Daniels. "Coping and Tolerance of Uncertainty: Predictors and Mediators of Mental Health During the COVID-19 Pandemic." *American Psychologist* 76, no. 3 (April 2021): 427–437. https://doi.org/10.1037/amp0000710.

Salari, Nader, Amin Hosseinian-Far, Rostam Jalali, Aliakbar Vaisi-Raygani, Shna Rasoulpoor, Masoud Mohammadi, Shabnam Rasoulpoor, and Behnam Khaledi-Paveh. "Prevalence of Stress, Anxiety, Depression Among the General Population During the COVID-19 Pandemic: A Systematic Review and Meta-Analysis." *Globalization and Health* 16, no. 1 (December 2020): 57. https://doi.org/10.1186/s12992-020-00589-w.

Satici, Begum, Mehmet Saricali, Seydi Ahmet Satici, and Mark D. Griffiths. "Intolerance of Uncertainty and Mental Wellbeing: Serial Mediation by Rumination and Fear of COVID-19." *International Journal of Mental Health and Addiction*, May 15, 2020. https://doi.org/10.1007/s11469-020-00305-0.

Smith, Brooke M., Alexander J. Twohy, and Gregory S. Smith. "Psychological Inflexibility and Intolerance of Uncertainty Moderate the Relationship between Social Isolation and Mental Health Outcomes During COVID-19." *Journal of Contextual Behavioral Science* 18 (October 2020): 162–174. https://doi.org/10.1016/j.jcbs.2020.09.005.

Spitzer, Robert L., Kurt Kroenke, Janet B.W. Williams, and Bernd Löwe. "A Brief Measure for Assessing Generalized Anxiety Disorder: The GAD-7." *Archives of Internal Medicine* 166, no. 10 (May 22, 2006): 1092. https://doi.org/10.1001/archinte.166.10.1092.

Stainback, Kevin, Brittany N. Hearne, and Monica M. Trieu. "COVID-19 and the 24/7 News Cycle: Does COVID-19 News Exposure Affect Mental Health?" *Socius: Sociological Research for a Dynamic World* 6 (January 2020): 237802312096933. https://doi.org/10.1177/2378023120969339.

Thomas, Justin, and Mariapaola Barbato. "Positive Religious Coping and Mental Health Among Christians and Muslims in Response to the COVID-19 Pandemic." *Religions* 11, no. 10 (September 29, 2020): 498. https://doi.org/10.3390/rel11100498.

Umarji, Osman, and Hassan Elwan. "Embracing Uncertainty: How to Feel Emotionally Stable in a Pandemic." Yaqeen Institute for Islamic Research, March 30, 2020. https://yaqeeninstitute.org/read/paper/embracing-uncertainty-how-to-feel-emotionally-stable-in-a-pandemic.

Umarji, Osman, Hassan Elwan, and Mustafa Umar. "A Punishment or a Mercy? What We Can Learn From COVID-19." Yaqeen Institute for Islamic Research, April 14, 2020. https://yaqeeninstitute.org/osman-umarji/a-punishment-or-a-mercy-what-we-can-learn-from-the-coronavirus/.

Umucu, Emre, and Beatrice Lee. "Examining the Impact of COVID-19 on Stress and Coping Strategies in Individuals with Disabilities and Chronic Conditions." *Rehabilitation Psychology* 65, no. 3 (August 2020): 193–198. https://doi.org/10.1037/rep0000328.

Victorson, David, Vered Hankin, James Burns, Rebecca Weiland, Carly Maletich, Nathaniel Sufrin, Stephanie Schuette, Bruriah Gutierrez, and Charles Brendler. "Feasibility, Acceptability and Preliminary Psychological Benefits of Mindfulness Meditation Training in a Sample of Men Diagnosed with Prostate Cancer on Active Surveillance: Results from a Randomized Controlled Pilot Trial: Mindfulness and Active Surveillance." *Psycho-Oncology* 26, no. 8 (August 2017): 1155–1163. https://doi.org/10.1002/pon.4135.

Wang, Sherry C., Aysha H. Raja, and Sabreen Azhar. "'A Lot of Us Have a Very Difficult Time Reconciling What Being Muslim Is': A Phenomenological Study on the Meaning of Being Muslim American." *Cultural Diversity and Ethnic Minority Psychology* 26, no. 3 (July 2020): 338–346. https://doi.org/10.1037/cdp0000297.

World Health Organization. "Depression and Other Common Mental Disorders: Global Health Estimates." Geneva: World Health Organization, 2017. WHO IRIS. https://apps.who.int/iris/handle/10665/254610.

Zauzmer Weil, Julie. "Ramadan During Coronavirus: A Holiday Like None Before It." *Washington Post*, April 22, 2020. https://www.washingtonpost.com/religion/2020/04/22/washingtons-muslim-community-begins-ramadan-like-no-other/.

CHAPTER 6

African-American Muslims' Reflections on the Pandemic

Diane Ameena Mitchell

1 Introduction

Watching the news and talking to friends and family, I began to think about how this COVID-19 pandemic is affecting the average person's thoughts and behaviors. I realized that the uncertainty of the present and of the immediate future influences people in ways not talked about in the public media. As I read more or watched more news, I became concerned because they were not reporting the coronavirus statistics about African Americans, and particularly African-American Muslims who were at risk. I was and continue to be wary of the advice about how to navigate life amid a pandemic because it does not always reflect the lifestyles of the marginalized. The news stories that were published tell about how COVID-19 stripped bare the ongoing disparities in areas such as healthcare, housing, and food availability for minorities. The media told many stories about the pandemic experiences of people, but the human-interest stories did not initially reflect the lived experiences of African-American Muslim families.

The aim of this article is to highlight the experiences and reactions of a small group of African-American Muslims living in the United States in the pandemic in the context of technology, food, housing, healthcare, and religion. I had informal phone conversations with each of seven African-American Muslims, four males and three females, ranging from 34 to the 70+ years old. I asked each of them questions about their personal experiences regarding areas where disparities for minorities exist. As they navigated their daily lives in the COVID-19 pandemic and its mutants, conversations with them reflected how food shopping, healthcare, housing, and religious practice changed because of the pandemic. I did not apply a formal methodology to these informal conversations, although they were directed toward specific questions and topics, and respondents' answers were placed inside of contextual information about disparities for minorities and the pandemic.

 | DOI:10.1163/9789004679771_008

2 Attending to Spiritual Matters

During the height of COVID from March to June 2020, rumors, mistruth on news and social media, and miscommunication from usually reliable government and international sources such as the Centers for Disease Control and Prevention (CDC) and the World Health Organization (WHO) meant that advice about the virus, how it spread and how to protect against it, changed constantly. Public health officials publicly cautioned about contact with other persons not living in one's household as contact with infected individuals was suspected as a major way of contracting the disease. American families along with at-home quarantines faced restrictions on gatherings.[1]

Initially, because houses of worship were considered as venues that brought many persons in contact with each other, the closing of mosques and other places of worship as part of COVID-19 shutdown was mandated or recommended in most states in the early spring 2020.[2] Later, in the fall 2020, limited worship gatherings were permitted, but restrictions required that only a few congregate at one time, and additional restrictions were in place about the use of face coverings and social distancing. Mosques and other places of worship were placed in the same category as other social outlets regarding openings and the number of people in the space, Later, the number of people that could gather changed again as new cases surged.

The closing of mosques as part of the mitigation efforts to curb the spread of COVID-19 was expressed by several interviewees as the worst effect of the pandemic on their religious worship. As one respondent said, Muslims seemed to be going "backwards" in how they practiced their faith. The Prophet began Islam in homes, and it grew into communities where the mosque was the focal point. Now, Muslims were forced to revert to doing everything religious/spiritual at home.

> I think if the prophet was alive right now I think he would say, "It's good … that you want to be in person, but right now for the sake of everybody you should stay in your houses", and at the same time spiritually it hurts

1 Adam Ferrise, "50 States of Coronavirus: How Every State in the U.S. has Responded to the Pandemic," *Cleveland.com*, March 21, 2020, accessed July 21, 2021, https://www.cleveland.com/metro/2020/03/50-states-of-coronavirus-how-every-state-in-the-us-has-responded-to-the-pandemic.html.

2 Saranac Hale Spencer, "Stay-at-Home Policies Treat Mosques Same as Churches," *FactCheck.org*, April 30, 2020, accessed July 21, 2021, https://www.factcheck.org/2020/04/stay-at-home-policies-treat-mosques-same-as-churches/.

> because at the time Islam started everyone was practicing in their homes in secret and we did that 180 [degree] turn ... and we are back to practicing Islam in our houses and not being a community. (Male, 34 years old)

Many found themselves wandering, questioning, and looking for answers about how to practice religious obligations traditionally done at the mosque or in religious gatherings. Questions and concerns were raised as to what could be practiced in one's home or virtually, and what practices must be done in congregation.

This was perplexing and frustrating for those who made daily prayers in congregation at the mosque or attended weekly religious classes because, interestingly, as other venues were permitted to reopen based on them providing essential services, religious gatherings were not included.

> everything I can, I am just doing it virtually ... Religiously, I think everyone from that is from this [State], you couldn't go to a gathering. So, you were forced to be virtual whether you wanted to or not ... going to Facebook to see if this masjid is streaming. (Female, 37 years old)

Interviewees indicated that saying their obligatory prayers in a timely manner was difficult. For one respondent, monitoring time was difficult.

> I don't sleep at the right times, you know. Making prayers on time. But once I was, then once I've decided this was a reckoning and, in many ways ... answers to lots of prayers that many myself and others had made, I settled. (Female, 70+ years old)

Finding time to make prayers became a dilemma for another respondent because colleagues presumed that unscheduled time during the workday meant time was available for work tasks such as virtual meetings.

> I would say just the whole virtualness I mean you would think that hey, I work from home now having time or having the opportunity to pray would have been at top of the list, but now everyone is like, "Oh, you're not [doing] anything. You're moving about the office. You must be free because of one hour of time you have." I am just saying that from the spiritual perspective to make sure you turn to the switch you know to make sure that you're getting the time you need. (Male, 39 years old)

When asked about changes in their obligations and traditions in Islam, interviewees generally agreed that the inability to participate in congregational prayers was the major change. "I would say, mainly Jumaat, going to the masjid because it is not accessible right now … that is the main one right now" (Male, 41 years old).

These circumstances caused many in the Muslim community to think about what was obligatory in congregation and what could be done without being in the mosque. Scholars, imams, and Muslims in general debated the efficacy of virtual religious services and worship practices. For example, ethico-legal debates around the religious permissibility of virtual religious worship practices centered on: Does it count? If not, then what is the recourse? For one interviewee, there was a question as to whether there was validity in participating in virtual rituals.

> Fundamental to worship for me as a Muslim is performing prayers in a congregational setting as much as five times a day. With most houses of worship being closed or in the alternative limited accessibility during the week … These times of these prayers would ordinarily take place during the day. This pandemic altered how valid that one of those aspects of worship is in terms of the fundamental one in praying, but it also is because for a lot of activities, as with many faith traditions, the house of worship itself is a focal point not only for direct worship but also for say social activities as well as volunteer activities, and all those have been curtailed right now. To the extent that they still do occur it's primarily by Zoom. (Male, 69 years old)

For another participant, the obligatory prayers made her aware of the importance of prayer.

> a couple of things became important to me during the pandemic … number one, like meditation is important … people describe it as different things but praying five time a day is a form of my meditation. I believe it is a form of meditation. A lot of things changed for me from my perspective a lot when I started meditating, so I was able to validate the importance of prayer because before meditation, and as you go throughout the day, there's so many things that come at you, knock you off your game, and you need that checkpoint to be like let's reset and have a clear mind to attack the next part of the day. (Female, 38 years old)

Virtual *Jumuʿa* prayers, classes, courses, and general talks were set up quickly. Women found more religious classes were available through technology and those sermons were easier to follow because sound and view were better. Interestingly, female respondents, although they missed contact with the Muslim community found virtual Friday prayers and religious classes helpful in fortifying them spiritually.

> As a female, I wasn't going to the Masjid anyway ... So that didn't change much, but as time wore on and various places began to have more activities on line, I listened and I enjoyed that there's people, more women ... but I also know women began to have classes online and seminars or webinars so I could avail myself of that and you don't have to worry about, oh, you gotta fly to someplace or is close enough for you to drive. You didn't have to worry about those things anymore. (Female, 70+ years old)

Interviewees were using technology to participate also in other religious activities. One interviewee mentioned that there were more religious programs available online since the pandemic hit. She was also surprised that the *khutbah*s did not address and help community members cope with these unprecedented events of 2020.

> there were just too many. So, you were choosing between things all the time, like one of these series that was on about the Black Companions of the Prophet Muhammad. I was determined I was going to listen to and any other thing that came on, I nixed it. You know there were some things that were almost once in a lifetime thing. So, I made sure I turned into ... one of the things that I found so interesting was that imams didn't make a switch to the pandemic. You, know, they were still giving *khutbah*s ... but they weren't giving guidance, you know. They were like the federal government. They didn't give any guidance on how to cope ... They didn't talk directly about the pandemic, but they should've given guidance you know in these days and times—let us think about, you know, this, that, the other, you know, but they [weren't] doing that. (Female, +70 years)

Virtual listeners could focus intently on what was being said. This situation also gave many Muslims the opportunity to hear a diversity of talks and enroll in many classes. It also provided women-led talks and classes, which would not have happened in person-to person circumstances.

The gradual reopening of mosques has had few guidelines from the government regarding when to reopen and how many people could gather. As previously stated, quarantines and restrictions turned the many Islamic traditions and rituals topsy turvy. This was evident in the restrictions imposed on Eid prayers and in-person community Eid celebrations in 2020 and now in 2021.

Ramadan began in the third week of April 2020. Traditionally, cultural and family celebrations centered on gathering for meals and prayers, but obligations and traditions changed in the pandemic since families from more than one household and members of mosques could not come together due to COVID-19 group restrictions. Eid was celebrated but as one participant indicated she became aware that Eid without the religious traditions was treated more like a "secular holiday" rather than an Islamic religious celebration even more during the pandemic: "it did make me, for example, think about Eid. What we are supposed to be celebrating and seeing so many of those around me turning Eid into Christmas" (Female, 70+ years old).

Virtual attempts at cultural and family traditional activities suffered from mosques and members' lack of technological skills and equipment. Participants said their traditions were modified by using virtual methods rather than face-to-face. One participant explained how the celebration of the birth of her baby was impacted by the pandemic.

> We did have the intention of having a micro, a little like actual *aqeeqah* [celebration for the birth and naming of a newborn], right. Invite people, but we just did like the overseas part (naming the baby officially) [with], like his [husband's] family [by phone] … We did have a time for *duʿāʾ* for the child. We did that part, but that was virtual, and then my mother and father joined in via phone [too]. (Female, 37 years old)

To add to the frustration, technical difficulties often stopped or cut short many virtual sessions. Lack of adequate technological equipment and internet access of presenters and audiences created difficulties that made virtual congregational gatherings many times frustrating.

3 Healthcare

The historical memory of abuse and ongoing presence of mistrust, lack of information, and racial discrimination complicates many African Americans' relationship with the healthcare system. Many patients of color come to a medical system already wary of the use of minorities historically as medical guinea pigs for various diseases and drugs and the racial stereotypes that characterize African Americans as patients with high pain tolerance and inability to understand medical diagnoses and treatments. Along with general racial biases that play an important role in instilling a lack of confidence in doctors and hospitals, many African Americans perceive the presence of a power differential between patient and medical personnel.[3]

In the context of a pandemic, how did respondents manage medical self-care or self-advocacy when healthcare was previously set on a routine schedule as attested to by an interviewee who was staying healthy by visiting their doctors and doing the prescribed tests?

> Well, with healthcare, oh a year before starting, about I guess two and half or almost three years ago, we have started as we're winding down to retirement. In return, I started to try to get as much of our healthcare stuff straightened out as much as possible. Colonoscopies and this and that and the other we had done before the pandemic hit. (Female, +70 years old)

Appointments to see the doctor or dentist, to get eyes checked for glasses, and taking various medical routine tests were delayed or avoided because of the pandemic.

> I would say the visits are not as frequent like I would have problems that I would've wanted my dentist about because of COVID and the fear, concern about possibly contracting it because of the close contact and liquids and stuff, I delayed it. So, I think it has to some extent compromised personal healthcare and my healthcare because of concerns about catching it. (Male, 69 years old)

> I had been putting off getting my eyes checked for the forever and then pandemic came and like oh great now I can't go get my eyes checked so that really like hit home that I should've did it when I had opportunity to and I finally did go get my eyes checked. (Female, 38 years old)

During this pandemic, in-person medical appointments were limited because of the precautions a medical office takes to prevent patients' exposure to coronavirus. One respondent explained how doctor's visits to check on a pregnancy, usually viewed with anticipation and joy turned into stressful events.

3 Ana Sandoiu, "Racial Inequalities in Covid-19: The Impact on Black Communities," *Medical News Today*, June 5, 2020, accessed July 22, 2021, https://www.medicalnewstoday.com/articles/racial-inequalities-in-covid-19-the-impact-on-black-communities.

> I mean I was pregnant. So, when I go I don't know … There is a picture you can hear heartbeat again you know something kind of fun. And it kind of something a bit more stressful, right? I had to wear my mask and wear my gloves this time, I have like disinfectant sprays. I have the hand sanitizer when you get in there the whole time you're thinking I have to be six feet apart from everybody. With their masks, like they are really going to stop anything if they are breathing next to you? … I mean even if they like take your blood pressure, they can't even be six feet from you … if you have a machine next to you and someone is standing next to the machine reading machine and then you are worried about if they have air circulating or why is the door shut all the way. (Female, 37 years old)

For some of the interviewees, in-person medical visits switched immediately to telehealth. A routine, in-person visit to the doctor usually involved consultation about the patient's health status and the doctor answering the patient's questions regarding diagnosis. Drug prescriptions are written by the doctor for the period between visits. The apprehension of medical staff and patients possibly infecting each other with the coronavirus led to routine virtual visits. Virtual appointments according to interviewees helped them stay in contact with their doctors and keep an eye out for any medical emergencies. A couple of interviewees indicated that they preferred the virtual visits because checking in with their doctor for the sole purpose of refills was much easier online than traveling physically to the doctor's office.

> A lot of things I was able to do by telehealth. So, I was able to have healthcare that allows me to see a doctor remotely. So, a lot of my health plans have gone from in person to remote. And that's a positive for me because having to get up and go to a doctor and check in even if it is for a consult or drug refill. That is a lot easier to have a remote session than it is to go in to get a prescription update. (Male, 34 years old)

> I find it actually more convenient that I don't have to get up and like leave to have a talk. I say like "I'll be back in an hour" and have my therapy session and then be back in the mix. (Female, 38 years old)

For others not so fortunate, many African Americans do not manage their health through the healthcare system unless absolutely necessary. Factors such as the complexities of the American health insurance system,[4] accessibility of

4 Healthcare disparities are obscured by the health insurance system in the United States. The

convenient medical consultations, diagnoses and treatments from websites are also critical in assessing the state of healthcare. Many families resorted to the use of herbal or folk remedies or procedures to diagnose and treat what they hoped will be minor illnesses. Sometimes, beginning chronic conditions that could have been contained had subsequently become emergencies.

Interviewees explained that their interests in homeopathic medicine was sparked by the realization that they must be aware of their own responsibility for treatment of their body's needs. In monitoring their health, homeopathic medicine helped.

> my perception of healthcare has changed and then another thing is that I really been looking a lot into just like homeopathic medicine and more, so natural medicine like provincial oil things like that. I've been studying a lot on using what is available to us to heal ourselves such as food exactly. Like I'm so concerned about making sure we eat the right stuff because diet is so important as well as we getting enough water. And so, if my son has headache, I'm like, "Like, all those things need to be checked off before I could go hand you the Tylenol." The pandemic has changed my perception of like my ability to heal myself ... I'm not saying that doctors aren't important but my common sense I know my body better than somebody else. (Female, 38 years old)

4 Housing

Although many families lived in multigenerational homes for a variety of reasons before, the pandemic increased the number doing so.[5] Families were motivated to include grandparents and/or children to their households during the pandemic for a variety of reasons, the most important of which became survival.[6] Many African-American multigenerational households not only live

---

system is based on "fee-for services" model meaning every service has a separate charge for which the patient is responsible. With health insurance, the patient is usually responsible for partial payments and/or full payments of services depending upon the contractual plan purchased. Plans with the most expensive premiums cover more services, and the patient has less out-of-pocket costs.

5 AARP, "Drivers and Barriers to Living in a Multigenerational Household: Pre-COVID–Mid-COVID," September 2020, accessed on July 26, 2021, https://www.aarp.org/content/dam/aarp/research/surveys_statistics/liv-com/2021/drivers-barriers-living-in-multigenerational-household-report.doi.10.26419-2Fres.00414.002.pdf.

6 AARP, "Drivers and Barriers to Living in a Multigenerational Household."

in homes designed for multigenerational occupants but also in homes, apartments, or mobile homes designed for nuclear families. External factors such as financial instability, care of grandchildren, or care of aging parents drive the decision for several generations to live under one roof.[7] A large percentage of Muslim families in the United States were multigenerational because of the Islamic tradition of children taking special care of parents and elderly relations.[8] These configurations also dictate the possibilities for how families who have to quarantine a member follow orders.

For some families under quarantine orders, the physical structure of the home allowed for private spaces for members of the household, and families occupied different levels or sections of a house. For these households, preventing COVID-19 from spreading in the home was easier than in households where family members shared common areas such as bedrooms, bathrooms, the living rooms and television/family rooms. The danger of spreading COVID-19 to elderly and infirmed members of a household increased when spaces served multiple functions such as a living room or family room doubling as a sleeping area at night.[9] Many families in these circumstances just ignored medical advice about quarantining but wore masks.

African-American Muslims experienced the same challenges that many multigenerational families experienced with limited living space. They were aware of their obligations to parents and elderly relations, but for many African-American Muslims, multigenerational living arrangements with family members came with an additional challenge of maneuvering differences in religious practices and dietary considerations between Muslim and non-Muslim members of the household.[10] Moving in with or allowing non-Muslim relations to reside in Muslim households led to difficult familial disagreements and arguments centering on religious beliefs and practices. It was for many an emotional dilemma as they toggled between what is perceived as Qurʾanic rules and familial obligations. Many forgo the usual experience of warmth and close contact of intergenerational living and arrange, when they can, to use regular visits and

7 D'Vera Cohn and Jeffrey S. Passell, "Record 64 Million Americans Live in Multigenerational Households," Pew Research Center, April 5, 2018, accessed July 25, 2021, https://www.pewresearch.org/fact-tank/2018/04/05/a-record-64-million-americans-live-in-multigenerational-households/.

8 Cohn and Passell, "Record 64 Million Americans Live in Multigenerational Households."

9 Laura Bliss and Lorena Rios, "Tracing the Invisible Danger of Household Crowding," *Bloomberg*, July 21, 2020, accessed July 26, 2021, https://www.bloomberg.com/news/articles/2020-07-21/gentrification-and-crowding-boost-covid-19-risk.

10 Cohn and Passell, "Record 64 Million Americans Live in Multigenerational Households."

telephone calls, video calls, or chats to care for elderly parents, which was often not enough.

Significant numbers of African-American families live in racially segregated urban and suburban areas where unhealthy environmental factors impact residents' health. The physical structures are only marginally sound and, in many cases, in need of basic repairs to utilities like plumbing and electricity. Some communities like Flint, Michigan suffer from lead and carcinogens infested water that is not usable for bathing or drinking directly from the spigot. More urban residents suffer from respiratory ailments from smoke and the fumes of transport vehicles. All of these factors impact how well urban and suburban residents prevent and fight COVID-19.[11]

Before the pandemic, renters who live in structurally poor houses or apartments usually also have pests such as rodents and insects, and struggled not to fall behind on paying the rent.[12] While monthly rents are increased, landlords frequently choose to or struggle to provide minimal maintenance of the property even though in some cities such as Chicago, ordinances have been imposed on landlords to make sure that they minimally care for the maintenance of the property. Missed mortgage payments threaten the security of shelter because foreclosures and evictions are initiated when repeatedly missed mortgage payments or monthly rent payments occur. As the pandemic set in, although some relief for past payments for shelter is being provided by state and local governments, mortgage payments remain recurring monthly costs.[13] With the uncertainty of how much income will be made in a household each month because of the declining economy, many Americans including African-American Muslims are always living on the edge of home foreclosure or eviction.[14]

Interestingly, interviewees who owned their homes did not address this issue directly. Those who were renting their homes did discuss the difference in costs before and during the pandemic. The renters were at different stages in the renting experience. It ranged from planning to move to another house to no intention of moving. However, all of them had comments about how their renting arrangements could be better.

---

11 Eugene Scott, "Analysis: 4 Reasons Coronavirus is Hitting Black Communities so Hard," *The Washington Post*, August 10, 2020, accessed July 26, 2021, https://www.washingtonpost.com/politics/2020/04/10/4-reasons-coronavirus-is-hitting-black-communities-so-hard/.

12 Jaboa Lake, "The Pandemic has Exacerbated Housing Instability for Renters of Color," Center for American Progress, October 30, 2020, accessed July 26, 2020, https://www.americanprogress.org/article/pandemic-exacerbated-housing-instability-renters-color/.

13 Scott, "Analysis: 4 Reasons Coronavirus is Hitting Black Communities so Hard."

14 Scott, "Analysis: 4 Reasons Coronavirus is Hitting Black Communities so Hard."

For one interviewee, there were plans to move out of the rented house before the pandemic began. As the pandemic unfurled, the lease expired, and plans to move to another city were abandoned when the interviewee lost his job. He moved in with his parents. Another interviewee also planned to move, but the pandemic stopped their search for a new house. They planned to terminate their lease because the present house is barely up to code. Because of the pandemic, they decided to continue renting the home until the circumstances are better.

> if any [of] this hadn't happened, we would have moved. But, I mean, because of the pandemic we ended up extending the lease for the house we feel uncomfortable in. Uncomfortable because of some of the things about the house that aren't as good as they could be. I want to say up to the code 'cause they're probably at the code but they're not the best. The landlord is not the greatest. I mean not even the neighbors. You wonder whether they are racist or if I believe it's they are more resentful because they, you know, see the upgrades we've done for our cars or the deliveries that we get during, you know, things like that and just creates an uncomfortable situation. (Female, 37 years old)

One renter had no plans to move but noticed that his rent schedule did not change even though the demand for apartments in his building had decreased. There had been no adjustment in the rent increase or decrease since the pandemic began.

> Rent has stayed the same. It's not like it went down even through there is less demand. Where I am at. So, the housing renting prices have not changed. I stay in the same apartment before the pandemic, after the pandemic. I pay the same way. I am not actually in a rent control apartment; so regardless I don't think this is going to affect me much. And I think they are reluctant to go down on the rent. I don't think housing is an issue. And luckily being in a privileged situation, I still have my job that I am working remotely and so, even though bills have shifted left to right, left to right, there is still that stability that I have, the foundation of paying for rent with my job. (Male, 34 years old)

5 Food and Shopping

As fears about the uncertainty of the pandemic grew, shoppers emptied grocery store shelves and created shortages of products that were readily available before the pandemic. Because of the hoarding, demand increased for basic food items and cleaning supplies and, consequently, prices increased. COVID-19 illnesses among manufacturing and trucking personnel, and logistical problems created a serious back-ordering of supplies in brick and mortar and online stores. Small stores, unable to restock inventory, gradually closed. For Muslims, the closing of small grocery stores made shopping unusually difficult because these stores provide halal meat and poultry.

Amid the pandemic, trying to follow the guidelines for a healthy diet to fight illness and fortify the immune system in communities where healthy food access means traveling outside of the community became a daily struggle without local access to healthy foods. A healthy diet that includes at the least the FDA daily requirements for vitamins, minerals, and proteins is necessary for good management of chronic diseases such as diabetes, heart disease, hypertension, and high cholesterol. Persons suffering from infectious diseases such as colds and flus benefit from the consumption of vegetables, fruits, and lean protein as their bodies combat the infections.

The level of stress about finding and affording healthy food was elevated because most African-American Muslims live in communities commonly called "food deserts." Food deserts are communities in which stores do not sell a variety of reasonably priced fresh produce and healthy food products. In some communities, stores selling food products that are high sugar and/or fat, low in nutrition, and laden with chemicals are common. If a large supermarket exists in the community, it is less likely to sell healthier food choices and fresh produce or, if it does, they cost more than community members can afford. More often, the supermarket stocks produce and food products that are near the end of their shelf life. Supermarkets that carry better and healthier food products are usually located outside of the community and are not readily accessible by public transportation, and so, are nearly impossible to reach unless one can afford private transportation.[15]

The convenience of less than fresh, semi-healthy food choices further complicated limited mealtimes because of distance learning for all grade levels,

15 Andy Weisbecker, "Few Healthy Food Choices in Urban Food Deserts," *Food Safety News*, May 21, 2010, accessed July 28, 2021, https://www.foodsafetynews.com/2010/05/few-healthy-food-choices-in-urban-food-deserts/.

working from home, and dealing with other issues resulting from the pandemic. In these circumstances, African-American Muslims turned to already prepared foods as a quick alternative as they sought non-pork and halal foods. Many restaurants with healthy menu choices were located outside of African-American communities.[16] So, the option is, when the money is available, to get meals without meat. Many delivery options were non-options for African Americans as restauranteurs were hesitant to deliver to these neighborhoods because of distance and stereotypes about the locales' crime and violence.

Food insecurity, not being sure if one would have enough food for the day, the week, or month, was becoming more prevalent in many communities during the pandemic, including African-American ones.[17] There are community and social services sponsored food pantries, but these places indicate that their food supplies are running low due to the increased demand. News media reported in Louisiana that cars started lining up in the early morning to receive food baskets from local food pantries.[18] Billboards along highways pleaded with motorists to donate food items to their local food pantries.

Interviewees' experiences with food choices and shopping before and during the pandemic revealed two themes. First, the interviewees felt that they had the freedom to shop whenever and wherever they found the products and prices desired before the pandemic. Most interviewees indicated that they would go to different stores based on their preferences. A few of them mentioned buying in bulk for many things, while others stated that they ordered online and either had it delivered or picked it up.

When the pandemic hit, food shopping habits changed. For one respondent, it was a shock to see the shelves emptying and realizing there were shortages on common items like toilet paper.

> The one thing that happened that was happening across the nation was that panic buying food. I was also panicked buying food. We couldn't get toilet paper, so we didn't get toilet paper or anything. I was following the coronavirus a little before the outbreak and saw some of this stuff hap-

16 Megan Horst, Subhashni Raj, and Catherine Brinkley, "Getting Outside the Supermarket Box: Alternatives to 'Food Deserts,'" PDXScholar, January 1, 2016, https://pdxscholar.library.pdx.edu/usp_fac/191.

17 Tamara Dubowitz et al., "Food Insecurity in a Low-Income, Predominantly African American Cohort Following the COVID-19 Pandemic," *American Journal of Public Health* 3, no. 3 (2021): 494–497, https://doi.org/10.2015/ajph.2020.306041.

18 Matt Haines, "Pandemic Worsens 'Food Deserts' for 23.5 Million Americans," *VOA: Voice of America*, May 19, 2020, accessed July 28, 2021, https://www.voanews.com/a/usa_pandemic-worsens-food-deserts-235-million-americans/6189526.html.

> pening ahead of time, about two days ahead of time. That way I was able to get some food, but I was under the impression that this would last a week or two. I think a lot of Americans thought this would last a week or two and blow over. And so, pre-pandemic, I would buy less food, I would go out more and I would not worry about food but now you buy it in bulk because you want to limit the time you go out and you want to buy more food because you are eating more at home. I guess, the little difference of eating is less going to restaurants, less going to coffee shops, things like that. (Male, 34 years old)

For other respondents, pre-pandemic shopping habits helped to prepare them.

> food, we have mostly a schedule because we're buying halal meat and then we had a variety of places we would go to get fresh vegetables … so we had a nice little rhythm. When the pandemic hit, however, we looked to fill things up to the brim. Because we didn't know how long. We had always bought goods you know like toilet paper, paper towels, Lysol, and that stuff. I had in overdrive but then I decided you know not knowing how long it would last, I wasn't going to try to buy out the store but I was going to add to it a little bit and then I found very quickly, because people were hoarding that stuff, it ran out already in most of those areas. I already had a six-month supply and mostly because I'm lazy and I wasn't going shopping every five minutes. So, I tended to buy in bulk. (Female, +70 years old)

The stores were opened but going to the stores heightened the risk of being exposed to the coronavirus. Fear of being exposed to the virus changed shopping habits to ordering everything online, for those who had means, even for groceries not ordered that way before.

> I think, across the board, before the pandemic, there were more options, right. I mean you could go out, I mean, we've been blessed that we were able right, we have a car we can go like over here and tried different places to get the foods that you want … now with the pandemic we rely so much on delivery to reduce the amount of exposure or possible exposures to COVID as much as possible. I mean delivery options they are much more limited … but you use it for like everything. (Female, 37 years old)

Another way that food choices changed was what interviewees decided to put in their pantries and the cost to do so.

> It changed … It's just that there's not enough time today; there's always, you know, you have to prioritize and, for me, I feel like we probably spend way too much money on food at this point because I felt I had more time previously … I felt as if I had more time to be more thoughtful about like what we purchased each week and, you know, meal planning ahead of time and things like that.

During the pandemic, interviewees indicated that dining out was no longer an option for two reasons. One reason is that restaurants and coffee shops for a time were not open to the public to dine in. Once eating establishments reopened, the concern became being able to practice social distancing while dining out.

> [Before the pandemic] … there was a lot of more liberal in terms of eating out. More liberal in term of going to the store … I go to the store and buy for one day and it wouldn't be too much concern … shopping there were less shopping trips or it would be more myself or my wife going to the store by ourselves and then I would say after how it changed. There's very limited eating out, maybe once a week or less, going to the stores every two weeks and it's also a collective effort, so I drive, my wife, she'll do the shopping and then, you know, we will come back. As opposed to before, you know, I would just go whenever you feel like it. (Males 41 years old)

6 The Emotional Toll

At the beginning of the lockdown, there was the assumption that the pandemic and all the restrictions and havoc caused would end like a severe weather experience, and everything would return to "normal," but people's lives changed forever. Americans were placed under unprecedented stress in this last year and a half from supply shortages, fear of contracting the coronavirus, mistrust and misinformation about the virus, isolation from family, friends, and co-workers, and the increasing number of surges that lead to severe illness and death for too many. The mental health of many Americans waned while looking for assistance from a health system with a history of ignoring or stigmatizing those who suffer from mental illness.

African-American communities have suffered especially because the rate of cases, hospitalizations, and deaths from COVID-19 is much higher than it is for some other ethnic groups. In these communities, mental health is not a primary concern, although mental crises are prevalent. Taking care of one's mental health is not a priority because of the community's stigmatization of mental illness.

Muslims rely on their faith in Allah to help them deal with mental health, but the need for human intervention is most times lacking. Stigmatization in Muslim communities is derived from the idea that mental illness or crises are the result of a person's wrongdoing or thinking, and so is deserved, or the product of supernatural forces. In many Muslim cultures, a family that has a member with a mental illness is considered problematic and the young people unmarriageable because mental illness is hereditary.

As respondents talked about the pandemic, the emotional toll of the pandemic was evident. One interviewee described her feelings toward the pandemic as "a whole gamut of emotions." Respondents described the pandemic as "uncertainty," "the unknown," "eye opening," "shocking," "a reckoning," "apprehensive," "scary," and "challenging," as they explained how the pandemic impacted their daily lives and plans for the future.

For the interviewees, the pandemic created the worst of times because of the stress from the uncertainty of living in the pandemic and the fear for self and loved ones. Stress came in different forms. For some, it was stress related to social and political events as they saw how the establishment treated marginalized communities. For other respondents, the pandemic was an indication that the government values money and the economy over human lives.

> how much are we trading off economy for health? Right now, everybody is [saying] we want the economy to be good, we want to open things up for the economy, the idea of abstract numbers in the stock market is worth more than a human life you can see and touch. I mean, it's sad ... We chose to put economy over people, over life. (Male, 34 years old)

Reflections about marginalized communities struggling before the pandemic and now, trying to endure without strong community ties for help was a concern also.

> I think it helped to put a lot of focus on resources that weren't there previously ... a lot of people who are struggling, who didn't have money to go out and buy a whole lot of resources or stockpile. I feel it was a lot harder for people of color to do that. And because it might have impacted their potential to get infected ... Then also a lot of blue-collar workers are right there on the front line ... African Americans do not really have strong communities to lean on, so a lot of people are just out there by themselves trying to do it. (Male, 39 years old)

Along with forming new habits that evolve from no indoor-eating restaurants, social distancing, and wearing masks in public or when around non-household family members, some participants indicated that there were stressors that they struggled with daily. For example, working while children are in the house was one of the biggest stressors.

> It's not actual technology that makes it hard with the kids … our current normal is that I'm using this technology, or I have to have video on or at a minimum a speaker on, right, and then most of time a mic … When you have a kid running around in the background, well. (Female, 37 years old)

Another major stressor was the instability. The fact that things were changing rapidly, and there was no way of knowing since every day was different. It was difficult just to keep children involved and occupied while watching how much screen time they devoted to their day.

> I would say, technologically it's been harder on, I would say, on the kids mostly because there's less opportunity to socialize with friends 'cause we're worried about … spreading things around the virus or catching it. The other part is since you can't do that then you're also confined to keep yourself occupied and that could mean more screen time in some sense, so, that is a little bit challenging to keep everybody, you know, not using technology as a crutch to keep yourself occupied. (Male, 41 years old)

Another interviewee indicated that she was stressed by the fact that now, publicly expressing support of black lives and valuing human life by attending protests and rallies could risk her family's lives and health from COVID-19.

Most participants expressed feelings of anxiety and stress.

> I think emotionally it's not being around people, feeling isolated wanting to see family, can't see family, wanting to see friends, can't see friends. Wanting to delay the plans. Coronavirus broke out at the same time that my wife and I wanted to go on our anniversary trip and so we had to cancel that. But there is definitely a lot of emotional changes that come about as a result of the pandemic. (Male, 34 years old)

Stress was reflected in eating habits. Interviewees mentioned eating, drinking coffee, and smoking more.

> Emotionally, I think it snuck up on me. And I realized that I was drinking more soda, smoking more cigarettes. I think my sleep cycle went off because for a while I was scared to sleep long. Because I was listening to the news. What's next? What's next? And the fact that until this day, we can't locate my son. I didn't have a way with any stability to get to my brother who is by himself ... Not being able to at least say: are you ok? Was and still am very worried. (Female, 70+ years old)

Interviewees used technology for social activities when possible since in-person social activities slowed or halted because of the pandemic. Other interviewees socialize but not as much as before. "We do Kahoots! At work but definitely nothing on the personal side" (Male, 39 years old).

> Activities is [sic] pretty much null and void because what you would ordinarily do you're not doing any more, you know, there is no hanging out. (Male, 69 years old)

> Social activities have changed. Now I think we, my wife and I before were very reclusive. We would hang out with people like once a month, and now it's like once every two months, but now we have remote or video meeting or more calls with friends, and we reach out more virtually than we see in person. (Male, 34 years old)

> For social things, you know, like having family and friends or talking, I find Skype. You do videos, WhatsApp, Zoom, Google Meets, too. You do whatever works for that group. (Female, 37 years old)

> We have the family meeting, oh which is good, I mean, that's something we could have done even before the pandemic but it's kind of nice that we have been forced to do it, you know, to socialize basically. (Male, 41 years old)

Special events like births and anniversaries were not as joyful because they could not be shared personally with family and friends.

> I mean it kind of takes away from the whole experience. Like we were able to get my husband was able to be there but you miss out on everything like my mom wasn't there. My dad wasn't there. These are things, you know, you expect, especially how much I enjoyed for my first birth ... To an extent, it did take away a bit of the joy of the experience, I mean,

> of course, you're happy and very emotional once you finally holding your baby, you see your baby but it's not the same as here you have like your full support group there with you. (Female, 37 years old)

Hospital stays, even if they were not based on the coronavirus, still isolated the person from family and friends.

> the whole part for giving birth in the hospital is all different. I came in two hours early. I had to get their coronavirus test, which is horrible because they stick the thing up your nose, all the way up your sinuses. So that your first welcome to the hospital. You get your temperature taken and then they give you the COVID test and then you know you go through the whole process. I had a C-section [Cesarean] everybody who you meet, the doctor, everybody has their masks on or it was a range of between a face mask and full PPE outfit. You know everything started to relax a bit more once my test finally came back that I didn't have COVID. It was the anxiety in the whole process. First of all, it's a hospital so it's a sterile environment but still there was an extra layer of stress about it and then that coupled with that most of your life support group has been significantly diminished. It becomes a much more stressful experience. (Female, 37 years old)

Trying to balance work and childcare also created stress. Being patient with family members and finding personal relaxation time were challenges.

> I would say just trying to find time to get away. (Male, 39 years old)

> Mostly, ah, I would say the most difficult has been trying to remain patient, in the sense that you don't know what's going to happen with the entire situation. It's like kind of taking it day by day and that's the hardest thing when you're not, you know, I have to realize that you're not in control when you think you are but now it's like more evident because you're not. (Male, 41 years old)

One interviewee indicated what made the pandemic emotionally difficult was the realization of the need to stop and reassess life to keep going on.

> I think for me the pandemic definitely brought me to a full stop … Emotionally empty, draining, I mean there's so many labels you can put on it but definitely was near the point of like, "OK. You have to stop and reassess

> life at this point or you won't make it till next year." The stress I was under was either perceived or real, but it was a lot of stress. (Female, 38 years old)

7 The Physical Toll

The most difficult thing for most interviewees was the lack of exercise. Several reasons explained why physical activities were reduced by the pandemic. One was the inability to enjoy outside activities as they did before the pandemic. Activities such as shopping trips and public outings were eliminated during the initial months of the pandemic for fear of exposure to the virus.

> not being able to spend as much time outside you normally would. Actually, because we had a quasi-spring [here]. You could not really enjoy it. Now, you have the summertime, and you have all the summertime stuff you would normally want to enjoy with your family and kids. You can't. You can't really do that. (Female, 37 years old)

Another reason that physical inactivity increased was that gyms were closed, and when they did reopen, were considered high-risk coronavirus places. "So, I just spent more than a year to going to the gym, loving it. Then, losing weight and getting muscle tone and some agility back and then, whoops gym closed" (Female, +70-year-old).

Interviewees stopped going to the gym because of the risk of exposure to the virus, "not being able to go to the gym. Trying to find other ways to be active … not getting exposed to, you know, other bacteria viruses, weakening our immune systems" (Male, 69 years old).

One interviewee explained that no gym means reaching no personal goals. Many interviewees mentioned gaining weight from not going outside. "Physically, it's like, gaining weight, eating at home, not going outside, [not] exercising. That's the hardest part physically" (Male, 34 years old).

One interviewee explained that the lack of sleep was the most difficult part physically because it influenced her mood throughout the day and week. She exchanged sleeping at night sometimes for a quiet time to surf the web, read, or do research, without distractions from family.

> Sleep. I have become aware, so to speak, how poorly I sleep on a regular night … I don't get a good night's rest I realize how it impacts me the next day. So, I'm foggy and takes me two hours just to get awake enough

> to actually do work … finding time to do everything that needs to be done but still finding time to take care of my body. That's challenging and like for me, sleep is the crux of it all … I even notice that like on the weekend. But I get a lot more sleep on Mondays. I'm like really, really focused motivated. I get a lot done but as the week goes on, as I make my way toward Friday every day gets harder and harder because I don't get much sleep during the week and trying to do things for kids and you know, make sure that the evening goes well. And then once everybody's in the bed and I'm like, oh this is my free time and I end up staying up too late. (Female, 38 years old)

Although some interviewees tried to find time, space, and resources to exercise, many distractions within the household stopped exercise activities.

> I would say trying to find time and space and I guess resources to exercise. Because you, you know, wake up in the morning, exercise, go to the gym and now you wake up and you try to exercise and then you got two kids coming to ask you would you know got the request [and] you're trying to focus on something else. (Male, 41 years old)

8 The Pandemic's Positive Side

As one interviewee said the pandemic has been the worst but also the best of times.

> I feel like fearfully it hasn't been very difficult. This has been a great time and the worst. It's been the best of times and the worst of times. I mean, yeah, that's the way I can describe it. Just like when I thought of the pandemic or 2020, I as like, it was the worst year and the best year all at the same time because I think throughout this and having to be in a position where I felt like I had to fix something in order to just move forward. (Female, 38 years old)

Despite the trauma and horrific effects of this pandemic, respondents found that the pandemic made them learn things that they would not otherwise realize. They created positive new habits, like reaching out to others using technology. They expanded their reach as to distance learning and found that learning can be done informally, not just seated inside of a building or institution. They learned more about their families and their children.

The interviewees indicated that they learned more about themselves. Spiritual journeys began or were enhanced. Interviewees indicated without the congregational prayers and community events, they took a closer look at their personal relationship with God. They found different meditation programs online and were using those to enhance their spirituality. "[I] go to a Buddhist seminar online that I probably would never have gone to if it wasn't offered remotely" (Male, 34 years old).

> I used it [Facebook] to study more so from a religious perspective not as much work or social so to speak but I did at one point like attend these … free meditation courses where you could like it with a couple of course weeks … get on the webinar that talks about meditation and benefits and then you have like a group meditation session. (Female, 38 years old)

They also reflected on their practices as Muslims, how important they were, and how important it was to give charity, venturing into things that they might not have except for the virtual experience. They expressed the hope that no one would give up as the pandemic continued. Life may not be the same as before; it could be even better. Television and social media dissected "the new normal" as Americans grappled with the fact that many activities and habits before the pandemic would not be returning. Part of this phrase embodied society's wish for a "comfort zone" from the unknown and inconsistency in everything from daily habits and activities to social contact with others. The idea of hope was expressed as each respondent described what "new normal" meant to them.

There was not consensus among the respondents as to what new normal would be, but there was a general feeling that new normal was hopeful. There was awareness that new habits were forming around protecting oneself and family from contracting the coronavirus. For some interviewees, they rejected the term, "new normal" completely and decided that "new normal" was the wrong term; it should be "current normal." The interviewee explained that the reason for using this term.

> I reject that terminology. I refuse to accept that this is my new normal. I mean it is current, yes, if we can calm down humanity especially like Americans can understand each other humanity and appreciate and value it. If people would put a darned mask on, distance themselves, and wash their hands, you know, we could dramatically decrease the time that we're all dealing with this. So, with that in mind, I refuse to accept the terminology of new normal. (Female, 37 years old)

Nevertheless, a couple of participants pointed out that there was no normal. Everything kept changing, and it was just that we have to keep adapting to whatever was presently happening and be prepared for the future.

> New normal? I have no idea what new normal is because everything's changing so how can you place the definition of normal on it when it is changing day to day. But I have a hope for what I want the new normal to be, that I hope we are moving forward. (Male, 34 years old)

> New normal means there is no normal. I think anything I realize that the world is going to continue to change in ways that we can't imagine, and you have to be in a state spiritually and mentally to be ready to adapt to change, and I think that normal, I guess, is being like spiritually grounded and being ready to react. (Female, 38 years old)

Some participants indicated that new normal would mean new opportunities since there was going to be a need for more products to protect people against the virus and the realization that new habits are not going to change anytime soon.

> I think it means additional precautions. I think once we get this vaccine, things will go back to normal from sporting and events perspective and the business world, and the ways things work there. I feel like there's gonna be this new market for looking for the product that has the cleanest products you know. Cleanest hotels and places in grocery stores … There are some negative aspects of what we found from the pandemic. I feel there's also other blessings. We just gotta keep moving. (Male, 39 years old)

> New normal really means to me that, as a result of this pandemic thing, how we interacted with each other, how we worked, how we socialize, how we worshiped is not going to return to the way it was before this pandemic. I think with the advent of so much work at home, that is, virtual meetings, that there are benefits to that that have been realized or that people would want to take, continue to take advantage of that, and the flip side of it is that so many businesses that closed, that they depended on this in-person contact like retail stores, restaurants, etc. uh with no business closed and that won't, I don't see that coming back. I think it'll be some sort of hybrid. The world already is witnessing where people will order, have it delivered but to return to where it is I think you will. If it does

> return it is going to take years, not just mere passage of this pandemic because I think new habits are being formed and they're not, I don't see them quickly changing back to where it was before. (Male, 69 years old)

Outlooks for a new normal reached beyond personal security and procurement of the necessities of life to include the welfare of society and the future in general. One participant indicated that new normal reflected that we were a society of risk takers.

> people won't do what they have been asked to do … you don't think prior to the pandemic you didn't know how much people wanted to do all the things they had been doing before. So even when you tell them their lives depend on not doing those things, they say, "ok, I'm going to die" because that's what they are saying when they refuse to adhere. (Female, 70+years old)

Protests for racial equality and the eruption of violence in cities complicated life during the pandemic but also brought to the forefront discussions about race and hope that these conversations would continue.

> I'm glad they are talking about races, and justice, and anti-Blackness because it is something a lot of Black Muslims experience growing up, unable to articulate it, but they feel it. So, the fact that this is now being talked about—it's like a weird catharsis or release for Black Muslims, so that's one thing where I think the new normal is that this doesn't go away, talking about Black lives in the Muslim community for sure. Or even in society in large. (Male, 34 years old)

For African-American Muslims, the struggle to adjust to a new religious reality was coupled with changes in healthcare, housing, and food areas due to the pandemic. African Americans suffered from the disparities in less accessible healthcare systems, poor housing, and inaccessible grocery stores and pharmacies. The pandemic made these disparities more evident while protests regarding Black lives increased the spotlight on the racism behind the disparities.

Stress from the pandemic caused eating habits to change for the worse, and a reduction in daily physical activity increased weight, threatening, for some, obesity. Social activities, possible outlets for stress and a mental health booster, slowed or halted during the pandemic. Outings to the park or playground or going to the gym were curtailed. Working out at home was difficult because of household and family distractions or lack of space and/or equipment. Inactivity also caused many experienced a change in sleep patterns. These changes in habits were aggravated by the realization that systemic racism was also creating stress and illness along with the pandemic.

African-American Muslims experienced the drama of systemic racism as others in the African-American community. One respondent explained that the Black Lives Matter Movement protests was an opportunity to delve deeply into how it feels to be Black and Muslim.

> Yeah. I think everybody feels like there is an obligation now for Black Lives like the fact is that as Black Muslims we're in this intersectionality of being Black but in the Black community there is this Islamophobia, and in the Muslim community, there is anti-Blackness. So, you're stuck in between these two like opposing forces and you are kind of in the middle. I think one thing the pandemic has changed is ... we are addressing anti-Blackness within the Muslim community, and I think that has brought it up, and I think now it's Black Muslims to bring up within their community about Islamophobia. ... what I can tell and what I grew up with, non-Muslim Black people don't have a positive attitude toward Islam and a lot of their exposure comes from civil rights movement and past history versus what is contemporary Black Islam. (Male, 34 years old).

For this small group of African-American Muslims, the revelation of disparities in healthcare, housing, food availability, and shopping choices for African Americans was coupled with restrictions on religious gatherings. The uncertainty felt during the pandemic was acerbated by the fact that mosques, the center of Muslim religious life, were closed by many states. For respondents, not being able participate in communal prayers and religious activities was the worst part of the pandemic. It was frustrating and perplexing not to be able to pray in congregation. Restrictions for Eid prayers and in-person community celebrations dampened 2020 and 2021 religious' holidays. Virtual attempts of cultural and family traditions suffered due to lack of technological skills and equipment. In practicing certain traditions through virtual gatherings on the Internet, rather than in person, many Muslims found themselves searching for answers as to how to practice their faith.

Despite protests against systemic racism, disparities in health, housing, and food choices, and the upending of religious traditions, the respondents persevered and perceived hope for a better day. This small group of African-American Muslims found positive new habits and discovered that learning can be done for the sake of growing personally and religiously by expanding their educational reach through virtual learning. They searched for ways to practice Islam and connect with Allah (God) even as the pandemic continued.

Bibliography

AARP. "Drivers and Barriers to Living in a Multigenerational Household: Pre-COVID–Mid-COVID." September 2020. https://www.aarp.org/content/dam/aarp/research/surveys_statistics/liv-com/2021/drivers-barriers-living-in-multigenerational-household-report.doi.10.26419-2Fres.00414.002.pdf.

Bliss, Laura, and Lorena Rios. "Tracing the Invisible Danger of Household Crowding." Bloomberg, July 21, 2020. https://www.bloomberg.com/news/articles/2020-07-21/gentrification-and-crowding-boost-covid-19-risk.

Cohn, D'Vera, and Jeffrey S. Passel. "Record 64 Million Americans Live in Multigenerational Households." Pew Research Center, April 5, 2018. https://www.pewresearch.org/fact-tank/2018/04/05/a-record-64-million-americans-live-in-multigenerational-households/.

Dubowitz, Tamara, Madhumita Ghosh Dastidar, Wendy M. Troxel, Robin Beckman, Alvin Nugroho, Sameer Siddiqi, Jonathan Cantor, et al. "Food Insecurity in a Low-Income, Predominantly African American Cohort Following the COVID-19 Pandemic." *American Journal of Public Health* 111, no. 3 (March 2021): 494–497. https://doi.org/10.2105/ajph.2020.306041.

Ferrise, Adam. "50 States of Coronavirus: How Every State in the U.S. Has Responded to the Pandemic." *Cleveland.com*, March 21, 2020. https://www.cleveland.com/metro/2020/03/50-states-of-coronavirus-how-every-state-in-the-us-has-responded-to-the-pandemic.html.

Haines, Matt. "Pandemic Worsens 'Food Deserts' for 23.5 Million Americans." *VOA: Voice of America*, May 19, 2020. https://www.voanews.com/a/usa_pandemic-worsens-food-deserts-235-million-americans/6189526.html.

Horst, Megan, Subhashni Raj, and Catherine Brinkley. "Getting Outside the Supermarket Box: Alternatives to 'Food Deserts.'" PDXScholar, January 1, 2016. https://pdxscholar.library.pdx.edu/usp_fac/191.

Lake, Jaboa. "The Pandemic has Exacerbated Housing Instability for Renters of Color." Center for American Progress, October 30, 2020. https://www.americanprogress.org/article/pandemic-exacerbated-housing-instability-renters-color/.

Sandoiu, Ana. "Racial Inequalities in Covid-19: The Impact on Black Communities." *Medical News Today*, June 5, 2020. https://www.medicalnewstoday.com/articles/racial-inequalities-in-covid-19-the-impact-on-black-communities.

Scott, Eugene. "Analysis: 4 Reasons Coronavirus Is Hitting Black Communities So Hard."

The Washington Post, August 10, 2020. https://www.washingtonpost.com/politics/2020/04/10/4-reasons-coronavirus-is-hitting-black-communities-so-hard/.

Spencer, Saranac Hale. "Stay-at-Home Policies Treat Mosques Same as Churches." *FactCheck.org*, April 30, 2020. https://www.factcheck.org/2020/04/stay-at-home-policies-treat-mosques-same-as-churches/.

Weisbecker, Andy. "Few Healthy Food Choices in Urban Food Deserts." *Food Safety News*, May 21, 2010. https://www.foodsafetynews.com/2010/05/few-healthy-food-choices-in-urban-food-deserts/.

CHAPTER 7

COVID-19 and US Islamic Schools: Responsive, Resourceful, and Resilient

Shaza Khan

1 Introduction

As a mother of three young children and the executive director of the Islamic Schools League of America (ISLA), a nonprofit that supports full-time Islamic schools in the United States, I was pushed into a whirlwind of professional activity at the onset of the pandemic that I never anticipated would occur at such an accelerated rate. Managing my children's remote learning at home while trying to support Islamic schools in the USA with the new demands facing them was challenging, to say the least. Yet, the need to network with other private school leaders, national medical and public health experts, and Muslim nonprofit professionals was unprecedented. In order to successfully provide educational services to Muslim students enrolled in Islamic schools, several questions needed to be immediately addressed, as they related to many facets of schooling, including adjusting modes of instruction, understanding constantly evolving health and safety protocols, maintaining compliance with local health guidelines, communicating effectively with parents, and understanding the mental health and well-being of staff, students, and their families. I begin the chapter with this personal perspective, not because I think that my experience was particularly unique, but because it likely mirrored the challenges that many other working Muslim parents of school-aged children faced, including those who lead or teach in full-time Islamic schools.

During the COVID-19 pandemic, leaders of Islamic schools, like their counterparts in educational institutions across the world, faced a number of challenges as they struggled to provide on-going quality education to their students. Globally, one of the first preventative measures enacted to curb the spread of COVID-19 was the initiation of in-person school closures.[1] The United Nations Educational, Scientific, and Cultural Organization (UNESCO) reports

1 Danilo Buonsenso et al., "Schools Closures During the COVID-19 Pandemic: A Catastrophic Global Situation," *The Pediatric Infectious Disease Journal* 40, no. 4 (2021): 146–150, https://doi.org/10.1097/INF.0000000000003052.

 | DOI:10.1163/9789004679771_009

that by June 2020, 75 percent of the world's population of pre-primary, primary, lower-secondary, upper-secondary, and tertiary learners were impacted by these measures.[2] In the United States alone, over 58 million students in pre-primary to secondary schools were impacted in 2020 by the initial closures, including thousands of students in full-time Islamic schools.[3] Over time, schools eventually reopened their doors by enacting changes to their instructional methods and implementing additional protocol to ensure the health and safety of their communities, bringing with it a host of new challenges that educators, students, and school leaders would have to manage or overcome.

In this chapter, I attempt to provide insight into the challenges and successes faced by Islamic school leaders during the COVID-19 pandemic. To inform this discussion, I draw upon emails sent by teachers and principals on ISLA's email listserv, the Islamic Educators' Communication Network (IECN), and the results of three surveys administered to full-time US Islamic school leaders from April 2020–June 2021. I begin by first providing an overview of the history of Islamic schools in the United States, a description of ISLA's services and network, and insight into Islamic school leaders' unfolding understanding of the impact of the pandemic on their school communities. Then, I describe the methods for the three surveys administered from April 2020–June 2021 (for survey questions, see Appendices). Next, I describe the findings from the three surveys, focusing on the impact of COVID-19 on Islamic schools' instructional delivery, enrollment, and finances. Finally, I discuss the implications of these findings, including the need for broad-based public support of Islamic education and for innovative and distinct Islamic schools that can maintain a strong value proposition amid an uncertain and volatile future.

2 Overview: Islamic Schools in the United States and ISLA

2.1 *Islamic Schools*

Since their inception in the 1930s, full-time Islamic schools have sought to provide a tailored curriculum and educational experience that responds to the unique needs of the diverse constituents and individuals that comprise Mus-

2 "Education: From Disruption to Recovery," United Nations Educational, Scientific and Cultural Organization, February 28, 2022, accessed September 27, 2021, https://en.unesco.org/covid19/educationresponse.

3 UNESCO, "Education: From Disruption to Recovery."

lims in America.[4] For example, the first known Islamic schools in the United States, called the University of Islam, were founded in the 1930s by Sister Clara and Elijah Muhammad. They established an educational system outside of the US public school system in order to allow African-American Muslim children to thrive, despite a harshly racist American society.[5] They did this by providing a curriculum that developed students' character and nurtured a strong understanding of one's self and God.[6] These schools were eventually renamed the Clara Muhammad Schools in the late 1970s. A second wave of development in Islamic schools occurred after immigrants from predominantly Muslim countries arrived in the country in the mid-1960s to study and work and eventually settled down after starting families of their own. The Islamic schools they and other American Muslims helped establish were driven by a desire to protect their children from external influences that were seen as threats to Muslim children's moral upbringing and to preserve their Islamic, ethnic, and linguistic heritage.[7]

Islamic schools have continued to evolve since their founding, striving to provide students with rigorous academic training and a firmly rooted American Muslim identity. Currently, there are an estimated 300 full-time Islamic schools in the United States that serve approximately 50,000 K-12 students.[8] Full-time Islamic schools in the United States are important educational institutions, which, due to their private non-profit status, depend largely upon tuition and charitable donations to achieve economic sustainability.[9] While they are responsible for educating only 3.8 percent of American Muslim children in the country,[10] I believe that the impact of full-time Islamic schools extends beyond their student enrollment. This is because, as registered schools,

4 S. Khan, P. Salahuddin, and S. Imam, "Looking Back and Re-Envisioning the Future: Full-Time Islamic Schools in the United States," in *Principles and Practices of Education in Islam*, ed. Shaikh Abdul Mabud (Oldham, UK: Beacon Books, forthcoming).

5 R. Zakiyyah Muhammad, *Mother of the Nation: Clara Evans Muhammad* (Anaheim, CA: Institute of Muslim American Studies, 2020).

6 R. Zakiyyah Muhammad, *Mother of the Nation: Clara Evans Muhammad* (Anaheim, CA: Institute of Muslim American Studies, 2020).

7 Yvonne Y. Haddad and Jane I. Smith, "Introduction: The Challenge of Islamic Education in North America," in *Educating the Muslims of America*, ed. Yvonne Y. Haddad, Farid Senzai, and Jane I. Smith (Oxford: Oxford University Press, 2009).

8 ISLA, Islamic Schools League of America, "ISLA Islamic School Registry Database," unpublished raw data, 2022.

9 Sabith Khan and Shariq Siddiqui, *Islamic Education in the United States and the Evolution of Muslim Nonprofit Institutions* (Northampton: Edward Elgar, 2017).

10 Karen Keyworth, "Islamic Schools of the United States: Data-Based Profiles," Institute for Social Policy and Understanding, Washington, DC, May 2011, 15, https://www.ispu.org/wp

they must follow federal and local laws that help them operate in a mature, structured fashion. Additionally, Islamic schools are one of the few places where young American Muslims can receive systematic instruction on Islam, wherein a measure of accountability is inherently built into the tuition-dependent financial structure of the schools. Finally, Islamic schools often offer many programs and services that are open to the broader community, including Eid carnivals, Ramadan *ifṭārs*, and more. Therefore, the impact of these schools is felt more broadly by the Muslim community and beyond the K-12 spectrum of a young Muslim's life.

2.2 *ISLA*

Established in 1998, the Islamic Schools League of America (ISLA), is a non-profit organization that seeks to create a professional network for Islamic school educators to ensure the long-term viability of Islamic schools in the United States. Additionally, ISLA seeks to put Islamic schools on the map, quite literally. To achieve this, ISLA hosts a directory of full-time Islamic schools and an interactive map on its website for individuals to easily identify and locate schools. Parents, researchers, and prospective staff, among other interest groups, utilize this directory for disparate reasons, such as identifying a suitable Islamic school for one's child or finding a job as an Islamic school educator. Islamic school administrators are requested to update their school information on a detailed online form regularly. The form has two parts: the first part populates data onto the public online directory of US Islamic schools, and the second portion populates an unpublished database that ISLA uses for research-related purposes, for example, to analyze the growth of Islamic schools or to gauge schools' current and future challenges.

ISLA also operates an email listserv that specifically caters to full-time Islamic school founders, board members, administrators, teachers, and dedicated volunteers, called the Islamic Educators' Communication Network (IECN). It has grown to over 1,000 email subscribers who are, or once were, professionally connected to full-time Islamic schools in one of the above-mentioned capacities. Uniquely, listservs facilitate discussion amongst subscribers by allowing them to send emails to everyone on the list. In other words, they are not uni-directional like many promotional email lists today; rather, they are designed to be multi-directional and therefore, conversational.

Throughout the pandemic, the IECN served as a platform for communicating and exchanging questions, concerns, ideas, and opportunities with teach-

-content/uploads/2011/04/2011_609_ISPU-Report_Islamic-Schools_Keyworth_WEB.pdf?x61645; and ISLA, "ISLA Islamic School Registry Database."

ers. The themes addressed in these emails included health and safety protocol, instructional technology, school financial sustainability, and the social and emotional well-being of students and teachers. Based on personal testimonials from Islamic school leaders, the IECN facilitated a strong sense of community and connection at a time when many educators felt isolated and confused.

3 Emergence of COVID-19 and Islamic School Leaders' Responses

Email exchanges on the IECN provide unique insight into how Islamic school leaders responded to the COVID-19 pandemic. The first communication sent on the listserv about COVID-19 was posted on March 2, 2020, in which Sufia Azmat, executive director of Council of Islamic Schools in North America (CISNA), encouraged school leaders to review their crisis management plans and to reach out to local health officials and school districts about suggested protocol regarding the novel coronavirus.[11] By March 12, 2020, Dr. Salman Shaikh, President of Baytul-Iman Academy in New Jersey started a thread on the email listserv asking what schools were doing to prepare for school closures,[12] to which ten replies were sent from school leaders with some sharing school closing plans and others requesting that a virtual meeting be rapidly organized for school leaders to discuss how to respond to the looming threat of forced school closures. An emerging sense of urgency and panic was palpable on the listserv during these initial weeks, with over eighty unique email threads, or conversation strands, created by Islamic school leaders and teachers sent through the IECN, each containing numerous replies, from March 2 to March 31, 2020.

In addition to providing a platform for discussion and resource-sharing through the IECN, ISLA sought to support Islamic school leaders and educators through a variety of other methods including hosting administrators' meetings, joining the National Muslim Task Force on COVID-19, and administering surveys to identify needs and support data-informed decision-making for school leaders. The first weekly administrator meeting ISLA hosted was on May 4, 2020. The meetings provided a virtual space for ISLA to disseminate important information regarding national health and safety guidelines, free resources for educators, and financial relief opportunities for Islamic schools, and for Islamic school leaders to discuss their most pressing concerns related to the pandemic. Attendees were most often principals, but also included administrative assis-

11 Sufia Azmat, Email to Islamic Educators' Communication Network, March 2, 2020. For Council of Islamic Schools of North America, see https://cisnausa.org.

12 Dr. Salman Shaikh, Email to Islamic Educators' Communication Network, March 12, 2020.

tants, school coordinators, and board members. There were on average twenty to thirty attendees at the weekly meetings until attendance began to dwindle in the winter of 2020. Several reasons may have led to the decline in attendance, including leaders' better understanding of the virus, availability of vaccines in the United States, and most likely from gradual burn-out due to the toll the virus was taking on educators' overall well-being.

In August 2020, ISLA joined the National Muslim Task Force on COVID-19, which grew from four founding organizations into a forty-member organization. The Task Force members worked collaboratively throughout the pandemic to identify areas of concern particular to American Muslim communities and to disseminate guidance, information, and statements relevant to American Muslim leaders and institutions. Notably, ISLA worked with the Task Force to produce a joint statement on school reopenings and COVID-19 vaccines published on September 1, 2021.[13]

Furthermore, throughout the pandemic, ISLA began to increasingly focus on collecting data that would provide more insight into the immediate and long-term impacts of COVID-19 on Islamic schools. In the following section, I describe three surveys ISLA administered at different points in the pandemic to achieve this goal.

4 Research and Methodology

The need for reliable data regarding the impact of COVID-19 became urgent especially as the US government began drafting relief bills to address the financial impact felt by schools and small companies, including nonprofits. In order to obtain data, ISLA began administering surveys to gauge the impact of COVID-19 on Islamic schools and to help ISLA respond to their emerging needs.

The first survey that was administered was launched in April 2020 to understand the immediate impact of COVID-19 on Islamic school leaders and institutions. It was an IRB-approved survey led by Principal Investigator, Dr. Shariq Siddiqui, Director of Muslim Philanthropy Initiative (MPI) at Indiana University's Lily School of Philanthropy, in collaboration with ISLA, CISNA, and the Center for Muslim Philanthropy (CMP). The survey was hosted on Qualtrics, a research software program. Directors of the partnering organizations met virtually to determine which questions were most urgently needed to gauge the

13 Islamic Schools League of America, "Keeping Students Safe: Joint Statement on School Re-Openings and COVID Vaccines," September 1, 2021, accessed September 29, 2021, https://theisla.org/keeping-students-safe.

emerging needs of Islamic schools. These questions were appended to an existing survey that was being administered by MPI to Muslim nonprofit leaders.

After Institutional Review Board (IRB) approval was obtained, ISLA and CISNA both disseminated the first survey electronically to their Islamic school contacts via email. Eligible participants included board members, school principals, and vice principals of US full-time Islamic schools. The survey was open for response from April to June 2020, resulting in a total of 252 responses. A total of sixty-six survey items were included, with eighteen items that asked questions specifically pertaining to Islamic schools, while the remaining questions addressed Muslim nonprofit institutions more broadly as part of the larger study being administered by MPI. The survey items sought to collect data about the existing and anticipated positive and negative impacts of the pandemic on Islamic schools as it related to enrollment, donations, volunteer hours, staffing and payroll, government pandemic relief aid, and more.

Two more surveys were administered by ISLA in subsequent months to Islamic school leaders about the ongoing impact of COVID-19 on Islamic schools: one was after the start of the new academic year in fall 2020;[14] and the other at the end of the school year in spring/summer 2021.[15] The purpose of administering the subsequent surveys was to understand the shifting ways Islamic school leaders were responding to COVID-19 over time and to use the data to learn about their current and emerging needs. These surveys were less extensive than the initial one and are better understood as "pulse surveys." A pulse survey is generally used by an organization to solicit quick feedback and/or data from internal members in order to better understand and respond to their needs. The survey is intentionally short and easy to answer to increase participation and response rates. Pulse surveys can be sent out regularly, addressing the same or new topics, depending on the purpose of the surveys.[16]

In contrast to the first survey, the second two surveys requested only one administrator of each US full-time Islamic school to respond, preferably the

14 Islamic Schools League of America, "The Impact COVID-19 on Enrollment in Full-Time Islamic Schools for the 2020–2021 Academic Year," November 2020, accessed September 30, 2021, https://theisla.org/covid-19-impact-on-islamic-school-enrollment; and Isra Brifkani and Shaza Khan, "The Impact of COVID-19 on Islamic Schools in the United States: Implications and Recommendations," *Journal of Education in Muslim Societies* 2, no. 2 (2021): 82–89, https://doi.org/10.2979/jems.2.2.05.

15 Islamic Schools League of America, "COVID-19 and Islamic Schools: 2020–2021 Year in Review," September 2021, accessed October 8, 2021, https://theisla.org/covid-19-islamic-schools-2020-2021-year-in-review.

16 J.B. Allen, S. Jain, and A.H. Church, "Using a Pulse Survey Approach to Drive Organizational Change," *Organizational Development Review* 52, no. 3 (2020): 62–68.

principal, head of school, or superintendent. This was made clear in the description of the survey and in the solicitation emails and social media posts. The surveys were hosted on Google Forms and sent out directly to the administrators of Islamic schools via email and on a WhatsApp group hosted by CISNA for Islamic school administrators. The second survey included fourteen survey items and was administered from October to November 2020, resulting in a total of eighty-one responses.[17] The third survey included nineteen survey items and was administered from May to June 2021, with a total of seventy-nine responses.[18]

Descriptive analysis of each of the surveys was performed using the survey platform; the first using Qualtrics, and the second and third using Google Forms. In the first survey, findings were interpreted simply as the percentage of Islamic school leaders reporting on a particular item, due to the potential duplicity in school leader responses from any particular school. For the second and third survey, findings were interpreted to depict the percentage of schools experiencing a particular phenomenon because responses were restricted to one per Islamic school. In the following sections, I discuss the findings from all three surveys separately, moving through each one sequentially. In doing so, I hope to share the unfolding story of how Islamic schools responded to the evolving COVID-19 pandemic. Each survey's findings are presented in four subsections: Enrollment Impact, Instructional Impact, Financial Impact, and Other Data.

5 Survey Findings

5.1 *First Survey: April–June 2020*

Enrollment Impact. The findings from the first survey administered to Islamic school leaders revealed that many Islamic schools immediately felt the impact of COVID-19 on their school enrollment, with 37 percent indicating a slight decrease and 19 percent reporting a significant decrease in enrollment. Nearly 26 percent reported no change or impact on enrollment. The remaining respondents reported an increase in enrollment.

Instructional Impact. Forty-five percent of respondents indicated that their Islamic schools reopened virtually, launching remote learning within one week of closing their physical doors, and another 30 percent of respondents indi-

17 For complete survey items, see Appendix B.

18 For complete survey items, see Appendix C.

cated that they launched within two weeks. Specifically, 32 percent of the respondents indicated that live remote instruction was being provided by their school, while 22 percent were offering education through asynchronous modes, in which students could access assignments or recorded lessons on their own time. The remaining respondents indicated that their school was using project-based learning or were sending materials home for student learning and engagement.

Financial Impact. Half of the respondents to this survey indicated that they planned to apply for federal funding to mitigate the negative financial impact on their schools, and another 13 percent indicated that they were still undecided about whether they would pursue government funding opportunities. Interestingly, 34 percent of respondents suspected the federal government might discriminate against Muslim nonprofits in allocating public funds. Despite the uncertainties, schools still felt confident that they would be able to fund their staff payroll in the next four weeks, but 64 percent worried that enrollment would decrease in the upcoming academic year, leading to more financial instability for the institutions. Additionally, 56 percent of respondents reported a decrease in charitable donations since the emergence of COVID-19, of which 29 percent indicated a significant decrease. Interestingly, however, 45 percent optimistically anticipated an increase in their Ramadan donations, while 40 percent worried about a decrease during this holy month.

Other Data. This survey also sought to understand Islamic schools' crisis readiness by asking respondents to identify specific technical and human resources they had in place before COVID-19 led to school closures. Survey respondents overwhelmingly noted that their schools had staff or volunteers with technical expertise that they could draw upon and that most students had prior access to personal devices. Respondents were also asked to identify from a checklist the leading positive and negative impacts of COVID-19 on their school. The most commonly selected positive impacts included: an enhanced use of technology among staff, increased parent involvement, and a sense of community, while the most commonly selected negative impacts included: financial impact, social emotional well-being of staff and students, and difficulty completing the curriculum.

5.2 *Second Survey: October–November 2020*

Enrollment Impact. The second survey, administered after the start of the new academic year, revealed that 79 percent of Islamic schools experienced a decline in enrollment for 2020–2021, with the majority of respondents indicating a 20–30 percent decline in overall enrollment. Survey participants indicated that the greatest decline in enrollment occurred in their preschool (43 percent) and elementary school grade levels (39 percent). When asked to speculate on the cause of enrollment decline, the school administrators believed that the financial standing of students' families was the greatest cause, followed by local school districts providing online schooling options, which notably, were free in comparison to the tuition-based Islamic schools.

Instructional Impact. Half of the respondents (49 percent) indicated that they opened their schools during the 2020–2021 academic year by offering only a virtual learning option, while 43 percent began the school year using hybrid instruction, offering both online and in-person options, and only 7 percent opened with exclusive in-person instruction.

Financial Impact. School leaders reported an increase in financial aid requests, noted by 67 percent of respondents. Sixty percent of the schools were able to increase their allocation for financial assistance for the new academic year. The high percentage of Islamic schools that increased their financial aid allocations seem to suggest that Islamic schools were able to leverage reserve funds or donor contributions to assist the households struggling to make tuition payments.

Other Data. School leaders were asked an open-ended question about how they were trying to mitigate the negative impact of COVID-19 on their schools. Some of their responses included: using clear and consistent communication to parents about health and safety protocol, creating individualized tuition plans for families that needed short-term support, enacting budget and staff pay cuts, providing hybrid instructional options to increase student retention, and increasing their social media presence.

5.3 *Third Survey: June–July 2021*

Enrollment Impact. The data from this survey was obtained at the end of the academic year and indicated that 78 percent of Islamic schools experienced enrollment declines in the 2020–2021 school year, which corroborates findings from ISLA's second survey in which 79 percent of respondents indicated a decline in enrollment.

Instructional Impact. Asked to report on their instructional method for the start of the school year, 63 percent stated that they began the academic year with hybrid instruction, followed by 32 percent with virtual instruction and no in-person option, and least commonly, 5 percent offering instruction in-person only, without any online options. By the end of the school year, the percentage of schools offering in-person only instruction more than doubled to 13 percent. Still, the majority (71 percent) offered a hybrid model of instruction. Notably, the percentage of schools offering exclusively virtual instruction reduced by nearly half, from 32 percent to 17 percent. Furthermore, the percentage of students attending in-person also gradually increased over the school year. Specifically, nearly 55 percent of respondents indicated that as the academic year progressed, increasingly more students' families decided to have their children learn in-person versus online.

Financial Impact. An overwhelming majority, 83 percent, of respondents indicated that their Islamic school applied for and received the federal relief program known as the Paycheck Protection Program (PPP), which was designed to support small businesses that suffered revenue/income loss due to COVID-19, which could be used towards employee wages, rent, mortgage and other eligible utilities.[19] Many other respondents (19 percent) stated that their Islamic school applied for another federal relief program, the Emergency Assistance to Non-Public Schools (EANS).[20] Per federal regulations, businesses could not receive both the first round of PPP and EANS; however, based on the survey, it appears some schools may have applied for both of the programs before deciding which federal aid would be more favorable to accept. The survey also found that nearly 40 percent of Islamic schools achieved their overall fundraising targets for the fiscal year. In contrast, almost an equal amount, about 39 percent, did not reach their fundraising goals during the 2020–2021 school year. Finally, 53 percent of the participants stated that their Islamic school did not have to reduce their staff due to budget cuts.

Other Data. The drop in student enrollment and, relatedly, tuition income, was reported as the biggest challenge faced by Islamic school leaders during the 2020–2021 academic year. The second oft-cited challenge faced during the school year was hybrid instruction; this mode of instruction was eventually offered by 70 percent of the Islamic schools responding to this survey. The two next biggest challenges reported by school leaders in this third survey included addressing students' learning needs and managing teacher burn-out. Overwhelmingly, school leaders predicted the top professional development needs for their teachers in the upcoming 2021–2022 school year to include addressing learning loss (53 percent), providing differentiated instruction (51 percent), and increasing student engagement and motivation (51 percent). The next highest need was integrating social emotional learning (SEL) into the curriculum (34 percent).[21] These topics all appear strongly related to one another and to

19 U.S. Department of the Treasury, "Paycheck Protection Program," 2021, accessed September 30, 2021, https://home.treasury.gov/policy-issues/coronavirus/assistance-for-small-businesses/paycheck-protection-program.

20 Office of Elementary and Secondary Education, "Emergency Assistance to Non-Public Schools," (2021), accessed September 30, 2021, https://oese.ed.gov/offices/education-stabilization-fund/emergency-assistance-non-public-schools.

21 The percentages do not add up to 100 percent because participants were to select the top three professional development needs for teachers and for school leaders' own needs.

the year and a half of disrupted schooling that occurred during the pandemic, resulting in stagnating interest, motivation, and academic gains for many students. Among the school leaders' own needs for the upcoming academic year were hiring and retaining highly qualified staff, selected by 52 percent of the participants, followed by curriculum redesign (38 percent), and strategies to increase enrollment (30 percent).

6 Discussion: Responsive, Resourceful, and Resilient Islamic Schools

The insights gleaned from discussions that took place on ISLA's email listserv, the IECN, and the data from the three surveys shared in this chapter, indicate that Islamic school leaders were remarkably responsive to their community's needs while attempting to understand and apply health guidelines issued by the federal government, local health departments, national experts—all while working within the limits of their school's resources.[22] The responsiveness of Islamic schools is especially evident when examining the data on schools' instructional methods and the ways they shifted over the academic year.

When the 2020–2021 school year began, COVID-19 vaccines were still not available, and many school leaders may have been reluctant to take on the associated risks of in-person learning. This seems likely, as only 5 percent of respondents stated that their Islamic school offered instruction exclusively in-person, while nearly 30 percent offered instruction exclusively online, and 62 percent offered a hybrid option. Each school operated its hybrid option differently, with some creating student pods segregated by grade or gender that had specific days or weeks that they attended on campus, whereas other schools allowed parents to choose whether their child would attend in person or online, irrespective of grade, gender, or other demographics. In comparison, 74 percent of the largest one hundred public school districts in the country began the school year with remote-only instruction, meaning only 26 percent of these largest public-school districts gave parents and students the option to attend school in person.[23] Based on this data, Islamic schools were far more likely

22 American Academy of Pediatrics, "COVID-19 Guidance for Safe Schools and Promotion of In-Person Learning" (2021), accessed September 30, 2021, https://www.aap.org/en/pages/2019-novel-coronavirus-covid-19-infections/clinical-guidance/covid-19-planning-considerations-return-to-in-person-education-in-schools; and Centers for Disease Control and Prevention, "Guidance for COVID-19 Prevention for K-12 Schools," (2021), accessed September 30, 2021, https://www.cdc.gov/coronavirus/2019-ncov/community/schools-childcare/k-12-guidance.html.

23 S. Shafer, "A Year of COVID-19: What it Looked Like for Schools," *Education Week*, March 4,

than large public school districts to have an in-person option available. Many factors could have impacted this reality, including the large influence of teachers' unions on public schools who expressed concerns for teachers' health and safety; on the other hand, tuition-dependent Islamic schools may have been forced to provide more options in order to retain student enrollment, which clearly impact Islamic schools' financial viability.

By the close of the 2020–2021 academic year, 70 percent of Islamic schools responding to the third survey reported that they offered hybrid instruction, an increase of nearly 8 percent over the academic year. The percentage of exclusive in-person instruction more than doubled to almost 13 percent. In order to safely provide an in-person learning option, the cumulative 83 percent of Islamic schools that offered in-person instruction, whether exclusively in-person or through a hybrid model, had to invest in sanitation equipment, face masks, and improved classroom and school ventilation. Furthermore, COVID-19 testing, communication, and quarantine procedures had to be established and followed in line with local and federal health guidance. Islamic schools' notable efforts to offer an in-person option demonstrate their commitment to the social-emotional needs of their students, as argued by the American Academy of Pediatrics, Centers for Disease Control, and other experts that stressed the importance of in-person learning for student well-being.[24]

Additionally, Islamic schools demonstrated exceptional resourcefulness in managing what could have been a financial crisis resulting in widespread, permanent school closures. With at least 78 percent of Islamic schools having experienced a decline in enrollment in 2020–2021, the financial impact of the pandemic on Islamic schools was indeed extensive. Yet, the data presented in this chapter demonstrates that the majority of Islamic schools were able to obtain federal relief funds, particularly the PPP, with 85 percent stating they applied for the funding. The CATO Institute report on the impact of COVID-19 on private schools cites private schools' ability to tap into the PPP and other federal relief packages as one reason they were not impacted as negatively as many originally feared.[25] Furthermore, fundraising during Ramadan was rel-

---

2021, accessed October 1, 2021, https://www.edweek.org/leadership/a-year-of-covid-19-what-it-looked-like-for-schools/2021/03.

24 Melissa Jenco, "Updated AAP School Reopening Guidance Calls for Layers of Protection, Flexibility," *American Academy of Pediatrics*, August 19, 2020, accessed September 30, 2021, https://www.aappublications.org/news/2020/08/19/schoolreentry081920.

25 Neil McCluskey, "Private Schooling After a Year of COVID-19: How the Private Sector has Fared and How to Keep It Healthy," CATO Institute Policy Analysis, April 13, 2021, accessed September 20, 2021, https://www.cato.org/sites/cato.org/files/2021-04/policy-analysis-no-914.pdf.

atively successful for nearly half of the Islamic schools (46 percent). Slightly less reported that they were able to achieve their overall fundraising goals for the year (40 percent). Yet, without comparative data from previous years, it is difficult to pinpoint the extent to which the pandemic was a factor impacting schools' missed Ramadan and overall fundraising targets.

7 Conclusion: The Pandemic Persists, and so will Islamic Schools

Despite the continued presence of COVID-19 at the time of writing this chapter, the data and insights presented indicate that Islamic schools were well poised to face the initial challenges presented by the pandemic and its aftermath. While schools will likely remain impacted on multiple fronts by COVID-19 for years to come, Islamic school leaders and teachers are more experienced, adept, and equipped to weather this storm in a manner that responds to the multifaceted needs of their staff, students, and communities.

These important institutions were born out of a deep-seated desire to provide an empowering and enriching alterative to Muslim families to simultaneously strengthen students' Muslim identities while enabling them to achieve success in this world and the next. As COVID-19 has pushed Islamic school leaders and educators to navigate never-before seen challenges, there seems to be no better time for innovative ideas to take shape regarding the future of Islamic education in America. What can Islamic schools do to differentiate themselves as distinctive and esteemed educational institutions, while holding firmly to the principles of Islam? By engaging with stakeholders in this moment, Islamic schools can enhance their value proposition even in the face of an uncertain and volatile future.

Appendix A—First Survey: Islamic Schools and COVID-19

Administered: April–May 2020

1. Please click "yes" if you are at least 18 years old and agree to participate in this study.
2. Please click "yes" if your organization is a nonprofit based in the United States AND if it is identified as an Islamic School.
3. Please select "Yes" if any of the following job or position titles most likely aligns with your job/position function. The position can be paid or unpaid.

4. What is your role at the school?
5. Is your school accredited by any state, regional, or national body?
6. How many students are enrolled in your school?
7. What grades are taught in your school?
8. What is the average annual tuition per student at your school?
9. What sect/denomination/school of thought does your school follow?
10. How has the COVID-19 pandemic impacted the number of students enrolled in your school?
11. What grades were most impacted by any dis-enrollment due to COVID-19 pandemic?
12. How is your school providing distance learning?
13. How long did your school take to initiate distance learning due to COVID-19 upon determining to close the physical location?
14. Which of the following tools did your school have prior to the COVID-19 pandemic in relation to distance learning?
15. How do you think the COVID-19 pandemic will impact your enrollment for 2020–2021?
16. Does your school have an endowment?
17. How do you expect the COVID-19 pandemic to impact your endowment during the 2020 calendar year?
18. If your school did not apply for the PPP and/or EIDL, what were the reasons? Choose all applicable responses.
19. In what ways has the COVID-19 pandemic negatively impacted your school this academic year?
20. In what ways has the COVID-19 pandemic positively impacted your school this academic year?
21. Does your school have a distance-learning contingency plan in case the school does not physically reopen in Fall 2020?
22. To what extent are you currently delivering your normal programs and/or services during the COVID-19 pandemic?
23. How has the COVID-19 pandemic impacted the amount of charitable donations your organization has received?
24. How has the COVID-19 pandemic impacted the number of volunteer hours your organization has received?
25. During the next four (4) weeks do you expect donations to your organization:
26. During the next four (4) weeks do you expect the number of volunteer hours to your organization:
27. During Ramadan this year do you expect donations to your organization:

28. During Ramadan this year do you expect the number of volunteer hours to your organization:
29. How likely is your nonprofit able to fully fund payroll for the next four (4) weeks?
30. How do you expect the COVID-19 pandemic to impact your donations for the 2020 calendar year?
31. Have you changed your communications and/or messaging given the COVID-19 pandemic?
32. Have you received a donation or pledge from a single donor after March 11, 2020 (date of COVID-19 pandemic declaration) in the following ranges?
33. Have you received any donation from a "donor advised fund" after March 11, 2020?
34. Has your organization launched a COVID-19 pandemic specific fundraising campaign?
35. How do you expect the COVID-19 pandemic to impact the number of volunteer hours your organization will receive during the 2020 calendar year?
36. How likely is your nonprofit able to fully provide services for the next four (4) weeks?
37. How likely is your nonprofit able to fully fund payroll for the next eight (8) weeks?
38. How concerned are you about the following?
39. Are there any other concerns not mentioned above?
40. What are the critical needs that your constituents are seeking in relation to COVID-19 pandemic? Please select all that apply.
41. What are the most urgent challenges your organization is facing because of the COVID-19 pandemic?
42. To what extent do you think the "CARES Act" funding can benefit your organization?
43. Does your organization intend to benefit from the "CARES Act"?
44. Does your organization have the capacity/capability to benefit from the "CARES Act"?
45. Do you believe Muslim nonprofits will be discriminated in receiving the "Cares Act" funding?
46. Which entity do you trust the most to get help from during this pandemic?
47. What leadership challenges do you expect to face as a result of the COVID-19 pandemic?
48. Are there any other concerns not mentioned above?
49. Have you hired a consultant for any purpose to assist the development of your nonprofit organization in the past?

50. What could the Muslim Philanthropy Initiative at Indiana University or the Center on Muslim Philanthropy do to assist you with? Please check your top five (5).
51. What is your gender?
52. What is your age?
53. Which of the following races do you consider yourself to be (select all that apply)?
54. What is the highest level of school you have completed or the highest degree you have received?
55. What is your total experience working for Islamic schools (both paid and volunteer work)?
56. Please select the job title that most likely aligns with your job function.
57. What is the main cause area of your organization?
58. Is your organization 501(c) registered?
59. For how many years has your organization been in existence?
60. Roughly what are your annual expenditures of your organization?
61. Roughly what is the annual revenue of your organization?
62. Roughly how many "full-time" employees worked for your organization before COVID-19 pandemic?
63. Roughly how many "part-time" employees worked for your organization before COVID-19 pandemic?
64. Roughly how many "volunteers" worked for your organization before COVID-19 pandemic?
65. Does your organization receive any government grants (local, state, or federal)?
66. In which city is your organization located/registered?

Appendix B—Second Survey: The Impact of COVID-19 on Islamic School Enrollment

Administered October–November 2021

1. Are you currently a principal/head of school at a full-time Islamic school?
2. When was your Islamic school established?
3. Where is your school located?
4. Which grade levels does your school serve? Please check all that apply.
5. When the 2020–2021 academic school year started, what was the method of instructional delivery at your school?
6. What is the current method of instructional delivery at your school?

7. How has COVID-19 impacted enrollment at your Islamic school for the 2020–2021 school year?
8. If your school experienced an enrollment decline, which grades were impacted most by enrollment decline at your school?
9. If your school experienced an enrollment decline for the 2020–2021 school year, what do you attribute the decline to?
10. How would you describe the percentage of families *requesting* financial assistance for tuition for the 2020–2021 school year compared to the previous year?
11. How would you describe the percentage of students *receiving* financial aid at your school for the 2020–2021 year compared to the previous year?
12. Please select the statement that best describes the tuition trend for the 2020–2021 school year compared to the previous academic year at your school.
13. If your school experienced enrollment challenges, how has your school tried to address these challenges?
14. Please share any additional comments you have regarding the impact of COVID-19 on enrollment at your school.

Appendix C—Third Survey: COVID-19 and Islamic Schools: 2020–2021 Year in Review

Administered May–June 2021

Eligibility

1. Were you a Principal or Head of School of a full-time Islamic school this past academic year (2020–2021)?
2. Is your full-time Islamic school located in the United States?

School Demographics

3. Which US region best describes the location of your full-time Islamic school?
4. Is your school located in a state that provides vouchers, tax credits, or scholarships to private schools or to eligible students attending private schools?
5. What grades does your full-time Islamic school serve? (Check all that apply)
6. When was your full-time Islamic school established?

Instructional Models: Trend Data for Academic Year 2020–2021

7. What instructional model was offered by your Islamic school at the *start* of the 2020–2021 school year?
8. What instructional method was offered by your Islamic school at the *END* of the 2020–2021 school year?
9. How would you describe your students' *onsite* attendance from the beginning of 2020–2021 school year to the end of the academic year?

Finance-Related: Trend Data for Academic Year 2020–2021

10. In 2020–2021, our school enrollment:
11. In 2020–2021, our school had to reduce staff to meet budget constraints.
12. In 2020–2021, our school was able to meet our Ramadan fundraising goals.
13. In 2020–2021, our school was able to meet our overall fundraising goals.
14. In 2020–2021, our school received PPP Funds.
15. In 2020–2021, our school received EANS Funds.

Biggest Challenges and Needs

16. What were the *Three Biggest Challenges* your school faced this academic year?
17. What are the *Top Three Professional Development Needs* for your *STAFF* to prepare for the upcoming school year?
18. What are your *Top Three Needs* as a *Principal/Head of School* for this upcoming year?

OPTIONAL: What's on Your Mind?

19. Tell us anything else related to how ISLA can support you and your school! We're listening and would love to better understand your needs, wants, and dreams. Add your email if you'd like a reply!

Bibliography

Allen, J.B., S. Jain, and A.H. Church. "Using a Pulse Survey Approach to Drive Organizational Change." *Organizational Development Review* 52, no. 3 (2020): 62–68.

American Academy of Pediatrics. COVID-19 Guidance for Safe Schools and Promotion of In-Person Learning. (2021). Accessed September 30, 2021. https://www.aap.org/en/pages/2019-novel-coronavirus-covid-19-infections/clinical-guidance/covid-19-planning-considerations-return-to-in-person-education-in-schools.

Azmat, Sufia. Email to Islamic Educators' Communication Network. March 2, 2020.

Brifkani, Isra, and Shaza Khan. "The Impact of COVID-19 on Islamic Schools in the

United States: Implications and Recommendations." *Journal of Education in Muslim Societies* 2, no. 2 (2021): 82–89. https://doi.org/10.2979/jems.2.2.05.

Buonsenso, Danilo, Damian Roland, Cristina De Rose, Pablo Vásquez-Hoyos, Bazlin Ramly, et al. "Schools Closures During the COVID-19 Pandemic: A Catastrophic Global Situation." *The Pediatric Infectious Disease Journal* 40, no. 4 (2021): 146–150. https://doi.org/10.1097/INF.0000000000003052.

Centers for Disease Control and Prevention. "Guidance for COVID-19 Prevention for K-12 Schools." (2021). Accessed September 30, 2021. https://www.cdc.gov/coronavirus/2019-ncov/community/schools-childcare/k-12-guidance.html.

Council of Islamic Schools of North America. Accessed March 5, 2021. https://cisnausa.org.

Haddad, Yvonne Y., and Jane I. Smith. "Introduction: The Challenge of Islamic Education in North America." In *Educating the Muslims of America*. Edited by Yvonne Y. Haddad, Farid Senzai, and Jane I. Smith. Oxford: Oxford University Press, 2009.

Islamic Schools League of America. "The Impact COVID-19 on Enrollment in Full-Time Islamic Schools for the 2020–2021 Academic Year." November 2020. Accessed September 30, 2021. https://theisla.org/covid-19-impact-on-islamic-school-enrollment.

Islamic Schools League of America. "COVID-19 and Islamic Schools: 2020–2021 Year in Review." September 2021. Accessed October 8, 2021. https://theisla.org/covid-19-islamic-schools-2020-2021-year-in-review.

Islamic Schools League of America. "ISLA Islamic School Registry Database." (2022). Unpublished raw data.

Islamic Schools League of America. "Keeping Students Safe: Joint Statement on School Re-Openings and COVID Vaccines." September 1, 2021. https://theisla.org/keeping-students-safe. Accessed September 29, 2021.

Jenco, Melissa. "Updated AAP School Reopening Guidance Calls for Layers of Protection, Flexibility." *American Academy of Pediatrics*, August 19, 2020. Accessed September 30, 2021. https://www.aappublications.org/news/2020/08/19/schoolreentry081920.

Keyworth, Karen. "Islamic Schools of the United States: Data-Based Profiles." Institute for Social Policy and Understanding, Washington, DC, May 2011. https://www.ispu.org/wp-content/uploads/2011/04/2011_609_ISPU-Report_Islamic-Schools_Keyworth_WEB.pdf?x61645.

Khan, Sabith, and Shariq Siddiqui. *Islamic Education in the United States and the Evolution of Muslim Nonprofit Institutions*. Northampton: Edward Elgar, 2017.

Khan, S., P. Salahuddin, and S. Imam. "Looking Back and Re-Envisioning the Future: Full-time Islamic schools in the United States." In *Principles and Practices of Education in Islam*, edited by Shaikh Abdul Mabud. Oldham, UK: Beacon Books, forthcoming.

McCluskey, Neal. "Private Schooling After a Year of COVID-19: How the Private Sector has Fared and How to Keep It Healthy." CATO Institute Policy Analysis. April 13, 2021. Accessed September 20, 2021. https://www.cato.org/sites/cato.org/files/2021-04/policy-analysis-no-914.pdf.

Muhammad, R. Zakiyyah. *Mother of the Nation: Clara Evans Muhammad*. Anaheim, CA: Institute of Muslim American Studies, 2020.

Office of Elementary & Secondary Education. "Emergency Assistance to Non-Public Schools." (2021). Accessed September 30, 2021. https://oese.ed.gov/offices/education-stabilization-fund/emergency-assistance-non-public-schools.

Rashid, Hakim M., and Zakiyyah Muhammad. "The Sister Clara Muhammad Schools: Pioneers in the Development of Islamic Education in America." *The Journal of Negro Education 61*, no. 2 (1992): 178–185.

Shafer, S. "A Year of COVID-19: What it Looked Like for Schools." *Education Week*. March 4, 2021. Accessed October 1, 2021. https://www.edweek.org/leadership/a-year-of-covid-19-what-it-looked-like-for-schools/2021/03.

Shaikh, Salman. Email to Islamic Educators' Communication Network. March 12, 2020.

UNESCO. "Education: From Disruption to Recovery." United Nations Educational, Scientific, and Cultural Organization, February 28, 2022. Accessed September 27, 2021. https://en.unesco.org/covid19/educationresponse.

UNESCO. "WHAT'S NEXT? Lessons on Education Recovery: Findings from a Survey of Ministries of Education amid the COVID-19 Pandemic." United Nations Educational, Scientific, and Cultural Organization, Paris, June 2021. http://uis.unesco.org/sites/default/files/documents/lessons_on_education_recovery.pdf.

U.S. Department of the Treasury. "Paycheck Protection Program." 2021. Accessed September 30, 2021. https://home.treasury.gov/policy-issues/coronavirus/assistance-for-small-businesses/paycheck-protection-program.

CHAPTER 8

An Examination of Ramadan Fasting and COVID-19 Outcomes in the UK

Karim Mitha, Salman Waqar, Miqdad Asaria, Mehrunisha Suleiman and Nazim Ghouri

1 Introduction

Many of the world's 1.8 billion Muslims fast during the month of Ramadan, abstaining from all food and drink from dawn to dusk—which, in some parts of the world, can be for up to nineteen hours. While the Islamic tradition exempts people suffering from acute or chronic illness from fasting, some people with significant comorbidities still choose to fast, often against medical advice.[1] The peak of the first wave of the COVID-19 pandemic in the UK coincided with the start of Ramadan, which took place in April–May 2020. This was also during a period of a government-imposed lockdown in which social and communal activities were severely restricted.

In the UK, home to approximately 3 million Muslims, many of whom fast during Ramadan, the Muslim community disproportionately suffered from the impacts of COVID-19 over multiple waves of the pandemic.[2] While some commentators have sought to explain this disproportionate impact with reference to "Muslim cultural practices," particularly during Ramadan, others have pointed to structural factors which have resulted in increased risk—for example, members of the Muslim community being over-represented in higher risk and public-facing jobs, being more likely to experience poorer living conditions, and existing inequalities in access to, uptake of, and experience within healthcare services, all of which increase exposure and affect coping with infection from the SARS CoV-2 virus.

In this chapter, we examine the contextual factors leading to health disparities among Muslims in the UK, and how they have played out during the

1 Nazim Ghouri et al., "Diabetes, Driving and Fasting During Ramadan: The Interplay Between Secular and Religious Law," *BMJ Open Diabetes Research & Care* 6, no. 1 (June 2018): e000520, https://doi.org/10.1136/bmjdrc-2018-000520.

2 " Deaths involving COVID-19 by religious group, England: 24 January 2020 to 28 February 2021, May 13 2021, https://www.ons.gov.uk/peoplepopulationandcommunity/birthsdeathsandmarriages/deaths/articles/deathsinvolvingcovid19byreligiousgroupengland/24january2020to28february2021

 | DOI:10.1163/9789004679771_010

COVID-19 pandemic. We then specifically consider whether ritual fasting during Ramadan contributed to inequalities. We finally assert that structural factors largely explain the disproportionate impacts on Muslims observed in the early stages of the pandemic.

2 British Muslims in Context

The most recent population estimates from the Office of National Statistics (ONS) suggest there are approximately 3.3 million Muslims in Great Britain, comprising 5 percent of its population.[3] It is a young population, with 50 percent under the age of 25,[4] and a diverse one, though roughly two-thirds have South Asian ancestry—as demonstrated by Figure 8.1.

It is a community which continues to experience substantial socio-economic disadvantage.[5] Sundas Ali examined 2011 census data on the Muslim population and mapped it to the 10 percent most deprived areas in England according to the 2010 Index of Multiple Deprivation (IMD)—this elucidated that nearly 50 percent of Muslims in England lived in the 10 percent most deprived areas of the country.[6] Changes in population distribution and in the distribution of levels of deprivation across England since that time have resulted in the most recent statistic being just under one-third of Muslims in England living in the 10 percent most deprived English local authority districts, according to the 2019 Index of Multiple Deprivation.[7] This is demonstrated in the Tables 8.1 and 8.2.

3 "Religion by Sex and Age-Group in Great Britain, 2018 to 2019," Office for National Statistics, December 13, 2019, https://www.ons.gov.uk/peoplepopulationandcommunity/culturalidentity/religion/adhocs/10999religionbysexandagegroupingreatbritain2018to2019.

NB: This estimate has been revised based on figures from the 2021 census, which puts the British Muslim population at 3.9 million in England and Wales. "Religion, England and Wales: Census 2021. November 29, 2022. https://www.ons.gov.uk/peoplepopulationandcommunity/culturalidentity/religion/bulletins/religionenglandandwales/census2021. Data has not been disaggregated by ethnicity, thus this chapter uses previous mid-census estimates from the ONS. The census in Scotland was postponed due to the COVID-19 pandemic and updated data will not be released until Autumn 2023.

4 Sundas Ali, "British Muslims in Numbers: A Demographic, Socio-Economic and Health Profile of Muslims in Britain drawing on the 2011 Census," *Muslim Council of Britain*, January 2015, https://mcb.org.uk/report/british-muslims-in-numbers/.

5 Ali, "British Muslims in Numbers"; and "Religion, Education and Work in England and Wales: February 2020," Office for National Statistics, February 26, 2020, https://www.ons.gov.uk/peoplepopulationandcommunity/culturalidentity/religion/articles/religioneducationandworkinenglandandwales/february2020.

6 Ali, "British Muslims in Numbers."

7 "Population Characteristics Research Tables," Office for National Statistics, December 4, 2019,

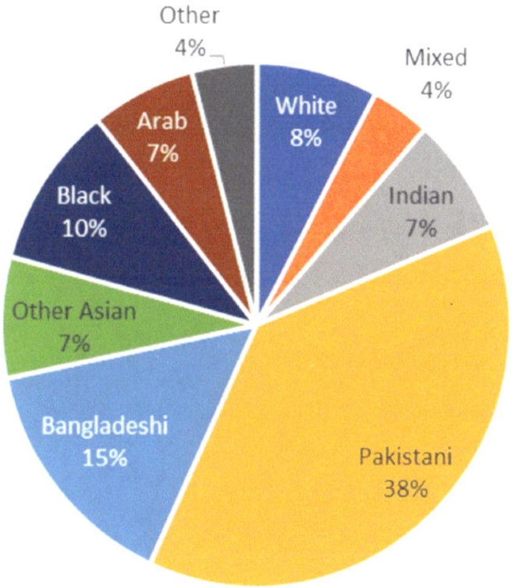

FIGURE 8.1
Ethnic breakdown of Muslim population in England and Wales, Census 2011

TABLE 8.1 Top 10 percent local authority districts in England and their Muslim population

Top 10% most deprived local authority districts, England—2010[a]	Muslim population (rounded to nearest 1,000)[b]	Top 10% most deprived local authority districts, England—2019[c]	Muslim population (rounded to nearest 1,000)[d]
Liverpool	15,000	Blackpool	1,000
Hackney	35,000	Knowsley	1,000
Newham	98,000	Liverpool	22,000
Manchester	79,000	Kingston upon Hull, City of	4,000
Knowsley	0	Middlesbrough	13,000
Blackpool	1,000	Manchester	100,000
Tower Hamlets	88,000	Birmingham	280,000
Middlesbrough	10,000	Burnley	5,000

https://www.ons.gov.uk/peoplepopulationandcommunity/populationandmigration/populationestimates/datasets/populationcharacteristicsresearchtables; and "English Indices of Deprivation 2019," Ministry of Housing, Communities & Local Government, September 26, 2019, https://www.gov.uk/government/statistics/english-indices-of-deprivation-2019; and "English Indices of Deprivation 2010", Ministry of Housing, Communities and Local Government, March 24, 2011; https://www.gov.uk/government/statistics/english-indices-of-deprivation-2010; and "Religion, usual place of residence", Nomis – Official census and labour market statistics, January 30, 2015 https://www.nomisweb.co.uk/census/2011/ks209ew

NB: IMD does not showcase changes in deprivation over time, but is a measure of relative deprivation at particular period. Thus, while areas may become more or less deprived over time, the IMD measures deprivation of the area relative to other areas at that point. IMD of local authorities are by "ranks", "scores", or "proportion of neighbourhoods in the 10% most deprived nationally. We have used ranks of scores in this comparison as it is least susceptible to variation of deprivation within a local authority area.

TABLE 8.1 Top 10 percent local authority districts in England and their Muslim population (*cont.*)

Top 10% most deprived local authority districts, England—2010[a]	Muslim population (rounded to nearest 1,000)[b]	Top 10% most deprived local authority districts, England—2019[c]	Muslim population (rounded to nearest 1,000)[d]
Birmingham	234,000	Blackburn with Darwen	42,000
Kingston upon Hull	5,000	Hartlepool	1,000
Burnley	9,000	Nottingham	30,000
Sandwell	25,000	Sandwell	34,000
Haringey	36,000	Bradford	113,000
Islington	20,000	Stoke-on-Trent	21,000
Waltham Forest	57,000	Rochdale	36,000
Stoke-on-Trent	15,000	Hyndburn	10,000
Blackburn with Darwen	40,000	Hastings	1,000
Salford	6,000	Salford	7,000
Hastings	1,000	Oldham	48,000
Nottingham	27,000	Great Yarmouth	1,000
Wolverhampton	9,000	Barking and Dagenham	41,000
Barking and Dagenham	26,000	Hackney	35,000
Rochdale	29,000	Halton	1,000
Hartlepool	1,000	Wolverhampton	10,000
Leicester	61,000	Walsall	25,000
Bradford	129,000	St. Helens	1,000
Halton	0	South Tyneside	3,000
Greenwich	17,000	Tameside	12,000
Lambeth	22,000	North East Lincolnshire	1,000
Walsall	22,000	Thanet	5,000
Lewisham	18,000	Barrow-in-Furness	2,000
Barrow-in-Furness	0	Leicester	69,000
Pendle	16,000		

a. There were 326 local authority districts at the time of the 2010 IMD (Index of Multiple Deprivation)
b. Muslim population as per the 2011 Census
c. There were 317 local authority districts at the time of the 2019 IMD
d. Muslim population as per the mid-census estimates (2016) by ONS

SOURCE: MINISTRY OF HOUSING, COMMUNITIES AND LOCAL GOVERNMENT, "ENGLISH INDICES OF DEPRIVATION 2019", SEPTEMBER 26, 2019; MINISTRY OF HOUSING, COMMUNITIES AND LOCAL GOVERNMENT, "ENGLISH INDICES OF DEPRIVATION 2010", MARCH 24 2011; OFFICE FOR NATIONAL STATISTICS, "POPULATION CHARACTERISTICS RESEARCH TABLES", DECEMBER 4 2019; NOMIS – OFFICIAL CENSUS AND LABOUR MARKET STATISTICS "RELIGION, USUAL PLACE OF RESIDENCE", JANUARY 30 2013

TABLE 8.2 Top 10 percent of local authorities with largest Muslim population

Top 10% of English local authority districts with the highest Muslim population—2011[a]	Muslim population (rounded to nearest 1,000)[b]	Top 10% of English local authority districts with highest Muslim population—2016[c]	Muslim population (rounded to nearest 1,000)[d]
Birmingham	230,000	Birmingham	280,000
Bradford	129,000	Newham	135,000
Newham	98,000	Tower Hamlets	128,000
Tower Hamlets	88,000	Bradford	113,000
Manchester	79,000	Manchester	100,000
Redbridge	65,000	Brent	78,000
Leicester	61,000	Redbridge	78,000
Kirklees	61,000	Kirklees	71,000
Brent	58,000	Leicester	69,000
Waltham Forest	56,000	Ealing	63,000
Ealing	53,000	Luton	57,000
Enfield	52,000	Waltham Forest	55,000
Luton	50,000	Enfield	54,000
Sheffield	43,000	Westminster	49,000
Leeds	41,000	Oldham	48,000
Westminster	40,000	Sheffield	46,000
Oldham	40,000	Hillingdon	43,000
Blackburn with Darwen	40,000	Blackburn with Darwen	42,000
Barnet	37,000	Barking and Dagenham	41,000
Haringey	36,000	Slough	40,000
Hounslow	36,000	Leeds	39,000
Hackney	35,000	Haringey	39,000
Slough	33,000	Bolton	37,000
Bolton	33,000	Rochdale	36,000
Harrow	30,000	Hackney	35,000
Croydon	30,000	Sandwell	34,000
Rochdale	29,000	Croydon	32,000
Hillingdon	29,000	Hounslow	32,000
Nottingham	27,000	Southwark	31,000
Camden	27,000	Wandsworth	31,000
Barking and Dagenham	26,000	Nottingham	30,000
Sandwell	25,000	Barnet	30,000
Wandsworth	25,000		

a. There were 326 local authority districts at the time of the 2010 IMD (Index of Multiple Deprivation)
b. Muslim population as per the 2011 Census
c. There were 317 local authority districts at the time of the 2019 IMD
d. Muslim population as per the mid-census estimates (2016) by ONS
SOURCE: OFFICE FOR NATIONAL STATISTICS, "POPULATION CHARACTERISTICS RESEARCH TABLES", DECEMBER 4 2019; NOMIS – OFFICIAL CENSUS AND LABOUR MARKET STATISTICS "RELIGION, USUAL PLACE OF RESIDENCE", JANUARY 30 2013

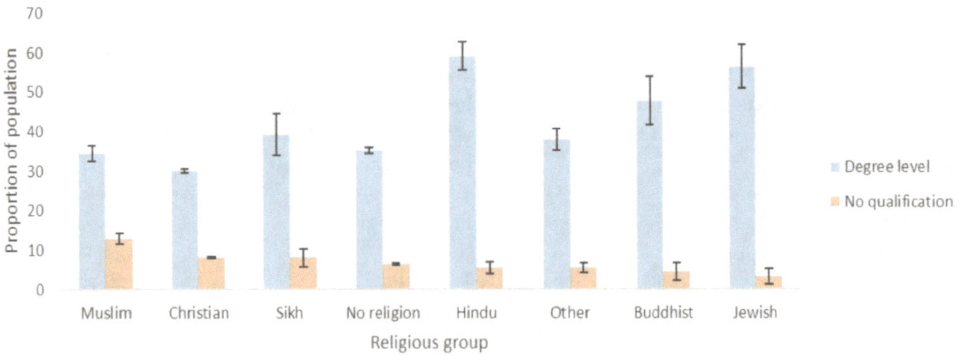

FIGURE 8.2 Highest level of educational attainment of those aged 16–64 by religious group in England and Wales, 2018
Note: error bars represent 95 percent confidence interval.
OFFICE FOR NATIONAL STATISTICS, "RELIGION, EDUCATION AND WORK IN ENGLAND AND WALES: FEBRUARY 2020," FEBRUARY 26, 2020

While 22 percent of the UK population live in relative low poverty after housing costs (meaning a household income of less than 60 percent the median income),[8] that figure varies by ethnic and religious groups. Anthony Heath and Yaojun Li note that approximately 50 percent of British Muslims live in poverty—with 57 percent of Pakistani Muslims, 56 percent of Black African Muslims, and 49 percent of Bangladeshi Muslims living in poverty.[9] Muslims in Britain experience substantial inequalities in terms of educational and employment. The ONS Annual Population Survey in England and Wales showed that among those aged sixteen and over in 2018, Muslims have statistically significantly the highest proportion of individuals with no qualifications (13 percent), and the second-lowest proportion of those with degree level qualifications (35 percent, compared to Christians with 30 percent).[10]

Muslims also have statistically significantly the lowest employment rate of all religious groups, with only 55 percent of those aged 16–64 in employment—which may be due to higher rates of economic inactivity among Muslim women

8 Brigid Francis-Devine, "Poverty in the UK: Statistics," House of Commons Library, October 16, 2021, https://commonslibrary.parliament.uk/research-briefings/sn07096/.

9 Anthony Heath and Yaojun Li, "Review of the Relationship Between Religion and Poverty: An Analysis for the Joseph Rowntree Foundation," Institute for Social and Economic Research, 2015, https://www.iser.essex.ac.uk/research/publications/523019.

10 Office for National Statistics, "Religion, Education and Work in England and Wales: February 2020."

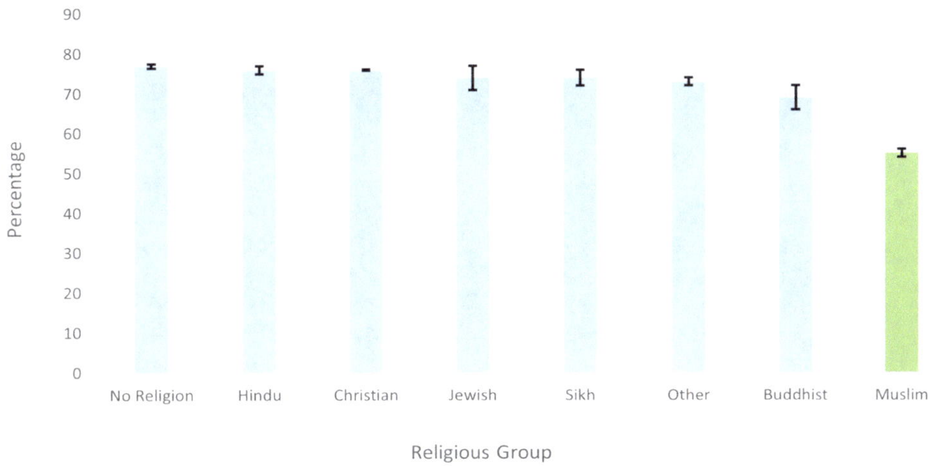

FIGURE 8.3 Employment rate among those aged 16–64 by religious group in England and Wales, 2018
Note: error bars represent 95 percent confidence interval.
OFFICE FOR NATIONAL STATISTICS, "RELIGION, EDUCATION AND WORK IN ENGLAND AND WALES: FEBRUARY 2020," FEBRUARY 26, 2020

(56 percent of Muslim women aged 16–64 being economically inactive, the highest of all religious groups), as demonstrated by Figures 8.3 and 8.4.[11]

Though there has been some change, as demonstrated by Figure 8.5, Muslims continue to lag behind their counterparts in other religious groups in the workforce. Among those aged sixteen and over in England and Wales, Muslims have the lowest proportion of individuals in professional occupations (21 percent) compared to all other religious groups, and the second highest proportion of people in low-skilled occupations (13 percent, compared to Buddhists at 17 percent) as seen in Figure 8.6.[12] As a consequence, Muslims have the lowest median wage across all religious groups—£9.63 per hour in 2018, half the wage of the highest earning religious group, as seen in Figure 8.7.[13]

Reasons for these inequalities experienced by Muslims are manifold ranging from the much younger demographic structure of the community, cultural views pertaining to gender and involvement in the mainstream workforce,

11 Office for National Statistics, "Religion, Education and Work in England and Wales: February 2020."

12 Office for National Statistics, "Religion, Education and Work in England and Wales: February 2020."

13 Office for National Statistics, "Religion, Education and Work in England and Wales: February 2020."

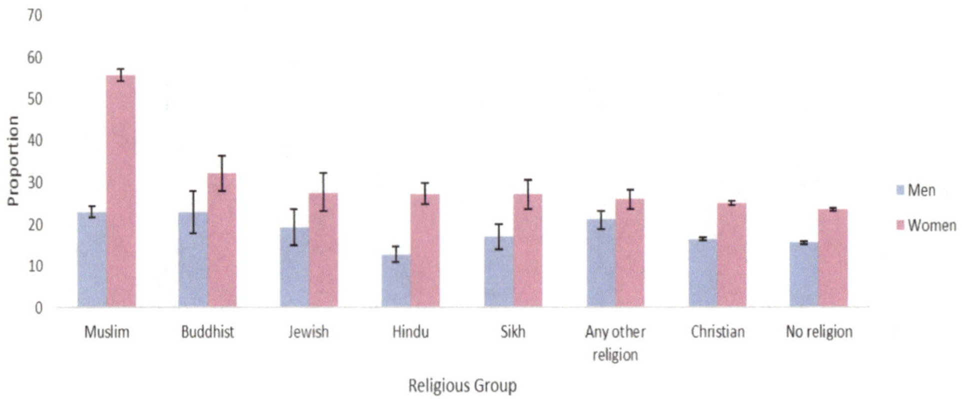

FIGURE 8.4 Proportion of 16–64-year-old population that is economically inactive, by religious group in England and Wales, 2018

Note: error bars represent 95 percent confidence interval.

OFFICE FOR NATIONAL STATISTICS, "RELIGION, EDUCATION AND WORK IN ENGLAND AND WALES: FEBRUARY 2020," FEBRUARY 26, 2020

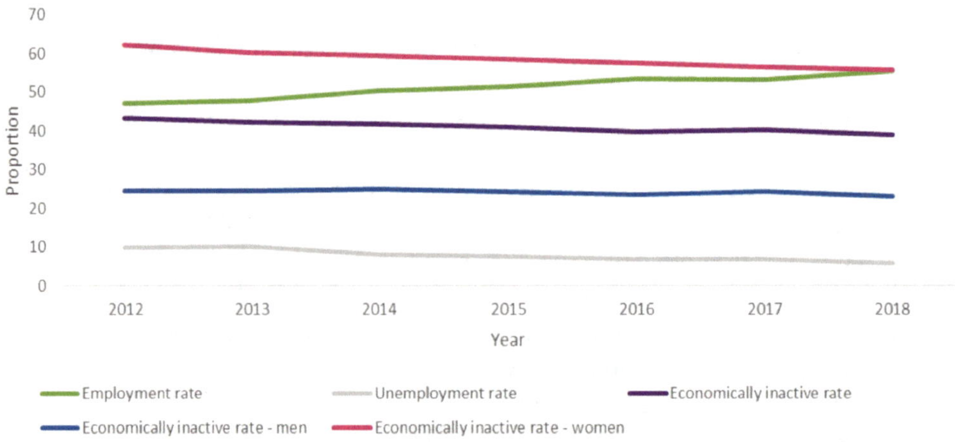

FIGURE 8.5 Proportion of employment type among 16–64-year-old Muslims in England and Wales, 2018

OFFICE FOR NATIONAL STATISTICS, "RELIGION, EDUCATION AND WORK IN ENGLAND AND WALES: FEBRUARY 2020," FEBRUARY 26, 2020

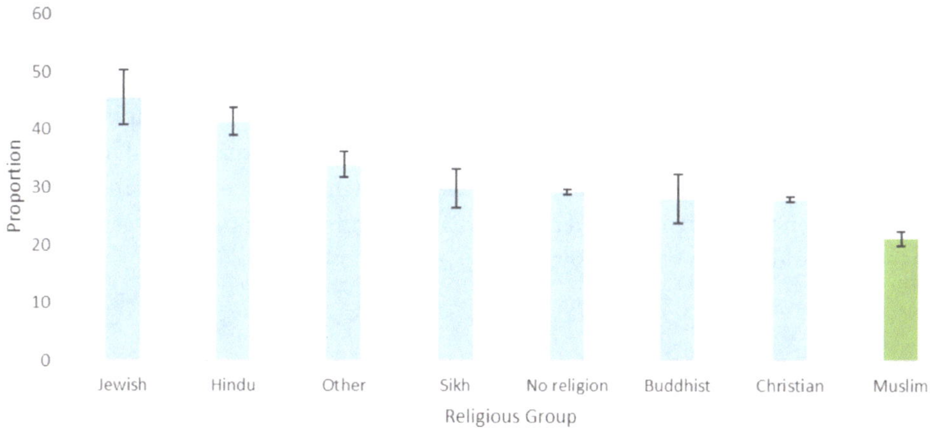

FIGURE 8.6 Proportion of 16–64-year-old population that is in a high-skilled occupation, by religious group in England and Wales, 2018
Note: error bars represent 95 percent confidence interval.
OFFICE FOR NATIONAL STATISTICS, "RELIGION, EDUCATION AND WORK IN ENGLAND AND WALES: FEBRUARY 2020," FEBRUARY 26, 2020

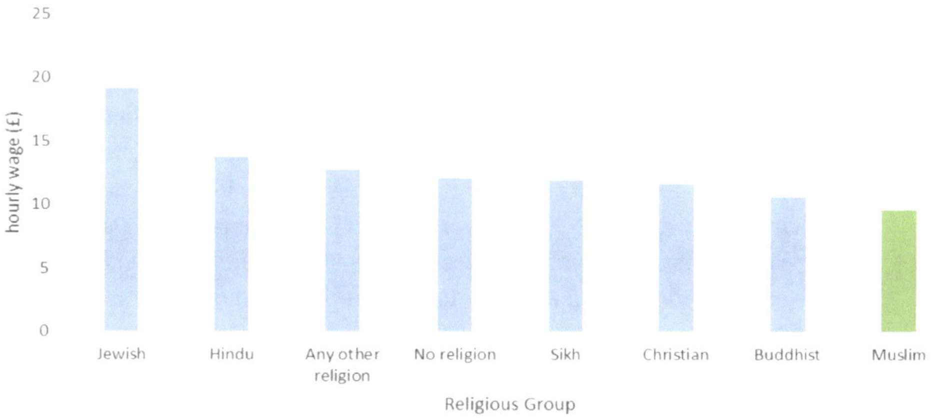

FIGURE 8.7 Median hourly wage among those aged 16–64 by religious group in England and Wales, 2018
OFFICE FOR NATIONAL STATISTICS, "RELIGION, EDUCATION AND WORK IN ENGLAND AND WALES: FEBRUARY 2020," FEBRUARY 26, 2020

social factors due to being a predominantly immigrant community and hence lacking wider social and cultural capital to facilitate upward social mobility, to broader factors of discrimination and systemic exclusion in mainstream workplace settings—all of which impede social mobility.[14] Through employing a social determinants of health framework, it is therefore unsurprising that these inequalities in education and employment influence broader health inequalities seen in and experienced by the Muslim community in the UK,[15] as will be discussed later in this chapter.

3 Attitudes Toward Minorities in Britain

Social vilification of British Muslim communities is often an "everyday" form of racism, which Philomena Essed describes as being those personal, daily, encounters of prejudice in day-to-day encounters—essentially a more "palatable" and "innocuous" form of racism, whereby overt acts of direct discrimination are now replaced by a more "British," subdued form of indirect discrimination.[16] The experiences of discrimination toward Muslim communities in Britain needs to be contextualized within broader inequalities experienced by ethnic minorities. Due to historical patterns of migration, and that nearly two-thirds of British Muslims are Asian (i.e., from the South Asian subcontinent), Muslims in Britain are often *racialized* as Asian.[17] Research by the Nuffield Trust showed that ethnic minorities in Britain have to send out 60 percent more CVs than White counterparts to be invited to interview for job applications—with that figure rising to 70 percent for Pakistani applicants, and 80 percent for Nigerian applicants.[18] Only 18 percent of Muslim students in higher education were awarded top grades, the lowest proportion out of any religious

14 Jacqueline Stevenson et al., "The Social Mobility Challenges Faced by Young Muslims," Social Mobility Commission, September 7, 2017, https://www.gov.uk/government/publications/social-mobility-challenges-faced-by-young-muslims.

15 Fran Darlington et al., "Exploring Ethnic Inequalities in Health: Evidence from the Health Survey for England, 1998–2011," *Diversity and Equality in Health and Care* 12, no. 2 (2015): 54–65.

16 Philomena Essed, *Everyday Racism: Reports from Women of Two Cultures* (Claremont, CA: Hunter House, 1990).

17 Nasar Meer, *Key Concepts in Race and Ethnicity*, 3rd ed. (Los Angeles, CA: SAGE, 2014).

18 Valentina Di Stasio and Anthony Heath, "Are Employers in Britain Discriminating Against Ethnic Minorities?" Nuffield Trust, accessed March 27, 2022, http://csi.nuff.ox.ac.uk/wp-content/uploads/2019/01/Are-employers-in-Britain-discriminating-against-ethnic-minorities_final.pdf.

group.[19] Katy Sian noted that institutional racism was endemic among UK higher education providers, with substantial racism experienced by Black and Asian academics.[20] Indeed, during the first COVID-19 lockdown it was reported that British universities were offering ham sandwiches to Muslim students quarantining in university-provided accommodation thus demonstrating institutional discrimination via ignorance regarding particularities of the Muslim faith.[21]

Experiences of institutional Islamophobia are rife in Britain. While the All-Party Parliamentary Group on British Muslims defined Islamophobia as "a type of racism that targets expressions of Muslimness or perceived Muslimness,"[22] this has not been without controversy—with some even denying Islamophobia is an issue.[23] Regardless of definitional semantics, the experiences of Muslims in Britain are laden with examples of discrimination. Aasma Day, for instance, noted how research findings from the British Islamic Medical Association (BIMA) noted that Muslim medics working within the National Health Service (NHS) face harassment and are taunted by co-workers and patients alike, with racial epithets hurled toward them, such as being called "terrorists," told to "go back to your country," and being taunted with bacon and alcohol.[24] Islamophobia has also been positioned as an "English problem" by (White) scholars of Muslims in Scotland—who suggest that due to Scotland's civic nationalism, that Muslims in Scotland have a Scottish accent, and that there are Muslims

19 Natasha Codiroli Mcmaster, "Research Insight: Religion and Belief in UK Higher Education," Advance HE, March 17, 2020, https://www.advance-he.ac.uk/knowledge-hub/research-insight-religion-and-belief-uk-higher-education.

20 Katy P. Sian, *Navigating Institutional Racism in British Universities* (Cham: Springer International Publishing, 2019), https://doi.org/10.1007/978-3-030-14284-1.

21 Daniel Hewitt, "University Covid Crisis: Muslim Student Stuck in Self-Isolation Served Ham Sandwiches," ITV News, September 29, 2020, https://www.itv.com/news/2020-09-29/university-covid-crisis-muslim-student-stuck-in-self-isolation-served-ham-sandwiches.

22 "Islamophobia Defined—The Inquiry into a Working Definition of Islamophobia," All-Party Parliamentary Group on British Muslims, 2018, https://appgbritishmuslims.org/publications.

23 Hugh Goddard, "Halal Haggis? An Introduction to Islam and Muslims in Scotland," Alwaleed Centre for the Study of Islam in the Contemporary World, University of Edinburgh, February 2015.

24 Aasma Day, "Exclusive: Muslim Medics Called 'Terrorists' and Told 'Go Back to Your Country'—By Patients," *HuffPost UK*, September 12, 2020, https://www.huffingtonpost.co.uk/entry/islamophobia-nhs-patients-muslims-religion-abuse-discrimination_uk_5f567984c5b62b3add4442b6; and Aasma Day, "Exclusive: Muslim Medics Taunted About Bacon and Alcohol—By Their Own NHS Colleagues," *HuffPost UK*, September 11, 2020, https://www.huffingtonpost.co.uk/entry/islamophobia-nhs-muslim-doctors-institutionalised_uk_5f562e80c5b62b3add43cccb.

in the Scottish Parliament, this means there is "nae problem here."[25] This view reframes the economic marginalization and exclusion of Scotland's Muslims from the mainstream workforce[26] as "economic resilience" due their greater levels of self-employment.[27] Indeed, this view that Islamophobia is an "English problem" due to "Caledonian exceptionalism" has been accepted by Scottish institutions,[28] despite criticisms and research from scholars such as Harris, Goldie, Davidson and Virdee, and Mitha, who have noted various examples of Muslims facing direct and indirect discrimination in Scotland at various levels from the everyday (i.e., assumptions of inability to speak or write in English), blatant (i.e., being told to "go back home", instances of rocks being thrown at hijabi women, firebombing of mosques), indirect (i.e., anecdotes of buses not stopping for visibly Muslim people, being passed for promotions in the workplace), and institutional (i.e., referring Muslim students to the Home Office Prevent counter-terrorism program).[29]

Hilary Aked notes that Muslims accessing mental health support are referred to the Prevent counter-terrorism program at a disproportionately greater rate than other religious groups, suggesting a systemic linking of religiosity, poor mental health, and radicalization.[30] Statistics from the Home Office note that in 2019/2020, half of all religiously motivated hate crimes were against Muslims and Muslim adults were the group most likely to experience a hate crime.[31]

25 Goddard, "Halal Haggis?"; and Stefano Bonino, *Muslims in Scotland: The Making of Community in a Post-9/11 World* (Edinburgh: Edinburgh University Press, 2017).

26 Khadijah Elshayyal, "Scottish Muslims in Numbers," University of Edinburgh, October 28, 2020, https://www.ed.ac.uk/literatures-languages-cultures/alwaleed/research/muslims-in-europe/scottish-muslims-in-numbers;

27 Goddard, "Halal Haggis?"; and Stefano Bonino, *Muslims in Scotland: The Making of Community in a Post-9/11 World* (Edinburgh: Edinburgh University Press, 2017).

28 Goddard, "Halal Haggis?"; and Bonino, *Muslims in Scotland.*

29 Scarlet Harris, "*Muslims in Scotland*: Integrationism, State Racism and the 'Scottish Dream,'" *Race & Class* 60, no. 2 (October 2018): 114–119, https://doi.org/10.1177/0306396818793583; Paul Goldie, "Cultural Racism and Islamophobia in Glasgow," in *No Problem Here: Understanding Racism in Scotland*, ed. Neil Davidson et al. (Edinburgh: Luath Press, 2018); Neil Davidson and Satnam Virdee, "Understanding Racism in Scotland," in *No Problem Here: Understanding Racism in Scotland*, ed. Neil Davidson et al. (Edinburgh: Luath Press, 2018); K. Mitha, "Identity, Islamophobia, and Mental Health: A Qualitative Investigation into Mental Health Needs Amongst Scotland's Muslims," *European Journal of Public Health* 28, no. suppl. 1 (May 1, 2018): 23, https://doi.org/10.1093/eurpub/cky047.013.

30 Hilary Aked, "UK Police are Making Muslim Mental Health a Terrorism Flag," *Al Jazeera*, June 8, 2021, https://www.aljazeera.com/opinions/2021/6/8/uk-police-is-making-muslim-mental-health-a-terrorism-flag.

31 "Hate Crime, England and Wales, 2019/2020," Home Office, October 13, 2020, https://www.gov.uk/government/statistics/hate-crime-england-and-wales-2019-to-2020.

Despite these substantial examples of Islamophobia, there has been a curious "myth of denial" in the public discourse as to the influence of systemic discrimination on health outcomes.

While first-generation migrant communities may have experienced, and even expected, outright racism during settlement, current racism experienced by second and subsequent generations and long-standing minority and migrant communities in Britain tends to be more subtle and micro-aggressive.[32] Addai notes that for racially minoritized individuals growing up in majority-White areas, everyday racism is part of their lived experience,[33] through encountering instances of direct discrimination (i.e., called racist language), subtle forms of racism, or everyday microaggressions,[34] and gaslighting by denying racist statements such as "where are you from?" and "you speak good English," or "prove you can write" are actually racist.[35] Indeed, Sarah Atayero notes there is often an onus on individuals experiencing racism to "prove" it exists,[36] despite evidence showing racialized individuals continue to experience subtle and blatant forms of racism.[37] Thind notes that experiences of subtle forms of racism cause the victim to question whether the experience was "real" or whether it was indeed racist, which in effect "Other"-ises individuals and excludes them from negotiating and taking part in a shared national identity due to social exclusion and not being considered part of the mainstream.[38] The UK Government Commission on Race and Ethnic Disparities, for instance, was called an example of institutional gaslighting by its con-

---

32 Sarah Atayero, "Decolonisation Among Clinicians," *The Psychologist*, March 2020, https://thepsychologist.bps.org.uk/volume-33/march-2020/decolonisation-among-clinicians; Essed, *Everyday Racism*; and Derald Wing Sue et al., "Racial Microaggressions in Everyday Life: Implications for Clinical Practice," *American Psychologist* 62, no. 4 (2007): 271–286, https://doi.org/10.1037/0003-066X.62.4.271.

33 C. Addai, "On Becoming a Psychologist," in *The Colour of Madness: Exploring BAME Mental Health in the UK*, ed. Samara Linton and Rianna Walcott (Edinburgh: Skiddaw Book, 2018).

34 Sue et al., "Racial Microaggressions in Everyday Life."

35 Hiraa Jamil, "What Are You?" *BDJ In Practice* 33, no. 4 (July 2020): 4, https://doi.org/10.1038/s41404-020-0446-0.

36 Atayero, "Decolonisation Among Clinicians."

37 Sean Bell, "'Scotland is not Immune from Hatred': Research Shows 'Persistent' Levels of Discrimination Against Black and Ethnic Minority Scots," *Source*, October 2, 2019, https://sourcenews.scot/scotland-is-not-immune-from-hatred-research-shows-persistent-levels-of-discrimination-against-black-and-ethnic-minority-scots/.

38 D. Thind, "Asian in a White Ward in a White Town," in *The Colour of Madness: Exploring BAME Mental Health in the UK*, ed. Samara Linton and Rianna Walcott (Edinburgh: Skiddaw Books, 2018).

clusion that there was no evidence of institutional racism in Britain or that racism impacts health outcomes.[39] This report was summarily denounced by several Royal Colleges and medical faculties in the UK, including the Royal College of Paediatrics and Child Health, Royal College of Psychiatrists, Faculty of Public Health, Royal College of General Practitioners, British Medical Association, Royal College of Midwives, Royal College of Obstetrics and Gynaecologists, and the Royal College of Nursing. The MacPherson report, in the wake of the police handling of the murder of Stephen Lawrence, a Black child, was notable for explicitly stating that institutional racism existed and was widespread within public services.[40] While the report was lauded as a watershed in race relations in the UK, the Lawrence Review, published in the wake of inequalities seen among ethnic minority mortality and morbidity in the first wave of COVID-19, was critical in noting that little practical changes have taken place in the two decades since the MacPherson report.[41] While a comprehensive overview of health inequalities experienced among ethnic minority communities in Britain is not with the scope of this chapter, readers are encouraged to read the work of Lawrence, Bhopal, and Karlsen, as well as more recent work by Raleigh and Holmes and Kapadia et al. for an overview.[42]

Concerningly, given the myth of denial of racism as a contributing factor in health inequalities, there has been a worrying resurgence in academic circles as to alternative explanations for health inequalities. Saffron Karlsen, for

39 Amanda Parker, "UK Report on Race is a Masterclass in Gaslighting," *Financial Times*, April 1, 2021, https://www.ft.com/content/feca1eb5-a50d-4698-8f43-c4d7c3d207b3.

40 William MacPherson, "The Stephen Lawrence Inquiry," February 1999, https://assets.publishing.service.gov.uk/government/uploads/system/uploads/attachment_data/file/277111/4262.pdf.

41 Doreen Lawrence, "An Avoidable Crisis: The Disproportionate Impact of Covid-19 on Black, Asian and Minority Ethnic Communities," United Nations Office for Disaster Risk Reduction, 2020, https://www.preventionweb.net/publication/avoidable-crisis-disproportionate-impact-covid-19-black-asian-and-minority-ethnic.

42 Laurence, "An Avoidable Crisis"; Raj S. Bhopal, *Migration, Ethnicity, Race, and Health in Multicultural Societies* (Oxford: Oxford University Press, 2013), https://doi.org/10.1093/med/9780199667864.001.0001; Karlsen, Saffron, "Ethnic Inequalities in Health: The Impact of Racism," Race Equality Foundation, March 2007, https://raceequalityfoundation.org.uk/wp-content/uploads/2018/03/health-brief3.pdf; Veena Raleigh and Jonathon Holmes, "The Health of People from Ethnic Minority Groups in England," The King's Fund, September 17, 2021, https://www.kingsfund.org.uk/publications/health-people-ethnic-minority-groups-england; and Dharmi Kapadia et al., "Ethnic Inequalities in Healthcare: A Rapid Evidence Review," NHS Race and Health Observatory, February 14, 2022, https://www.nhsrho.org/publications/ethnic-inequalities-in-healthcare-a-rapid-evidence-review/.

instance, noted that there is often a presumption and assumption by others of inherent ability based on race,[43] with some even placing inequalities experienced by minority communities as a consequence of *inherent* differences within racialized minorities themselves or, in the case of religious minorities (and particularly Muslims), framing their religion as a "hindrance" to social integration and to health and well-being.[44] Indeed, this worrying return to "race science" demonstrates the British "palatable" form of racism,[45] wherein with the Equalities Act (2010) legislation enacted by the UK Government to address discrimination in workplace and public settings prohibiting outright discrimination, indirect discrimination still occurs and is framed as "cultural differences."

4 Racism, Health Inequalities, and COVID-19

Nasar Meer notes that systematic inequalities experienced by racialized minorities in Britain sets up "patterns of disadvantage," whereby racialized individuals continue to experience a "racial penalty" in access to opportunities throughout the life course—in effect, becoming a racial underclass, largely concentrated in the service sector, due to systemic disadvantage and lack of opportunities.[46] Thus, employing a social determinants of health framework, the substantial challenges Muslim communities experience have an impact on their health outcomes. Data on health outcomes by religious group is not routinely collected nor is it readily available in the UK, with ethnicity often used as a proxy, which can be problematic as it masks heterogeneity within population groups. Nevertheless, from what is available and through being influenced by wider social and living conditions, Muslim communities experience substantial health inequalities, including greater prevalence of cardiovascular disease, diabetes, respiratory illness, obesity, infant mortality, and mental ill health, and lower levels of physical activity, smoking, alcohol consumption, and cancer

43 Karlsen, "Ethnic Inequalities in Health."

44 Nancy Foner and Richard Alba, "Immigrant Religion in the U.S. and Western Europe: Bridge or Barrier to Inclusion?" *International Migration Review* 42, no. 2 (June 2008): 360–392, https://doi.org/10.1111/j.1747-7379.2008.00128.x; and Hugh Goddard and L. Bradley, "Progress Report: Minutes of Meeting Reported to School of Literature, Languages, and Culture, February 2017," Alwaleed Centre for Study of Islam in the Contemporary World, University of Edinburgh, 2017.

45 Angela Saini, *Superior: The Return of Race Science* (Boston, MA: Beacon Press, 2019).

46 Meer, *Key Concepts in Race and Ethnicity*.

incidence, as well as poorer experiences of care.[47] Muslims also have the lowest recovery rate in terms of use of mainstream psychological services.[48]

Marmot employed a social determinants of health framework to evaluate progress made in reducing health inequalities in England over the past decade, noting that with the impacts of austerity and wider systemic policies (particularly in housing and employment/benefits), health inequalities in England worsened—with life expectancy stagnating for men in the most deprived areas since 2010 and even decreasing among women in the most deprived areas.[49] Values for countries within Great Britain are seen in Figures 8.8 and 8.9.

Cutbacks to social services during a decade of austerity have been particularly felt by those in deprived areas, who already experience greater levels of socio-economic adversity, childhood obesity, poorer quality of life, greater years of life-limiting illness, and lower health-adjusted life expectancy. Rather than acknowledge and act on its own systemic policy failures, the government's focus instead on xenophobic policies and a "hostile environment" has resulted in, what Mitha notes as a "fraying of social cohesion,"[50] where vulnerable and marginalized communities were politically "written off"—essentially what Marmot terms as "left behind" communities, where deprived communities experience cyclical poverty due to continued disinvestment and worsening social and health outcomes.[51]

47 Peter C. Corry, "Consanguinity and Prevalence Patterns of Inherited Disease in the UK Pakistani Community," *Human Heredity* 77, nos. 1–4 (2014): 207–216, https://doi.org/10.1159/000362598; Saffron Karlsen and James Y. Nazroo, "Religious and Ethnic Differences in Health: Evidence from the Health Surveys for England 1999 and 2004," *Ethnicity & Health* 15, no. 6 (December 2010): 549–568, https://doi.org/10.1080/13557858.2010.497204; Ghazala Mir and Aziz Sheikh, "'Fasting and Prayer Don't Concern the Doctors ... They Don't Even Know What It Is': Communication, Decision-Making and Perceived Social Relations of Pakistani Muslim Patients with Long-Term Illnesses," *Ethnicity & Health* 15, no. 4 (August 2010): 327–342, https://doi.org/10.1080/13557851003624273; Kapadia et al., "Ethnic Inequalities in Healthcare"; and Raleigh and Holmes, "The Health of People from Ethnic Minority Groups in England."

48 Carl Baker, "Mental Health Statistics: Prevalence, Services and Funding in England," House of Commons Library, December 13, 2021, https://commonslibrary.parliament.uk/research-briefings/sn06988/.

49 Michael Marmot et al., "Health Equity in England: The Marmot Review 10 Years On," Health Foundation, February 2020, https://www.health.org.uk/publications/reports/the-marmot-review-10-years-on.

50 Karim Mitha, "'England Is Faltering': The Marmot Review, 10 Years On," *Psychologists for Social Change* (blog), April 15, 2020, http://www.psychchange.org/blog/england-is-faltering-the-marmot-review-10-years-on.

51 Marmot et al., "Health Equity in England."

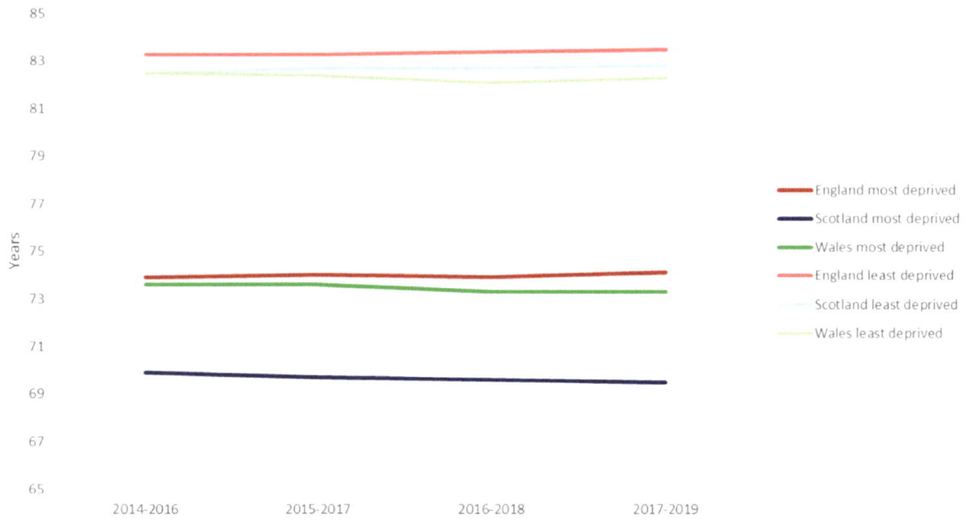

FIGURE 8.8 Life expectancy of males at birth, countries within Great Britain
OFFICE FOR NATIONAL STATISTICS, "HEALTH STATE LIFE EXPECTANCIES BY INDEX OF MULTIPLE DEPRIVATION (IMD 2015 AND IMD 2019), ENGLAND, AT BIRTH AND AGE 65 YEARS", MARCH 22 2021; OFFICE FOR NATIONAL STATISTICS, "HEALTH STATE LIFE EXPECTANCIES BY WELSH INDEX OF MULTIPLE DEPRIVATION (WIMD 2014 AND WIMD 2019), WALES, AT BIRTH AND AGE 65 YEARS". MARCH 22 2021; SCOTTISH GOVERNMENT, "LONG-TERM MONITORING OF HEALTH INEQUALITIES: MARCH 2022 REPORT" MARCH 1 2022

These existing factors were therefore compounded during the COVID-19 pandemic. Despite government rhetoric of us "being all in this together," policies and messaging by the government exacerbated existing inequalities, with members of minority communities, and Muslims, facing disproportionate burden of mortality and morbidity as well as media coverage of "bringing it upon themselves" due to a perception of flouting government guidelines.[52] Indeed, data from the first wave of the COVID-19 pandemic showed that mortality rate was 3.0× and 1.9× higher among Bangladeshi males and females respectively compared to White British males and females, and for Pakistani males and females the mortality rates were 2.2× and 2.0× higher respectively.[53] In the sec-

52 Elizabeth Poole and Milly Williamson, "Disrupting or Reconfiguring Racist Narratives About Muslims? The Representation of British Muslims During the Covid Crisis," *Journalism*, July 2, 2021, 146488492110301, https://doi.org/10.1177/14648849211030129.

53 "Updating Ethnic Contrasts in Deaths Involving the Coronavirus (COVID-19), England: 24 January 2020 to 31 March 2021," Office for National Statistics, May 26, 2021, https://www.ons.gov.uk/peoplepopulationandcommunity/birthsdeathsandmarriages/deaths/article

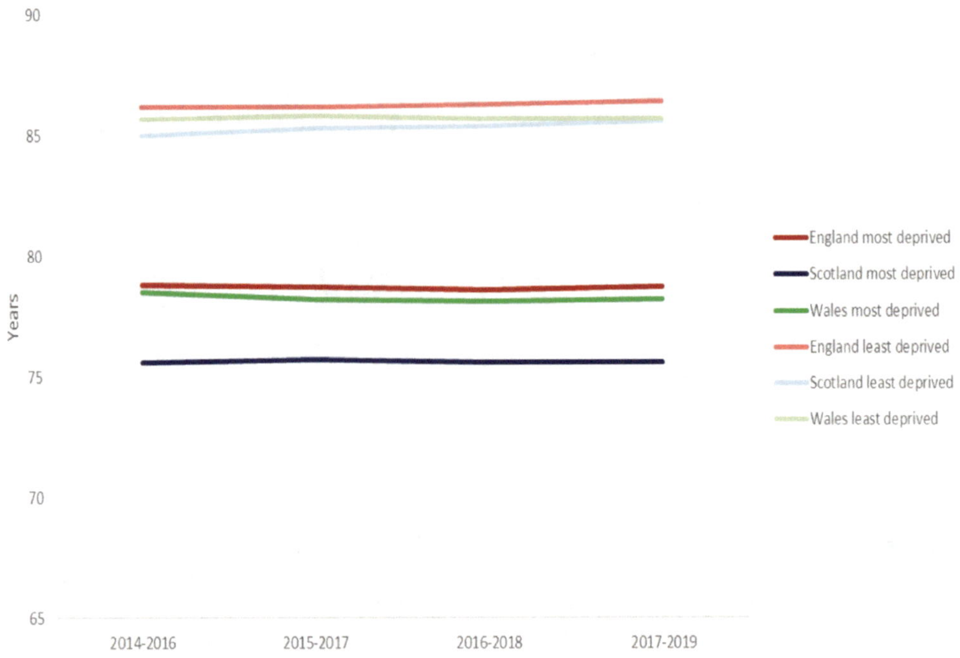

FIGURE 8.9 Life expectancy of females at birth, countries within Great Britain
OFFICE FOR NATIONAL STATISTICS, "HEALTH STATE LIFE EXPECTANCIES BY INDEX OF MULTIPLE DEPRIVATION (IMD 2015 AND IMD 2019), ENGLAND, AT BIRTH AND AGE 65 YEARS", MARCH 22 2021; OFFICE FOR NATIONAL STATISTICS, "HEALTH STATE LIFE EXPECTANCIES BY WELSH INDEX OF MULTIPLE DEPRIVATION (WIMD 2014 AND WIMD 2019), WALES, AT BIRTH AND AGE 65 YEARS". MARCH 22 2021; SCOTTISH GOVERNMENT, "LONG-TERM MONITORING OF HEALTH INEQUALITIES: MARCH 2022 REPORT" MARCH 1 2022

ond wave, the mortality rates for Bangladeshi males and females were 5× and 4.1× higher than White British males and females, whereas for Pakistani males and females the mortality rates were 3.4× and 2.8× higher than White British respectively.[54] This increased risk continued into the third wave, with increased risk in Bangladeshi males (2.2×), Bangladeshi females (2.1×), and Pakistani males (1.2×) higher than White British when demographic, socio-economic, vaccination status, and pre-existing health conditions were controlled for.[55]

s/updatingethniccontrastsindeathsinvolvingthecoronaviruscovid19englandandwales/24january2020to31march2021.

54 Office for National Statistics, "Updating Ethnic Contrasts in Deaths Involving the Coronavirus (COVID-19), England: 24 January 2020 to 31 March 2021."

55 "Updating Ethnic Contrasts in Deaths Involving the Coronavirus (COVID-19), England: 8 December 2020 to 1 December 2021," Office for National Statistics, January 26, 2022,

While Public Health England noted the disproportionate burden of Covid-19 in minoritized groups during the first wave of the pandemic,[56] marking the impacts of "social and structural determinants of health," Mitha and colleagues noted that it also favored a narrow, biomedical focus—attributing disproportionately in mortality and morbidity to diet and vitamin D—than focusing on underlying social and structural determinants as contributory factors.[57] Indeed, Razaq and colleagues asserted that systemic discrimination was a contributory factor in COVID-19 mortality and morbidity among racialized groups, with racially minoritized individuals more likely to be frontline workers or in service industries which precluded isolating during "lockdowns" or being disempowered to request access to personal protective equipment (PPE), particularly given existing health inequalities due to social and economic deprivation among the racially minoritized.[58] Mitha and colleagues noted political factors such as the government's Hostile Environment policy, "No recourse to public funds" for migrants, and lack of engagement with minoritized groups, as additional barriers placed onto minoritized communities, which influence health outcomes.[59] These social determinants, embedded systemically and pervasively, and their role in health inequalities were particularly salient during the COVID-19 pandemic and how British Muslims were framed, despite experiencing greater inequalities in mortality and morbidity.[60]

---

https://www.ons.gov.uk/peoplepopulationandcommunity/birthsdeathsandmarriages/deaths/articles/updatingethniccontrastsindeathsinvolvingthecoronaviruscovid19englandandwales/8december2020to01december2021.

56 "Beyond the Data: Understanding the Impact of COVID-19 on BAME Groups," Public Health England, June 2020, https://assets.publishing.service.gov.uk/government/uploads/system/uploads/attachment_data/file/892376/COVID_stakeholder_engagement_synthesis_beyond_the_data.pdf.

57 Karim Mitha et al., "Racism as a Social Determinant: COVID-19 and Its Impacts on Racial/Ethnic Minorities," *Discover Society*, December 22, 2020, https://archive.discoversociety.org/2020/12/22/racism-as-a-social-determinant-covid-19-and-its-impacts-on-racial-ethnic-minorities/.

58 Abdul Razaq et al., "BAME COVID-19 Deaths—What Do We Know? Rapid Data & Evidence Review," Centre for Evidence-Based Medicine, May 5, 2020, https://www.cebm.net/covid-19/bame-covid-19-deaths-what-do-we-know-rapid-data-evidence-review/.

59 Mitha et al., "Racism as a Social Determinant."

60 Office for National Statistics, "Coronavirus (COVID-19) Related Deaths by Religious Group, England and Wales: 2 March to 15 May 2020."

5 British Muslims and COVID-19

The first case of COVID-19 recorded in the UK was on January 31, 2020, in York, and the first death was on March 5, 2020, in Reading. Despite the World Health Organization (WHO) declaring COVID-19 a global pandemic on March 11, 2020, a work from home directive did not occur until March 16, 2020, after several festivals, concerns, and football matches had taken place the previous weekend. Schools did not close until March 20, 2020, and the UK officially entered its first lockdown on March 23, 2020. This lockdown immediately preceded several religious events, including Easter on April 12, 2020, in which the Queen sent out a televised address, as well as the start of Ramadan on April 23, 2020. Ramadan is a holy month for Muslims and fasting during this time is viewed as one of the central pillars for adherents to Islam. Observational practice of religious prescriptive behavior can be central to identity to Muslims, particularly observance of Ramadan fasting, and among British Muslims performativity of religious identity is often important to sense of self-identity.[61] Thus, while people suffering from acute or chronic illness are exempt from ritual fasting during Ramadan, some people may still choose to fast, often against medical advice.[62] Ramadan is also a period of community solidarity—thus, concerns of Ramadan during COVID-19 were in relation to community adherence to lockdowns (i.e., observing cessation of communal *ifṭār* and *tarāwīḥ* prayers) as well as the impact of fasting on exacerbating or predisposing people to COVID-19. WHO issued a statement outlining that healthy individuals fasting should have no increased risk from Covid,[63] and an evidence review prior to Ramadan concluded the same.[64]

Public health concerns and measures during the pandemic were focused on the spread and containment of COVID-19, via use of masks, handwashing, social distancing, ventilation—promoted in NHS campaigns as "Hands, face, space, ventilation." As the number of deaths due to COVID-19 rose in April 2020, it became clear there was a disproportionality observed in terms of deaths among people from Black and Asian backgrounds. As mentioned earlier, there were

---

61 Tariq Modood et al., *Ethnic Minorities in Britain: Diversity and Disadvantage* (London: Policy Studies Institute, 1997).

62 Ghouri et al., "Diabetes, Driving and Fasting During Ramadan."

63 World Health Organization, "Safe Ramadan Practices in the Context of the COVID-19: Interim Guidance, 15 April 2020," Geneva: World Health Organization, 2020, WHO IRIS, https://apps.who.int/iris/handle/10665/331767.

64 Asli Kalin et al., "Is it Safe for Patients with COVID-19 to Fast in Ramadan?" Centre for Evidence-Based Medicine, April 22, 2020, https://www.cebm.net/covid-19/is-it-safe-for-patients-with-covid-19-to-fast-in-ramadan/.

various hypotheses put forth—and suggestions of further outreach needed with minority communities who, due to general government distrust particularly in relation to austerity and immigration rules, were felt to either not have access to or take stock of government guidance, which, at that time, was primarily in English and not adapted for minority communities. Given the transmissibility of the SARS-CoV-2 virus via airborne secretions and increased susceptibility of transmission from close quarters, guidance on social distancing was recommended—and emphasized particularly to Muslim communities at the start of Ramadan in April 2020. Gaughan et al.'s later work noted the importance of lockdowns in curbing risk among religious communities, examining mortality by religious groups pre- and post-lockdown, and noted that: Muslim males had a 4× greater risk of COVID-19 mortality compared to Christians; for Muslim women, this was 3.6× greater risk, while post-lockdown, this risk reduced to 2× and 1.5× for Muslim men and women respectively.[65] Evidence on the necessity for specific targeted messaging for Muslim communities stem from advice pertaining to viral surveillance for respiratory illnesses during other Muslim congregational occasions, such as during *Hajj*, another central pillar of the Islamic faith, where Muslims who are able perform pilgrimage to Mecca during the period of Eid al-Adha.[66]

As mentioned previously, traditional celebrations which take place during Ramadan, include communal breaking of the fast (*ifṭār*), daily prayers, and additional nightly congregational prayers (*tarāwīḥ*). Due to the lockdown, these were not legally possible to hold during the first wave of COVID-19. Nevertheless, there was concern among some parties that Muslims would continue to partake in communal activities, despite government guidance. There were also additional concerns regarding adherence to guidance during the end of Ramadan, during the Eid period, which also occurred during lockdown.[67] To address these concerns and to ensure messaging was being transmitted effectively, there was substantial religious and secular guidance developed targeted toward the Muslim community. These included posters, campaigns, messages on websites, and information leaflets from the WHO, Muslim Council of Britain, British Islamic Medical Association, and even local authorities in England (e.g.,

---

65 Charlotte Hannah Gaughan et al., "Religious Affiliation and COVID-19-Related Mortality: A Retrospective Cohort Study of Prelockdown and Postlockdown Risks in England and Wales," *Journal of Epidemiology and Community Health* 75, no. 6 (June 2021): 509–514, https://doi.org/10.1136/jech-2020-215694.

66 A. Rashid Gatrad et al., "Hajj and the Risk of Influenza," *BMJ* 333, no. 7580 (December 9, 2006): 1182–1183, https://doi.org/10.1136/bmj.39052.628958.BE.

67 S. Hanif et al., "Covid-19 and Ramadan 2020: Time for Reflection," *The BMJ*, July 3, 2020, https://blogs.bmj.com/bmj/2020/07/03/covid-19-and-ramadan-2020-time-for-reflection/.

Waltham Forest).[68] Additional campaigns included efforts from the Mayor of London to translate government guidance into mother tongue languages of the British Muslim community,[69] as well as having British Muslim celebrities state this advice in various languages via video messages on government websites and YouTube.[70] Muslim communities themselves took initiative in the COVID-19 effort, by offering up premises in mosques for testing and vaccination. Nevertheless, media portrayal tended to present British Muslims as not adhering to government guidance and focused on high profile British Muslims who were observed flouting guidance, such as the Mayor of Luton, a Pakistani Muslim, photographed holding Eid festivities in his house, thus giving credence to the media portrayal that ethnic communities, particularly Muslims, were not heeding government advice.[71] This "victim-blaming" was largely unjustified given it was small instances being generalized to a community, and this was particularly problematic when it later emerged that during this same time government ministers themselves were flouting their own guidance, including the prime minister's special advisor taking a family domestic holiday,[72] and the Prime Minister himself holding a "working lunch" in the garden of his residence in May 2020, when mixing of individuals outwith one's household was prohibited, as well as having Christmas parties in his office during the third national lockdown in December 2020.[73]

---

68 World Health Organization, "Safe Ramadan Practices in the Context of the COVID-19"; "Ramadan at Home," Muslim Council of Britain, April 20, 2020, https://mcb.org.uk/press-releases/ramadan2020_guidance/; "Ramadan Rapid Review," British Islamic Medical Association, 2020, https://britishima.org/ramadan-rapid-review; and "Ramadan During COVID-19," London Borough of Waltham Forest, 2020, https://www.walthamforest.gov.uk/content/ramadan-during-covid-19.

69 "Mayor Provides Covid Health Guidance in Urdu, Punjabi, Bengali & Hindi," Mayor of London, September 4, 2020, https://www.london.gov.uk/press-releases/mayoral/mayor-provides-covid-19-health-advice.

70 "British Asian Celebrities Unite for Video to Dispel Covid Vaccine Myths," *BBC News*, January 26, 2021, https://www.bbc.com/news/entertainment-arts-55809355.

71 Poole and Williamson, "Disrupting or Reconfiguring Racist Narratives about Muslims?"; and "Coronavirus: Luton Councillors 'Sorry' for Lockdown Breach," *BBC News*, July 24, 2020, https://www.bbc.com/news/uk-england-beds-bucks-herts-53531782.

72 Matthew Weaver, "'People Won't Forget Dominic Cummings' Visit': Barnard Castle Learns to Live with Notoriety," *The Guardian*, December 17, 2020, https://www.theguardian.com/lifeandstyle/2020/dec/17/people-wont-forget-dominic-cummings-visit-barnard-castle-learns-to-live-with-notoriety.

73 Rowena Mason, Heather Stewart, and Peter Walker, "Boris Johnson and Staff Pictured with Wine in Downing Street Garden in May 2020," *The Guardian*, December 19, 2021, https://www.theguardian.com/politics/2021/dec/19/boris-johnson-and-staff-pictured-with-wine-in-downing-street-garden-in-may-2020; and Peter Walker, Aubrey Allegretti, and Jamie

6 Evidence Regarding the Impact of Ramadan During COVID-19

To understand whether Ramadan fasting had an impact on mortality seen during the first wave of COVID-19, a data review was conducted using publicly available datasets.[74] The key concerns identified in the review were the potential for dehydration to worsen illness and the risk of rapid deterioration in those patients who had significant co-morbidities such as diabetes, which may be aggravated by fasting. Previous papers had explored the risk of infection during Ramadan, and no conclusive findings were demonstrated due to studies being either animal models or of poor quality.[75] Indeed, some animal model studies have suggested that fasting, including regular intermittent fasting, may be associated with a better immune response.[76] A study specifically dedicated to British Pakistanis and British Bangladeshis examined prescriptions during and after Ramadan over a ten-year time-span saw no statistically significant result compared to before Ramadan (IRR: 0.994; 95 percent CI: 0.988–1.001 and IRR: 1.006; 95 percent CI: 0.999–1.013, respectively).[77]

This debate demonstrated that evidence-based clinical guidance was inconclusive for patients wishing to fast during Ramadan with chronic health conditions. As a result, the British Islamic Medical Association (BIMA) undertook a rapid review to systematically profile risk in a patient-centered way, outlining an algorithmic approach for care providers to advise patients on fasting based on a risk stratification of age, frailty, and co-morbidity.[78] This review suggested, like Qureshi,[79] that there was no evidence to suggest an adverse

Grierson, "PM Accused of Lying after No 10 Officials Caught Joking About Christmas Party," *The Guardian*, December 7, 2021, https://www.theguardian.com/politics/2021/dec/07/leaked-video-shows-no-10-officials-joking-about-holding-christmas-party.

74 Salman Waqar et al., "Assessing the Impact of Ramadan Fasting on COVID-19 Mortality in the UK," *Journal of Global Health* 11 (March 27, 2021): 03060, https://doi.org/10.7189/jogh.11.03060.

75 Imran Qureshi, "Immunity and Infection Risk: COVID-19 Ramadan Rapid Review," *Journal of the British Islamic Medical Association* 4, no. 2 (2020): 38–41.

76 Ruth E. Patterson and Dorothy D. Sears, "Metabolic Effects of Intermittent Fasting," *Annual Review of Nutrition* 37, no. 1 (August 21, 2017): 371–393, https://doi.org/10.1146/annurev-nutr-071816-064634.

77 Munerah Almulhem et al., "Ramadan is not Associated with Increased Infection Risk in Pakistani and Bangladeshi Populations: Findings from Controlled Interrupted Time Series Analysis of UK Primary Care Data," ed. Md Jamal Uddin, *PLOS ONE* 17, no. 1 (January 13, 2022): e0262530, https://doi.org/10.1371/journal.pone.0262530.

78 British Islamic Medical Association, "Ramadan Rapid Review"; Salman Waqar and Nazim Ghouri, "Managing Ramadan Queries in COVID-19," *BJGP Open* 4, no. 2 (June 2020): bjgpopen20X101097, https://doi.org/10.3399/bjgpopen20X101097.

79 Qureshi, "Immunity and Infection Risk."

effect for asymptomatic immuno-competent individuals, though those with prolonged illnesses or development of COVID-19-like symptoms should refrain from fasting. The risk matrix enabled a clear pathway of fasting recommendations and a guide for clinicians to use when faced with queries from Muslim patients. To undertake the data review, Waqar et al. examined fifteen local authorities (LAs) where the Muslim population as measured at the 2011 census made up at least one-fifth of the population and used the other local authorities within the most deprived quintiles as a control.[80] Mortality rates for the two groups (the fifteen LAs with at least 20 percent Muslim population, the remaining LAs in the most deprived quintile) are plotted in Figure 8.10. They found that deaths were falling steadily in both Muslim areas and control areas in the immediate period preceding Ramadan and continued over the Ramadan period in 2020. This trend continued in both groups post-Ramadan suggesting that there was no lagged detrimental effect of fasting in the Muslim areas. Age adjusted death rates were higher than raw death rates in the Muslim areas due to their younger than average populations. This is seen in Figure 8.10.

These age-adjusted death rates suggest that, if anything, death rates fell faster in the Muslim areas than in the control areas over Ramadan, albeit from a higher initial peak level. While this was reassuring, it is important to recognize that these data were from a period when England was in lockdown, and thus was without the usual congregational activity during Ramadan which otherwise may have facilitated the spread of COVID-19. Nonetheless, this was a strong indicator that the Ramadan fast *ipso facto* did not affect mortality from COVID-19.

Given that this study examined data during the first lockdown in the first wave of the pandemic, it may be the case that a similar analysis examining Ramadan 2021, when the UK was experiencing partial restrictions, had a partially vaccinated population (with eligibility based on age), and social gatherings permitted to some extent though discouraged, may reveal an additional disease burden from COVID-19 in the Muslim community, given that some of the communal practices that traditionally occur during Ramadan were able to continue. While further analyses elucidated a continued burden among the Muslim community—with ONS data noting an increased risk of mortality in the first and second wave respectively among Muslim men 1.15× and 1.7× that of Christians, and for women 0.78× and 1.26×, after adjusting for factors such as

80 Waqar et al., "Assessing the Impact of Ramadan Fasting on COVID-19 Mortality in the UK."

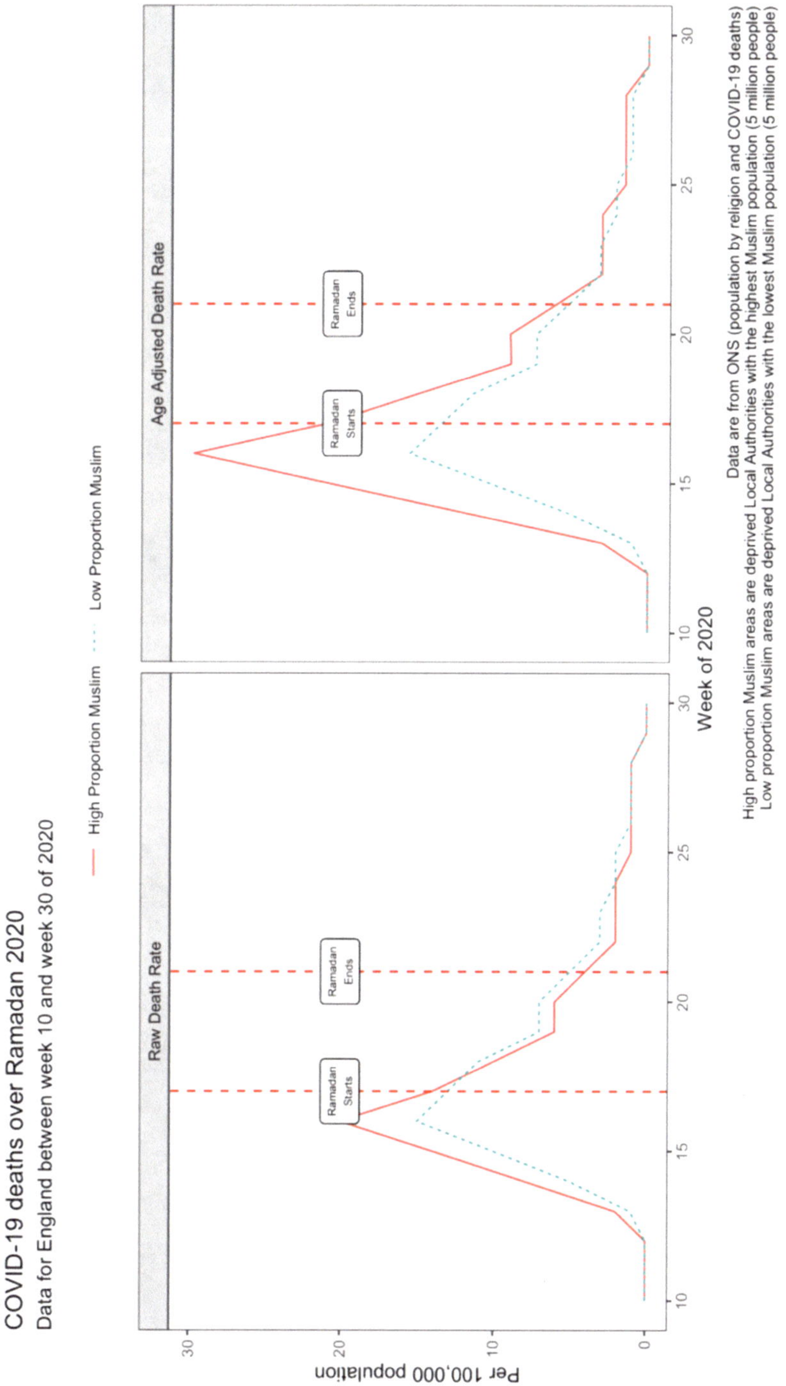

FIGURE 8.10 Examination of mortality rates in high-density and low-density Muslim population local authorities before, during, and after Ramadan 2020

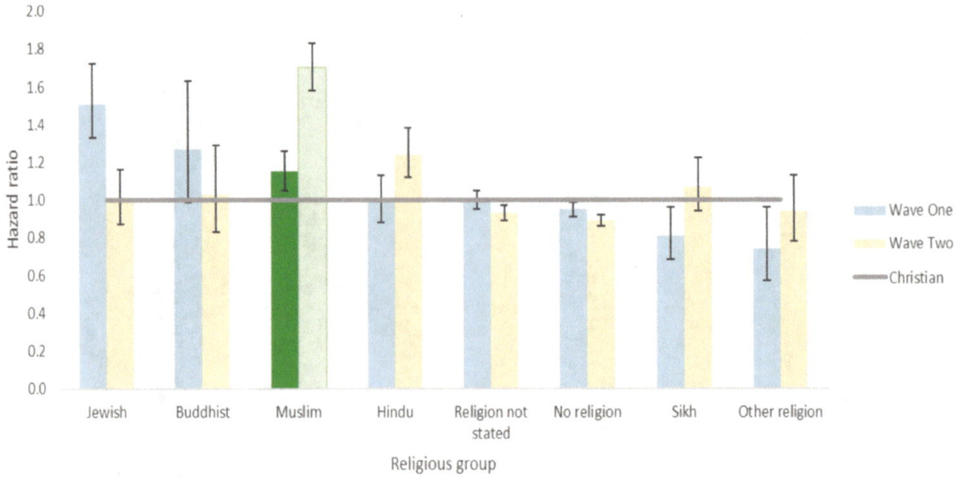

FIGURE 8.11 Hazard ratio of COVID-19 mortality among 30–100-year-old males by religious group
Note: error bars represented 95 percent confidence interval.
Note: Wave one defined here as January 24, 2020 to September 11, 2020 and wave two defined here as September 12, 2020 to February 28, 2021.
OFFICE FOR NATIONAL STATISTICS, "DEATHS INVOLVING COVID-19 BY RELIGIOUS GROUP, ENGLAND: 24 JANUARY 2020 TO 28 FEBRUARY 2021," MAY 13, 2021.

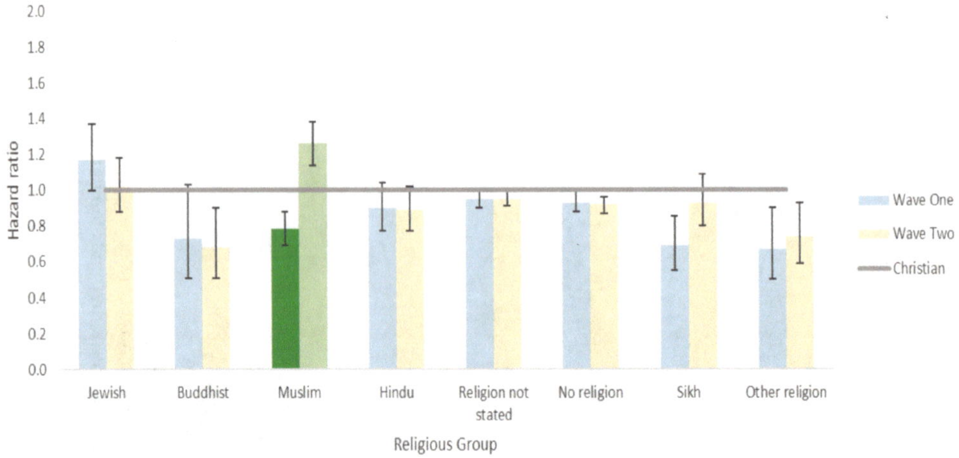

FIGURE 8.12 Hazard ratio of COVID-19 mortality among 30–100-year-old females by religious group
Note: error bars represented 95 percent confidence interval.
Note: Wave one defined here as January 24, 2020 to September 11, 2020 and wave two defined here as September 12, 2020 to February 28, 2021.
OFFICE FOR NATIONAL STATISTICS, "DEATHS INVOLVING COVID-19 BY RELIGIOUS GROUP, ENGLAND: 24 JANUARY 2020 TO 28 FEBRUARY 2021," MAY 13, 2021

age, socio-economic status, and ethnicity[81]—to these authors' knowledge, no further work has examined the impact of Ramadan on mortality in subsequent waves/lockdowns of the pandemic.

7 Conclusion

There has been much media commentary suggesting that the behaviors and cultural practices of minority communities explain their increased exposure to the pandemic.[82] These claims are not evidence based. Rather, they are unhelpful distractions from inequalities in the social determinants of health—particularly inequalities in living and working conditions—that have been key drivers of health inequalities for all socially disadvantaged groups prior to as well as during the COVID-19 pandemic.[83]

Bibliography

Addai, C. "On Becoming a Psychologist." In *The Colour of Madness: Exploring BAME Mental Health in the UK*, edited by Samara Linton and Rianna Walcott. Edinburgh: Skiddaw Book, 2018.

Aked, Hilary. "UK Police are Making Muslim Mental Health a Terrorism Flag." *Al Jazeera*, June 8, 2021. https://www.aljazeera.com/opinions/2021/6/8/uk-police-is-making-muslim-mental-health-a-terrorism-flag.

Ali, Sundas. "British Muslims in Numbers: A Demographic, Socio-Economic and Health Profile of Muslims in Britain Drawing of the 2011 Census." Muslim Council of Britain, January 2015. https://mcb.org.uk/report/british-muslims-in-numbers/.

All-Party Parliamentary Group on British Muslims. "Islamophobia Defined: The Inquiry into a Working Definition of Islamophobia." 2018. https://appgbritishmuslims.org/publications.

Almulhem, Munerah, Rasiah Thayakaran, Shahjehan Hanif, Tiffany Gooden, Neil Thomas, Jonathan Hazlehurst, Abd A. Tahrani, Wasim Hanif, and Krishnarajah

81 Office for National Statistics, "Deaths Involving COVID-19 by Religious Group, England: 24 January 2020 to 28 February 2021," May 13, 2021.

82 Zubaida Haque, Laia Becares, and Nick Treloar, "Over-Exposed and Under-Protected—The Devastating Impact of COVID-19 on Black and Minority Ethnic Communities in Great Britain," Runnymede Trust, August 2020, https://www.runnymedetrust.org//publications/over-exposed-and-under-protected.

83 Marmot et al., "Health Equity in England."

Nirantharakumar. "Ramadan is not Associated with Increased Infection Risk in Pakistani and Bangladeshi Populations: Findings from Controlled Interrupted Time Series Analysis of UK Primary Care Data." Edited by Md Jamal Uddin. *PLOS ONE* 17, no. 1 (January 13, 2022): e0262530. https://doi.org/10.1371/journal.pone.0262530.

Atayero, Sarah. "Decolonisation Among Clinicians." *The Psychologist*, March 2020. https://thepsychologist.bps.org.uk/volume-33/march-2020/decolonisation-among-clinicians.

Baker, Carl. "Mental Health Statistics: Prevalence, Services and Funding in England." House of Commons Library, December 13, 2021. https://commonslibrary.parliament.uk/research-briefings/sn06988/.

BBC News. "British Asian Celebrities Unite for Video to Dispel Covid Vaccine Myths." January 26, 2021. https://www.bbc.com/news/entertainment-arts-55809355.

BBC News. "Coronavirus: Luton Councillors 'Sorry' for Lockdown Breach." July 24, 2020. https://www.bbc.com/news/uk-england-beds-bucks-herts-53531782.

Bell, Sean. "'Scotland is not Immune from Hatred': Research Shows 'Persistent' Levels of Discrimination against Black and Ethnic Minority Scots." *Source*, October 2, 2019. https://sourcenews.scot/scotland-is-not-immune-from-hatred-research-shows-persistent-levels-of-discrimination-against-black-and-ethnic-minority-scots/.

Bhopal, Raj S. *Migration, Ethnicity, Race, and Health in Multicultural Societies*. Oxford: Oxford University Press, 2013. https://doi.org/10.1093/med/9780199667864.001.0001.

Bonino, Stefano. *Muslims in Scotland: The Making of Community in a Post-9/11 World*. Edinburgh: Edinburgh University Press, 2017.

British Islamic Medical Association. "Ramadan Rapid Review." 2020. https://britishima.org/ramadan-rapid-review.

Corry, Peter C. "Consanguinity and Prevalence Patterns of Inherited Disease in the UK Pakistani Community." *Human Heredity* 77, no. 1–4 (2014): 207–216. https://doi.org/10.1159/000362598.

Darlington, Fran, Paul Norman, Dimitris Ballas, and Daniel John Exeter. "Exploring Ethnic Inequalities in Health: Evidence from the Health Survey for England, 1998–2011." *Diversity and Equality in Health and Care* 12, no. 2 (2015): 54–65.

Davidson, Neil, and Satnam Virdee. "Understanding Racism in Scotland." In *No Problem Here: Understanding Racism in Scotland*, edited by Neil Davidson, Minna Liinpaa, Maureen McBride, and Satnam Virdee. Edinburgh: Luath Press, 2018.

Day, Aasma. "Exclusive: Muslim Medics Called 'Terrorists' and Told 'Go Back to Your Country'—by Patients." *HuffPost UK*, September 12, 2020. https://www.huffingtonpost.co.uk/entry/islamophobia-nhs-patients-muslims-religion-abuse-discrimination_uk_5f567984c5b62b3add4442b6.

Day, Aasma. "Exclusive: Muslim Medics Taunted About Bacon and Alcohol—by Their Own NHS Colleagues." *HuffPost UK*, September 11, 2020. https://www.huffingtonpost

.co.uk/entry/islamophobia-nhs-muslim-doctors-institutionalised_uk_5f562e80c5b62b3add43cccb.

Di Stasio, Valentina, and Anthony Heath. "Are Employers in Britain Discriminating Against Ethnic Minorities?" Nuffield Trust. Accessed March 27, 2022. http://csi.nuff.ox.ac.uk/wp-content/uploads/2019/01/Are-employers-in-Britain-discriminating-against-ethnic-minorities_final.pdf.

Elshayyal, Khadijah. "Scottish Muslims in Numbers." University of Edinburgh, October 28, 2020. https://www.ed.ac.uk/literatures-languages-cultures/alwaleed/research/muslims-in-europe/scottish-muslims-in-numbers.

Essed, Philomena. *Everyday Racism: Reports from Women of Two Cultures*. Claremont, CA: Hunter House, 1990.

Foner, Nancy, and Richard Alba. "Immigrant Religion in the U.S. and Western Europe: Bridge or Barrier to Inclusion?" *International Migration Review* 42, no. 2 (June 2008): 360–392. https://doi.org/10.1111/j.1747-7379.2008.00128.x.

Francis-Devine, Brigid. "Poverty in the UK: Statistics." House of Commons Library, October 16, 2021. https://commonslibrary.parliament.uk/research-briefings/sn07096/.

Gatrad, A Rashid, Shuja Shafi, Ziad A. Memish, and Aziz Sheikh. "Hajj and the Risk of Influenza." BMJ 333, no. 7580 (December 9, 2006): 1182–1183. https://doi.org/10.1136/bmj.39052.628958.BE.

Gaughan, Charlotte Hannah, Daniel Ayoubkhani, Vahe Nafilyan, Peter Goldblatt, Chris White, Karen TIngay, and Neil Bannister. "Religious Affiliation and COVID-19-Related Mortality: A Retrospective Cohort Study of Prelockdown and Postlockdown Risks in England and Wales." *Journal of Epidemiology and Community Health* 75, no. 6 (June 2021): 509–514. https://doi.org/10.1136/jech-2020-215694.

Ghouri, Nazim, Sufyan Hussain, Ruzwan Mohammed, Salem Arifi Beshyah, Tahseen A. Chowdhury, Naveed Sattar, and Aziz Sheikh. "Diabetes, Driving and Fasting During Ramadan: The Interplay Between Secular and Religious Law." *BMJ Open Diabetes Research & Care* 6, no. 1 (June 2018): e000520. https://doi.org/10.1136/bmjdrc-2018-000520.

Goddard, Hugh. "Halal Haggis? An Introduction to Islam and Muslims in Scotland." Presented at the Alwaleed Centre for the Study of Islam in the Contemporary World, University of Edinburgh, February 2015.

Goddard, Hugh, and L. Bradley. "Progress Report: Minutes of Meeting Reported to School of Literature, Languages, and Culture, February 2017." Alwaleed Centre for Study of Islam in the Contemporary World, University of Edinburgh, 2017.

Goldie, Paul. "Cultural Racism and Islamophobia in Glasgow." In *No Problem Here: Understanding Racism in Scotland*, edited by Neil Davidson, Minna Liinpaa, Maureen McBride, and Satnam Virdee. Edinburgh: Luath Press, 2018.

Hanif, S., W. Hanif, Kamlesh Khunti, and Sarah N. Ali. "Covid-19 and Ramadan 2020:

Time for Reflection." *The BMJ*, July 3, 2020. https://blogs.bmj.com/bmj/2020/07/03/covid-19-and-ramadan-2020-time-for-reflection/.

Haque, Zubaida, Laia Becares, and Nick Treloar. "Over-Exposed and Under-Protected—The Devastating Impact of COVID-19 on Black and Minority Ethnic Communities in Great Britain." Runnymede Trust, August 2020. https://www.runnymedetrust.org//publications/over-exposed-and-under-protected.

Harris, Scarlet. "*Muslims in Scotland*: Integrationism, State Racism and the 'Scottish Dream.'" *Race & Class* 60, no. 2 (October 2018): 114–119. https://doi.org/10.1177/0306396818793583.

Heath, Anthony, and Yaojun Li. "Review of the Relationship Between Religion and Poverty: An Analysis for the Joseph Rowntree Foundation." Institute for Social and Economic Research, 2015. https://www.iser.essex.ac.uk/research/publications/523019.

Hewitt, Daniel. "University Covid Crisis: Muslim Student Stuck in Self-Isolation Served Ham Sandwiches." ITV News, September 29, 2020. https://www.itv.com/news/2020-09-29/university-covid-crisis-muslim-student-stuck-in-self-isolation-served-ham-sandwiches.

Home Office. "Hate Crime, England and Wales, 2019/2020." October 13, 2020. https://www.gov.uk/government/statistics/hate-crime-england-and-wales-2019-to-2020.

Jamil, Hiraa. "What Are You?" *BDJ In Practice* 33, no. 4 (July 2020): 4. https://doi.org/10.1038/s41404-020-0446-0.

Kalin, Asli, Ammad Mahmood, Salman Waqar, Asim Yusuf, Nazim Ghouri, Naveed Sattar, Tahseen Chowdhury, and Nazim Ghouri. "Is it Safe for Patients with COVID-19 to Fast in Ramadan?" Centre for Evidence-Based Medicine, April 22, 2020. https://www.cebm.net/covid-19/is-it-safe-for-patients-with-covid-19-to-fast-in-ramadan/.

Kapadia, Dharmi, Jingwen Zhang, Sarah Salway, James Nazroo, Andrew Booth, Nazmy Villarroel-Williams, Laia Becares, and Aneez Esmail. "Ethnic Inequalities in Healthcare: A Rapid Evidence Review." NHS Race and Health Observatory, February 14, 2022. https://www.nhsrho.org/publications/ethnic-inequalities-in-healthcare-a-rapid-evidence-review/.

Karlsen, Saffron. "Ethnic Inequalities in Health: The Impact of Racism." Race Equality Foundation, March 2007. https://raceequalityfoundation.org.uk/wp-content/uploads/2018/03/health-brief3.pdf.

Karlsen, Saffron, and James Y. Nazroo. "Religious and Ethnic Differences in Health: Evidence from the Health Surveys for England 1999 and 2004." *Ethnicity & Health* 15, no. 6 (December 2010): 549–568. https://doi.org/10.1080/13557858.2010.497204.

Laurence, Doreen. "An Avoidable Crisis: The Disproportionate Impact of Covid-19 on Black, Asian and Minority Ethnic Communities." United Nations Office for Disaster Risk Reduction, 2020. https://www.preventionweb.net/publication/avoidable-crisis-disproportionate-impact-covid-19-black-asian-and-minority-ethnic.

London Borough of Waltham Forest. “Ramadan During COVID-19.” 2020. https://www.walthamforest.gov.uk/content/ramadan-during-covid-19.

MacPherson, William. “The Stephen Lawrence Inquiry.” February 1999. https://assets.publishing.service.gov.uk/government/uploads/system/uploads/attachment_data/file/277111/4262.pdf.

Marmot, Michael, Jessica Allen, Tammy Boyce, Peter Goldblatt, and Joana Morrison. “Health Equity in England: The Marmot Review 10 Years On.” Health Foundation, February 2020. https://www.health.org.uk/publications/reports/the-marmot-review-10-years-on.

Mason, Rowena, Heather Stewart, and Peter Walker. “Boris Johnson and Staff Pictured with Wine in Downing Street Garden in May 2020.” *The Guardian*, December 19, 2021. https://www.theguardian.com/politics/2021/dec/19/boris-johnson-and-staff-pictured-with-wine-in-downing-street-garden-in-may-2020.

Mayor of London. “Mayor Provides Covid Health Guidance in Urdu, Punjabi, Bengali & Hindi.” September 4, 2020. https://www.london.gov.uk/press-releases/mayoral/mayor-provides-covid-19-health-advice.

Mcmaster, Natasha Codiroli. “Research Insight: Religion and Belief in UK Higher Education.” Advance HE, March 17, 2020. https://www.advance-he.ac.uk/knowledge-hub/research-insight-religion-and-belief-uk-higher-education.

Meer, Nasar. *Key Concepts in Race and Ethnicity*, 3rd ed. SAGE Key Concepts. Los Angeles, CA: SAGE, 2014.

Ministry of Housing, Communities and Local Government. “English Indices of Deprivation 2019.” September 26, 2019. https://www.gov.uk/government/statistics/english-indices-of-deprivation-2019.

Ministry of Housing, Communities and Local Government, “English Indices of Deprivation 2010” March 24, 2011. https://www.gov.uk/government/statistics/english-indices-of-deprivation-2010

Mir, Ghazala, and Aziz Sheikh. “‘Fasting and Prayer Don’t Concern the Doctors … They Don’t Even Know What It Is’: Communication, Decision-Making and Perceived Social Relations of Pakistani Muslim Patients with Long-Term Illnesses.” *Ethnicity & Health* 15, no. 4 (August 2010): 327–342. https://doi.org/10.1080/13557851003624273.

Mitha, K. “Identity, Islamophobia, and Mental Health: A Qualitative Investigation into Mental Health Needs amongst Scotland’s Muslims.” *European Journal of Public Health* 28, no. suppl. 1 (May 1, 2018): 23. https://doi.org/10.1093/eurpub/cky047.013.

Mitha, Karim. “‘England Is Faltering’: The Marmot Review, 10 Years On.” *Psychologists for Social Change* (blog), April 15, 2020. http://www.psychchange.org/blog/england-is-faltering-the-marmot-review-10-years-on.

Mitha, Karim, Kaveri Qureshi, Shelina Adatia, and Hiten Dodhia. “Racism as a Social Determinant: COVID-19 and Its Impacts on Racial/Ethnic Minorities.” Discover Society, December 22, 2020. https://archive.discoversociety.org/2020/12/22/racism-as-a-social-determinant-covid-19-and-its-impacts-on-racial-ethnic-minorities/.

Modood, Tariq, Richard Berthoud, Jane Lakey, James Nazroo, Patten Smith, Satnam Virdee, and Sharon Beishon. *Ethnic Minorities in Britain: Diversity and Disadvantage*. London: Policy Studies Institute, 1997.

Muslim Council of Britain. "Ramadan at Home." April 20, 2020. https://mcb.org.uk/press-releases/ramadan2020_guidance/.

Nomis – Official Census and Labour Market Statistics "Religion, usual place of residence", January 30 2013. https://www.nomisweb.co.uk/census/2011/ks209ew

Office for National Statistics. "Population Characteristics Research Tables." December 4, 2019. https://www.ons.gov.uk/peoplepopulationandcommunity/populationandmigration/populationestimates/datasets/populationcharacteristicsresearchtables.

Office for National Statistics. "Religion by Sex and Age-Group in Great Britain, 2018 to 2019." December 13, 2019. https://www.ons.gov.uk/peoplepopulationandcommunity/culturalidentity/religion/adhocs/10999religionbysexandagegroupingreatbritain2018to2019.

Office for National Statistics. "Religion, Education and Work in England and Wales: February 2020." February 26, 2020. https://www.ons.gov.uk/peoplepopulationandcommunity/culturalidentity/religion/articles/religioneducationandworkinenglandandwales/february2020.

Office for National Statistics. "Health state life expectancies by Index of Multiple Deprivation (IMD 2015 and IMD 2019), England, at birth and age 65 years" March 22 2021. https://www.ons.gov.uk/peoplepopulationandcommunity/healthandsocialcare/healthinequalities/datasets/healthstatelifeexpectanciesbyindexofmultipledeprivationengland

Office for National Statistics. "Health state life expectancies by Welsh Index of Multiple Deprivation (WIMD 2014 and WIMD 2019), Wales, at birth and age 65 years". March 22 2021. https://www.ons.gov.uk/peoplepopulationandcommunity/healthandsocialcare/healthinequalities/datasets/healthstatelifeexpectanciesbywelshindexofmultipledeprivationwimd14walesatbirthandage65years

Office for National Statistics. "Deaths Involving COVID-19 by Religious Group, England: 24 January 2020 to 28 February 2021." May 13, 2021. https://www.ons.gov.uk/releases/deathsinvolvingcovid19byreligiousgroupenglanddeathsoccurringbetween24january2020and28february2021.

Office for National Statistics. "Updating Ethnic Contrasts in Deaths Involving the Coronavirus (COVID-19), England: 24 January 2020 to 31 March 2021." May 26, 2021. https://www.ons.gov.uk/peoplepopulationandcommunity/birthsdeathsandmarriages/deaths/articles/updatingethniccontrastsindeathsinvolvingthecoronaviruscovid19englandandwales/24january2020to31march2021.

Office for National Statistics. "Updating Ethnic Contrasts in Deaths Involving the Coronavirus (COVID-19), England: 8 December 2020 to 1 December 2021." January 26, 2022. https://www.ons.gov.uk/peoplepopulationandcommunity/birthsdeathsandm

arriages/deaths/articles/updatingethniccontrastsindeathsinvolvingthecoronaviru scovid19englandandwales/8december2020to1december2021.

Parker, Amanda. "UK Report on Race is a Masterclass in Gaslighting." *Financial Times*, April 1, 2021. https://www.ft.com/content/feca1eb5-a50d-4698-8f43-c4d7c3d207b3.

Patterson, Ruth E., and Dorothy D. Sears. "Metabolic Effects of Intermittent Fasting." *Annual Review of Nutrition* 37, no. 1 (August 21, 2017): 371–393. https://doi.org/10.1146/annurev-nutr-071816-064634.

Poole, Elizabeth, and Milly Williamson. "Disrupting or Reconfiguring Racist Narratives about Muslims? The Representation of British Muslims During the Covid Crisis." *Journalism*, July 2, 2021, 146488492110301. https://doi.org/10.1177/14648849211030129.

Public Health England. "Beyond the Data: Understanding the Impact of COVID-19 on BAME Groups." June 2020. https://assets.publishing.service.gov.uk/government/uploads/system/uploads/attachment_data/file/892376/COVID_stakeholder_engagement_synthesis_beyond_the_data.pdf.

Qureshi, Imran. "Immunity and Infection Risk: COVID-19 Ramadan Rapid Review." *Journal of the British Islamic Medical Association* 4, no. 2 (2020): 38–41.

Raleigh, Veena, and Jonathon Holmes. "The Health of People from Ethnic Minority Groups in England." The King's Fund, September 17, 2021. https://www.kingsfund.org.uk/publications/health-people-ethnic-minority-groups-england.

Razaq, Abdul, Dominic Harrison, Sakthi Karunanithi, Ben Barr, Miqdad Asaria, Ash Routen, and Kamlesh Khunti. "BAME COVID-19 Deaths—What Do We Know? Rapid Data & Evidence Review." Centre for Evidence-Based Medicine, May 5, 2020. https://www.cebm.net/covid-19/bame-covid-19-deaths-what-do-we-know-rapid-data-evidence-review/.

Saini, Angela. *Superior: The Return of Race Science*. Boston, MA: Beacon Press, 2019.

Scottish Government. "Long term monitoring of health inequalities: March 22 report". March 1 2022. https://www.gov.scot/publications/long-term-monitoring-health-inequalities-march-2022-report/pages/6/

Sian, Katy P. *Navigating Institutional Racism in British Universities*. Cham: Springer International Publishing, 2019. https://doi.org/10.1007/978-3-030-14284-1.

Stevenson, Jacqueline, Sean Demack, Bernie Stiell, Muna Abdi, Lisa Clarkson, Farhana Ghaffar, and Shaima Hassan. "The Social Mobility Challenges Faced by Young Muslims." Social Mobility Commission, September 7, 2017. https://www.gov.uk/government/publications/social-mobility-challenges-faced-by-young-muslims.

Sue, Derald Wing, Christina M. Capodilupo, Gina C. Torino, Jennifer M. Bucceri, Aisha M.B. Holder, Kevin L. Nadal, and Marta Esquilin. "Racial Microaggressions in Everyday Life: Implications for Clinical Practice." *American Psychologist* 62, no. 4 (2007): 271–286. https://doi.org/10.1037/0003-066X.62.4.271.

Thind, D. "Asian in a White Ward in a White Town." In *The Colour of Madness: Exploring BAME Mental Health in the UK*, edited by Samara Linton and Rianna Walcott. Edinburgh: Skiddaw Books, 2018.

Walker, Peter, Aubrey Allegretti, and Jamie Grierson. "PM Accused of Lying after No 10 Officials Caught Joking about Christmas Party." *The Guardian*, December 7, 2021. https://www.theguardian.com/politics/2021/dec/07/leaked-video-shows-no-10-offi cials-joking-about-holding-christmas-party.

Waqar, Salman, Miqdad Asaria, Nazim Ghouri, Mehrunisha Suleman, Halima Begum, and Michael Marmot. "Assessing the Impact of Ramadan Fasting on COVID-19 Mortality in the UK." *Journal of Global Health* 11 (March 27, 2021): 03060. https://doi.org/10.7189/jogh.11.03060.

Waqar, Salman, and Nazim Ghouri. "Managing Ramadan Queries in COVID-19." *BJGP Open* 4, no. 2 (June 2020): bjgpopen20X101097. https://doi.org/10.3399/bjgpopen20X 101097.

Weaver, Matthew. "'People Won't Forget Dominic Cummings' Visit': Barnard Castle Learns to Live with Notoriety." *The Guardian*, December 17, 2020. https://www.thegu ardian.com/lifeandstyle/2020/dec/17/people-wont-forget-dominic-cummings-visi t-barnard-castle-learns-to-live-with-notoriety.

World Health Organization. "Safe Ramadan Practices in the Context of the COVID-19: Interim Guidance, 15 April 2020." Geneva: World Health Organization, 2020. WHO IRIS. https://apps.who.int/iris/handle/10665/331767.

CHAPTER 9

An Islamic Ethico-Legal Framework for Pandemics: The Case for COVID-19

Rafaqat Rashid

1 Introduction

The World Health Organization declared COVID-19 a pandemic on March 11, 2020 because there were serious concerns that COVID-19 was affecting a large proportion of the population and had spread to 114 countries. This declaration advised countries to contain the virus by detecting, testing, treating, isolating, tracing, and mobilizing their people in the response.[1] The spread of the disease was to be slowed down in order to ease the burden of overstretched healthcare services and prevent avoidable deaths. Social distancing measures are essential to slowing the speed of the outbreak, so that healthcare services can manage increasing admissions in the absence of vaccines. Population deaths and morbidity will be reduced by preventing mass transmission using these measures. Social distancing requires people to stay at home as much as possible and not to spread the virus, which profoundly limits and restricts the use of communal places of worship for Muslims like the mosque. Communal prayers in the mosque are a mandatory form of worship and any public policy which restricts this, conflicts with important communal and individual Islamic obligations for Muslims. Vaccines are the most important solution to eliminate or diminish COVID-19 and most vaccines currently in use are free from impure animal ingredients, or ingredients which would normally be prohibited by Muslims. It is yet to be seen what the Muslim response would be if the only vaccines available were those which contain impure ingredients.

In circumstances like this, because of the COVID-19 pandemic, where there is significant harm to public interests, difficult and complex decisions need to be made about priorities related to the preservation of the higher objectives of the Shariʿa in conflicting situations, while drawing the right balance between

1 "WHO Director-General's Opening Remarks at the Media Briefing on COVID-19—11 March 2020," World Health Organization, March 11, 2020, accessed December 2020, https://www.who.int/director-general/speeches/detail/who-director-general-s-opening-remarks-at-the-media-briefing-on-covid-19---11-march-2020.

 | DOI:10.1163/9789004679771_011

competing public harms. In order to save lives, we may be required to make tough decisions about the restriction of rights of populations—like limiting freedom of movement through imposition of quarantine, restricting freedom of choice with interventions like compulsory vaccination programs, and limiting freedom of religious practice, by curbing or stopping certain mandatory religious acts of worship which preserve religion and faith in our communities, such as closure of mosques during lockdown to avoid spread. There may also be compelling reasons to permit the prohibited when there are no other alternatives, like ritually impure ingredients in vaccines, that is, porcine gelatin, as part of mass vaccination programs in Muslim populations or countries.

Furthermore, spiritual and psychological approaches are also a must in any calamity inflicting Muslim populations. If an approach is not balanced, in that it does not provide both physical solutions as well spiritual/psychological ones, then this can lead to worsening the mental and social well-being of communities, which in turn will increasingly burden services.[2] Sometimes we can be too focused on mortality and morbidity figures and neglect the harm caused to our psychological and spiritual coping mechanisms, individually and as a community. When it comes to solutions, Muslims accept that physical means should be taken, coupled with trust in God. The means are not just limited to the physical and material (*asbāb ẓahiriyya*), but also transcend beyond that to the metaphysical and spiritual (*asbāb bāṭiniyya*), through increasing worship and supplication. It can be a challenge to get this balance right, especially when one conflicts with the other. Unclear theological positions and an imbalance of priorities can lead to confusion and dissenting views. This can lead to discord and divisions between members of the Muslim public and among Muslim scholars and leaders in an important time requiring unity. Quoting science and epidemiological figures to justify stringent interventions which conflict with religious imperatives do not always address nor resolve this discord, because standard epidemiological models of viral spread do not take account of human factors such as religious ideologies and values.[3] Any guidance on getting this balance right requires that we engage with our Islamic theological and legal tradition in

2 Kathryn Mansfield et al., "Indirect Acute Effects of the COVID-19 Pandemic on Physical and Mental Health in the UK: A Population-Based Study," *Lancet* 3, no. 4 (2021): 217–230, https://doi.org/10.1016/S2589-7500(21)00017-0; Souvik Dubey et al., "Psychosocial Impact of COVID-19," *Diabetes and Metabolic Syndrome* 14, no. 5 (2020): 779–788, https://doi.org/10.1016/j.dsx.2020.05.035; and Reza Shahriarirad et al., "The Mental Health Impact of COVID-19 Outbreak: A Nationwide Survey in Iran," *International Journal of Mental Health Systems* 15, no. 19 (2021), https://doi.org/10.1186/s13033-021-00445-3.

3 Wesley J. Wildman et al., "Religion and the COVID-19 Pandemic," *Religion, Brain & Behavior* 10, no. 2 (2020): 115–117, https://doi.org/10.1080/2153599X.2020.1749339.

order to develop an ethico-legal framework, which addresses concerns related to pandemics like COVID-19 and not just rely upon a secular or scientific model.

This chapter is an effort to address intersections between the Islamic ethico-legal tradition, medical science, and public health policy, in order to provide direction and guidance at times of conflict between public health interventions and mandatory Islamic legal imperatives during pandemics like COVID-19. I will begin by explaining the Islamic theological and legal principles associated with public harm considerations. I will then show how related risks to public interests, when there are competing harms to life and religion can be addressed, using an impact assessment tool that can help to determine Islamic ethico-legal rulings. This tool can be applied to different phases of an epidemic, addressing respective stages of response. An Islamic framework for the COVID-19 pandemic will be offered using a "five conditions approach."

2 Islamic Principles Related to Harm from COVID-19

It is important for any effective working framework to take into consideration theological precepts or principles that regulate Muslim behavior or thought. Questions about illnesses and disease, like COVID-19, and whether preventing disease contravenes reliance on God, are two such examples of what needs to be known. Other questions include the role of God's decree, and whether taking up physical means to avert public harm of COVID-19 infringes belief in such decree. How does Islam describe and perceive plagues and epidemics/pandemics like COVID-19, and whether there are any associated rulings from classical Muslim scholars on preventing harm from them. All these considerations are to be informed by the Islamic tradition, which will frame the Muslim response to the COVID-19 pandemic.

3 Islamic Theological Precepts Related to Public Harm

The Qur'an informs us that all illnesses, diseases, and trials are tests from God, and are seen as the natural course of life. They have their benefits, rewards, and should not viewed solely as punishment. It is only through the instruction of God that life is saved and taken. It should therefore not be surprising when such tests become real, like in pandemics, because they have a purpose. God says, "We shall certainly test you with fear and hunger, and loss of property, lives, and crops. But give glad tidings to those who are patient." (Q.2:155). The Prophet said, "Whatever trouble, illness, anxiety, grief, hurt or sorrow afflicts any Muslim, even the prick of a thorn, God removes some of his sins by it."[4] These tests are not in vain but are rewarded if patience and steadfastness is maintained.

Islam requires us to put both our trust in God (*tawakkul*) and utilize the means to protect ourselves when possible. God says, "Say: Nothing will afflict us except what God has decided for us." (Q.9:51). A Muslim accepts that all is from God and recognizes that the means to prevent harm are destined by God, and it is for us to utilize those means to overcome hardships. The means do not conflict with trust in God's decree, just like taking medicine does not reduce one's trust in God's plan—rather it is seen as part of the plan. During the lifetime of the Prophet, some people thought that using medicine defies the trust and reliance in God (*tawakkul*). They therefore asked the Prophet, "O Messenger of God, should we use medicine?" The Prophet replied, "Yes, you may use medicine. God has not created any disease without also creating its cure, except one: old age."[5] The Prophet clarified that the use of medicine is permissible and even encouraged, and that this does not violate the concept of trust in God. Anas, the Companion of the Prophet, narrates that a man asked: "O Messenger of God, shall I tie my camel and rely upon God, or leave it untied and rely upon God?" The Messenger of God replied: "Tie your camel and rely upon God."[6] The Messenger of God said, "An ill person should not mix with healthy people."[7] The Prophet also said, "Avoid a [contagious] disease the way a person flees from a lion."[8] Therefore, taking precaution by taking up means to avoid a bad outcome or the spread of infectious disease, like in COVID-19, is something prescribed in Islam. This also extends to the use of other effective physical means to avert public harm. In pandemics, social distancing, using face coverings, and regular handwashing are common practices, which the public is obliged to strictly adhere to. These are means which do not violate the concept of trust in God.

The Companions of the Prophet demonstrated how practical means of prevention should be balanced while upholding theological understandings of decree. The caliph ʿUmar was informed by ʿAbd al-Raḥmān ibn ʿAwf that he heard from the Messenger of God: "If you hear that it (the plague) is in a land,

4 Muḥammad ibn Ismāʿīl al-Bukhārī, *Ṣaḥīḥ al-Bukhārī* (Dār al-Salām: Al-Kutub al-Sitta, 2000), *ḥadīth* no. 5641.

5 Abū Dāwūd, *Sunan Abī Dāwūd* (Riyadh: Al-Kutub al-Sitta, 2000), *ḥadīth* no. 3855.

6 Muḥammad Ibn ʿĪsā Tirmidhī, *Sunnan al-Tirmidhī* (Riyadh: Al-Kutub al-Sitta, 2000), *ḥadīth* no. 2517.

7 Ibn Ḥajjāj Muslim, *Ṣaḥīḥ Muslim* (Riyadh: Al-Kutub al-Sitta, 2000), *ḥadīth* no. 2221b.

8 Al-Bukhārī, *ḥadīth* no. 5707.

do not go there, and if it breaks out in a land where you are, do not leave, fleeing from it."[9] Also Usāma ibn Zayd said: The Messenger of God said:

> The plague is a calamity (or a punishment) that was sent upon the Children of Israel, or upon those who came before you. If you hear of it in some land, do not go there, and if it breaks out in a land where you are, do not leave, fleeing from it.[10]

This advice is in line with one of the higher objectives of the Shariʿa, that Muslims are obligated to preserve life and prevent harm to life.

There have been many historical accounts of plagues in the Muslim world, and Muslim scholars have observed certain legal rulings that stem from advice sought from the prophetic tradition that relates to using preventative means to avoid spread of plagues. Classical Muslim scholars however, differed on the definition of the plague (*ṭāʿūn*), differentiating it from an epidemic (*wabāʾ*). This has led to dissenting views among contemporary Muslim scholars, where some claim the preventative rulings of fleeing and leaving a land with plague are obligatory. However, they are specific to plagues and do not apply to *wabāʾ*, which most associate with the COVID-19 pandemic.[11]

The word *ṭāʿūn* (plague) was used interchangeably with *wabāʾ* (epidemic) by people of different historical contexts because, in the medieval past, people were often unable to identify whether the source of widespread sickness was the same, and hence did not associate it to the same illness.[12] Generally, the word *wabāʾ* was ascribed to the spread of increased disease among the population, where the source was not clear and could have been due to multiple causes or illnesses. The word "plague" was attributed to an exceptionally high number of deaths when the cause was clear, because the unique characteristic symptoms and signs which would identify the illness were the same. Because

---

9 Al-Bukhārī, *ḥadīth* no. 5739; and Muslim, *ḥadīth* no. 2219.

10 Al-Bukhārī, *ḥadīth* no. 3473; and Muslim, *ḥadīth* no. 2218.

11 I.S. Irfan et al., "Pandemic and Islamic Point of View Based on Hadith Plague," *Journal of Critical Reviews* 7, no. 8 (2020): 1017–1020; and Nazir Khan and Muntasir Zaman, "The Prophetic Promises for Martyrs and Medina: Is COVID-19 a Plague?" Yaqeen Institute for Islamic Research, April 5, 2020, accessed December 2020, https://yaqeeninstitute.org/muntasir-zaman/the-prophetic-promises-for-martyrs-and-medina-is-covid-19-a-plague.

12 An epidemic today is defined as "the occurrence in a community or region of cases of an illness ... clearly in excess of normal expectancy." A pandemic is defined as "an epidemic occurring over a very wide area, crossing international boundaries, and usually affecting a large number of people." See Miquel Porta, ed., *A Dictionary of Epidemiology*, 6th ed. (Oxford: Oxford University Press, 2014).

the plague had its own defining, somatic, characteristic signs, there was certainty that the illness was the same, whereas this would not have been the case for many epidemics, which shared similar symptoms, because they would have been indistinguishable.

If there was a COVID-19 pandemic in the medieval past, it would have been difficult for the people to ascertain that the high death rates were from the same illness, that is, COVID-19, because majority of its symptoms are no different to other common viral illnesses. COVID-19 would have therefore been considered a *wabāʾ*. Obligatory rulings related to containing the spread, like in the case of plague, would not have been applied or justified. However, we now have advanced epidemiological research capabilities and advanced diagnostic/screening technology to accurately confirm the source of the sickness and high death rates, and so it can be argued that epidemics and pandemics would also be included within the legal rulings of plagues, if these factors of spread and fatality is confirmed to be from the same infective source, like in the case of COVID-19.[13]

Rulings by classical Muslim scholars, regarding avoiding and entering a zone of a plague, were to prevent harm to public, and its obligation was not unique to plagues. It was because plagues caused widespread deaths, that such stringent rulings were implemented.[14] These rulings, therefore, should also extend to epidemics or pandemics like COVID-19 because we are more certain about the

13 In a strictly biological sense, the plague is usually understood as an infection caused by the Yersinia pestis bacillus, identified in 1894 by Alexandre Yersin. Many Muslim scholars also identified plague to a particular disease condition, which resembled the bubonic plague. One to seven days after exposure to the bacteria, flu-like symptoms develop. These symptoms include fever, headaches, and vomiting. Swollen and painful lymph nodes occur in the area closest to where the bacteria entered the skin. The plague was the cause of the Black Death that swept through Asia, Europe, and Africa in the fourteenth century and killed an estimated 50 million people. The disease was also responsible for the Plague of Justinian, originating in the Eastern Roman Empire in the sixth century CE, as well as the third epidemic, affecting China, Mongolia, and India, originating in the Yunnan Province in 1855; see Raoult Didier et al., "Plague: History and Contemporary Analysis," *Journal of Infection* 66 (2013): 18–26, https://doi.org/10.1016/j.jinf.2012.09.010.

14 A group of Mālikī jurists consider this as solely recommendation, and guidance (*taʾdīb wa irshād*), and not an obligation, however, the correct view is that the ruling in the hadith is of prohibition and this is the view of the majority of scholars and the prophetic traditions indicate that the prohibition applies specifically to one who leaves the land where the plague is occurring, with the intention of fleeing from it. As for one who leaves for another purpose, such as trade, study, or work, the prohibition does not apply to him. Yaḥyā bin Sharaf al-Nawawī, *Ṣaḥīḥ Muslim bī Sharḥ al-Nawawī* (Beirut: Dār al-Kutub al-ʿIlmiyya, 2006), Vol. 14, 205; and Ibn Qayyim al-Jawziyya, *Zād al-Maʿād* (Beirut: Muʾassasat al-Risālah, 1998), Vol. 4, 39.

cause being COVID-19, which is leading to widespread deaths.[15] Social distancing, self-isolation, quarantine, compulsory use of face coverings, and acts of hygiene can be made mandatory on the population if there is a high incidence of deaths during peaking pandemic waves. The current state travel restrictions imposed by many countries would be consistent with this. Many Muslim countries introduced travel restrictions as a way of curbing fatal deaths, especially the annual *Hajj* pilgrimage to Mecca.[16]

Classical Muslim jurists have detailed many legal principles related to harm, which allow dispensations when there is conflict between important religious imperatives and preventing harm to life. These principles of harm can also be applied to the COVID-19 pandemic, because COVID-19 leads to fatal outcomes that must be prevented.

4 Islamic Legal Principles of Public Interest and Harm: Necessity *and* Need

Goal setting, planning and prevention strategies, to achieve objectives and reduce harm to public, are all important Islamic acts prescribed by Islamic law. The higher objectives *maqāṣid al-sharīʿa* of Islam must be preserved, which are principled extrapolations derived from sets of normative rulings that protect our faith, life, lineage, mind, and wealth. Anything that harms these necessities is to be reduced and/or eliminated. Islam describes harms that impact essential public interests (*maṣlaḥa*). The concept of *maṣlaḥa* has been discussed at length by several jurists in the past and increasingly more so today.[17]

---

15 Muhammad Adnan Shereen et al., "COVID-19 Infection: Emergence, Transmission, and Characteristics of Human Coronaviruses," *Journal of Advanced Research* 24 (2020): 91–98, https://doi.org/10.1016/j.jare.2020.03.005.

16 The Saudi Arabian Ministry of Hajj and Umrah announced that *Hajj* in 2021 would be limited to citizens and residents from within the Kingdom of Saudi Arabia only, in similarity to 2020. No foreign pilgrims residing in the other countries were allowed to enter and pilgrims were advised not to make any bookings or pay any deposits for *Hajj* packages. See "According to the Precautionary Measures, the Ministry of Hajj and Umrah Announces the Regulations and Procedures of Hajj 1442H/2021," Ministry of Hajj and Umrah, June 12, 2021, accessed July 6, 2021, https://www.haj.gov.sa/en/News/Details/12513.

17 The two most prominent reformers known for their writings on the subject, which have often been referred to due to their aspiring recognition and global acclaim are the Shāfiʿī jurist and Ashʿarī theologian, Abū Ḥāmid al-Ghazālī (d. 505 AH) and the Mālikī jurist Abū Isḥāq al-Shāṭibī (d. 790 AH). Al-Ghazālī was one of the first to provide the original formulation of the concept from its rudimentary form, while the latter developed and refined the concept. Some recognised figures include Ibn al-Muqaffa (d. 139 AH), Abu Bakr al-Jaṣṣāṣ

The institution of *maṣlaḥa* is derived from the survey of Islamic teachings and injunctions found and derived from the Qur'an and prophetic tradition, which address obligations and duties which bring benefit, prosperity to public interests, and preventing them from harm and hardship. This institution relates that the Shari'a in all its teachings aims at the attainment of good, welfare, advantage, benefits, etc., and the warding off evil, injury, and loss, for the public interest.

Based on the concept of *maṣlaḥa*, projects can be classified into five categories related to the higher objectives of the Shari'a (*maqāṣid al-sharī'a*). These five categories are related to the protection, improvement, and amelioration of man's five basic elements, namely, religion (*dīn*), life (*nafs*), mind (*'aql*), lineage (*nasl*), and wealth (*māl*). However, these five elements are not equal in importance. Even though Muslim jurists agree that these are the five higher objectives of the Shari'a that protect public interest from harm, and that preservation of life and religion precede others as a weightier normative objective requiring preservation,[18] there remains a difference of opinion about whether preserving religion precedes preserving life. In circumstances like the COVID-19 pandemic, where there is significant risk of life to public, there is a need to determine which higher objective is the weightier to preserve when they compete. Are Muslims permitted to compromise mandatory rulings, which are promoted in preserving religion, for the sake of mitigating loss of life? These hard questions are usually the most difficult to answer and require us to justify the importance of life and the requirement of its preservation relative to other priorities in religion. Classical Muslim scholars provide their legal reasoning in support of their conclusions.[19]

(d. 370 AH), al-Juwaynī (d. 478 AH), Fakhr al-Dīn al-Rāzī (d. 606 AH), al-Qarāfī (d. 684 AH), and Najm al-Dīn al-Ṭūfī (d. 716 AH). For a good analysis of the historical development of the concept of *maṣlaḥa*, see Felicitas Opwis, *Maṣlaḥa and the Purpose of the Law: Islamic Discourse on Legal Change from the 4th/10th to 8th/14th Century* (Leiden: Brill, 2010).

18 'Alī Ibn Muḥammad al-Āmidī, *al- Iḥkām fī Uṣūl al-Aḥkām*, 2nd ed. (Beirut: al-Maktab al-Islāmī, 2015), Vol. 4, 381; Abū Ḥāmid al-Ghazālī, *al-Mustaṣfā min 'Ilm al-Uṣūl* (Beirut: Mu'assasat al-Risāla, n.d.), Vol. 1, 287; Muḥammad ibn Muḥammad Laknawī al-Anṣārī, *Fawātiḥ al-Raḥmūt bī Sharḥ Musallam al-Thubūt* (Beirut: Dār al-Kutub al-'Ilmiyya, 2002), Vol. 2, 262; and 'Abd al-Raḥīm Ibn al-Ḥasan Isnawī, *Nihāyat al-Sūl fī Sharḥ Minhāj al-Uṣūl* (Cairo: 'Alim al-Kutub, 2009), Vol. 4, 184.

19 The majority consider religion precedes life and a few argue that life precedes religion, like the Ḥanafī jurist Ibn Amīr al-Ḥāj (d. 879 AH); Ibn Amīr al-Ḥāj, *al-Taqrīr wa al-Taḥrīr* (Beirut: Dār al-Kutub al-'Ilmiyya, 1999). He does so on the basis that this is a human right, which is a weightier objective of the Shari'a. The legal reasoning behind this is that when both the right of God (*ḥaqq Allāh*) and human right (*ḥaqq al-ādmī*) compete, then human right is given precedence like the dispensation of shortened prayer and postponement of

For the majority, preservation of life is a greater priority compared to other higher objectives, as long as it does not compete with interests which are the complete right of God like completely suspending obligatory prayer altogether.[20]

To address complex questions around closure of mosques and suspension of congregational prayers (i.e., acts which are obligatory) to reduce spread, we will need to view *maṣlaḥa* according to grades of need (*ḥāja*) and necessity (*ḍarūra*). These grades of need and necessity will determine whether the need to introduce an intervention, that will reduce the risk of spread or loss of life, is serious enough, to qualify or allow for change in important competing Islamic rulings or dispensations when there is hardship. The greater the need, the higher it is in priority and requires preserving. The greater the harm to

---

fast for those traveling and for the sick, to safeguard their health. Here, these acts of worship are a right of God, whereas removing hardship and preserving health is a human right. The response that Muslim scholars give to this is that each of these cases represents situations of need and necessity where the dispensation is such that the human right does not precede over the complete right of God. In situations of travel and sickness, there is the right of the individual that he is not harmed, and the right of God that he reads his obligatory prayer. When fasting or traveling, the right of God supersedes that of the human right, where dispensation is acceptable by God on the basis that the individual will have to either postpone the act, like fasting an alternate day (*qaḍā*) or the act is lightened to remove hardship, like reducing the units of prayer, and if they are not possible, then expiation (*fidyā*) is to be paid. Al-Āmidī, *al-Iḥkām fī Uṣūl al-Aḥkām*, Vol. 4, 379; and ʿIzz al-Dīn ʿAbd al-ʿAzīz ibn ʿAbd al-Salām, *Qawāʿid al-Aḥkām fī Maṣāliḥ al-Anām* (Beirut: Dār al-Maʿārif, n.d.), Vol. 1, 167 and 173, There are verses of the Qur'an that stipulate these rulings see:

> O you who believe! Fasting is prescribed for you, even as it was prescribed for those before you, that you may ward off (evil); (Fast) a certain number of days; and (for) him who is sick among you, or on a journey, (the same) number of other days; and for those who can afford it there is a ransom: the feeding of a man in need. (Q.2:183–187)

20 In situations of travel and sickness, there is the right of the individual that he is not harmed, and the right of God that he reads his obligatory prayer. When fasting or traveling, the right of God supersedes that of the human right where dispensation is acceptable by God on the basis that the individual will have to either postpone the act, like fasting an alternate day (*qaḍā*) or the act is lightened to remove hardship, like reducing the units of prayer, and if they are not possible, then expiation (*fidyā*) is to be paid. Al-Āmidī, *al-Iḥkām fī Uṣūl al-Aḥkām*, Vol. 4, 379; and ʿIzz al-Dīn ʿIbn ʿAbd al-Salām, *Qawāʿid al-Aḥkām fī Maṣāliḥ al-Anām*, Vol. 1, 167 and 173. There are verses of the Qur'an that stipulate these rulings see, "O you who believe! Fasting is prescribed for you, even as it was prescribed for those before you, that you may ward off (evil); (Fast) a certain number of days; and (for) him who is sick among you, or on a journey, (the same) number of other days; and for those who can afford it there is a ransom: the feeding of a man in need …" (Q.2:183–187).

public interests, the likelier that dispensations of rulings would be acceptable. Two categories are recognized that describe the degree of harm to public interests, if at all. They are *al-maṣlaḥat al-ḍarūriyyā* (necessities) and *al-maṣlaḥat al-ḥājiyya* (needs).[21]

4.1 Al-MaṣLaḥat al-ḌArūRiyyā (*Necessities*)

These necessities are defined as those activities and interventions that are essential to the preservation of the five foundations of individual and social life according to Islam, that is, religion, life, mind, lineage, and wealth. Their neglect leads to total disruption and chaos in life.

Muslim scholars all agree that *ḍarūra* refers to preservation of life's interests from harms of both this world and hereafter. This does not just refer to individuals but can extend to public needs. In *ḍarūra* one is compelled to act contrary to what God has ordered in the Islamic sources (i.e., to abstain from congregational Friday prayers) to preserve what the Shariʿa considers of greater importance and a higher objective (i.e., prevent deaths from COVID-19). In a technical sense, God's right is waived to one of greater priority.

Al-maṣlaḥa al-ḍarūriyya upholds the *maṣlaḥa* (public good and its interest) and is utilized when referring to any harm that threatens to seriously damage life or bodily parts and not necessarily lead to their loss. This harm is not just limited to immediate circumstances in a state of compulsion, but also encompasses future inevitabilities that are certain or close to certain.[22]

According to this level of need, if individuals or vulnerable groups are at high risk of contracting COVID-19 and there is a high probability that this could lead

21 Abū Isḥāq al-Shāṭibī, *al-Mawāfaqāt fī Uṣūl al-Sharīʿā* (Beirut: Dār al-Iḥyāʾ al-Turāth al-ʿArabī, 2001), Vol. 2, 17. There is also *al-maṣlaḥat al-taḥsīniyya* (embellishments), which refer to activities and things that go beyond the limits of conveniences and whose realization leads to the improvement and attainment of that which is desirable such as fashionable clothes, voluntary acts of worship, different types of luxury food, and good behavior and speech. Going beyond refinements into extravagance and self-indulgence is perceived by Islam as a disutility for both individuals and society, and is disapproved. This will not be explored in this chapter as, even though it holds some importance in the welfare of people, it is not relevant to our discussion on issues of need and necessity during epidemics where the expectation is that embellishments will inevitably be compromised to support more important priorities.

22 Al-Wahbah al-Zuhaylī, *Naẓariat al-Ḍarūrat al-Sharʿiyya* (Beirut: Muʾassasat al-Risāla, 1985), 66–68; Muṣtafa Aḥmad al-Zarqāʾ, *Sharḥ al-Qawāʿid al-fiqhiyya* (Damascus: Dār al-Qalam, 1989), 155; al-Ghazālī, *al-Mustaṣfā min ʿIlm al-Uṣūl*, 251; al-Shāṭibī, *al-Mawāfaqāt fī Uṣūl al-Sharīʿā*, Vol. 6, 2; and Jalāl al-Dīn al-Suyūṭī, *al-Asbāh wa al-Naẓāʾir fī qawāʿid wa furūʿfiqh al-Shāfiʿī* (Beirut: Dār al-Kutub al-ʿIlmiyya, 1990), 76.

to loss of life or serious illness, then such groups and individuals are excused and offered dispensation on obligatory rulings like not attending the mosque for Friday congregational prayers.[23]

The next level of need is *al-Maṣlaḥat al-Ḥājiyya.*

4.2 al-Maṣlaḥat al-Ḥājiyya (*Needs*)

This category comprises all activities and things that are not vital to the preservation of the five higher objectives but are necessary to relieve or remove related impediments and difficulties and hardships in life. These needs promote and supplement the necessities and their neglect leads to hardship but not to the total disruption of normal life.[24]

The main distinction, agreed by contemporary jurists, between *al-maṣlaḥat al-ḍarūriyya* and *al-ḥājiyya* is the severity of the outcome if such necessity or need is not overcome. With *ḍarūra*, the individual is likely to perish and in *ḥāja* he is likely to undergo a comparatively less severe outcome of difficulty and hardship.[25] It is important to know that if the rule of *ḥāja* is extended from an individual to a general group or to the general public, then widespread public *ḥāja* achieves the normative force of *ḍarūra*. The legal maxim used to describe this: "*Ḥāja* is given the status of *ḍarūra*, [when it is] general [to a population] *al-ḥājat al-ʿāmma* or specific [to a group] *al-ḥājat al-khāṣa*."[26]

Al-ḥājat al-khāṣa (also termed *al-ḥājat al-fiqhiyya*) does not provide dispensation to everyone, but is limited to only one or a group of people that undergo hardship (*al-muḥtāj*), whereas *al-ḥājat al-ʿāmma* (or *al-ḥājat al-uṣūliyya*) is

23 Al-Zuhaylī, *Naẓariat al-Ḍarūrat al-Sharʿiyya*, 66–68; al-Zarqā', *Sharḥ al-Qawāʿid al-fiqhiyya*, 155; al-Ghazālī, *al-Mustaṣfā min ʿIlm al-Uṣūl*, 251; al-Shāṭibī, *al-Mawāfaqāt fī Uṣūl al-Sharīʿā*, Vol. 6, 2; and al-Suyūṭī, *al-Asbāh wa al-Naẓāʾir fī qawāʿid wa furūʿfiqh al-Shāfiʿī*, 76.

24 Imām Shāṭibī defines *ḥāja* as the expansion of measures in cases of need in order to relieve serious difficulty from that which is harmful to that of ease, where the hardship is diminished with that which is sought. Imām Suyūṭī further elucidates:

> that this is a state when a starving person [is in need of food] and he is unable to find that which he can eat; he does not perish from not eating but suffers difficulty and hardship. [The ruling of this state is that] it does not permit the prohibited.

Al-Shāṭibī, *al-Mawāfaqāt fī Uṣūl al-Sharīʿā*, Vol. 2, 11; and Badr al-Dīn al-Zarkashī, *al-Manthūr fī l-Qawāʿid* (Beirut: Dār al-Kutub al-ʿIlmiyya, 2000), Vol. 2, 320.

25 Al-Suyūṭī, *al-Asbāhu w'al-Naẓāʾir fī qawāʿid wa furūʿfiqh al-Shāfiʿ*, 80.

26 Al-Suyūṭi, *al-Asbāhu w'al-Naẓāʾir fī qawāʿid wa furūʿfiqh al-Shāfiʿ*, 88; Zain al-Dīn bin Ibrāhīm Ibn Nujaym, *Al-Asbāhu w'al-Naẓāʾir ʿalā Madhhab Abī Ḥanīfah al-Nuʿmān* (Beirut: Dār al-Kutub al-ʿIlmiyya, 1999), 91; and Nūr Muḥammad, ed., *Majallat al-Aḥkām al-ʿAdaliyya* (Karachi: Kārkhāna Tijārat Kutub, 2010), *mādah* (32), Vol. 1, 19.

given the status of *ḍarūra* in its normative force and hence provides dispensation to everyone, those undergoing hardship as well as those who are not undergoing hardship directly (*al-muḥtāj wa ghayr al-muḥtāj*), but are members of the public concerned, and are impacted indirectly.[27]

In other words, if the majority of the public are undergoing hardship at level of *ḥāja*, when public interests are threatened related to the higher objectives of the Shariʿa, like preservation of religion (i.e., closure of mosques), life (i.e., high death rates), mind (i.e., increasing mental health issues), lineage (i.e., negative impact on family relations and care of children), and wealth (i.e., a strained economy and financial situation), then the principle of *ḍarūra* can be implemented at a public level in support of public health policy. The COVID-19 pandemic has had a major impact on restrictions and closure of mosques, on lives lost, on deteriorating mental health of people due to lockdown and closure of businesses, and on loss of work and general economy, and hence would qualify as a situation of general public need, affecting everyone, or at least majority of the people.

If the public are threatened by a pandemic illness like COVID-19, which is fatal, and one which threatens our higher Islamic objectives, then we can apply the principle of *al-maṣlaḥat al-ḍarūriyya* to the cases of vulnerable groups like the elderly and those who have underlying disease conditions which put them at risk, and *ḥājat al-ʿāmma*, related to all individuals who are negatively impacted by public policy around social distancing.

What is yet to be clarified or be determined is *how* we assess and measure the degree of impact of harm and hardship to the public, which satisfy the conditions required, allowing dispensations using the principle of *ḍarūra* or *ḥājat al-ʿāmma*.

This process of determination must be both conducive to the Islamic framework relating public harm considerations and be practical in that it is simple to use. What we need is an impact assessment tool (IAT). An IAT would inform Muslim scholars, leaders, health professionals, and the public about the seriousness of potential health, economic, social, and environmental outcomes. This would improve transparency of decision-making, contribute to increasing partner and public participation, and clarify how public policy helps to achieve goals aligned to the Shariʿa requirements, by determining priorities through policy indicators. The impact assessment tool could contribute to con-

27 ʿAbd al-Malik al-Juwaynī, *al-Burhān fī Uṣūl al-Fiqh* (Beirut: Dār al-Kutub al-ʿIlmiyya, 1997), 945; for more details, see also Hishām ibn Sulaymān al-Saʿīd, *Tanzīl al-Ḥājat Manzalat al-Ḍarūrah, Fiqh al-Aqalliyyāt*, 42.

tinuous learning in policy development and the effective application of the utility of principles of need and necessity by identifying causalities that inform and influence the decision-making process.[28]

5 Shariʿa Considerations and Measuring Risk

There is a need to provide holistic, well-informed Islamic guidance to Muslim scholars, imāms, Muslim leaders, healthcare professionals, the Muslim population, and Islamic organizations. This is not to suggest that there is only one opinion, and everyone must follow it, rather there should be a systematic approach or a framework that we can use to ensure that our conclusions are thought through and adhere to the Islamic traditional approach when dealing with the welfare of communities. The guidance needs to be timely, at a local and global footprint, consistent, easy to follow, authentic in its sources from the Islamic tradition, and informed by both medical science and intelligence from public health. An impact assessment tool would provide a structured approach that can be applied at all levels of decision-making, from policies to specific projects. An impact assessment would enable the identification, prediction, and evaluation of the likely changes in the level of harm to the population due to the pandemic, both positive and negative (single or collective) of a policy program and plan, or development action on a defined population. These changes may be direct and immediate or indirect and delayed.[29] Its purpose is to add value to the decision-making process.[30] It aims to assist decision makers by clarifying the various ways in which a policy could influence health and by ensuring that health considerations are not overlooked.[31] An impact assessment tool should also recognize the phases and stages of epidemics and their crucial stages of response, so that they can be effectively aligned.

28 Klaus Jacob et al., "Sustainability in Impact Assessments: A Review of Impact Assessment Systems in Selected OECD Countries and the European Commission," OECD. SG/SD(2011)6 /FINAL, accessed January 2021, http://www.oecd.org/gov/regulatory-policy/Sustainability%20in%20impact%20assessment%20SG-SD%282011%296-FINAL.pdf.

29 D. Morgan, ed., *Health and Environmental Impact Assessment* (London: Earthscan, 1998).

30 "Developing Health Impact Assessment in Wales," National Assembly for Wales, Cardiff, Wales, 1999, accessed June 20, 2022, http://www.wales.nhs.uk/sites3/Documents/522/developing_hia_in_wales.pdf.

31 Karen Lock, "Health Impact Assessment," *British Medical Journal* 320, (2000): 1395–1398, https://doi.org/10.1136/bmj.320.7246.1395.

6 Impact Assessment Tool (IAT)

Epidemics this century can spread more widely and quickly, as is evident from the COVID-19 pandemic, because of our modern modes of transport affecting greater numbers of people than ever before. They can destroy lives and severely impact the economy of affected countries including travel and trade, and hence the greater need to be prepared for such major events.[32]

Epidemics occur by either one of these two ways. Either as new-emerging pathogens and re-emerging pathogens—these are pathogens that are known for some time and have re-emerged and threaten other populations or those populations, which are not immunized against them. They can sometimes present as different variants like with the COVID-19 virus.[33]

The Islamic bioethics framework of need and necessity can be employed when there is some evidence that the epidemic is leading to loss of life or severe physical harm, either to the whole population or a vulnerable group of people in that population. This requires us to develop measurable key indicators which will fulfill the conditions required for the application of the principle of *al-ḍarūra* or *al-ḥājat al-ʿāmma*. This will be based on the level of risk of outbreaks to the public, and depends on three factors:[34]

1. **The characteristics of the COVID-19 virus**: the rate of spread between people (its virulence) and hence its transmission rate, are key characteristics that determine the immediacy and intensity of response if the illness is fatal.
2. **The severity of resulting illness**: This is best measured from mortality and morbidity figures and their trends, as a direct result of those infected. The rate of mortality will determine the fatality of the illness and trends will allow us to predict when we are heading toward a wave of increasing mortality and morbidity and hence plan to mitigate.
3. **The ability to control the impact**: Public health measures like social distancing, hygiene measures, lockdowns, vaccines, or medications that can treat the illness, and other policy measures, may be used to control or mitigate the impact of the virus. The level of effectiveness in reducing the negative impact and demand on health systems is essential to this. Each disease requires a different set of public health interventions. The

32 *Managing Epidemics: Key Facts About Major Deadly Diseases* (Geneva: World Health Organization, 2018), 14.

33 Jacqui Wise, "Covid-19: New Coronavirus Variant is Identified in UK," *BMJ* 371 (2020): m4857, https://doi.org/10.1136/bmj.m4857.

34 World Health Organization, *Managing Epidemics*, 36.

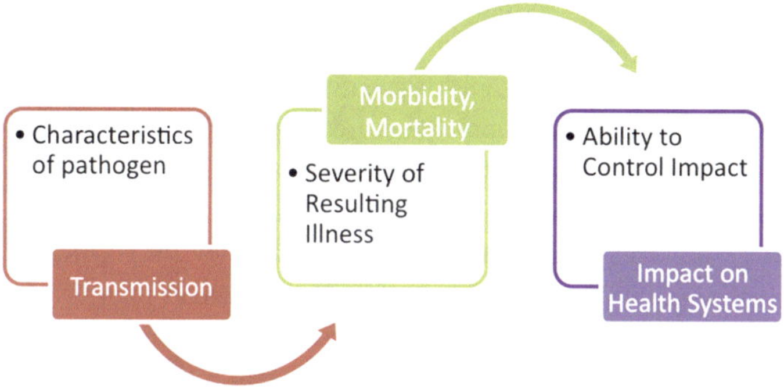

FIGURE 9.1 Factors to determine severity of epidemics and their measurable indicators

objectives of these interventions are to reduce transmission, morbidity, and mortality and to reduce burden on health systems and other associated systems to preserve the higher objectives of the Shariʿa which may also include economic stability.

There are three main measurable key indicators that effectively measure the risk posed by the three above-mentioned factors and require consideration when deciding on Islamic rulings for groups of people. These three key indicators will determine the severity of risk, taking into consideration the multiple contributing factors (see Fig. 9.1).

7 Transmission of the Disease and Rate of Spread

The following are four considerations for decision makers regarding transmission:

1. **Speed of Transmission**: in local areas, the number of cases and demand for services can be expected to increase, requiring an agile and a coordinated response. If capacity needs are not met, then this can lead to serious demand issues where services that care for the ill and vulnerable like primary care, hospitals, and even community nursing services will be heavily impacted. Ensuring everyone impacted receives the right care at the right time may prove difficult to maintain, and if this capacity is not met, then mortality and morbidity figures will surge. These factors will need to be considered when deciding on Islamic rulings which provide dispensations in cases when there does not seem to be an apparent direct link between factors which are causing fatalities, yet they contribute significantly if not controlled.

2. **The infectious hazard**: its severity, lethality, modes of transmission, how it can be diagnosed, treated, or managed are important when relating the degree of concern and the thresholds for employing rulings of hardship and need. If the infection is lethal, then more caution and lower thresholds will be required in accepting dispensations.
3. **Local hotspots**: the demands of the pandemic are unlikely to be uniform, but different areas will be under pressure at different times (and some not at all), requiring flexibility of approach, as well as planning for easy access to antiviral medicines. In such situations, the *fiqh* (substantive law) that may apply to one locality, may differ from that of another. Generalized *fatāwā* (sing. *fatwā*)[35] may prove problematic and may cause public anxieties because the target group is not identified and this may cause unnecessary panic and disorder for those not affected, or complacency, non-compliance of safety measures for those affected, if not appropriated effectively. There will be a need to refer to *fatāwā* that address rulings related to the degree of threat to specific groups of people and to articular localities.
4. **The geography and demographics of the outbreak**: this may be contained, or widely distributed. It may be national or international and can affect certain vulnerable communities where there is a larger elderly population, ethnic minorities, or the general population. It may be in a remote forgotten village or major city. It may be affecting the poor in poverty areas or affecting travel and trade. Different communities and localities may require a different approach and appropriate advice should be sought for each community.

8 Severe Morbidity and Mortality as a Direct Result of the Epidemic

The following are six considerations for decision makers regarding morbidity and mortality:

1. **Uncertainty**: there will be little or no information at the outset of a new pandemic about the severity of the illness. This will require accurate and detailed surveillance data, including numbers affected, hospital and crit-

35 *Fatwā* (pl. *fatāwā*) is an authoritative, but non-binding legal opinion or interpretation on a point of Islamic law given by a qualified legal scholar (known as a mufti) or collectively, comprising a number of Muslim scholars with an interdisciplinary team of biomedical scientists. A fatwa is usually issued in response to questions from individuals or Islamic courts.

ical care admissions, which will need to be gathered as an early priority. The level of certainty required to associate a public health, political, economic intervention in eradicating an epidemic would need to be estimated, for example, mass containment of individuals or communities against their wishes. In such cases, it is expected that rules of need and necessity can only be utilized when there is dominant probability (*ghalabat al-ẓann*) of benefit of an intervention. Reliable knowledge may not be evident and may require further time, however, when there is some historical evidence and experience (*tajriba*) that a fatal outcome will occur, either through equivalent historical cases or evidence from other countries where the outbreak is serious, then this will suffice to verify and justify use of principles of need and necessity.

2. **Profile:** the media, public and professional appetite for information is likely to be intense at times, requiring frequent, consistent, and coordinated communications. This is the time when misinformation, conspiracies, and misguidance become more apparent. Muslim leaders and Muslim scholars must make sure that they are well informed and updated regularly about the science, politics, and the economic situation, so that they can advise appropriately and accurately ensuring consistency in messages. This is best dealt with using reliable governmental websites and the voice of trusted bodies and individuals.
3. **Duration:** a pandemic wave can be expected to continue for many weeks or even months, requiring robust arrangements to support individuals involved in the response. In time, further waves may also occur. All these inevitabilities and trends need to be calculated and interim *fatāwā* should be released at their appropriate times to ensure the consumers of the information are given timely and appropriate advice particular to them.
4. **The levels of trust** that exists between the affected or at-risk populations and authorities, experts, or the response teams are essential. Conspiracies and misinformation should be responded to when advising, as non-adherence to a community-wide or nation-wide plan can lead to higher mortalities.
5. **Peoples' underlying beliefs, cultures, traditions, values, and practices.** Muslims belong to different ethnicity, sects, schools of thought, and different spiritual leadership and affiliation. It is essential that rulings account for these differences, are holistic, are not too narrow, and do not critique the other. Ensure information dissipated does not suite only one affiliation.
6. **Education and different levels of awareness:** It is important that all have access to understandable information, and trusted channels of communi-

cation. Different levels of knowledge are appropriate for different groups of people. The advice should be presented in a way that it is not complex and confusing. Advice for Muslim healthcare professionals will be quite different to the general Muslim public.

9 The Impact on Health Systems and Other Systems (Economy), Political and Other Sectors

The following are four considerations for decision makers regarding the impact on health systems:

1. **Cross-sector**: while the health sector will be under particular pressure, the response will span different sectors and organizations, requiring close working and mutual support. It is for this reason that a multidisciplinary approach should be sought to ensure rulings are well thought out, true, and inclusive. Muslim scholars and Muslim physicians may require input from those who have expertise in public health, local politics, social and economic issues, and epidemiology.
2. **Wider applicability**: the response to the H1N1 (2009) influenza pandemic enhanced its response to more routine pressures such as those arising from severe weather. These seasonal factors should also be considered. The season of transmission and escalation will impact outcomes and issues of capacity and response. Demographic factors, climatic conditions, and school cycles influence transmission dynamics.[36]
3. **Self-efficacy**: do communities have the ability, resources, and environment to follow health advice? It is essential that common mediums of social media release the appropriate advice quickly and smoothly at the most appropriate times. Confusion, complacency, and panic are all factors which can cause fatalities if present at scale.
4. **Level of Epi-features**: There are several epi-features that need to be considered when evaluating the potential impact on health services and other important public services.[37] The demand on these services is

36 Gerardo Chowell et al., "The Influence of Climatic Conditions on the Transmission Dynamics of the 2009 A/H1N1 Influenza Pandemic in Chile," *BMC Infectious Diseases* 12, no. 298 (2012), https://doi.org/10.1186/1471-2334-12-298.

37 For a list of definitions of different Epidemiologically Relevant features (Epi-features) like: peak value, peak time, total attack rate, speed of epidemic, intensity duration etc., see Farzaneh Sadat Tabataba et al., "A Framework for Evaluating Epidemic Forecasts," *BMC Infectious Diseases* 17, no. 1 (May 2017): 345.

paramount in concluding the level of hardship especially when these services are overwhelmed. Different regions may have different levels of demand based on this, and a lot of this will vary according to public health strategies and resources.

The Islamic response needs to accommodate these essential factors when applying rulings related to hardship, need, and necessity to the COVID-19 pandemic. If transmission rate is rapid in any locality, then rules of need and necessity will apply more immediately, depending on the response and based on experiences of other countries and regions. If there is severe morbidity and mortality, well beyond the regular rate of influenza, then this will justify the introduction of rules of Shariʿa need and necessity because of the worsening fatality.

There are further considerations that need to be met which go beyond the concern of the direct outcomes of the epidemic. They encroach on issues of politics, economy, and trading. It is likely that morbidity and mortality rates may increase at a much greater rate if the political, economic, and social situation cannot withstand the pressure and demand.

Islamic rulings of *al-maṣlaḥat al-ḍarūriyya* and *ḥājat al-ʿāmma* may be employed, having taken into consideration the key measurable indicators detailed above related to transmission, morbidity/mortality, and the impact on health systems. Determining the level of threat using a simple scoring system for each of these three main key indicators will indicate to us the seriousness of the condition, informed by science and the level of national and local response and resilience. It is also important to understand the phases of epidemics and the crucial stage of response that relates to each phase. Understanding these phases will provide geographical and time bound projections of the level of hardship and demands in addressing need and necessity in different localities.

10 Phases and Stages of Epidemics with Their Crucial Stages of Response

The stages of epidemic and pandemic diseases like COVID-19 typically and predominantly go through four phases (see Fig. 9.2):[38]

First phase *Emergence*—the introduction or emergence of the pathogen and disease in a community.

38 World Health Organization, *Managing Epidemics*, 28.

FIGURE 9.2 Four stages of epidemics

Second phase *Outbreak*—this is localized transmission, where sporadic infections with the pathogen occur.

Third phase *Amplification*—this is when the outbreak amplifies into an epidemic or pandemic—the pathogen is able to transmit from human to human and causes a sustained outbreak in the community, threatening to spread beyond it.

Fourth phase *Reduced Transmission*—when human-to-human transmission of the pathogen decreases, owing to acquired population immunity or effective interventions to control the disease.

It is important for Muslim scholars and those who provide Islamic legal advice to the Muslim community to recognize which phase of the COVID-19 pandemic their rulings relate to. Each phase represents different levels of response, in terms of interventions and hence the level of stringency and importance required for each one of these interventions. Some of these interventions may not be religiously permitted in normal circumstances and, depending on the severity of public harm considerations, dispensations may be made at locality level, regional, or even national and international levels—all of which will be determined by the phase of the epidemic and expected stage of response. Examples may include quarantine, containment of public places, and the closure of Islamic institutes like the mosque, and consequently, congregational Friday prayers may have to be suspended within localities.

Then there are responses to the above-mentioned phases and the sequence of interventions.[39] These responses aim to reduce harm, and it is important to understand how the principles of need and necessity in the Shariʿa are employed in line with these responses to produce a good outcome.

11 Stages of Response to Phases of Epidemics

There are five stages of response, which are as follows: (1) anticipation; (2) early detection; (3) containment; (4) control and mitigation; and (5) elimination or eradication (see Fig. 9.3).

39 World Health Organization, *Managing Epidemics*, 29–30.

FIGURE 9.3 Stages of response to phases of epidemics

11.1 *Anticipation*

In this early stage, introduction and emergence of a pathogen can be anticipated even though it cannot be predicted. The anticipation of risks will allow early planning and focus on eradicating the threat. Because of the low levels of certainty, questions arise as to whether dispensations in utilizing certain preventative measures which are contrary to Islamic rulings are allowed, for example, the free mixing and physical examination of non-related individuals of opposite gender in situations where there is a need to screen populations by taking deep throat swabs, take blood tests or even examine.[40] Other examples may be the prophylactic use of vaccines, which may contain impure prohibited animal ingredients and whether Muslims are religiously permitted to take them.

11.2 *Early Detection*

Diseases can be emerging and re-emerging. New ones may appear and there is little scientific knowledge about them. While investigations are made to investigate their source, coordinated, rapid-containment measures should also be considered and there should be preparedness for new interventions for new diseases. At this stage there is a balance to be made between the potential seriousness of the emerging disease and its harm to individuals and the population, with the need to maintain Shariʿa rulings without having to resort to the dispensations of need *ḥāja* or even necessity *ḍarūra*. There will be a lot of reliance on the emerging knowledge from scientific health bodies to come to this conclusion. The difficulty here is the ambivalence and lack of assurance of the impending consequences and their seriousness, and to what degree Shariʿa dispensations can be applied.

11.3 *Containment*

Even if the source is not known, rapid containment should be started immediately. This is just as important as early detection. If there is a risk of an epidemic,

40 *Khalwah* is a state of seclusion in the Shariʿa, in which two people, male and female, are alone and are *non-maḥram*. It is a state from which they ought to remove themselves. A *non-mahram* is anyone of opposite sex who is not a close family member like parents, siblings, spouse, and children.

depending on the seriousness of the disease outcome, Shariʿa dispensations may apply. Some complex areas include deciding on individual, local, regional containment, and its wider implications. If there is a risk of harm to wider society and this harm cannot be contained due to non-compliance, or there is difficulty or hardship *mushaqqah*, to control a large population, then the rules of need may be employed or even necessity, depending on individual circumstances of people and geography. This stage can lead to a lot of public non-adherence as the impact of the epidemic may not have reached communities, but just pockets of communities.

11.4 *Control and Mitigation*

Mitigating and reducing the impact of the disease is essential when the threat reaches an epidemic or pandemic level. The incidence, morbidity, mortality, and disruptions to economic, political, and social systems should be reduced as much as is possible. The wider implications related to other systems present additional hardship, which may indirectly impact mortality and morbidity in addition to the direct outcome of the epidemic. These additional system burdens and hardship will need to be taken into consideration when deciding on interventions which would normally be religiously prohibited, such as the use of porcine-derived vaccines to prevent further harm to the public. Importance of herd immunity would require even those who have not contracted the infection to be immunized. Other decisions may also be pertinent such as whether such mass immunization schemes would be permitted and be made compulsory for all. Also, whether the risk of the responsibility accepted of physicians and first responders, to put their health and lives at risk in combating epidemics is acceptable, and to what degree. What if a physician, who may have the symptoms, refuses to seek diagnosis, would that be considered acceptable? How should Muslim physicians balance their dual obligations to family and society if they are asked to stay and treat patients during an epidemic? Can use of experimental treatments be justified in times of epidemics when we are not sure of the adverse effects? This stage can cause panic and confusion if not managed properly and on time, as well as mistrust in governmental interventions.

11.5 *Elimination or Eradication*

Elimination of a disease requires that the disease is controlled so that there is no re-occurrence in a defined geographical area—the disease is no longer considered a major public health issue. However, intervention measures (surveillance and control) should continue to prevent its re-emergence. At what stage would the Shariʿa rules of need and necessity no longer apply? How would the maxims *qawāʿid* of need and necessity be employed to address the limits of the

TABLE 9.1 Phases of epidemics and their associated shariʿa rulings of need and necessity

Phase of epidemic	Stage of response	Shariʿa rulings
The First Phase: Emergence	Anticipation Early detection	Rulings of need and necessity may just be limited to individuals or localities
The Second Phase: Outbreak, Localized Transmission	Containment	Rulings of need and necessity may be just limited to localities where there are outbreaks
The Third Phase: Amplification	Control and mitigation	Rulings of need and necessity may apply to all where there are outbreaks and beyond
The Fourth Phase: Reduced Transmission	Elimination or eradication	Rules of need and necessity may continue and extend well into this phase until there is assurance that safety can be maintained, and another wave is unlikely to occur

exceptions? When would it be safe for mosques to reopen and congregations to continue as normal without social distancing?

It is important to note that the eradication of a disease is difficult and rarely achieved. It involves the permanent elimination of its incidence worldwide. Three criteria need to be met to eradicate a disease:[41]

1. there must be an available intervention to interrupt its transmission, that is, vaccinations;
2. there must be available efficient diagnostic tools to detect cases that could lead to transmission; and
3. humans must be the only reservoir.

Achieving all three criteria is not always possible and hence the complexity of withdrawing Islamic legal rulings pertaining to *ḥāja* (need) and *ḍarūra* (necessity) may not seem as straightforward.

The principles of Shariʿa necessity and need will vary in application according to the phases of the epidemic, where rulings of *ḥāja* and *ḍarūra* may just be limited to individuals or localities and *al-maṣlaḥat al-ḍarūriyya* and *al-ḥājat al-ʿāmma* to wider public, and be maintained until the level of risk subsides or is eliminated (see Table 9.1).

41 World Health Organization, *Managing Epidemics*, 30.

We shall refer to these phases and their crucial stages of response while applying our Islamic framework for pandemics to COVID-19. I will describe how contemporary Islamic legal rulings engaged with such factors, their value in the debate, and whether there were gaps in the ethico-legal reasoning applied. The different thresholds of application by different groups of people, based on important and common conditional factors, will be explored using the framework.

12 Application: Case of COVID-19

The following "five conditions approach" will provide the guidance, which will ensure that our responses are well thought through and informed by both the science as well as our Islamic legal tradition. This framework will guide decision-making related to the permissibility of interventions or acts, which would normally be prohibited in Islam, but because of public interest need and necessity, are permitted (see Fig. 9.4). I will provide examples of how this "five conditions approach" is be utilized, using the example of the contemporary responses to two main areas of contention during the COVID-19 pandemic—the first being the closure of mosques to reduce spread, and the second, the use of vaccines which contain impure ingredients to eliminate COVID-19.

12.1 *Condition 1: The Epidemic/Pandemic Illness Must Be a Fatal Illness*

The first condition requires that there be strong evidence that the COVID-19 pandemic is leading to loss of life or severe physical harm, either to the whole population or a vulnerable group of people in that population.[42] There is a need to measure the significance of this harm by measuring the seriousness of the key indicators mentioned as part of our IAT. This will identify whether the fatality justifies the application of the principle of *ḍarūra* or *ḥājat al-ʿāmma*. The fatality may vary with varying: (1) transmission rates, (2) mortality figures, and (3) pressures on services, dependent on the phase of the epidemic.

The IAT will score higher in all domains as we come closer to an outbreak or another wave and will indicate when there is a serious threat to the whole population, and to particular vulnerable groups such as the elderly, those with multiple co-morbidities, as well as frontline key workers. It is argued that the Muslim community is at higher risk compared to the general population. This

42 Muḥammad Amīn Ḥāshiā ibn ʿĀbidīn Ibn ʿĀbidīn, *Radd al-Muḥtār ʿalā Durr al-Mukhtār Sharḥ Tanwīr al-Abṣār* (Beirut: Dār al-Kutub al-ʿIlmiyya, 2003), Vol. 7, 480.

is because of a higher prevalence of chronic illnesses such as diabetes and heart disease in Muslims compared to other ethnic populations, as a result of extended families living with each other, and the practice of frequent and regular community and communal gatherings for both social and religious purposes.[43]

If the score is high, then rulings related to *ḍarūra* will have more normative/legal force in supporting the closure of mosques or in the use of vaccinations which contain impure substances, if alternative permissible ones are not available.

12.2 *Condition 2: The Proposed Intervention or Action, Which Is Normally Prohibited, Must Be Effective*

An evaluation is to be made of the effectiveness of the intervention or act proposed.[44] This requires that the level of certainty required for an intervention or action to be effective, will need to be of (1) dominant probability (*ghalabat al-ẓann*). This should ideally be (2) evidenced through good peer-reviewed science and epidemiological studies. It is possible to (3) use expert opinion or experience of previous similar cases in other geographical areas to determine this effectiveness if the source and conclusion are reliable and confirmed to be accurate.

Muslim scholars have had dissenting views regarding the act of closing mosques and suspending congregational prayers to contain spread. Some claim that such an intervention will not be effective enough to control spread, mainly because there is little if any evidence that gatherings in mosques are a significant source of spread. It is viewed by some that the risk of the mosque, as a contributing factor to spread, is minimal, relative to other venues, which are to remain open like superstores, schools, and colleges. So, why should mosques be targeted and not be seen as a necessary venue that is needed for the spiritual and psychological welfare of people during such a traumatizing time for many, especially when risks can be mitigated through social distancing measures, shorter prayers, hygiene measures, monitoring worshipers, and using face coverings?[45] Closing mosques is seen as an intervention, which is likely to have little benefit in containing spread if the right measures are in place. This opin-

43 British Islamic Medical Association, "An Open Letter to the Muslim Community," 2020, accessed January 2021, https://www.britishima.org/covid-open-letter-to-muslim-community/.

44 Ibn ʿĀbidīn, *Radd al-Muḥtār ʿalā Durr al-Mukhtār Sharḥ Tanwīr al-Abṣār*, Vol. 1, 365–356.

45 Yusuf Shabbir, "Coronavirus: Should Masjids Close?" *Islamic Portal*, March 17, 2020, accessed January 2021, https://islamicportal.co.uk/coronavirus-should-masjids-close/.

ion appeals to the lack of certainty of evidence of spread, which would justify closure of mosques. It also appeals to the idea of ensuring spiritual support is maintained for Muslim communities.

The contrary view advises the closure of mosques and suspension of congregational prayers. This is argued using anecdotal reports of outbreaks at mosques internationally like in the four-day meeting in Malaysia where there were claimed to be 673 identified cases, stressing the importance of closure.[46] Some estimated the level of threat through experiences gained and lessons learned from other neighboring countries, like the worsening death rate and increasing hospital admissions in Italy, while others provided an estimate of the risk factors based on the science of transmission of the virus, in view of normal practices in the mosque such as handshaking, physical contact with carpets during prostration, the sharing of washing facilities for the purpose of ritual ablution, and the fear that healthy individuals could end up transmitting the virus to vulnerable members of their household, as well as the question of the unlikelihood of such measures being stringently upheld at the risk of a seriously bad outcome.[47] This opinion appeals to the science behind the different routes of COVID-19 transmission and infection and how the mosque is a high-risk environment, as well as expert opinion and experience of previous similar cases in other geographical areas.

Both ends of the argument require reliable evidence, which is not always certain at a level of dominant probability but is estimated. The demand to provide strong "enough" evidence for the risk of spread, particularly in the mosque, and evidence of whether the risk can be mitigated through stringent measures, and whether those measures are likely to be adhered to by worshipers can be an impractical and risky process. The dominant argument remains that even if stringent mitigating measures are put in place, there is still an unacceptable risk of spread, and to undergo an evaluation of this is too risky as it will be at the cost of life. Most took the cautionary position and advised the closure of mosques.[48] All agreed that if the government made it a legal requirement to

---

46 "Made in Malaysia: How Mosque Event Spread Virus to SE Asia," *Al-Jazeera*, March 18, 2020, accessed January 2021, https://www.aljazeera.com/news/2020/3/18/made-in-malaysia-how-mosque-event-spread-virus-to-se-asia.

47 British Islamic Medical Association, "An Open Letter to the Muslim Community."

48 British Board of Imams and Scholars (BBSI), "UK Community Briefing Paper for Imams, Mosques, and Madrasas for the Coronavirus Pandemic," March 16, 2020, https://www.bbsi.org.uk/uk-community-briefing-paper-for-imams-mosques-and-madrasas-for-the-coronavirus-pandemic/; Shaykh (Dr) Sajid Umar, "Closing Mosques—Islamic Justifications for Coronavirus Lockdowns," *Islam21c*, March 23, 2020, accessed January 2021, https://www.islam21c.com/islamic-law/closing-mosques-islamic-justifications-for-coronavirus-lockd

close the mosques for the benefit of Muslims, then Muslims should adhere to this. This is evident from many traditional Islamic sources, which describe the importance of upholding governmental rulings if they are for public interest according to the Shariʿa.[49]

COVID-19 vaccines, which have been approved by the regulatory bodies, are proving to be very effective (between 65–95 percent) and, luckily, there have been no current approved vaccines that contain animal products or impure substances that would be considered prohibited.[50] If such a vaccine was approved and contained impure ingredients, then the discourse would be pivotal on its effectiveness and if there is a permissible alternative—which leads on to our next condition.

12.3 *Condition 3: There Is No* Alternative *Permissible Intervention or Act* Reasonably Available *and of Equal or Greater* Effectiveness

There are two evaluations to be made here: (1) whether there are alternative interventions or actions which are equally or more effective; and (2) whether these alternatives are practical, feasible, or reasonably available.

It is argued that there are alternative options before deciding on closing mosques, which can mitigate the risk of spread, like social distancing measures, shorter prayers, hygiene measures, monitoring worshipers, and using face coverings. They are not as effective as closing the mosque entirely, however, if the risk of spread in the mosque is shown to be minimized significantly through

owns/; Zulfiqar Ali Shah, "*Fiqh* Council of North America Covid Statement: Rulings on Daily and Weekly Congregational Prayers During Coronavirus Pandemic," June 25, 2020, https://www.sfinterfaithcouncil.org/sites/default/files/files/Fiqh%20Council%20of%20North%20America.pdf; and Zulfiqar Ali Shah, "Fiqh Council Guidelines for Coronavirus Epidemic," April 9, 2020, http://fiqhcouncil.org/fiqh-council-guidelines-for-coronavirus-epidemic/.

49 Muftī al-Saʿūdiyyah, "yūḍiḥ ḥukm man yukhālif walī al-amr wa yaskharu min juhūd," April 1, 2020, *Al-Ghad*, accessed July 2021, https://alghad.com/%D9%85%D9%81%D8%AA%D9%8A-%D8%A7%D9%84%D8%B3%D8%B9%D9%88%D8%AF%D9%8A%D8%A9-%D9%8A%D9%88%D8%B6%D8%AD-%D8%AD%D9%83%D9%85-%D9%85%D9%86-%D9%8A%D8%AE%D8%A7%D9%84%D9%81-%D9%88%D9%84%D9%8A-%D8%A7%D9%84%D8%A3/.

50 There have been some doubts expressed by particular religious institutes and scholarly individuals about use of foetal germ line, see Amin Kholwadia and Hisham Dawood, "Fatwā on COVID Vaccines," *Darul Qasim*, April 21, 2021, accessed July 2021, https://darulqasim.org/wp-content/uploads/2021/04/DI00489-Fatwa-COVID-Vaccine.pdf; and Mawlana Mateen A. Khan et al., "Islamically Permissible COVID-19 Vaccines: Viral Vector Page," *MuslimMed.org*, February 3, 2021, accessed July 2021, https://muslimmed.org/2021/02/03/viral-vector-page/.

mitigating measures, then there is an argument that they are not significantly less effective. If this reduction of spread cannot be verified, then some may maintain that the risk to worshipers is far too great and outweighs any speculation that mitigating spread is effective. Unlike other faiths, communal worship in Islamic law is congregational and not individual, and so the congregational prayer, which represents the central ritual of worship in mosques, does increase the risk.

Islam has also permitted alternative rulings in cases of hardship, for example, the substitute (*badal*) for Friday congregational prayers (*jumuʿa*) in the mosque is reading the *ẓuhr* prayer at home or other venues (ideally in a small congregation), if excused. Islamic law allows for a number of exemptions to the obligation to attend Friday prayer based on relative minor degrees of threat or harm such as excessive rain, cold, and fear of illness. Valid opinions also exist in Islamic law, which allow the Friday prayer to be conducted outside of the mosque with a minimum of three congregants, which could be offered as an alternative to attending Friday prayer at the mosque.[51]

Feasibility and practicality of adherence is the second evaluation to be made, and some would argue that to monitor worshipers and even having to remove those who do not adhere can prove quite difficult. Maintaining this level of adherence and compliance may be difficult as worshipers become more complacent over time. Hardship is also a factor which allows one to resort to means which would normally be prohibited; in line with the legal maxim hardship begets facility (*al-mushaqqah tajlib al-taysīr*), where due to hardship in maintaining order and compliance, some mosques may opt to close.

Similar evaluations can be made of vaccines containing impure ingredients. The first is that if there are alternative permissible vaccines, which are pure and of equal or greater effectiveness, then they must be used. If the effectiveness of the impure vaccine exceeds the effectiveness of the pure one, then it can be used. However, it may be that the pure alternative vaccine is unavailable, it has not yet been approved by drug monitoring bodies, there are processing issues, or it is significantly more expensive, then the notion of hardship related to the legal maxim of begetting facility can be applied, permitting its use.

51 British Board of Imams and Scholars (BBSI), "UK Community Briefing Paper for Imams, Mosques, and Madrasas for the Coronavirus Pandemic (BBSIG-02): Individual Institutional, and Collective Responsibilities," March 16, 2020, accessed January 2021, https://www.bbsi.org.uk/wp-content/uploads/2020/03/BBSI_G02_CoronaVirus.pdf.

12.4 *Condition 4: The Benefits of the Intervention Must Outweigh Its Harms*

Even if there are evident benefits from closing mosques or utilizing vaccines which contain impure substances, the adverse effects or harms of these interventions must not be significant enough to outweigh these benefits. There are certain legal maxims, which provide guidance to preferred outcomes. There are many examples of these legal maxims found in the *fiqh* literature (*al-qawāʿid al-fiqhīyya*).[52] These maxims are used by jurists when they need to judge between competing harms.[53] One of the five leading maxims relates to harm principles, "harm must be eliminated" (*al-ḍararu yuzāl*) and "there is to be no harm and no reciprocating harm" (*lā ḍarar wa lā ḍirār*), and they have branching maxims.[54] Commonly used maxims are: a greater harm is eliminated by [tolerating] a lesser harm (*al-ḍarar al-ashaddu yuzālu bī al-ḍarar al-akhaff*); harm must not be eliminated by an equal harm (*al-ḍararu lā yuzālu bi mithlihī*); and the lesser of the two evils is to be chosen (*yukhtār ahwan al-sharrayn*). These legal maxims indicate that when there is conflict between two harms then the least of the two is to be preferred and the other tolerated. An evaluation is made of the normative force or weight of the ruling and whether the stringency of the ruling can be compromised in pressing circumstances.

With regards to the COVID-19 pandemic, an evaluation is to be made of the weight of the ruling of keeping mosques open and preventing Muslims from taking impure medication to preserve religion or rights of God. This evaluation is made by assessing whether the force of these rulings can be compromised when competing with the need to save lives through social distancing or taking vaccinations which contain impure ingredients.

---

52 Unless they reaffirm a ruling of the Qur'an or Sunnah, the legal maxims do not bind the jurist in delivering a judgment, but they do provide an important influence in exercising *ijtihād* in arriving at legal decisions (*ḥukm*) and opinions (*fatwā*). Legal maxims, like legal theories (*naẓarīyāt al-fiqhīyya*), are designed to elucidate a refined understanding of the subject matter rather than address enforcement. The legal maxims are not similar to *uṣūl al-fiqh* (principles of Islamic jurisprudence) since maxims are based on the *fiqh* itself and represent rules and principles that are derived from the detailed rules of *fiqh* on various issues. *Uṣūl al-fiqh* is concerned with the sources of law, the rules of interpretation, methodology of legal reasoning, dealing with the meaning and implication of commands and prohibitions and so on. On the other hand, a maxim is defined as "a general rule, which applies to all or most of its related particulars," M.H. Kamali, *Shari'ah Law: An Introduction* (Oxford: Oneworld, 2012).

53 See ʿIzz al-Dīn, *Qawāʿid al-Aḥkām fī Maṣāliḥ al-Anām*, Vol. 1, 64–65.

54 See Ibn Nujaym, *Al-Ashbāhu wa al-Naẓāir ʿalā Madhhab Abī Ḥanīfah al-Nuʿmān*.

Muslim scholars determine the level of obligation in the opening of mosques and their congregations, and whether there are justifications which allow for their closure and suspension of congregational prayers. There are claims that it is not permissible to close mosques and suspend congregational prayers as this would be tantamount to harming the *maṣlaḥa* of preserving religion and faith. Other arguments are presented in support of temporary closure of mosques that congregational prayer in the mosque is not a direct and immediate detriment to the preservation of faith, because individuals can still temporarily pray in congregation with their families at home and will be preserving their faith, and it is not that mosques are to be permanently closed.[55] Some claim that mosques have never been closed even at the time of plagues,[56] whereas others provide evidence that even when conditions are not considered severe such as heavy rain, bad weather or illness, that one is excused from attending the mosque. The Ḥanbalī scholar Ibn Qudāmah (d. 620 AH) wrote, "A man may be excused for not praying Friday prayer [*jumuʿa*] … because of rain that makes the clothes wet, or mud that causes annoyance or stains the clothes." It was narrated that Ibn ʿAbbās said to the caller of prayer on a very rainy day:

> When you say: I bear witness that there is no god, but God and I bear witness that Muhammad is the Messenger of God, do not say "come to prayer" but rather say "pray in your houses." Some people found that strange, so he responded to them: "Are you surprised by what I just said? A person better than me did just that (referring to the Prophet)."[57]

It is also claimed that protecting the community from harm takes precedence over the acquiring of religious benefits, like the legal maxim which states: "Averting harm takes precedence over acquiring benefit." Therefore, protecting public from the harm of COVID-19 is seen as weightier than the obligation and benefit of keeping the mosques open or maintaining congregational prayers, especially since valid opinions exist in Islamic law which allow the Friday prayer to be conducted outside of the mosque with the minimum of three congregants, which could offer an alternative to attending Friday prayer at the mosque.[58]

---

55 Umar, "Closing Mosques."

56 Shabbir, "Coronavirus: Should Masjids Close?"

57 Abdullah ibn Aḥmad Ibn Qudāmah, *al-Mughnī* (Beirut: Dār al-Fikr, 1980), Vol. 1, 366.

58 British Board of Imams and Scholars, "UK Community Briefing Paper for Imams, Mosques, and Madrasas for the Coronavirus Pandemic."

When it comes to closing mosques, the balance of opinion may sway toward their temporary closure if the assessment tool shows that fatality scores are worsening, especially if it is seen that this is affecting the Muslim community disproportionately.

As for vaccines, there are many accounts in the prophetic tradition and in the writings of classical Muslim jurists permitting treatment with impure medication (*tadāwī b'il-muḥarram*) like carrion, camel urine, pig meat, blood, intoxicants (*al-khamr*), and other prohibited substances, when there is state of need and necessity in someone who requires such treatment.[59] The point of contention is that these cases have mainly been applied and are limited to individuals who are sick, and not to those who are well for the benefit of those who are at risk of being sick. So are healthy individuals able to take them as a preventative measure, to achieve herd immunity and benefit their community, when there is risk of serious disease or death of the vulnerable?

It is argued that if the risk of death in the community as a whole is significant enough, and the only means of removing the harm is through mass vaccine programs, to achieve herd immunity, then even if the vaccines contain impure substances, those who are not of major risk can be vaccinated to prevent harm to the vulnerable. This is because it is known that the risk to the larger population can only be removed and reduced if majority of the population is vaccinated. The low-risk population have a responsibility to the higher-risk groups, where some contemporary Muslim jurists even consider it an obligation to take vaccines, even if it contains impure substance.[60]

Important maxims which are quite pertinent in epidemics are maxims like: harm to an individual is tolerated in removing a public harm (*yutaḥammal al-ḍarar al-khāss lī dafʿ al-ḍarar al-ʿāmm*), which points to the bigger discussion

59 Al-Ḥaskafī, *Radd al-Mukhtār ʿalā Durr al-Mukhtār Sharḥ Tanwīr al-Abṣār* (place: pub, year), 210; Abū Bakr al-Rāzī al-Jaṣṣāṣ, *Aḥkām al-Qur'ān* (Beirut: Dār al-Iḥyā' al-Kutub al-ʿArabiyya, 1992), Vol. 1, 107; al-Khaṭīb al-Shirbīnī, *Mughnī al-Muḥtāj* (Beirut: Dār al-Maʿrifah, 1997), Vol. 4, 307; Yaḥyā bin Sharaf al-Nawawī, *al-Majmūʿ Sharḥ al-Muhadhdhab l-il-shirāzī* (Jeddah: Maktaba al-Irshād, 2008), Vol. 9, 43; Ibn Rushd, *Bidayat al-Mujtahid wa al-nihāyat al-muqtaṣid* (Cairo: Maktabah Ibn Taymiyyah, 1994), Vol. 1, 476; Abu Bakr Ibn ʿArabī, *Aḥkām al-Qur'ān* (place: pub, year), Vol. 1, 55; ʿ Ibn Qudāmah, *al-Mughnī*, Vol. 13, 335; Ibn Mufliḥ, Kishāf al-Qināʿ (place: pub, year), 6:194; Ibn Ḥazm, *al-Muḥallā bi-l Āthār* (Beirut: Dār al-Kutub al-ʿIlmiyya, n.d.), Vol. 7, 426; and al-Dardīr, *al-Sharḥ al-Saghīr* (Cairo: Dār al-Maʿārif, n.d.), Vol. 2, 184.

60 Muṣtafa K, "*al-Qaradāghī yufta bu wujūb talaqqi liqāḥ cūrūna ʿalā kulli Muslim*," *Rūdaw*, January 24, 2021, accessed July 2021, https://www.rudaw.net/arabic/kurdistan/240120219.

of *māslaḥat al-ḍarūriyya* and *ḥājat al-ʿāmma* considerations. These considerations are employed while recognizing that avoiding [harm] takes precedence over bringing about benefit (*darʾ al-mafāsid awlā min jalb al-maṣāliḥ*).

Even if it was argued that there is very little risk of death or serious illness to the low-risk groups and hence the principle of *ḍarūra* cannot be employed, then this can be addressed using two main approaches. The first is that it is a responsibility for the whole population to protect the most at risk in their population and if there is no other alternative then such means can be taken as *māslaḥat al-ḥājiyya*, where even those who are not in need directly (*ghayr al-muḥtāj*), have dispensation on the basis of this ruling. The second is that the pandemic has many other harms to society as a whole, with repeated lockdowns, there is risk to the economy, poverty, and psychological harms and trauma of losing loved ones which qualify as *ḥājat al-ʿāmma* and hence the rulings of *ḍarūra* can be applied.

12.5 *Condition 5: The Permissibility of the* Intervention *Remains as Long as the Threat of Harm Remains*

The permissibility of the *intervention* remains as long as the threat of harm remains, but efforts should also be made to find *acceptable* alternatives at all times. This is based on the maxims: harm is to be eliminated within reasonable limits (*al-ḍararu yudfaʿu bi qadr al-imkān*); and a thing which is permissible out of excuse ceases to be permissible with the disappearance of that excuse (*mā jāza li ʿudhri baṭala bi zawālihi*).

The IAT can be used to determine the level of stringency of rulings required for both the closure of mosques, suspension of congregational prayers, as well as the permissibility in use of impure vaccines. If the risk of transmission and death rates increase, then mosques should be closed if necessary and open, when risk has subsided, while maintaining mitigating measures. If we are compelled to use vaccines containing impure ingredients, then as soon as other permissible pure vaccines become available of equal or greater effectiveness, then it would no longer be permissible to use the impure vaccine, while maintaining that there should remain a consistent effort to produce vaccines which are pure or the Muslim public should push for their availability.

This "five conditions approach" in conjunction with the different phases of epidemics should be utilized to systematically discuss and determine important rulings related to need and necessity. They will ensure that conversations are constructive, informed, and appropriate at a time when things can be complex and confusing.

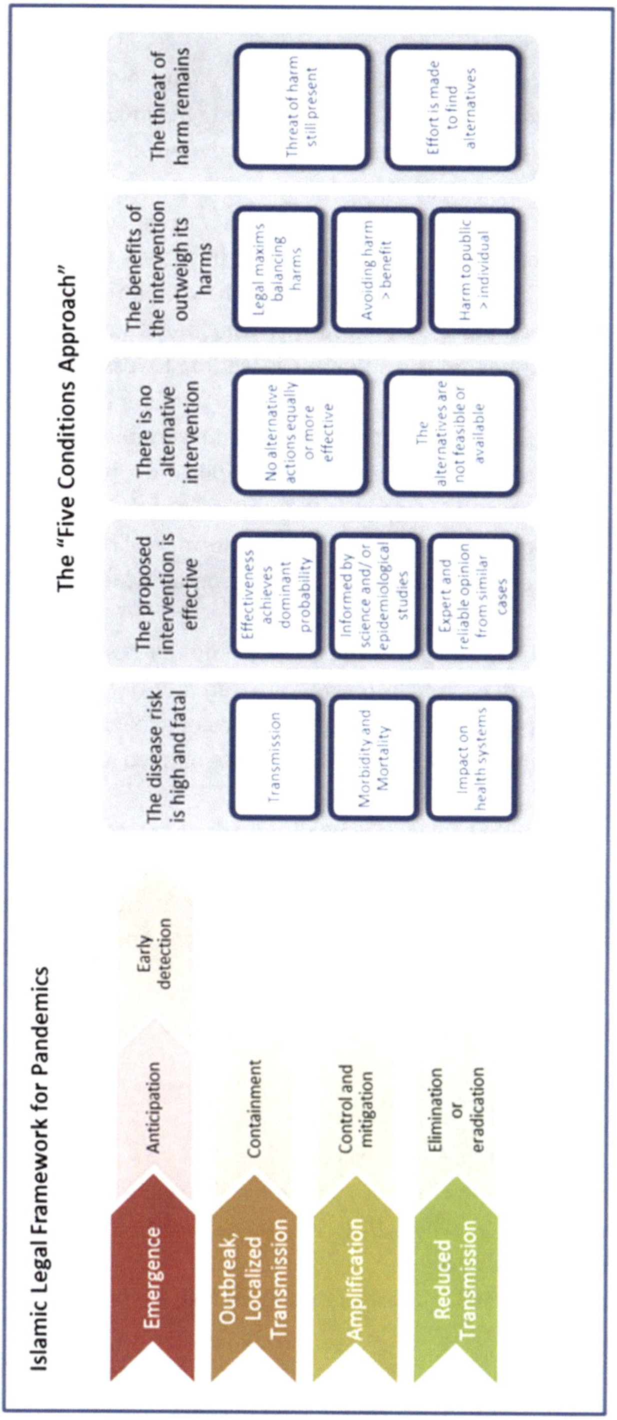

FIGURE 9.4 Islamic legal framework for pandemics

13 Conclusion

Illnesses, diseases, and trials are tests from God, and they have benefits and rewards. Islam requires trust in God (*tawakkul*) and utilizing the means to protect us when possible, and this does not deny or defy the decree of God. Muslim scholars have observed certain legal rulings that stem from advice sought from the prophetic tradition. The rulings stipulated by classical Muslim scholars regarding fleeing and entering a zone of plague or epidemic was to prevent harm to the public. Islam has its own ethico-legal approach to public harm consideration, which aims to protect essential public interests (*maṣlaḥa*).

There must be some evidence that the epidemic is leading to loss of life or severe physical harm either to the whole population or to a vulnerable group of people in that population. This requires us to develop measurable key indicators, which will fulfill the conditions required for the application of the principle of *ḍarūra* or *ḥājat al-ʿāmma*. It is important to understand the phases of epidemics and the crucial stages of response which will inform us of the level of hardship in addressing need and necessity from both a geographical and time perspective.

The "five conditions approach," in light of the phases of epidemics and their response, has been offered as an Islamic framework for pandemics, which will provide the criterion for the permissibility of interventions or acts, that would normally be prohibited in Islam, but because of the fatality of need and necessity of what may ensue, will be permitted.

It is also important to note that this is a start of a working framework and can only improve with further appraisal from expert advice and constructive and informed criticism. What is required is education and training in the use of such a framework for community leaders, Muslim scholars, health professionals, and other important figures in the public domain.

Bibliography

Abū Dāwūd. *Sunan Abī Dāwūd*. Riyadh: Al-Kutub al-Sitta, 2000.

Alfani, Guido, and Tommy E. Murphy. "Plague and Lethal Epidemics in the Pre-Industrial World." *The Journal of Economic History* 77, no. 1 (March 2017): 314–343. https://doi.org/10.1017/S0022050717000092.

Al-Āmidī, ʿAlī ibn Muḥammad. *Al-Iḥkām fī Uṣūl al-Aḥkām*, 2nd ed., 4 vols. Beirut: al-Maktab al-Islāmī, 2015.

Al-Anṣārī, Muḥammad ibn Muḥammad al-Laknawī. *Fawātiḥ al-Raḥmūt bī Sharḥ Musallam al-Thubūt*, 2 vols. Beirut: Dār al-Kutub al-ʿIlmiyya, 2022.

British Board of Imams and Scholars (BBSI). UK Community Briefing Paper for Imams, Mosques, and Madrasas for the Coronavirus Pandemic (BBSIG-02): Individual Institutional, and Collective Responsibilities. March 16, 2020. Accessed January 2021, https://www.bbsi.org.uk/wp-content/uploads/2020/03/BBSI_G02_CoronaVirus.pdf.

British Board of Imams and Scholars (BBSI). UK "Community Briefing Paper for Imams, Mosques, and Madrasas for the Coronavirus Pandemic." March 16, 2020. https://www.bbsi.org.uk/wp-content/uploads/2020/03/BBSI_G02_CoronaVirus.pdf.

Ibn ʿĀbidīn, Muḥammad Amīn Ḥāshiā ibn ʿĀbidīn. *Radd al-Muḥtār ʿalā Durr al-Mukhtār Sharḥ Tanwīr al-Abṣār*, 14 vols. Beirut: Dār al-Kutub al-ʿIlmiyya, 2003.

Ibn Amīr al-Ḥāj. *Al-Taqrīr wa al-Taḥrīr*. Beirut: Dār al-Kutub al-ʿIlmiyya, 1999.

Ibn ʿArabī, Abu Bakr. *Aḥkām al-Qur'ān*. place: pub, year.

Ibn Ḥazm. *Al-Muḥallā bi-l Āthār*, 12 vols. Beirut: Dār al-Kutub al-ʿIlmiyya, n.d.

Ibn Mufliḥ. *Kishāf al-Qināʿ*. place: pub, year.

Ibn Nujaym, Zain al-Dīn bin Ibrāhīm. *Al-Āshbāh wa al-Naẓāir ʿalā Madhhab Abī Ḥanīfah al-Nuʿmān*. Beirut: Dār al-Kutub al-ʿIlmiyya, 1999.

Ibn Qayyim al-Jawziyya, Shams al-Dīn Abī ʿAbd Allah. *Zād al-Maʿād*, 6 vols. Beirut: Mu'assasat al-Risālah, 1998.

Ibn Qudāmah, ʿAbdullah ibn Aḥmad. *Al-Mughnī*, 15 vols. Beirut: Dār al-Fikr, 1980.

Ibn Rushd, Abī Walīd Muḥammad Ibn Aḥmad. *Bidāyat al-mujtahid wa al-nihāyat al-muqtaṣid*, 4 vols. Cairo: Maktabah Ibn Taymiyyah, 1994.

Irfan, I.S., Mohd Daud Awang, Suhaimi Ab Rahman, and Aznan Hasan. "Pandemic and Islamic Point of View Based on Hadith Plague." *Journal of Critical Reviews* 7, no. 8 (2020): 1017–1020.

Isnawī, ʿAbd al-Raḥīm Ibn al-Ḥasan. *Nihāyat al-Sūl fī Sharḥ Minhāj al-Uṣūl*, 4 vols. Cairo: ʿAlim al-Kutub, 2009.

ʿIzz al-Dīn ʿAbd al-ʿAzīz, Ibn ʿAbd al-Salām al-Silmī. *Qawāʿid al-Aḥkām fī Maṣāliḥ al-Anām*, 2 vols. Beirut: Dār al-Maʿārif, n.d.

Jacob, Klaus, Johanna Ferretti, Anna-Lena Guske, John Turnpenny, Andrew Jordan, and Camilla Adelle. "Sustainability in Impact Assessments A Review of Impact Assessment Systems in Selected OECD Countries and the European Commission." OECD. (2011). SG/SD(2011)6/FINAL. Accessed January 2021, http://www.oecd.org/gov/regulatory-policy/Sustainability%20in%20impact%20assessment%20SG-SD%282011%296-FINAL.pdf.

Al-Jaṣṣāṣ, Abū Bakr al-Rāzī. *Aḥkām al-Qurān*, 5 vols. Beirut: Dār al-Iḥyā' al-Kutub al-ʿArabiyya, 1992.

Al-Juwaynī, ʿAbd al-Malik. *Al-Burhān fī Uṣūl al-Fiqh*. Beirut: Dār al-Kutub al-ʿIlmiyya, 1997.

Kamali, Mohammad Hashim. *Shari'ah Law: An Introduction*. Oxford: Oneworld, 2012.

Khan, Mawlana Mateen A., Ramzan Judge, Sama Tirmizi, and Adil Farooki. "Islamically Permissible COVID-19 Vaccines: Viral Vector Page." *MuslimMed.org*, February 3, 2021. Accessed July 2021, https://muslimmed.org/2021/02/03/viral-vector-page/.

Khan, Nazir, and Muntasir Zaman. "The Prophetic Promises for Martyrs and Medina: Is COVID-19 a Plague?" Yaqeen Institute for Islamic Research, April 5, 2020. Accessed December 2020, https://yaqeeninstitute.org/muntasir-zaman/the-prophetic-promises-for-martyrs-and-medina-is-covid-19-a-plague.

Kholwadia, Amin, and Hisham Dawood. "Fatwā on COVID Vaccines." *Darul Qasim*, April 21, 2021. https://darulqasim.org/wp-content/uploads/2021/04/DI00489-Fatwa-COVID-Vaccine.pdf.

Lock, Karen. "Health Impact Assessment." *British Medical Journal* 320 (2000): 1395–1398. https://doi.org/10.1136/bmj.320.7246.1395.

"Made in Malaysia: How Mosque Event Spread Virus to SE Asia." *Al-Jazeera*, March 18, 2020. Accessed January 2021, https://www.aljazeera.com/news/2020/3/18/made-in-malaysia-how-mosque-event-spread-virus-to-se-asia.

Mansfield, Kathryn, Rohini Mathur, John Tazare, Alasdair D. Henderson, Amy R. Mulick, Helena Carreira, et al. "Indirect Acute Effects of the COVID-19 Pandemic on Physical and Mental Health in the UK: A Population-Based Study." *Lancet* 3, no. 4 (2021): 217–230. https://doi.org/10.1016/S2589-7500(21)00017-0.

Ministry of Hajj and Umrah. "According to the Precautionary Measures, the Ministry of Hajj and Umrah Announces the Regulations and Procedures of Hajj 1442H/2021." June 12, 2021. Accessed July 6, 2021, https://www.haj.gov.sa/en/News/Details/12513.

Morgan, D., ed. *Health and Environmental Impact Assessment*. London: Earthscan, 1998.

Muḥammad, Nūr, ed. *Majallat al-Aḥkām al-ʿAdaliyya*. Karachi: Kārkhāna Tijārat Kutub, 2010.

Muslim, Ibn Ḥajjāj. *Ṣaḥīḥ Muslim*. Riyadh: Al-Kutub al-Sitta, 2000.

Muṣtafa, K. "*Al-Qaradāghī yufta bu wujūb talaqqi liqāḥ cūrūna ʿalā kulli Muslim.*" *Rūdaw*, January 24, 2021. Accessed July 2021, https://www.rudaw.net/arabic/kurdistan/240120219.

National Assembly for Wales. "Developing Health Impact Assessment in Wales." Cardiff, Wales, 1999. Accessed June 20, 2022, http://www.wales.nhs.uk/sites3/Documents/522/developing_hia_in_wales.pdf.

Al-Nawawī, Yaḥyā bin Sharaf. *Ṣaḥīḥ Muslim bī Sharḥ al-Nawawī*, 9 vols. Beirut: Dār al-Kutub al-ʿIlmiyya, 2006.

Al-Nawawī, Yaḥyā bin Sharaf. *Al-Majmūʿ Sharḥ al-Muhadhdhab l-il-shirāzī*, 23 vols. Jeddah: Maktabat al-Irshād, 2008.

Opwis, Felicitas. Maṣlaḥa *and the Purpose of the Law: Islamic Discourse on Legal Change from the 4th/10th to 8th/14th Century*. Leiden: Brill, 2010.

Porta, Miquel, ed. *A Dictionary of Epidemiology*, 6th ed. Oxford: Oxford University Press, 2014.

Shabbir, Yusuf. "Coronavirus: Should Masjids Close?" Islamic Portal, March 17, 2020. Accessed January 2021, https://islamicportal.co.uk/coronavirus-should-masjids-close/.

Shah, Zulfiqar Ali. "*Fiqh* Council of North America Covid Statement: Rulings on Daily and Weekly Congregational Prayers During Coronavirus Pandemic." June 25, 2020. https://www.sfinterfaithcouncil.org/sites/default/files/files/Fiqh%20Council%20of%20North%20America.pdf.

Shah, Zulfiqar Ali. "Fiqh Council Guidelines for Coronavirus Epidemic." April 9, 2020. http://fiqhcouncil.org/fiqh-council-guidelines-for-coronavirus-epidemic/.

Shahriarirad, Reza, Amirhossein Erfani, Keivan Ranjbar, Amir Bazrafshan, and Alireza Mirahmadizadeh. "The Mental Health Impact of COVID-19 Outbreak: A Nationwide Survey in Iran." *International Journal of Mental Health Systems* 15, no. 19 (2021). https://doi.org/10.1186/s13033-021-00445-3.

Al-Shāṭibī, Abū Isḥāq. *Al-Mawāfaqāt fī Uṣūl al-Sharīʿā*, 6 Vols. Beirut: Dār al-Iḥyāʾ al-Turāth al-ʿArabī, 2001.

Shereen, Muhammad Adnan, Suliman Khan, Abeer Kazmi, Nadia Bashir, and Rabeea Siddique. "COVID-19 Infection: Emergence, Transmission, and Characteristics of Human Coronaviruses." *Journal of Advanced Research* 24 (2020): 91–98. https://doi.org/10.1016/j.jare.2020.03.005.

Al-Shirbīnī, al-Khaṭīb. *Mughnī al-Muḥtāj*, 4 vols. Beirut: Dār al-Maʿrifah, 1997.

Al-Suyūṭī, Jalāl al-Dīn. *Al-Ashbāh wa al-Naẓāʾir fī qawāʿid wa furūʿfiqh al-Shāfiʿī*. Beirut: Dār al-Kutub al-ʿIlmiyya, 1990.

Tabataba, Farzaneh Sadat, Prithwish Chakraborty, Naren Ramakrishnan, and Srinivasan Venkatramanan. "A Framework for Evaluating Epidemic Forecasts." *BMC Infectious Diseases* 17, no. 1 (May 2017): 345. https://doi.org/10.1186/s12879-017-2365-1.

Tirmidhī, Muḥammad Ibn ʿĪsā. *Sunnan al-Tirmidhī*. Riyadh: Al-Kutub al-Sitta, 2000.

Umar, Sajid. "Closing Mosques—Islamic Justifications for Coronavirus Lockdowns." *Islam21c*, March 23, 2020. Accessed January 2021. https://www.islam21c.com/islamic-law/closing-mosques-islamic-justifications-for-coronavirus-lockdowns/.

Wildman, Wesley J., Joseph Bulbulia, Richard Sosis, and Uffe Schjoedt. "Religion and the COVID-19 Pandemic." *Religion, Brain & Behavior* 10, no. 2 (2020): 115–117. https://doi.org/10.1080/2153599X.2020.1749339.

Wise, Jacqui. "Covid-19: New Coronavirus Variant is Identified in UK." *BMJ* 371 (2020): m4857. https://doi.org/10.1136/bmj.m4857.

World Health Organization. *Managing Epidemics: Key Facts About Major Deadly Diseases*. Geneva: World Health Organization, 2018. Accessed December 2020, https://apps.who.int/iris/handle/10665/272442. Licence: CC BY-NC-SA 3.0 IGO.

World Health Organization. "WHO Director-General's opening remarks at the media briefing on COVID-19—11 March 2020." March 11, 2020. Accessed December 2020. https://www.who.int/director-general/speeches/detail/who-director-general-s-opening-remarks-at-the-media-briefing-on-COVID-19---11-march-2020.

Al-Zarkashī, Badr al-Dīn. *Al-Manthūr fī al-Qawāʿid*, 2 vols. Beirut: Dār al-Kutub al-ʿIlmiyya, 2000.

Al-Zarqā’, Muṣtafa Aḥmad. *Sharḥ al-Qawā‘id al-fiqhiyya*. Damascus: Dār al-Qalam, 1989.

Al-Zuhaylī, al-Wahbah. *Naẓariat al-Ḍarūrat al-Shar‘iyya*. Beirut: Mu’assasat al-Risāla, 1985.

Glossary

aqeeqahs joyous sacrifice of an animal on the occasion of childbirth
ʿaql mind
asbāb bāṭiniyyah metaphysical and spiritual means
asbāb ẓahiriyyah physical and material means
ḍarūra dire necessity
dhuhr midday prayers
dīn religion
duʿāʾ supplication
fard religious obligation or duty
fardh kifaya moral religious duties
***fatwa* (pl. *fatāwā*)** an authoritative, but non-binding ethico-legal opinion
fidyā expiation
fiqh Islamic Bioethics, substantive law
hadith Prophetic statements
ḥāja need
***ḥājat al-ʿāmma* (or *ḥājat al-uṣūliyya*)** a general/universal need
***ḥājat al-khāṣa* (also termed *ḥājat al-fiqhiyya*)** a specific need
Hajj pilgrimage to Mecca
ḥalāl permissible to use
ḥaqq al-ādmī human right
ḥaqq Allāh *right of God*
ḥifz al-dīn preservation of religion
ḥifz al-nafs preservation of life
ḥukm legal decisions
ibada service to God through service to humankind
ifṭār fast-breaking meals
ijtihād ethico-legal normative analysis
imam Literally a Muslim prayer leader but the term also can apply to a religious scholar
Jumuʿa Friday prayer
maṣlaḥa public interest
maṣlaḥa ʿāmm a public good
maṣlaḥat al-ḍarūriyya necessities
maṣlaḥat al-ḥājiyya needs
maṣlaḥat al-taḥsīniyya embellishments
muḥtāj hardship
nafs life
nasl lineage
qawāʿid maxims
Qurʾan the Muslim sacred text believed to be the literal word of God revealed to the Prophet Muhammad via the angel Gabriel
qurra lots
rukhaṣ exemptions or allowances
sharīʿa Islamic sacred law based on scriptural and formal sources
taʾdīb wa irshād guidance
tajriba historical evidence and experience
tarāwīḥ night vigil prayers
al-ṭāʿūn plague
tawakkul trust in God
ʿUmra "lesser" pilgrimage to Mecca
uṣūl al-fiqh principles of Islamic jurisprudence
wabāʾ epidemic
wudu ablution

 | DOI:10.1163/9789004679771_012

Index

Page numbers followed by *f* refer to figures, page numbers followed by *n* refer to footnotes (19*n*8), and page numbers followed by *t* refer to tables (74*t*).